ANDROID™ BOOT CAMP FOR DEVELOPERS USING JAVA™, COMPREHENSIVE: A BEGINNER'S GUIDE TO CREATING YOUR FIRST ANDROID APPS

CORINNE HOISINGTON

COURSE TECHNOLOGY
CENGAGE Learning®

Australia • Brazil • Japan • Korea • Mexico • Singapore • Spain • United Kingdom • United States

COURSE TECHNOLOGY
CENGAGE Learning·

Android Boot Camp for Developers Using Java, Comprehensive: A Beginner's Guide to Creating Your First Android Apps
Corinne Hoisington

Executive Editor: Marie Lee

Senior Product Manager: Alyssa Pratt

Development Editor: Lisa Ruffolo

Associate Product Manager:
  Stephanie Lorenz

Content Project Manager:
  Heather Hopkins

Art Director: Faith Brosnan

Marketing Manager: Shanna Shelton

Compositor: Integra

Cover Designer: Wing-ip Ngan, Ink
  design, inc. ©

Cover Image Credits:
  istockphoto.com/zentilia
  istockphoto.com/thesuperph
  istockphoto.com/franckreporter
  iQoncept/Shutterstock.com

Library of Congress Control Number: 2012932024

ISBN-13: 978-1-133-59720-9

Course Technology
20 Channel Center Street
Boston, MA 02210

Cengage Learning is a leading provider of customized learning solutions with office locations around the globe, including Singapore, the United Kingdom, Australia, Mexico, Brazil, and Japan. Locate your local office at:
international.cengage.com/region

Cengage Learning products are represented in Canada by Nelson Education, Ltd.

For your lifelong learning solutions, visit **course.cengage.com**

Visit our corporate website at **cengage.com**.

Some of the product names and company names used in this book have been used for identification purposes only and may be trademarks or registered trademarks of their respective manufacturers and sellers.

Any fictional data related to persons or companies or URLs used throughout this book is intended for instructional purposes only. At the time this book was printed, any such data was fictional and not belonging to any real persons or companies.

Course Technology, a part of Cengage Learning, reserves the right to revise this publication and make changes from time to time in its content without notice.

The programs in this book are for instructional purposes only.

They have been tested with care but are not guaranteed for any particular intent beyond educational purposes. The author and the publisher do not offer any warranties or representations, nor do they accept any liabilities with respect to the programs.

Printed in the United States of America
1 2 3 4 5 6 7 18 17 16 15 14 13 12

Brief Contents

Contents

x

Preface

Welcome to *Android Boot Camp for Developers Using Java, Comprehensive: A Beginner's Guide to Creating Your First Android Apps*! This book is designed for people who have some programming experience or are new to Java programming and want to move into the exciting world of developing apps for Android mobile devices on a Windows or Mac computer. Google Android is quickly becoming the operating system of choice for mobile devices, including smartphones and tablets, with nearly half of the world's mobile devices running on the Android platform. To help you participate in the growing Android market, this book focuses on developing apps for Android devices.

Approach

The approach used in *Android Boot Camp for Developers Using Java, Comprehensive* is straightforward. You review a completed Android app and identify why people use the app, the tasks it performs, and the problems it solves. You also learn about the programming logic, Java tools, and code syntax you can use to create the app. Next, you work through a hands-on tutorial that guides you through the steps of creating the Android app, including designing the user interface and writing the code. After each step, you can compare your work to an illustration that shows exactly how the interface should look or what the code should contain. Using the illustrations, you can avoid mistakes in creating the app and finish the chapter with an appealing, real-world Android app.

The main tool used in *Android Boot Camp for Developers Using Java, Comprehensive* is a standard one developers use to create Android apps: Eclipse Classic, a free, open-source integrated development environment (IDE). Eclipse includes an emulator for testing your apps, so you don't need a smartphone or tablet to run any of the apps covered in this book. Instructions for downloading and setting up Eclipse are provided later in this preface.

What This Book Is

This book introduces you to writing apps for Android mobile devices. It familiarizes you with the development software for creating Android apps, programming logic used in the apps, and Java code that puts the software design and logic into practice. You don't need an Android device because you can run the apps you create in this book by using an Android emulator.

What This Book Is Not

Because this book is targeted to those new to developing Android apps, it doesn't cover advanced topics, such as application programming interfaces (APIs) for each platform. Instead, this book provides a launch pad to begin your journey into creating Android apps for fun and for profit.

In addition, this book isn't an exhaustive information resource. You can find a wealth of information, tutorials, examples, and other resources for the Android platform online. You should learn enough from this book that you can modify and make use of code you find to fit your needs. The best way to learn how to create Android apps is to write code, make mistakes, and learn how to fix them.

Organization and Coverage

Chapter 1 introduces the Android platform and describes the current market for Android apps. You create your first Android project using Eclipse and become familiar with the Eclipse interface and its tools. As programming tradition mandates, your first project is called Hello Android World, which you complete and then run in an emulator.

Chapter 2 focuses on the Android user interface. While developing an app for selecting and displaying healthy recipes, you follow a series of steps that you repeat every time you create an Android app. You learn how to develop a user interface using certain types of controls, select a screen layout, and learn how to write code that responds to a button event (such as a click or tap). While creating the chapter project, you develop an app that includes more than one screen and can switch from one screen to another. Finally, you learn how to correct errors in Java code.

Chapter 3 covers user input, variables, and operations. You develop an Android app that allows users to enter the number of concert tickets they want to purchase, and then click a button to calculate the total cost of the tickets. To do so, you create a user interface using an Android theme and add controls to the interface, including text fields, buttons, and spinner controls. You also declare variables and use arithmetic operations to perform calculations, and then convert and format numeric data.

Chapter 4 discusses icons and decision-making controls. The sample app provides health care professionals a mobile way to convert the weight of a patient from pounds to kilograms and from kilograms to pounds. You create this project using a custom application icon, learn how to fine-tune the layout of the user interface, and include radio buttons for user selections. You also learn how to program decisions using If statements, If Else statements, and logical operators.

Chapter 5 describes how to use lists, arrays, and Web browsers in an Android app. You design and create an Android app that people can use as a traveler's guide to popular attractions in San Francisco, California. To do so, you work with lists, images, and the Switch decision structure. You also learn how to let users access a Web browser while using an Android app.

Chapter 6 explains how to include audio such as music in Android apps. The sample app opens with a splash screen and then displays a second screen where users can select a song to play. To develop this app, you create and set up a splash screen, learn about the Activity life cycle, pause an Activity, and start, play, stop, and resume music playback.

Chapter 7 demonstrates how to use an Android layout tool called a Gallery view, which shows thumbnail images in a horizontally scrolling list. When the user clicks a thumbnail, the app displays a larger image below the Gallery view. You also learn how to use an array to manage the images.

In **Chapter 8**, you design a calendar program that includes a DatePicker control for selecting a date to book a reservation. Because this app is designed for a larger tablet interface, you also learn how to design an app for a tablet device and add an Android Virtual Device specifically designed for tablets.

Chapter 9 continues to explore Android apps designed for tablet devices. In this chapter, you create a tabbed interface with each tab displaying a different layout and Activity. To create the tabbed interface, you work with TabHost and TabWidget controls.

Chapter 10 explains how to create two types of animation. Using a frame-by-frame animation, you animate a series of images so that they play in sequence. Using a motion tween animation, you apply an animated effect to a single image.

Chapter 11 shows you how to create an Android app that includes Google Maps to display a map users can zoom in and out. You also learn how to display pushpins to mark special locations on the map. Because using Google Maps requires special permissions, you learn how to add these permissions to the Android Manifest file to access the Internet and the Google library.

In **Chapter 12**, you learn how to publish an Android app to the Android Market, which is currently part of Google Play. Before publishing the app, you test it, prepare it for publication, create a package and digitally sign the app, and then prepare promotional materials.

Features of the Book

Android Boot Camp for Developers Using Java, Comprehensive includes the following features:

- *Objectives*—Each chapter begins with a list of objectives as an overview of the topics discussed in the chapter and as a useful study aid.

- *GTKs and In the Trenches*—GTK stands for Good to Know. These notes offer tips about Android devices, Android apps, and the Android development tools. The In the Trenches features provide programming advice and practical solutions to typical programming problems.

- *Figures and tables*—Chapters contain a wealth of screen shots to guide you as you create Android apps and learn about the Android marketplace. In addition, many tables are included to give you an at-a-glance summary of useful information.

- *Step-by-step tutorials*—Starting in Chapter 1, you create complete, working Android apps by performing the steps in a series of hands-on tutorials that lead you through the development process.

- *Code syntax features*—Each new programming concept or technique is introduced with a code syntax feature that highlights a type of statement or programming structure. The code is analyzed and explained thoroughly before you use it in the chapter project.

- *Summaries*—At the end of each chapter is a summary list that recaps the Android terms, programming concepts, and Java coding techniques covered in the chapter so that you have a way to check your understanding of the chapter's main points.

- *Key terms*—Each chapter includes definitions of new terms, alphabetized for ease of reference. This feature is another useful way to review the chapter's major concepts.

- *Developer FAQs*—Each chapter contains many short-answer questions that help you review the key concepts in the chapter.

- *Beyond the Book*—In addition to review questions, each chapter provides research topics and questions. You can search the Web to find the answers to these questions and further your Android knowledge.

- *Case programming projects*—Except for Chapter 12, each chapter outlines six realistic programming projects, including their purpose, algorithms, and conditions. For each project, you use the same steps and techniques you learned in the chapter to create a running Android app on your own.

- *Quality*—Every chapter project and case programming project was tested using Windows 7 and Mac OS X computers.

Student Resources

Source code and project files for the chapter projects and case programming projects in *Android Boot Camp for Developers Using Java, Comprehensive* are available at *www.cengagebrain.com*.

For complete instructions on downloading, installing, and setting up the tools you need to perform the steps in this book, see the section titled "Prelude! Installing the Android Eclipse SDK" later in this preface.

For the Instructor

Android Boot Camp for Developers Using Java, Comprehensive is intended to be taught as a complete course dedicated to the mobile programming of the Android device or as an exploratory topic in a programming class or literacy course. Students can develop Android applications on a Windows or Mac computer using the Eclipse emulator in a traditional or online class. Offering such an exciting topic that is relative to today's huge growth in the mobile environment brings excitement to the programming classroom. The Eclipse/Android platform is fully free and open-source, which means all students can access these tools on their home computers.

Instructor Resources

The following teaching tools are available on the Instructor Resources CD or through *login.cengage.com* to instructors who have adopted this book:

Instructor's Manual. The electronic Instructor's Manual follows the book chapter by chapter to assist in planning and organizing an effective, engaging course. The manual includes learning objectives, chapter overviews, ideas for classroom activities, and abundant additional resources. A sample course syllabus is also available.

ExamView®. This book is accompanied by ExamView, a powerful testing software package that allows instructors to create and administer printed, computer (LAN-based), and Internet exams. ExamView includes hundreds of questions corresponding to the topics covered in this book, enabling students to generate detailed study guides that include page references for further review. These computer-based and Internet testing components allow students to take exams at their computers and save instructors time by grading each exam automatically. Test banks are also available in Blackboard, WebCT, and Angel formats.

PowerPoint presentations. This book comes with PowerPoint slides for each chapter. They're included as a teaching aid for classroom presentations, to make available to students on the network for chapter review, or to be printed for classroom distribution. Instructors can add their own slides for additional topics or customize the slides with access to all the figure files from the book.

Solution files. Solution files for all chapter projects and the end-of-chapter exercises are provided.

Prelude! Installing the Android Eclipse SDK

Setting Up the Android Environment

To begin developing Android applications, you must first set up the Android programming environment on your computer. To establish a development environment, this section walks you through the installation and setup for a Windows or Mac computer. The Android Software Development Kit (SDK) allows developers to create applications for the Android platform. The Android SDK includes sample projects with source code, development tools, an emulator, and required libraries to build Android applications, which are written using the Java programming language.

The Android installation is quite different from a typical program installation. You must perform the following tasks in sequence to correctly prepare for creating an Android application. Before you write your first application in Chapter 1, complete the following tasks to successfully install Android SDK on your computer:

1. Prepare your computer for the installation.
2. Download and unzip the Eclipse Integrated Development Environment (IDE).
3. Download and unzip the Android SDK package.
4. Install the Android Development Tools (ADT) Plugin within Eclipse.
5. Set the location of the ADT within Eclipse.
6. Set up the Android emulator.

Preparing Your Computer

The Android Software Development Kit is compatible with Windows XP (32-bit), Windows Vista (32- or 64-bit), Windows 7 (32- or 64-bit), Windows 8 (32-, 64-, or 128-bit), and Mac OS X (Intel only). To install the basic files needed to write an Android application, your hard drive needs a minimum of 400 MB of available space.

Downloading Eclipse

Before downloading the necessary files, create a folder on the hard drive (C:) of your computer named Android. Next, you must download and unzip the software in the C:\Android folder. Windows Vista and Windows 7 automatically unzip files, but if you are using Windows XP, you will need to first download an unzip program such as WinZip at *download.com*.

The preferred Java program development software is called Eclipse. Eclipse is a free and open-source IDE. To download Eclipse:

1. Open the Web page *www.eclipse.org/downloads* and look for the most recent version of Eclipse Classic as shown in Figure 1.

Figure 1   Eclipse Downloads page (*www.eclipse.org/download*)

2. Select the most recent version of Eclipse Classic. If you are downloading to a Macintosh computer, click the **Windows** list arrow and then click **Mac OS X (Cocoa)**. If you are downloading to a Windows computer, click **Windows 32 Bit** or **Windows 64 Bit** based on the system on your computer.

3. After downloading the Eclipse package, unzip the downloaded eclipse file into a subfolder of the Android folder at C:\Android on your local computer. The unzipped file contains the contents of the Eclipse development environment (Figure 2). You may want to create a shortcut on the desktop to make it easy to start Eclipse.

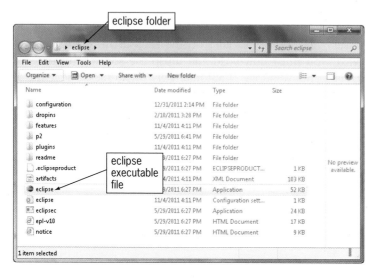

Figure 2   Contents of the Eclipse folder

Downloading the SDK Starter Package

After unzipping the Eclipse package, the next step is to download the Android Software Development Kit (SDK), which is a collection of files and utilities that work with Eclipse to create Android applications. The SDK starter package includes only the core SDK tools, which you can use to download the rest of the SDK components such as the latest Android platform. To download the Android SDK:

1.   Go to the Android developers Web site at *http://developer.android.com/sdk*.

2.   Download the latest SDK for your computer's platform (Figure 3).

Figure 3 Android SDK download site (*http://developer.android.com/sdk*)

3. After downloading the SDK, unzip its contents into the C:\Android folder.

Setting Up the Android Development Tools in Eclipse

After you install Eclipse and the Android SDK, the next step is to install the ADT (Android Development Tools) plug-in from Eclipse. The ADT plug-in for Eclipse is an extension to the Eclipse IDE that creates Android applications, debugs the code, and exports a signed application file to the Android Market. To download the Android Development Tools:

1. In the Android folder on your computer, open the **eclipse** folder and double-click the **eclipse.exe** file to open Eclipse. (If an Open File - Security Warning dialog box opens, click the **Run** button.)

2. In Eclipse, click **Help** on the menu bar and then click **Install New Software** to open the Install dialog box.

3. Click the **Add** button in the upper-right corner of the dialog box.

4. In the Add Repository dialog box, type **ADT Plugin** for the Name and the following URL for the Location: ***https://dl-ssl.google.com/android/eclipse/*** (Figure 4).

xxii

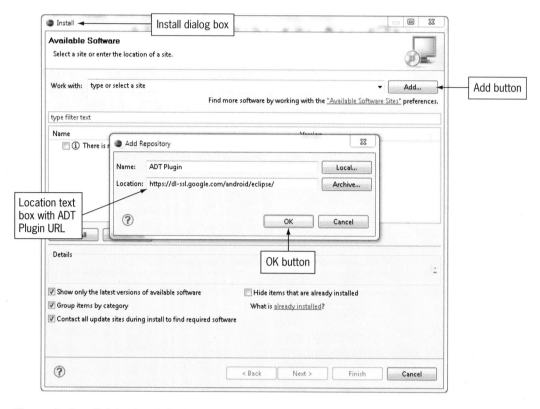

Figure 4 Install dialog box in Eclipse

5. Click the **OK** button.

6. In the Available Software dialog box, select the **Developer Tools** check box and then click the **Next** button.

7. In the next window, click the **Next** button.

8. Read and accept the license agreements, and then click the **Finish** button. If a security warning appears indicating that the authenticity or validity of the software can't be established, click **OK**. When the installation is finished, restart Eclipse.

Configuring Eclipse with the Location of the ADT Plugin

After successfully downloading the ADT plug-in, the next task is to modify your ADT preferences in Eclipse to use the Android SDK directory. Next, you install the repositories for Android 4.0 SDK, Google API, and the emulator.

1. In Eclipse, click **Window** on the menu bar and then click **Preferences** to open the Preferences dialog box.

   On Mac OS X, click **Eclipse** on the menu bar and then click **Preferences**.

2. Select **Android** in the left pane. To set the SDK Location, type **C:\android\android-sdk-windows** to enter the path to the installed files (Figure 5).

On Mac OS X, set the SDK Location to **/Library/android**.

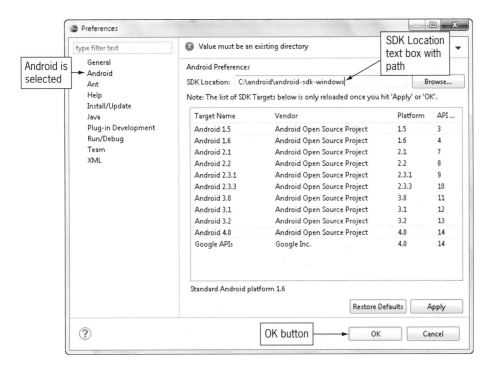

Figure 5 Setting the SDK Location in Eclipse

3. Click the **OK** button. To install the repositories for the Android 4.0 SDK, click **Window** on the Eclipse menu bar and then click **Android SDK Manager** to open the Android SDK Manager dialog box.

4. Click **Android 4.0 (API 14)** to select it, and then click the **Install packages** button.

5. In the next window, click **Install** to install the Android 4.0 SDK in Eclipse (Figure 6). The installation may take some time to complete.

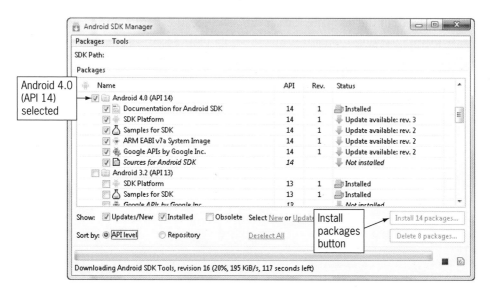

Figure 6   Installing Android 4.0 using the SDK Manager in Eclipse

Setting up the Android Emulator

The Android SDK includes a phone and tablet emulator that allows you to develop and test your Android applications. Android mobile devices come in many shapes and sizes and must be tested on a host of emulator layout sizes to verify the configuration and usability. Each Android device configuration is stored in an Android Virtual Device (AVD).

The Android SDK and AVD Manager within Eclipse provide multiple emulators for test-driving your application without using a physical device. When you run an Android app, it runs in an emulator so you can interact with the emulated mobile device just as you would an actual mobile device. You can simulate touching the screen of the emulator with the pointing device on your computer.

To use the emulator, you first must create one or more AVD configurations. In each configuration, you specify an Android platform to run in the emulator and the set of hardware options and emulator skin you want to use. When you launch the emulator, you specify the AVD configuration that you want to load. In this book, the Android 4.0 Ice Cream Sandwich version emulator is used, although based on your actual Android device, you can add multiple emulators to test the devices on which you plan to deploy your apps.

You must name the emulator that you set up to use to deploy your Android apps. By selecting an emulator, you choose the skin, or resolution, that the Android emulator displays. To specify the Android 4.0 emulator:

1. In Eclipse, click **Window** on the menu bar and then click **AVD Manager** to open the Android Virtual Device Manager dialog box.

2. Click the **New** button to open the Create new Android Virtual Device (AVD) dialog box.

3. To name your Android emulator, type **IceCream** in the Name text box.

4. To target your Android app to appear in the Android 4.0 version, select **Android 4.0 – API Level 14** in the Target list (Figure 7). You can select newer Android versions, but most devices are not using the newest platform.

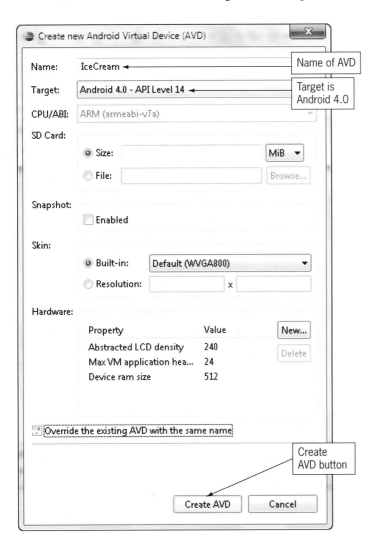

Figure 7 Create new Android Virtual Device (AVD) dialog box

5. Click the **Create AVD** button. The Android Virtual Device Manager dialog box lists the AVD Name (IceCream) for the Android 4.0 target device (Figure 8).

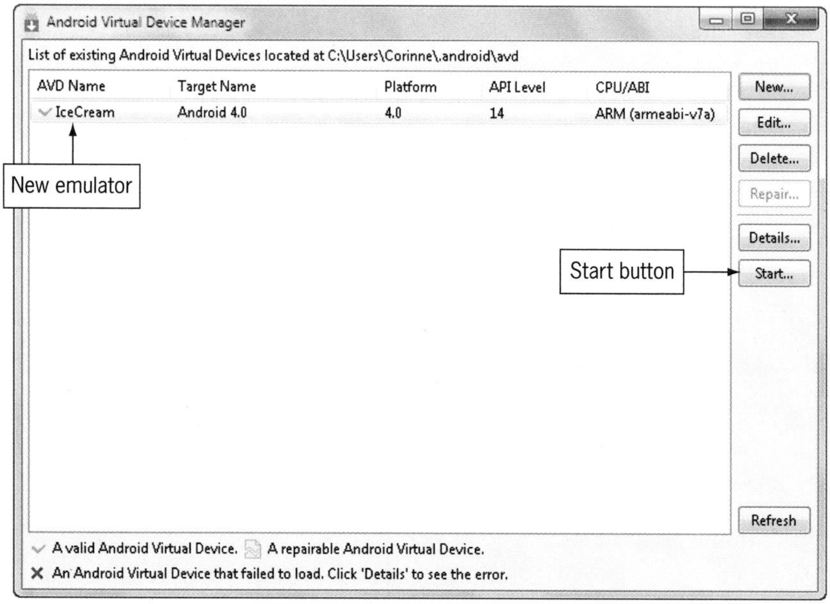

Figure 8   Android Virtual Device Manager dialog box

6. Your AVD is now ready to use. To launch and test the emulator with the AVD, click the **IceCream** emulator and then click the **Start** button. If a Launch Options dialog box opens, click the **Launch** button. After a few moments, the Ice Cream Sandwich Android 4.0 emulator starts (Figure 9).

Figure 9   Android emulator

7.   Close Eclipse by clicking **File** on the menu bar and then clicking **Exit**. Close all other open windows. You are now ready to create your first application.

Android Software Development Kit (SDK) Installation Instructions for Mac

To develop Android apps, you need to install the Android Software Development Kit (SDK). In addition, you need another application in which to run the SDK. The most popular version, and the one you use here, is Eclipse. This section provides instructions for installing the Android SDK and Eclipse.

Android currently provides online installation instructions at *http://developer.android.com/sdk/installing.html*. Eclipse currently provides online installation instructions at *http://developer.android.com/sdk/eclipse-adt.html#installing*. Use the online instructions as a backup if you encounter any unique issues with the installation not covered in this chapter.

System Requirements

Before you install the software, be sure that your Mac meets the following system requirements by completing the following steps.

1. Your operating system should be Mac OS X 10.5.8 or later (x86 only). Click the Apple icon on the Mac toolbar, and then click About this Mac to open the About This Mac dialog box and view your current operating system version. In the About This Mac dialog box, also verify that your Mac has an Intel processor.

    The operating system is later than 10.5.8 and the processor is by Intel (Figure 10).

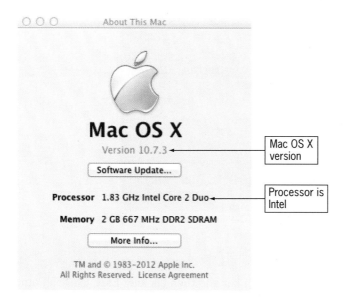

Figure 10   About This Mac dialog box

2. Eclipse 3.6.2 (Helios) or greater is installed on your machine. Eclipse Indigo is installed for this book and the installation instructions appear later in this section.

Installing the Android Software Development Kit (SDK)

Now that you know your system meets the requirements, you can install the SDK starter package. The Android SDK zip file contains only the core tools. Complete the following steps to install the SDK.

1. Use your browser to go to **http://developer.android.com/sdk/index.html** and download the latest Mac OS X SDK starter package zip file. At the time of publication, this file is named is android-sdk_r18-macosx.zip. Click android-sdk_r18-macosx.zip to download the file.

Download the android-sdk_r18-macosx.zip installation zip file (Figure 11).

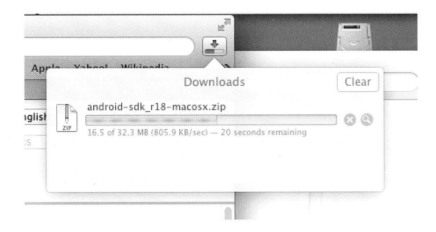

Download the Android SDK

Welcome Developers! If you are new to the Android SDK, please read the steps below, for an overview of how to set up the SDK.

If you're already using the Android SDK, you should update to the latest tools or platform using the *Android SDK and AVD Manager*, rather than downloading a new SDK starter package. See Adding SDK Components.

Platform	Package	Size	MD5 Checksum
Windows	android-sdk_r18-windows.zip	37448775 bytes	bfbfdf8b2d0fdecc2a621544d706fa98
	installer_r18-windows.exe (Recommended)	37456234 bytes	48b1fe7b431afe6b9c8a992bf75dd898
Mac OS X (intel)	android-sdk_r18-macosx.zip	3390372...	...a5531c9d6f6f1a0261cb97af36
Linux (i386)	android-sdk_r18-linux.tgz	29731463 bytes	6cd716d0e04624b865ffed3c25b3485c

Installation zip file

Here's an overview of the steps you must follow to set up the Android SDK:

1. Prepare your development computer and ensure it meets the system requirements.
2. Install the SDK starter package from the table above. (If you're on Windows, download the installer for help with the initial setup.)
3. Install the ADT Plugin for Eclipse (if you'll be developing in Eclipse).
4. Add Android platforms and other packages to your SDK.
5. Explore the contents of the Android SDK (optional).

To get started, download the appropriate package from the table above, then read the guide to Installing the SDK.

Figure 11   The Android SDK installation zip file

2. Open your browser's Downloads folder. In Safari, click the Show downloads button in the upper-right corner of the browser.

The list of recently downloaded files appears in a pop-up window (Figure 12).

Figure 12   android-sdk_r18-macosx.zip file in Downloads list

3. Click the Show in Finder icon next to android-sdk_r18-macosx.zip, and then move the folder to your Applications folder.

Installing Eclipse

The tool this book uses to develop Android apps is Eclipse. Use Eclipse 3.6.2 or greater to be compatible with the Android SDK. Android, Inc., recommends Eclipse Classic, though they state that a Java or RCP version is also adequate. Install the 32-bit or 64-bit (OS X Lion, some installations, only) version. If you are running the Lion OS, check the following file in a text editor to see if your version of Lion is booting in 64-bit or 32-bit: /Library/Preferences/SystemConfiguration/com.apple.Boot.plist.

1. To download Eclipse, use your browser to go to **http://www.eclipse.org/downloads/**.

    The Eclipse Downloads page is displayed (Figure 13).

Figure 13   Eclipse Downloads page

2. On the Eclipse Downloads page, next to the version of Eclipse you want to download such as Eclipse Classic 3.7.2, click the Mac OS X 32 Bit or Mac OS X 64 Bit link to open the Eclipse downloads – mirror selection page.

The Eclipse downloads – mirror selection page is displayed (Figure 14).

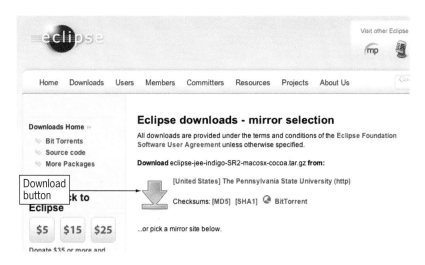

Figure 14 Eclipse downloads – mirror selection page

3. On the Eclipse downloads – mirror selection page, click the Download button.
   The Eclipse download begins (Figure 15).

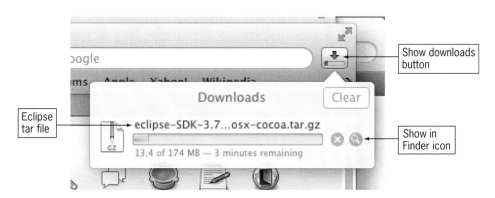

Figure 15 Eclipse tar file in Downloads list

4. After a minute or so, when the download is complete, open the Downloads folder. In Safari, click the Show downloads button in the upper-right corner of the browser. Click the Show in Finder icon next to the eclipse file. Double-click the tar file (eclipse-eclipse-SDK-3.7.2-macosx-cocoa.tar in this case) to expand the files. Move the eclipse folder from your Downloads folder to the Applications folder. Open the eclipse folder, and then double-click eclipse.app. Click Open if a warning dialog box appears regarding this application having been downloaded from the Internet.

Eclipse starts and the Workspace Launcher appears (Figure 16).

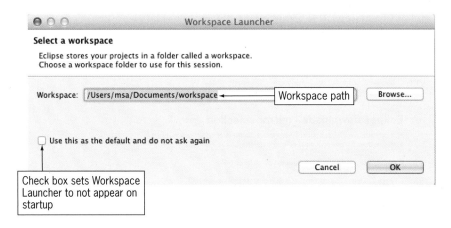

Figure 16   The Workspace Launcher

5. Enter a Workspace path in the Workspace Launcher dialog box. This path is where your Android projects will be saved. (For this book, the projects are saved to a USB drive but this path is entered by project.) For now, enter a path that makes sense for the projects to such as *username*/workspace where *username* is the username associated with your Mac. Type ***username*/workspace** in the Workspace text box or click the Browse button, navigate to the desired location, and then open the location. The Workspace Launcher appears each time you start Eclipse. You can change that default so it will not appear by clicking the "Use this as the default and do not ask again" check box. You may want to hold off on changing this default until you are sure that the location is working for you. Click OK.

The Eclipse application is now fully installed and open.

Installing Android Development Tools (ADT) Plugin for Eclipse

Now that Eclipse is installed, the Android Development Tools (ADT) Plugin needs to be added to the program.

1. With Eclipse running, click Help on the menu bar and then click Install New Software.

The Install wizard starts (Figure 17).

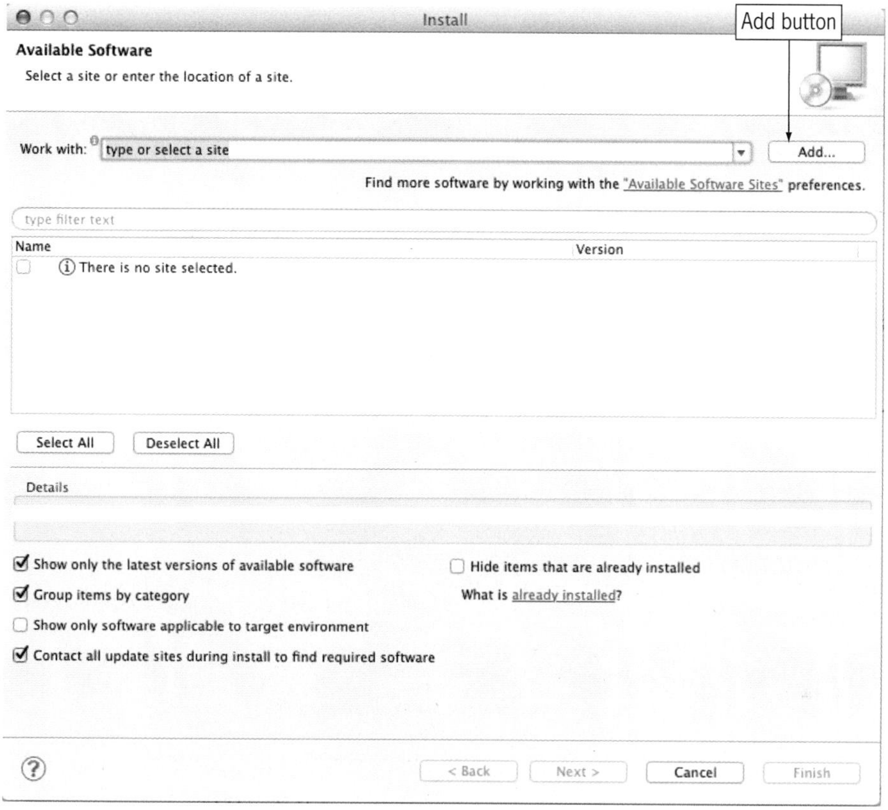

Figure 17 Install wizard

2. Click the Add button to open the Add Repository dialog box. In the Name text box, type **ADT Plugin** and then type **https://dl-ssl.google.com/android/eclipse/** in the Location text box. Click OK. If this fails for some reason, then try the prefix http instead of https, which is a less secure option to use if the secure option fails.

The criteria are entered in the Add Repository dialog box (Figure 18).

Figure 18   Add Repository dialog box

3. Click the Developer Tools check box, and then click Next.

    Developer Tools is selected (Figure 19).

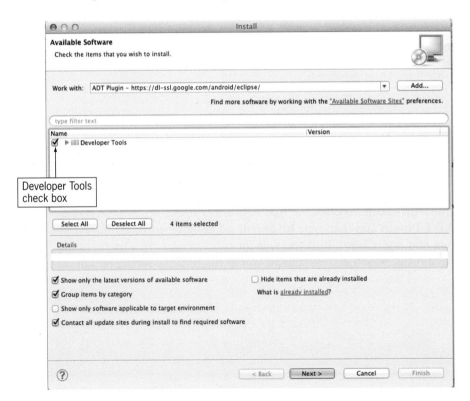

Figure 19   Install wizard – Available Software page

4. Leave the defaults in the Install Details list box and then click Next. Select a license agreement in the Licenses box, read the license agreement, and then repeat for all other license agreements. Click the "I accept the terms of the license agreements" option button.

Read each license agreement and accept them all (Figure 20).

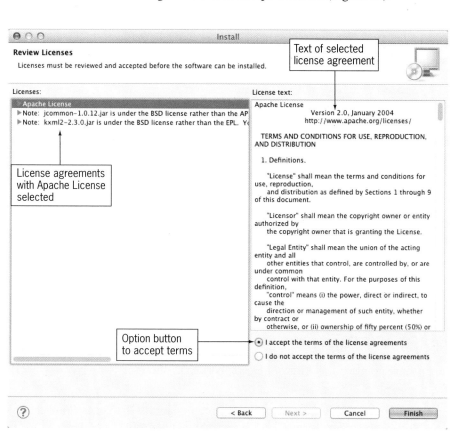

Figure 20   Install wizard – Review Licenses page

5. Click the Finish button to open the Installing Software dialog box. Click Run in Background to complete the installation while doing other tasks. If a Security Warning dialog box appears regarding the authenticity of the software, click OK to clear it. When the installation completes, click Restart Now to restart Eclipse. Click OK in the Workspace Launcher dialog box to accept the default location you entered earlier.

Eclipse begins to launch (Figure 21).

Figure 21   Eclipse launches

Leave Eclipse open for the next set of instructions. See *http://developer.android.com/sdk/ eclipse-adt.html#installing* for more installation information, if necessary.

Configuring the ADT Plugin

The ADT Plugin must point to the Android Developers SDK directory for it to work correctly.

1. Start Eclipse, if necessary. Click Eclipse on the menu bar and then click Preferences to open the Preferences dialog box. Click the Android category.

The Eclipse Preferences dialog box displays the Android Preferences (Figure 22).

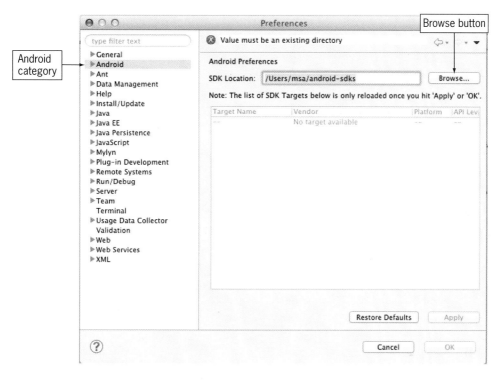

Figure 22 Eclipse Preferences dialog box

2. Click the Browse button next to SDK Location. Navigate to the Applications folder, and then select the android-sdk-macosx folder.

The android-sdk-macosx folder is selected (Figure 23).

Figure 23   android-sdk-macosx folder

3. Click the Open button. Click the Apply button and then click OK to set the SDK location and close the Preferences dialog box. Leave Eclipse open for the next set of instructions.

The ADT Plugin now points to the correct directory. See *http://developer.android.com/sdk/ eclipse-adt.html#installing* for more instructions, if necessary.

Adding Android Platforms and Other Packages to SDK

The final step in this installation is to download essential SDK packages using the Android SDK Manager. To program applications, you need to install at least one Android platform.

1. Start Eclipse, if necessary. Click Window on the menu bar and then click Android SDK Manager. In the Android SDK Manager dialog box, click the Tools check box, if necessary, to select the packages.

The packages are selected for installation (Figure 24).

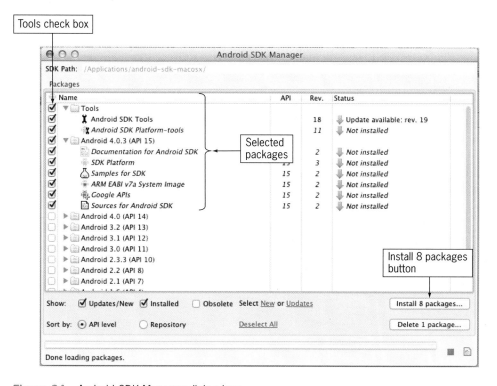

Figure 24 Android SDK Manager dialog box

2. Click the Install 8 packages button. In the Choose Packages to Install dialog box, select and read the license agreements, click the Accept all option button, and then click Install. The Android SDK Manager Log shows the detailed progress of the download, which might take a few minutes. If the Android Tools Updated dialog box appears, click OK. When the Done loading packages message appears, click Close to close the Android SDK Manager Log dialog box. Click the Close button on the title bar to close the Android SDK Manager dialog box. Click Check for Updates on the Help menu. Install any updates that may appear.

See *http://developer.android.com/sdk/installing.html* for more installation information, if necessary, and details regarding these packages. Your development environment is now ready for you to use to create Android apps.

Acknowledgements

xl

Android Boot Camp for Developers Using Java, Comprehensive: A Beginner's Guide to Creating Your First Android Apps is the product of a wonderful team of professionals working toward a single goal: providing students with pertinent, engaging material to further their knowledge and careers. Thank you to the folks at Cengage—specifically Acquisitions Editor Brandi Shailer; Senior Product Manager Alyssa Pratt; Content Project Manager Heather Hopkins; Karen Annett, the copyeditor; Suzanne Huizenga, the proofreader; and Susan Whalen and Susan Pedicini, the MQA testers.

Thank you to the reviewers of this book: Sam Abraham, Siena Heights University; Marilyn Achelpohl, Galesburg High School; Jay Bohnsack, Moline High School; Arshia Khan, College of Saint Scholastica; Larry Langellier, Moraine Valley Community College; and Roseann Rovetto, Horry-Georgetown Technical College. It's because of their insights and experience that *Android Boot Camp for Developers Using Java* is a book that can actually be used in the classroom.

Writing a book is similar to entering a long-term relationship with an obsessive partner. Throughout the journey, life continues around you: teaching classes full time, presenting across the country, and attending family events at every turn. As the world continues, those closest to you allow you to focus on your reclusive writing by assisting with every other task. My husband, Timothy, is credited with learning to cook dinner, to cheer me on, and most of all for his love. Special thanks to my six children Tim, Brittany, Ryan, Daniel, Breanne, and Eric for providing much needed breaks filled with pride and laughter. A heartfelt thanks to my dear sister Shirley who has encouraged me for a lifetime. And a special thanks to Lisa Ruffolo as my developmental editor and master wordsmith who provided the perfect polish for every chapter.

Voilà! Meet the Android

In this chapter, you learn to:

- ◎ Understand the market for Android applications
- ◎ State the role of the Android device in the mobile market
- ◎ Describe the features of the Android phone
- ◎ Identify which languages are used in Android development
- ◎ Describe the role of the Android Market in the mobile marketplace
- ◎ Create an Android project using Eclipse
- ◎ Explain the role of the Package Explorer
- ◎ Specify the use of layout and widget controls in the user interface
- ◎ Execute an Android application on an emulator
- ◎ Open a saved Android project in Eclipse

Welcome to the beginning of your journey in creating Android phone applications and developing for the mobile device market. Mobile computing has become the most popular way to make a personal connection to the Internet. Mobile phones and tablets constitute the fastest growing category of any technology in the world. Mobile phone usage has quickly outgrown the simple expectation of voice calls and text messaging. An average data plan for a mobile device, often called a **smartphone**, typically includes browsing the Web, playing popular games such as Angry Birds, using business applications, checking e-mail, listening to music, recording live video, and mapping locations with a GPS (global positioning system).

When purchasing a phone, you can choose from many mobile operating systems, including the iOS for the iPhone, Google Android, Microsoft Phone 7, and BlackBerry OS. Recently the Android phone has become the sales leader, outselling its competitors. The Android market is exploding with more than 50 million Android phones now being used worldwide. Nearly one-half of the world's mobile devices run on the Android platform.

IN THE TRENCHES
More than 25 percent of all U.S. households have canceled their landlines for the convenience of receiving only one bill from a mobile carrier.

Creating mobile applications, called apps, for the Android phone market is an exciting new job opportunity. Whether you become a developer for a technology firm that creates professional apps for corporations or a hobbyist developer who creates games, niche programs, or savvy new applications, the Android marketplace provides a new means to earn income.

Meet the Android

The Android phone platform is built on a free operating system primarily created by a company called Android, Inc. In 2005, Google obtained Android, Inc., to start a venture in the mobile phone market. Because Google intended the Android platform to be open source, the Android code was released under the Apache license, which permits anyone to download the full open-source Android code for free. Two years later, Google unveiled its first open-standards mobile device called the Android (Figure 1-1). In less than a decade, the Android phone market has grown into the world's best-selling phone platform.

Figure 1-1   Android phone

iStockphoto.com/Alexandru Nika

Android is the first open-source technology platform for mobile devices. Being an open-source operating system effectively means that no company or individual defines the features or direction of the development. Organizations and developers can extract, modify, and use the code for creating any app. The rapid success of the Android phone can be attributed to the collaboration of the **Open Handset Alliance** (*http://openhandsetalliance.com*), an open-source business alliance of 80 firms that develop standards for mobile devices. The Open Handset Alliance is led by Google. Other members include companies such as Sony, Dell, Intel, Motorola, Qualcomm, HTC, Texas Instruments, Samsung, Kyocera, and LG. Competitors such as Apple, which produces the iPhone, and Research In Motion (RIM), which produces the BlackBerry, do not have an open-source coding environment, but instead work with proprietary operating systems. The strength of the open-source community lies in the developers' ability to share their source code. Even though the open-source Android software is free, many developers are paid to build and improve the platform. For example, proprietary software such as the Apple operating system is limited to company employees licensed to build a program within the organization. The Android open-source platform allows more freedom so people can collaborate and improve the source code.

Many phone manufacturers install the Android operating system (OS) on their brand-name mobile phones due to its open-source environment. The open-source structure means that manufacturers do not pay license fees or royalties. With a small amount of customization, each manufacturer can place the Android OS on its latest devices. This minimal overhead allows manufacturers to sell their phones in the retail market for relatively low prices, often less than $100. Low prices on Android mobile devices have increased the sales and popularity of these devices.

One of the key features that make Android phones so attractive for consumers is the openness of the Android OS. Android has a large community of developers writing apps that extend the functionality of the devices. Users, for example, can benefit from over 250,000 apps available in the Android marketplace, many of which are free. Because the Android phone platform has become the leader in sales in the mobile market, the Android application market is keeping pace.

Android Phone Device

The Android phone is sold by a variety of companies under names you may recognize, such as EVO, Droid X, Galaxy, Echo, Optimus, Xperia, Cliq, Inspire, Thunderbolt, Atrix, Desire, Nexus, Infuse, Pyramid, and Revolution (Figure 1-2).

Figure 1-2   Android on many types of devices

IN THE TRENCHES

Android has ventured into the television market as well. Google TV integrates Google's Android operating system and the Linux version of the Google Chrome browser to create an interactive Internet television.

Android devices come in many shapes and sizes, as shown in Figure 1-2. The Android OS powers all types of mobile devices, including smartphones, tablets, netbooks, e-readers, MP4 players, and Internet TVs. The NOOK, a color e-book reader for Barnes and Noble, is based on the Android OS as well. Android devices are available with a variety of screen dimensions and many devices support a landscape mode where the width and height are spontaneously reversed depending on the orientation of the device. As you design Android apps, the screen size affects the layout of the user interface. To take full advantage of the capabilities of a particular device, you need to design user interfaces specifically for that device. For example, a smartphone and a tablet not only have a different physical screen size, but also different screen resolutions and pixel densities, which change the development process. As you develop an Android app, you can test the results on an emulator, which duplicates how the app looks and feels on a particular device. You can change the Android emulators to simulate the layout of a smartphone with a 3.5-inch screen or a tablet with a larger screen, both with high-density graphics. Android automatically scales content to the screen size of the device you choose, but if you use low-quality graphics in an app, the result is often a poorly pixelated display. As a developer, you need to continue to update your app as the market shifts to different platforms and screen resolutions.

The Android phone market has many more hardware case and size options than the single 3.5-inch screen option of an iPhone. Several Android phones such as the Atrix, Droid X, EVO, and Nexus offer screens 4 inches or larger. This extra space is excellent for phone users who like to watch movies, play games, or view full Web pages on their phone. In addition, tablets, also called slates, are now available on the Android platform. The Xoom Android tablet is produced by Google/ Motorola and offers a 10.1-inch screen with a very high resolution of 1280 × 800 pixels. Amazon also has a 7-inch Android slate device called the Kindle Fire (Figure 1-3), currently available for $199. The Android tablets are in direct competition with other tablets and slate computers such as the iPad (various generations), BlackBerry PlayBook, and Galaxy Tab.

Figure 1-3   Kindle Fire Android tablet

KEVIN DIETSCH/UPI/Newscom

Features of the Android

As a developer, you must understand a phone's capabilities. The Android offers a wide variety of features that apps can use. Some features vary by model. Most Android phones provide the features listed in Table 1-1.

Feature	Description
Flash support	Flash video plays within the Android Web browser. (The iPhone does not support Flash capabilities.)
Power management	Android identifies programs running in the background using memory and processor resources. You can close those apps to free up the phone's processor memory, extending the battery power.
Optimized gaming	Android supports the use of gyroscope, gravity, barometric sensors, linear acceleration, and rotation vector, which provide game developers with highly sensitive and responsive controls.
Onscreen keyboard	The onscreen keyboard offers suggestions for spelling corrections as well as options for completing words you start typing. The onscreen keyboard also supports a voice-input mode.
Wi-Fi Internet tethering	Android supports tethering, which allows a phone to be used as a wireless or wired hot spot that other devices can use to connect to the Internet.
Multiple language support	Android supports multiple human languages.
Front- and rear-facing camera	Android phones can use either a front- or rear-facing camera, allowing developers to create applications involving video calling.
Voice-based recognition	Android recognizes voice actions for calling, texting, and navigating with the phone.
3D graphics	The interface can support 3D graphics for a 3D interactive game experience or 3D image rendering.
Facial recognition	Android provides this high-level feature for automatically identifying or verifying a person's face from a digital image or a video frame.

Table 1-1   Android platform features

Writing Android Apps

Android apps are written using the Java programming language. **Java** is a language and a platform originated by Sun Microsystems. Java is an **object-oriented programming language** patterned after the C++ language. Object-oriented programming encourages good software engineering practices such as code reuse. The most popular tool for writing Java programs is called Eclipse, an integrated development environment (IDE) for building and integrating application development tools and open-source projects.

As shown in the preface of this book, the first step in setting up your Android programming environment is to install the free Eclipse IDE. After installing Eclipse, the next step is to install the plug-in called the Android Software Development Kit (SDK), which runs in Eclipse. The Android SDK includes a set of development tools that help you design the interface of the program, write the code, and test the program using a built-in Android handset emulator. To write Android programs, you must also add an Eclipse plug-in called the Android Development Tools (ADT), which extends the capabilities of Eclipse to let you quickly set up new Android projects, create an application user interface, and debug your applications. Another language called **XML** (Extensible Markup Language) is used to assist in the layout of the Android emulator.

GTK
Eclipse can be used to develop applications in many programming languages, including Java, C, C++, COBOL, Ada, and Python.

Android Emulator

The Android emulator lets you design, develop, prototype, and test Android applications without using a physical device. When you run an Android program in Eclipse, the emulator starts so you can test the program. You can then use the mouse to simulate touching the screen of the device. The emulator mimics almost every feature of a real Android handset except for the ability to place a voice phone call. A running emulator can play video and audio, render gaming animation, and store information. Multiple emulators are available within the Android SDK to target various devices and versions from early Android phones onward. Developers should test their apps on several versions to confirm the stability of a particular platform. The first Android version, release 1.0, was introduced in September 2008. Each subsequent version adds new features and fixes any known bugs in the platform. Android has adopted a naming system for each version based on dessert items, as shown in Table 1-2. After the first version, dessert names have been assigned in alphabetical order.

Version	Name	Release Date
1.0	First version	September 2008
1.5	Cupcake	April 2009
1.6	Donut	September 2009
2.0	Éclair	October 2009
2.2	Froyo (Frozen Yogurt)	May 2010
2.3	Gingerbread	December 2010
3.0	Honeycomb	February 2011
4.0	Ice Cream Sandwich	May 2011

Table 1-2   Android version history

Getting Oriented with Market Deployment

The Android platform consists of the Android OS, the Android application development tools, and a marketplace for Android applications. After you write and test a program, you compile the app into an Android package file with the filename extension .apk.

Programs written for the Android platform are sold and deployed through an online store called the **Android Market** (*http://market.android.com*), which provides registration services and certifies that the program meets minimum standards of reliability, efficiency, and performance. The Android Market requires that you sign an agreement and pay a one-time registration fee (currently $25). After registration, you can publish your app on the Android Market, provided the app meets the minimum standards. You can also release updates as needed for your app. If your app is free, the Android Market publishes your app at no cost. If you want to charge for your app, the standard split is 70 percent of sales for the developer and 30 percent for the wireless carriers. For example, if you created an app for your city that featured all the top restaurants, hotels, attractions, and festivals and sold the app for $1.99, you would net $1.39 for each app sold. If you sell 5,000 copies of your app, you would earn almost $7,000. You can use the Android Market to sell a wide range of content, including downloadable content, such as media files or photos, and virtual content such as game levels or potions (Figure 1-4). As an Android developer, you have the opportunity to develop apps for a fairly new market and easily distribute the app to the millions of Android mobile device owners.

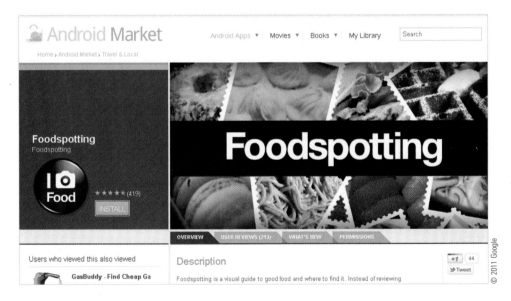

Figure 1-4 Android Market

IN THE TRENCHES
The Apple iTunes App Store charges a $99 yearly registration fee to publish an app through the iPhone Dev Center. The iTunes App Store has a much more rigorous standards approval process than the Android Market.

The online company Amazon also has a separate Appstore (*http://amazon.com/appstore*) where Android apps can be deployed and sold. The Amazon Appstore is a category listed on Amazon.com. Customers can shop for apps from their PCs and mobile devices. The Amazon Appstore has an established marketing environment and search engine that displays a trusted storefront and creates app recommendations based on customers' past purchases. The Amazon Appstore charges a $99 annual developer program fee, which covers the application processing and account management for the Amazon Appstore Developer Program. Amazon also pays developers 70 percent of the sale price of the app; in addition, you can post free apps.

First Venture into the Android World

After installing the Eclipse IDE, installing the Android SDK, and creating the Android Virtual Device (AVD) as instructed in the preface of this book, the next step is to create your first Android application. As programming tradition mandates, your first program is called Hello Android World. The following sections introduce you to the elements of the Android SDK and provide a detailed description of each step to create your first app.

Opening Eclipse to Create a New Project

To create a new Android project, you first open Eclipse and then select an Android project. As you create your first project, you provide the following information:

- *Project name*—The Eclipse project name is the name of the directory that will contain the project files.

- *Application name*—This is the human-readable title for your application, which will appear on the Android device.

- *Package name*—This is the Java package namespace where your source code will reside. You need to have at least a period (.) in the package name. Typically, the recommended package name convention is your domain name in reverse order. For example, the domain name of this book is androidbootcamp.net. The package name would be net.androidbootcamp. HelloAndroidWorld. The package name must be unique when posted on the Android Market, so it is vital to use a standard domain-style package name for your applications.

- *Create Activity*—As the Activity name, use the name for the class that is generated by the plug-in. This will be a subclass of Android's Activity class. An Activity is a class that can run and do work, such as creating a user interface. Creating an Activity is optional, but an Activity is almost always used as the basis for an application.

- *Minimum SDK*—This value specifies the minimum application programming interface (API) level required by your application.

Creating the Hello World Project

A project is equivalent to a single program or app using Java and the Android SDK. Be sure you have a blank USB (Universal Serial Bus) drive plugged into your computer so you can store the Android project on this USB drive. To create a new Android project, you can take the following steps:

1. Open the Eclipse program. Click the first button on the Standard toolbar, which is the New button.

   The New dialog box opens (Figure 1-5).

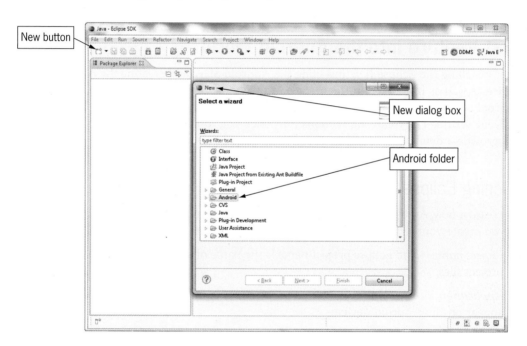

Figure 1-5   New dialog box

2. Expand the Android folder and then select the Android Project icon.

   Android Project is selected in the New dialog box (Figure 1-6).

Figure 1-6 Selecting an Android project

3. Click the Next button. In the New Android Project dialog box, enter the Project Name **Hello Android World**. To save the project on your USB drive, click to remove the check mark from the Use default location check box. In the Location text box, enter **E:\Workspace** (E: identifies the USB drive; your drive letter might differ). Throughout the rest of this book, the USB drive is called the E: drive, though you should select the drive on your computer that represents your USB device.

If you are using a Mac, enter **\Volumes***USB_DRIVE_NAME* *instead of* E:\Workspace.

The New Android project has a project name and a location of E:\Workspace, a folder on a USB drive (Figure 1-7).

12

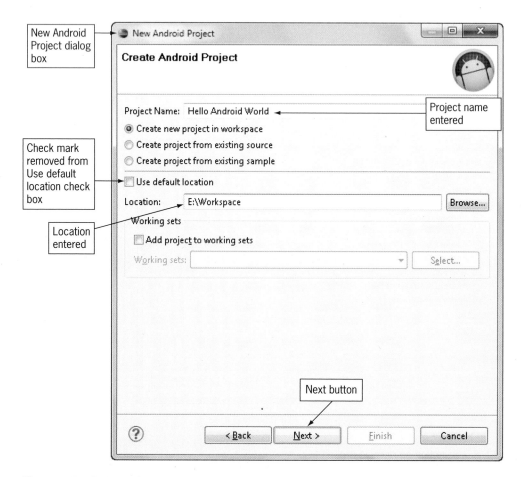

Figure 1-7   Project information entered

4.   Click the Next button. To select a build target that works on most Android phones, accept Android 4.0 for the Build Target, which is selected by default. (If you are deploying to an earlier model of an Android phone, you can select an earlier version for the Build Target.) Click the Next button.

For the Application Info, type the Package Name **net.androidbootcamp. helloandroidworld**. Enter **Main** in the Create Activity text box. Notice the Minimum SDK uses the API number of 14 from the selected Build Target of the Android 4.0.

The new Android project has an application name, a package name, and an Activity (Figure 1-8).

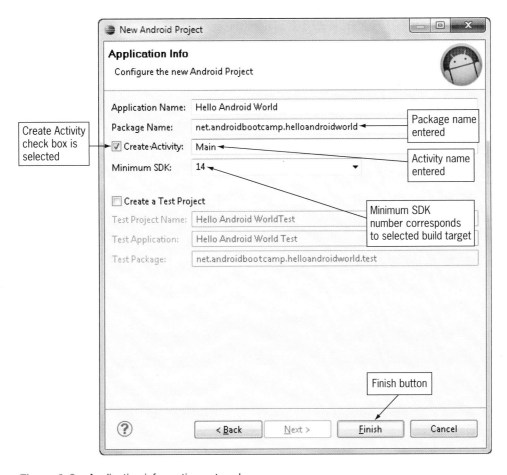

Create Activity check box is selected

Package name entered

Activity name entered

Minimum SDK number corresponds to selected build target

Finish button

Figure 1-8 Application information entered

5. Click the Finish button.

    The Android project files are created on the USB drive. The project Hello Android World appears in the left pane.

Building the User Interface

This first Android app will display the simple message, "Hello World – My First Android App." Beyond the tools and gadgets of the Android environment, what will stand out most is the user experience—how a user feels while using a particular device. Ensuring an intuitive user interface that does not detract from functionality is the key to successful usage. Android supports two ways of building the user interface of an application: through Java code and through XML layout files. The XML method is preferred as it allows you to design the user interface of an application without needing to write large amounts of code. Both methods and more details about building the user interface are covered in later chapters.

Taking a Tour of the Package Explorer

The **Package Explorer** on the left side of the Eclipse program window contains the Hello Android World application folders. When the project folder Hello Android World is expanded (Figure 1-9), the Android project includes files in the following folders:

- The **src folder** includes the Java code source files for the project.

- The **gen folder** contains Java files that are automatically generated.

- The **Android 4.0 Library** contains a single file, android.jar. The android.jar file contains all the class libraries needed to build an Android application for this version.

- The **assets folder** holds any asset files that are accessed through classic file manipulation.

- The **res folder** contains all the resources, such as images, music, and video files, that your application may need. The user interface is in a subfolder of the res folder named layout.

- The **AndroidManifest.xml** file contains all the information about the application that Android needs to run.

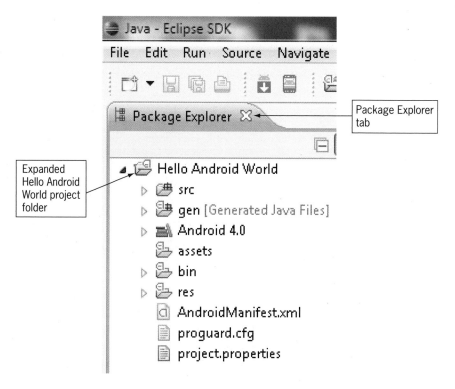

Figure 1-9   Expanded Hello Android World project folder

Designing the User Interface Layout

To assist in designing the Android user interface, the Android SDK includes layout files. You can create a layout and then add widgets to the layout. A **layout** is a container that can hold as many widgets as needed. A **widget** is a single element such as a TextView, Button, or CheckBox control, and is also called an object. Upcoming chapters demonstrate many layouts, each with unique properties and characteristics. To open the layout files, follow these steps:

1. Close any tabs that are open on the right side of the Eclipse window and minimize the Console pane that appears at the bottom of the window, if necessary. Open the Package Explorer (if necessary) by clicking Window on the menu bar, pointing to Show View, and then clicking Package Explorer.

    Expand the Hello Android World project in the Package Explorer. Expand the res folder to display its subfolders. Expand the layout subfolder. Double-click the main. xml file. To select an emulator, click the emulator button directly above the Palette, and then click 3.7in WVGA (Nexus One), if necessary. You can use many phone emulators, but throughout this text, select the 3.7in WVGA (Nexus One) emulator. Click the Zoom In button on the right side of the window to make the emulator screen as large as possible.

    The main.xml tab and the contents of the main.xml file are displayed in the Project window. The main.xml tab includes an asterisk (*) to indicate that project changes have not been saved. Note that Android placed a default TextView control in the emulator window (Figure 1-10).

Emulator is 3.7in WVGA
(Nexus One)

main.xml tab

Emulator window

main.xml

Zoom In button

Default TextView
control

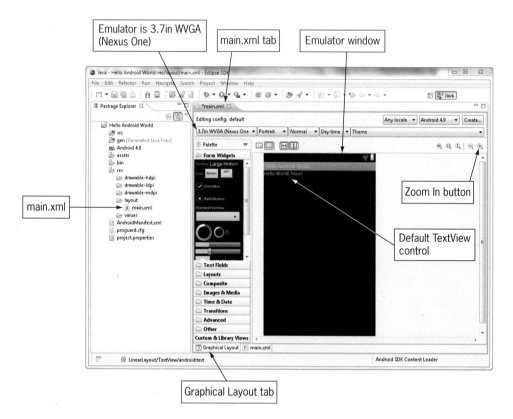

Graphical Layout tab

Figure 1-10   Layout displayed in the Eclipse window

2. In the emulator window, select the default TextView control, which reads Hello
    World, Main!.

    *The default TextView control is selected and displayed in a blue selection box
    (Figure 1-11).*

Figure 1-11   Selected TextView control

3.   Press the Delete key.

The default TextView control that Android placed in the user interface is deleted.

GTK

The default Android device shown in the Graphical Layout view when using some of the latest platforms is a 10.1-inch tablet. You can select a different device at the top of the Graphical Layout tabbed window. It is best not to target your program for the latest platform because older phones cannot run the application.

Adding a Form Widget to the User Interface Layout

The Android User Interface Layout editor displays form widgets that you place on the user interface using the drag-and-drop method. Technically, a widget is a View object that functions as an interface for interaction with the mobile user. In other words, a widget is a control such as a message users read or a button users click. The tabs at the bottom of the emulator identify the Graphical Layout window and the main.xml window, which displays the code behind each form widget. Each window displays a different view of the project: The Layout view allows you to preview how the controls will appear on various screens and orientations, and the XML view shows you the XML definition of the resource.

To display a message on the Android device, you must first place a TextView form widget on the emulator and then select the main.xml tab to open the code behind the TextView control. The main.xml coding window is written in XML code, not Java code. To add a form widget to the user interface layout, follow these steps:

1. In the main.xml tab, select TextView in the Form Widgets list. Drag the TextView control to the emulator window and drop it below the title Hello Android World.

   The TextView control is placed in the emulator window (Figure 1-12).

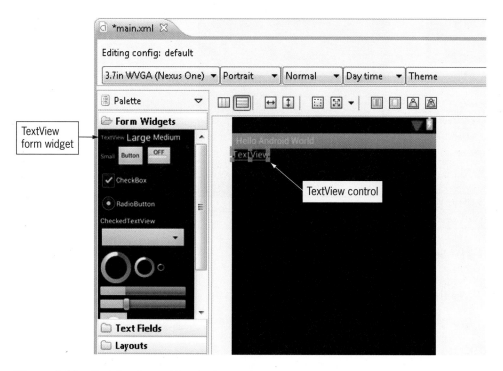

Figure 1-12   TextView form widget in the emulator

2. Click the main.xml tab below the emulator window.

   The main.xml code window is displayed. The TextView code that is associated with the TextView control contains the text android:text="TextView" /> (Figure 1-13).

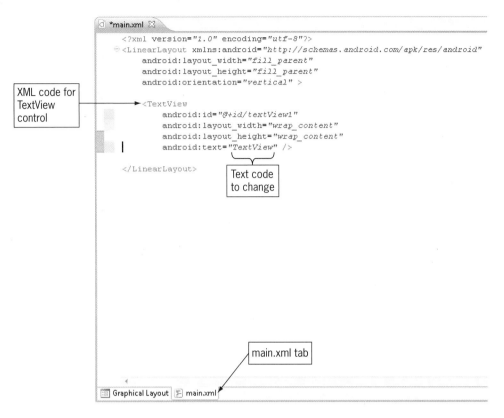

XML code for TextView control

Text code to change

main.xml tab

Figure 1-13 Displaying the XML code for the TextView control

3. To change the text displayed in the TextView control when the program is executed, select the word TextView in the next-to-last line of code, android:text="TextView". Change "TextView" to **"Hello World – My First Android App"**. Do not change any other text on this line of code.

The next-to-last code line now begins with android:text="Hello World – My First Android App" (Figure 1-14).

```
  *main.xml ⊠
      <?xml version="1.0" encoding="utf-8"?>
    ⊖<LinearLayout xmlns:android="http://schemas.android.com/apk/res/android"
          android:layout_width="fill_parent"
          android:layout_height="fill_parent"
          android:orientation="vertical" >

          <TextView
              android:id="@+id/textView1"
              android:layout_width="wrap_content"
              android:layout_height="wrap_content"
              android:text="Hello World - My First Android App" />

      </LinearLayout>
```
New text entered

Figure 1-14   Changing the TextView control text

4.   Click the Graphical Layout tab to display the revised text in the TextView control. Click File on the menu bar and then click Save All to update your project.

The Hello World – My First Android App TextView control fits on one line in the emulator (Figure 1-15).

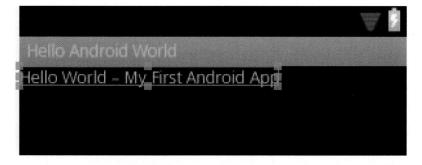

Figure 1-15   Displaying the revised text in the emulator

GTK

To deploy your app to an actual Android device instead of the emulator, you first need to install a USB driver for your device from *http://developer.android.com/sdk/win-usb.html*. On the Android device, the "USB Debugging Mode" must be checked on the Application menu. On a Mac, no USB driver installation is needed.

Testing the Application in the Emulator

Time to see the finished result! Keep in mind that the Android emulator runs slowly. It can take over a minute to display your finished results in the emulator. Even when the emulator is idling, it consumes a significant amount of CPU time, so you should close the emulator when you complete your testing. To run the application, follow these steps:

1. Click Run on the menu bar, and then click Run.

   The first time an application is run, the Run As dialog box opens (Figure 1-16).

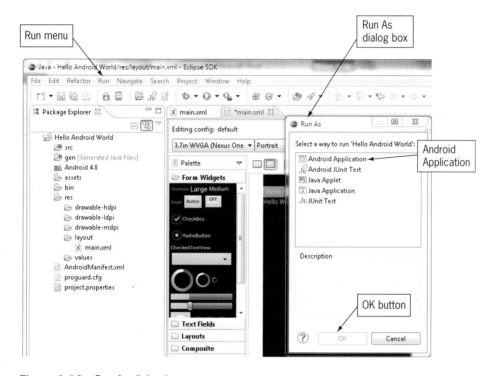

Figure 1-16   Run As dialog box

2. Click Android Application in the Run As dialog box, and then click the OK button.

   The program slowly begins to execute by displaying the Android logo and then an application window with the Android splash screen on the left. This may take up to one full minute. Next, the Android main screen appears with a lock icon (Figure 1-17).

Android
main screen

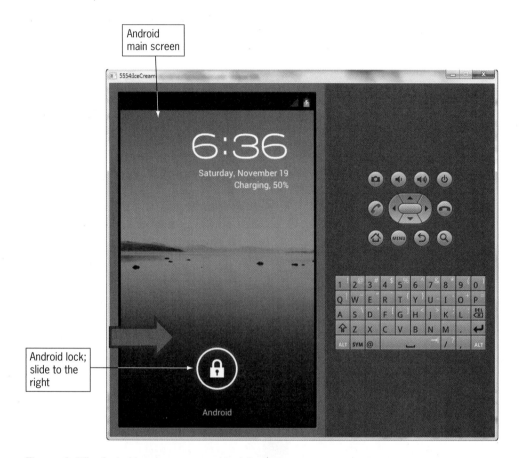

Android lock;
slide to the
right

Figure 1-17   Android main screen and lock icon

3. Click the lock icon and slide it across the screen to the right until you see a green dot
    to unlock the simulated device.

    If you are using a Mac, drag the lock icon until it changes to an unlock icon.

    *After the Android device is unlocked, the emulator displays the text message
    (Figure 1-18).*

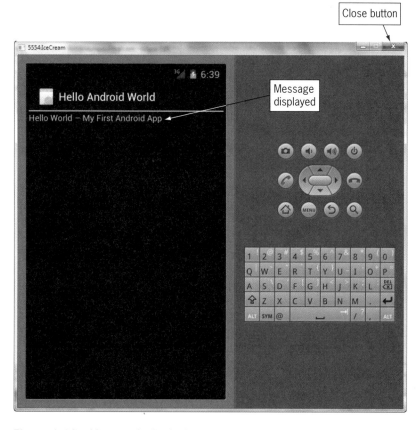

Close button

Message displayed

Figure 1-18 Message in the Android emulator

4. Close the application by clicking the Close button.

The emulated application window closes. The program is saved each time the program is run. You can close Eclipse by clicking File on the menu bar and then clicking Exit if you are working on a Windows computer. Click Quit Eclipse if you are working on a Mac.

GTK

Ctrl+F11 is the Windows shortcut key combination for running your Android application in Eclipse. On a Mac, the shortcut keys are Command+Shift+F11.

Opening a Saved App in Eclipse

After you save a project and close Eclipse, you might need to open the project and work on it again. To open a saved project, you can follow these steps with Eclipse open:

1. If the project is not listed in the Package Explorer, click File on the Eclipse menu bar and select Import. In the Import dialog box, expand the General folder, if necessary, and then click Existing Projects into Workspace.

   The Import dialog box opens and in the Select an import source area, the Existing Projects into Workspace folder is selected (Figure 1-19).

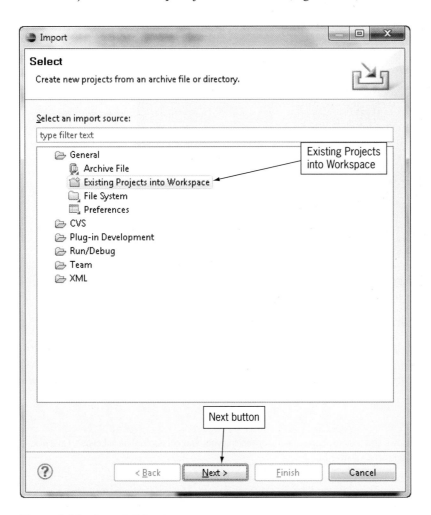

Figure 1-19   Import dialog box

2. Click the Next button. Click the Browse button next to the Select root directory text box. Click Computer and then click the USB drive on a Windows computer. (If you are using a Mac, click the USB DEVICE in the left pane of the Finder.) Click the Workspace folder. Click the OK button (or the Open button on a Mac). Insert a check mark in the Hello Android World check box, if necessary. Insert a check mark in the Copy projects into workspace check box.

    In the Import dialog box, the root directory is selected. The Hello Android World project is selected, and the Copy projects into workspace check box is checked (Figure 1-20).

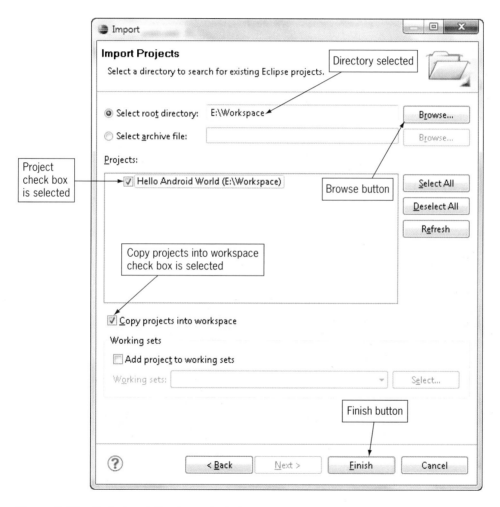

Figure 1-20 Project and directory selected

3. Click the Finish button.

    The program loads into the Package Explorer. You can now continue working on your user interface and code.

GTK

To delete a project from the project workspace, right-click the project name in the Package Explorer. Select Delete on the shortcut menu. Click the OK button. The project is still saved on the USB drive, but is no longer in the Package Explorer.

Wrap It Up—Chapter Summary

This chapter has provided an overview of the Android open-source platform, which is positioned for fast innovation without the restraints of a proprietary system. With the largest market share and its rich feature set, the Android environment allows you to develop useful, inventive Android apps. In the first chapter project, Hello Android World, you completed steps that start your journey to create more interesting applications in future chapters.

- The Android operating system is released under the Apache license, which permits anyone to download the full open-source Android code for free. Android is the first open-source technology platform for mobile devices.

- The Android OS powers all types of mobile devices, including smartphones, tablets, netbooks, e-readers, MP4 players, and Internet TVs.

- To write Android apps, you can use Eclipse, an integrated development environment for building applications, including Android apps, using Java, an object-oriented programming language.

- The Android emulator lets you design, develop, prototype, and test Android applications without using a physical device. When you run an Android program in Eclipse, the emulator starts so you can test the program as if it were running on a specified Android mobile device.

- The Android platform consists of the Android OS, the Android application development platform, and the Android Market, a marketplace for Android applications.

- Android supports two ways of building the user interface of an application: through Java code and through XML layout files. The XML method is preferred as it allows you to design the user interface of an application without needing to write large amounts of code.

- The Package Explorer on the left side of the Eclipse program window contains the folders for an Android project.

- To design a user interface for an Android app, you can create a layout, which is a container that displays widgets such as TextView, Button, and CheckBox controls, also called objects.

- After you create an application, you can run it in the Android emulator to test the application and make sure it runs correctly.

Key Terms

Android 4.0 Library—A project folder that contains the android.jar file, which includes all the class libraries needed to build an Android application for the specified version.

Android Market—An online store that sells programs written for the Android platform.

AndroidManifest.xml—A file containing all the information Android needs to run an application.

assets folder—A project folder containing any asset files that are accessed through classic file manipulation.

gen folder—A project folder that contains automatically generated Java files.

Java—An object-oriented programming language and a platform originated by Sun Microsystems.

layout—A container that can hold widgets and other graphical elements to help you design an interface for an application.

object-oriented programming language—A type of programming language that allows good software engineering practices such as code reuse.

Open Handset Alliance—An open-source business alliance of 80 firms that develop open standards for mobile devices.

Package Explorer—A pane on the left side of the Eclipse program window that contains the folders for the current project.

res folder—A project folder that contains all the resources, such as images, music, and video files, that an application may need.

smartphone—A mobile phone with advanced computing ability and connectivity features.

src folder—A project folder that includes the Java code source files for the project.

widget—A single element such as a TextView, Button, or CheckBox control, and is also called an object.

XML—An acronym for Extensible Markup Language, a widely used system for defining data formats. XML assists in the layout of the Android emulator.

Developer FAQs

1. In which year did Google purchase the company Android, Inc.?

2. What is the one-time cost for a developer's account at the Android Market?

3. When you post an Android app at the Android Market, what percentage of the app price does the developer keep?

4. How much is Amazon's annual fee for a developer's account?

5. Which three manufacturers' operating systems can be used to program an Android app?

6. Which two languages are used in creating an Android app in Eclipse?

7. What would be the recommended package name if your domain was karencodeworld.net and your project name was AndroidMap?

8. Name three widgets mentioned in this chapter.

9. What is the name of the widget that was used in the Hello Android World app?

10. Which two key combinations can you press to execute an Android app in Eclipse?

11. Which Android version is Ice Cream Sandwich?

12. Using the alphabetical theme for Android version names, list three possible future names for the next versions of Android device operating systems.

13. What does XML stand for?

14. What does SDK stand for?

15. Where are music and image files saved within the Package Explorer?

Beyond the Book

Using the Internet, search the Web for the following answers to further your Android knowledge.

1. Research a particular model of a popular Android mobile device and write a paragraph on this device's features, specifications, price, and manufacturer.

2. Name five Android mobile device features not mentioned in the "Meet the Android" section of Chapter 1.

3. What is the current annual cost for a developer's account at the Phone 7 app store called the Windows Phone 7 Marketplace?

4. Go to the Android Market Web site and take a screen shot of each of the following app categories: education, gaming, mapping, travel, and personal hobby. Place screen shots in a word processor document and label each one to identify it.

Case Programming Projects

Complete one or more of the following case programming projects. Use the same steps and techniques taught within the chapter. Submit the program you create to your instructor. The level of difficulty is indicated for each case programming project.

Easiest: ★

Intermediate: ★ ★

Challenging: ★ ★ ★

Case Project 1–1: Quote of the Day App ★

Requirements Document

Application title: Quote of the Day App

Purpose: In the Quote of the Day app, a famous quotation of your choice
                  is displayed.

Algorithms: The opening screen displays the quotation of the day.

Conditions: You may change the quotation to your own (Figure 1-21).

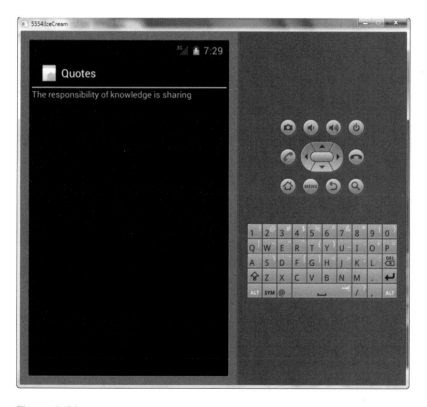

Figure 1-21

Case Project 1–2: Android Terminology App ★ ★

Application title:	Android Terminology App
Purpose:	In the Android Terminology app, three terms introduced in Chapter 1 and their definitions are displayed.
Algorithms:	The opening screen displays three different terms from this chapter and their definitions.
Conditions:	Multiple TextView controls are required.

Case Project 1–3: Business Card App ★ ★ ★

Application title:	Business Card App
Purpose:	In the Business Card app, your address and information are displayed.
Algorithms:	The opening screen displays a simple business card with your personal information. The first line should include your name. The second line should include your future dream job title. The third line should include your address. The fourth line should include your city, state, and postal code. The last line should include your phone number.
Conditions:	Multiple TextView controls are required.

Simplify! The Android User Interface

Unless otherwise noted in the chapter, all screenshots are provided courtesy of Eclipse.

In this chapter, you learn to:

- ◎ Develop a user interface using the TextView, ImageView, and Button controls
- ◎ Create an Android project that includes a Button event
- ◎ Select a Linear or Relative layout for the user interface
- ◎ Create multiple Android Activities
- ◎ Add activities to the Android Manifest file
- ◎ Add a Java class file
- ◎ Write code using the onCreate method
- ◎ Display content using the setContentView command
- ◎ Open a second screen using a Button event handler
- ◎ Use an OnClickListener to detect user interaction
- ◎ Launch a second screen using a startActivity method
- ◎ Correct errors in Java code
- ◎ Run the completed app in the emulator

Before a mobile app can be coded using Java, it must be designed. Designing a program can be compared with constructing a building. Before cement slabs are poured, steel beams are put in place, and walls are erected, architects and engineers must design the building to ensure it will perform as required and be safe and reliable. The same holds true for a computer app developer. Once the program is designed within the user interface, it can be implemented through the use of Extensible Markup Language (XML) and Java code to perform the functions for which it was designed.

Designing an Android App

To illustrate the process of designing and implementing an Android app, in this chapter you will design and code the Healthy Recipes application shown in Figure 2-1 and Figure 2-2.

Figure 2-1   Healthy Recipes Android app

Figure 2-2   Second window displaying the recipe

The Android app in Figure 2-1 could be part of a larger app that is used to display Healthy Recipes. The Healthy Recipes app begins by displaying the recipe name, which is Simple Salsa for this recipe, and an image illustrating the completed recipe. If the user taps the View Recipe button, a second window opens displaying the full recipe, including the ingredients and preparation for the salsa.

IN THE TRENCHES
If you own a data plan phone, tablet, or slate device, download the free app called Epicurious to get an idea of how this Healthy Recipes app would be used in a much larger application.

The Big Picture

To create the Healthy Recipes application, you follow a set of steps that you repeat every time you create an Android application.

1. Create the user interface, also called an XML layout, for every screen in the application.

2. Create a Java class, also called an Activity, for every screen in the application.

3. Update the Android Manifest file for each Java class in the application.

4. Code each Java class with the appropriate objects and actions as needed.

Using the Android User Interface

Before any code can be written for an Android application, the project structure of the user experience must be designed by means of the user interface. For an Android application, the user interface is a window on the screen of any mobile device in which the user interacts with the program. The user interface is stored in the res/layout folder in the Package Explorer. The layout for the user interface is designed with XML code. Special Android-formatted XML code is extremely compact, which means the application uses less space and runs faster on the device. Using XML for layout also saves you time in developing your code; for example, if you developed this recipe app for use in eight human languages, you could use the same Java code with eight unique XML layout files, one for each language. To open the layout of the user interface of the Healthy Recipes app, follow these steps to begin the application:

1. Open the Eclipse program. Click the New button on the Standard toolbar. Expand the Android folder, if necessary, and select Android Project. Click the Next button. In the New Android Project dialog box, enter the Project Name **Healthy Recipes**. To save the project on your USB drive, click to remove the check mark from the Use default location check box. Type **E:\Workspace** (if necessary, enter a different drive letter that identifies the USB drive). Click Next. For the Build Target, select Android 4.0, if necessary. Click Next. Type the Package Name **net.androidbootcamp. healthyrecipes**. Type **Main** in the Create Activity text box.

Notice the Minimum SDK text box displays the API number from the selected Build Target (Android 4.0). If you are deploying to an earlier model of an Android phone, you can select an earlier version.

The new Android Healthy Recipes project has an application name, a package name, and a Main Activity (Figure 2-3).

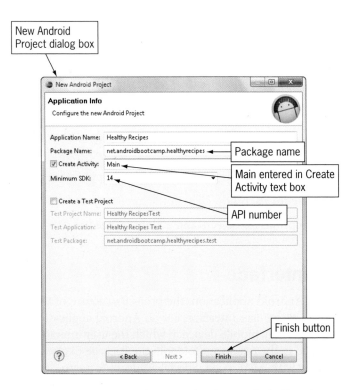

Figure 2-3   Application information for the new Android project

2.   Click the Finish button. Expand the Healthy Recipes project in the Package Explorer. Expand the res folder to display its subfolders. Expand the layout subfolder. Double-click the main.xml file. Click the Hello World, Main! TextView (displayed by default). Press the Delete key.

The main.xml file is displayed on the Graphical Layout tab and the Hello World TextView widget is deleted (Figure 2-4).

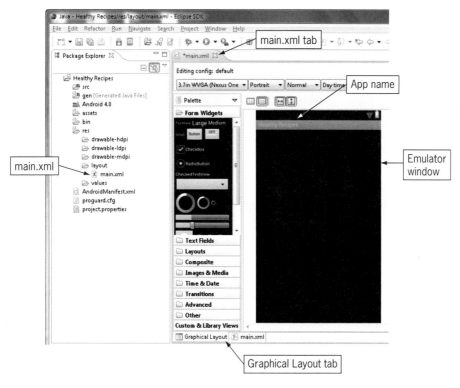

Figure 2-4 Displaying the emulator window for the Healthy Recipes project

Linear Layouts and Relative Layouts

The Android user interface includes a layout resource designer that organizes how controls appear on the app's various screens. When you click the Graphical Layout tab as shown in Figure 2-4, you display the default user interface for main.xml, which uses a resource file defined as a Linear layout. A **Linear layout** organizes layout components in a vertical column or horizontal row. In Figure 2-5, multiple ImageView controls (Android icons) were dragged onto the emulator window. By default, the Linear layout places each control directly below the previous control to form a vertical column. You can change the Linear layout's orientation from vertical to horizontal by right-clicking the emulator window, pointing to Orientation on the shortcut menu, and then clicking Horizontal. If you select a horizontal Linear layout, the controls are arranged horizontally in a single row, as shown in Figure 2-6.

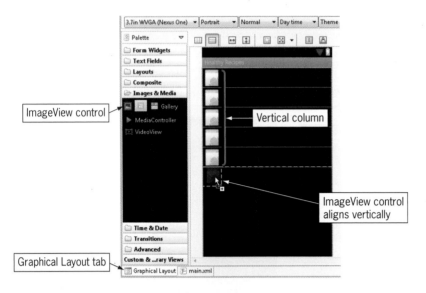

Figure 2-5　Linear layout with a vertical orientation (default)

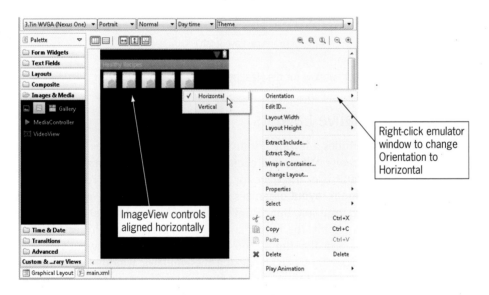

Figure 2-6　Linear layout with a horizontal orientation

Linear layouts are common for forms that display controls in a single row or column. Android user interface designers typically use another layout called a Relative layout. A **Relative layout** organizes layout components in relation to each other. This provides more flexibility in positioning controls than Linear layouts. To change the default Linear layout to a Relative layout, right-click the emulator window and click Change Layout. In the Change Layout dialog box, click the New Layout Type button and then click RelativeLayout. Click the OK button to change the emulator to a Relative layout. As shown in Figure 2-7, five ImageView controls are placed anywhere the developer desires. Using a Relative layout, you can place an ImageView, TextView, RadioButton, or Button control to the left of, to the right of, above, or below another control. Layout resources are stored as XML code in the res/layout resource directory for the Android application corresponding to the user interface template.

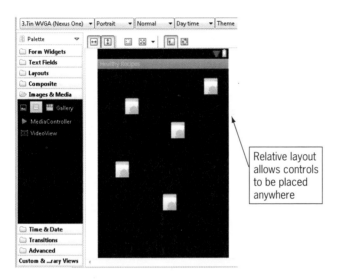

Relative layout allows controls to be placed anywhere

Figure 2-7   Relative layout

GTK

Other layouts you can use include a Frame layout, Table layout, and Table Row layout. You also can use a combination of layouts, which means you can nest controls within one another.

Designing the Healthy Recipes Opening User Interface

When the Healthy Recipes app opens, the initial screen as shown in Figure 2-1 displays a TextView control with the text Simple Salsa, an ImageView control with a picture of the finished salsa, and a Button control with the text View Recipe. Notice that the controls are not in a Linear layout, but use a Relative layout so they are placed freely on the screen. Instead of using XML code to change the text of each control, in this chapter you modify a control's properties using the Properties pane. To change the property of a control, select the control first, and then change the appropriate property, such as the text or size, in the Properties pane.

Android Text Properties

The most popular text properties change the displayed text, modify the size of the text, and change the alignment of the text. The **Text property** changes the text written within the control. The **Text size property** can use various units of measurement, as shown in Table 2-1. The preferred unit of measurement is often **sp**, which stands for scaled-independent pixels. The reason for using this unit of measurement is that if a user has set up an Android phone to display a large font size for more clarity and easier visibility, the font in the app will be scaled to meet the user's size preference.

Unit of Measure	Abbreviation	Example
Inches	in	"0.5in"
Millimeters	mm	"20mm"
Pixels	px	"100px"
Density-independent pixels	dp or dip	"100dp" or "100dip"
Scaled-independent pixels	sp	"100sp"

Table 2-1   Measurements used for the Text size property

On the opening screen of the Healthy Recipes app, the TextView control for the title, ImageView control for the salsa picture, and Button controls can all be centered on the screen using a guide, a green dashed vertical line that appears when a control is dragged to the emulator window. The Relative layout allows controls to be placed anywhere, but the green dashed line centers each control perfectly.

GTK
All Palette controls such as TextView and ImageView can use a property called Layout margin top. For example, if you type 50dp to the right of the Layout margin top property, the control is placed 50 pixels from the top of the screen to help you design an exact layout. You can also center using the Layout center horizontal property by changing the setting to true.

To place all three centered controls on the form using a Relative layout, follow these steps:

1. In the main.xml window, right-click the emulator window, and then click Change Layout on the shortcut menu. In the Change Layout dialog box, click the New Layout Type button, and then click RelativeLayout.

   The Change Layout dialog box opens and the RelativeLayout is selected (Figure 2-8).

Change Layout
dialog box

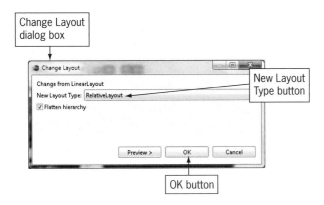

New Layout
Type button

OK button

Figure 2-8   Change Layout dialog box

2.   Click the OK button. In the Form Widgets Palette, select the Form Widget named
     TextView. Drag the TextView control to the emulator window and drop it below the
     Healthy Recipes title. To center the TextView control, drag the control to the center
     of the window until a green dashed vertical line identifying the window's center is
     displayed. To open the Properties pane, right-click the emulator window, point to
     Show In on the shortcut menu, and then click Properties. With the TextView control
     selected, scroll down the Properties pane, and then click the Text property.

     *The TextView object is placed in the emulator window, the Properties pane is opened,
     and the Text property is selected (Figure 2-9).*

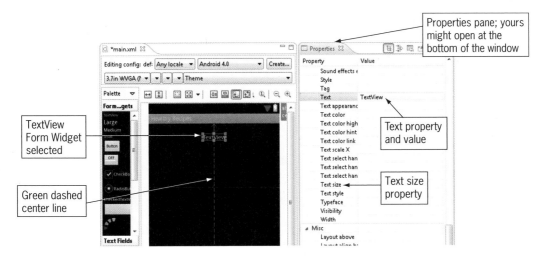

Figure 2-9   Text property in the Properties pane

3. Change the Text property to **Simple Salsa**. In the Properties pane, scroll to the Text size property, type **40sp** to represent the scaled-independent pixel size, and then press Enter.

The TextView object has the Text property of Simple Salsa and the Text size is 40sp (Figure 2-10).

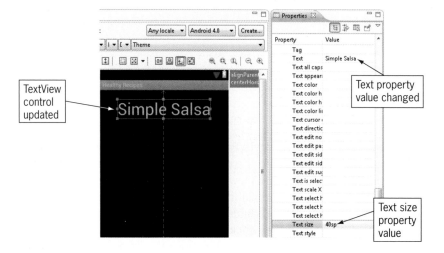

TextView control updated

Text property value changed

Text size property value

Figure 2-10   Updated Text property

GTK
The top free Android apps are Google Maps, YouTube, Facebook, Pandora, and Netflix, in that order.

GTK
Throughout the book, note that Windows computers have an Enter key, but Mac computers use the Return key.

Adding a File to the Resources Folder

In the Healthy Recipes application, an image of salsa is displayed in an ImageView control. Before you can insert the ImageView control in the emulator window, you must place the appropriate picture file in the resources folder. In the Package Explorer in the left pane of the Eclipse program window, the res (resource) folder contains three subfolders whose names start with *drawable*. The graphics used by the application can be stored in these folders. Android supports three types of graphic formats: .png (preferred), .jpg (acceptable), and .gif (discouraged). Android creates a Drawable resource for any of these files when you save them in the res/drawable folder. The three drawable folders are identified with the following dpi (dots per inch) densities shown in Table 2-2.

Name	Description
hdpi	Resources for high-density screens
mdpi	Resources for medium-density screens
ldpi	Resources for low-density screens

Table 2-2   Drawable folders

Place the salsa image in the res/drawable-hdpi folder to be used by the ImageView control, which links to the resource image. You should already have the student files for this text that your instructor gave you or that you downloaded from the Web page for this book (*www.cengage.com*). To place a copy of the salsa image from the USB drive into the res/drawable-hdpi folder, follow these steps:

1. If necessary, copy the student files to your USB drive. Open the USB folder containing the student files. In the Package Explorer pane, expand the drawable-hdpi folder. A file named ic_launcher.png (the Android logo) is typically contained within this folder already. To add the salsa.png file to the drawable-hdpi resource folder, drag the salsa.png file to the drawable-hdpi folder until a plus sign pointer appears. Release the mouse button.

The File Operation dialog box opens (Figure 2-11).

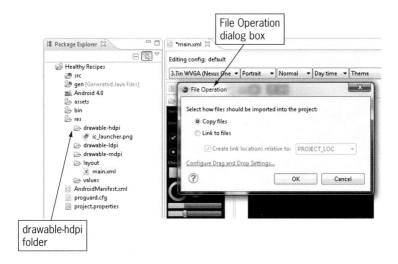

Figure 2-11   File Operation dialog box

2. If necessary, click the Copy files option button, and then click the OK button.

    A copy of the salsa.png file appears in the drawable-hdpi folder.

GTK

High-density graphics have 240 dots per inch, medium-density graphics have 160 dots per inch, and low-density graphics have 120 dots per inch.

Adding an ImageView Control

After an image is placed in a drawable resource folder, you can place an ImageView control in the emulator window. An **ImageView control** can display an icon or a graphic such as a picture file or shape on the Android screen. To add an ImageView control from the Images & Media category of the Palette, follow these steps:

1. Close the Properties pane to create more room to work. Click the Images & Media category in the Palette on the Graphical Layout tab. Drag an ImageView control (the first control in this category) to the emulator window. Drag the control to the center until a green dashed vertical center line appears. Release the mouse button.

    The ImageView control is centered and the Resource Chooser dialog box opens (Figure 2-12).

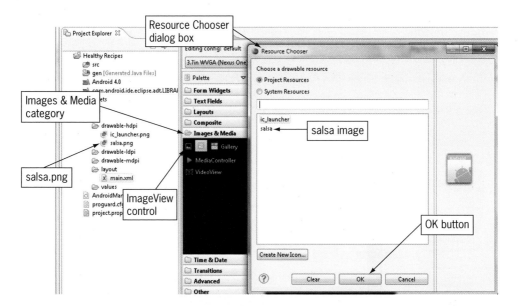

Figure 2-12   Resource Chooser dialog box

2. Click salsa in the Resource Chooser dialog box, and then click the OK button.

The salsa image is displayed in the emulator window.

IN THE TRENCHES
If you have an image that you want to use in your Android app, but the file type is not .png, open the image in Microsoft Paint or a similar type of program. You can convert the file type by saving the image as a .png file.

Adding a Button Control

A Button control is a commonly used object in a graphical user interface. For example, you probably are familiar with the OK button used in many applications. Generally, when the program is running, buttons are used to cause an event to occur. The Android SDK includes three types of button controls: Button, ToggleButton, and ImageButton. The Button control is provided in the Form Widgets category in the Palette. In the Healthy Recipes app, the user taps a Button control to display the salsa recipe on a second screen. To name the Button control, you use the Id property. For example, use btnRecipe as the Id property for the Button control in the Healthy Recipes app. The prefix btn represents a button in the code. If you intend to use a control in the Java code, it is best to name that control using the Id property. To add a Button control from the Form Widgets category of the Palette, follow these steps:

1. Click the Form Widgets category in the Palette. Drag the Button control to the emulator window below the ImageView control until a green dashed vertical center line appears. Release the mouse button. To open the Properties pane, right-click the emulator window, point to Show In on the shortcut menu, and then select Properties. Click the Button control, and then scroll the Properties pane to the Id property, which is set to @+id/button1 by default. Change the Id property to **@+id/btnRecipe** to provide a unique name for the Button control. Scroll down to the Text property. Change the text to **View Recipe**. Change the Text size property to **30sp** and press Enter.

The Button control is named btnRecipe and displays the text View Recipe, which has the text size of 30sp (Figure 2-13).

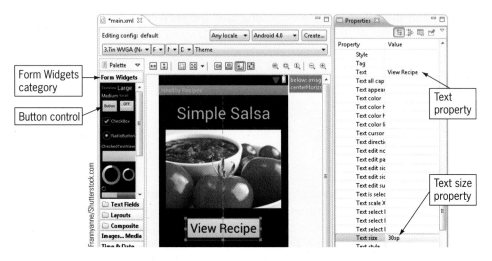

Figure 2-13   Button control

Planning a Program

As you learn the skills necessary to design an Android user interface, you are ready to learn about the program development life cycle. The program development life cycle is a set of phases and steps that developers follow to design, create, and maintain an Android program. Following are the phases of the program development life cycle:

1. *Gather and analyze the program requirements*—The developer must obtain the information that identifies the program requirements and then document these requirements.

2. *Design the user interface*—After the developer understands the program requirements, the next step is to design the user interface. The user interface provides the framework for the processing that occurs within the program.

3. *Design the program processing objects*—An Android app consists of one or more processing objects that perform the tasks required in the program. The developer must determine what processing objects are required, and then determine the requirements of each object.

4. *Code the program*—After the processing object has been designed, the object must be implemented in program code. Program code consists of the instructions written using XML and Java code that ultimately can be executed.

5. *Test the program*—As the program is being coded, and after the coding is completed, the developer should test the program code to ensure it is executing properly.

Creating Activities

The Healthy Recipes application displays two screens, as shown in Figures 2-1 and 2-2. The system requirement for this app is for the user to select a recipe name and then tap the button to display the recipe details. Screens in the Android environment are defined in layout files. Figure 2-13 shows the completed main.xml design. Next, a second screen named recipe.xml must be created and designed. Each of the two screens is considered an Activity. An **Activity**, one of the core components of an Android application, is the point at which the application makes contact with your users. For example, an Activity might create a menu of Web sites, request a street address to display a map, or even show an exhibit of photographs from an art museum. An Activity is an important component of the life cycle of an Android app. In the chapter project, each screen is an Activity where you capture and present information to the user. You can construct Activities by using XML layout files and a Java class.

Creating an XML Layout File

All XML layout files must be placed in the res/layout directory of the Android project so that the Android packaging tool can find the layout files. To create a second XML layout file to construct the second Activity, follow these steps:

1. Close the Properties pane. In the Package Explorer, right-click the layout folder. On the shortcut menu, point to New and then click Other. In the New dialog box, click Android XML Layout File, and then click Next. In the New Android Layout XML File dialog box, type **recipe.xml** in the File text box to name the layout file. In the Root Element list, select RelativeLayout.

   The XML file is named and the layout is set to RelativeLayout (Figure 2-14).

New Android
Layout XML
File dialog box

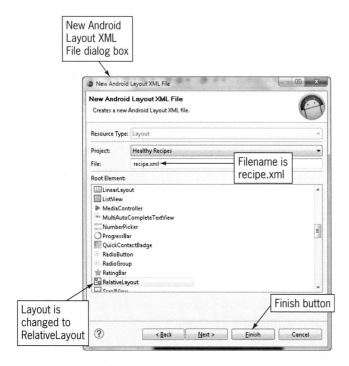

Filename is
recipe.xml

Layout is
changed to
RelativeLayout

Finish button

Figure 2-14 Naming the XML file

2. Click the Finish button. Using the techniques taught earlier in the chapter, create the second user interface, recipe.xml, as shown in Figure 2-15.

The second user interface, recipe.xml, is designed (Figure 2-15).

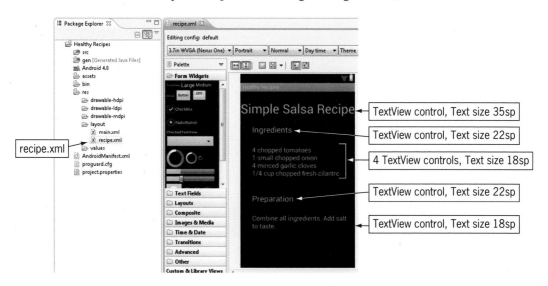

recipe.xml

TextView control, Text size 35sp

TextView control, Text size 22sp

4 TextView controls, Text size 18sp

TextView control, Text size 22sp

TextView control, Text size 18sp

Figure 2-15 User interface for recipe.xml

GTK

You can use comments to document your code. Comments are ignored by the Java compiler. When you want to make a one-line comment, type "//" and follow the two forward slashes with your comment. For example:

// This is a single-line comment

Another way to comment is to use block comments. For example:

/* This is a

block comment

*/

Adding a Class File

In the src folder in the Package Explorer is the Main.java file. This file contains the Main class that opens the main.xml screen, which you designed for the app's user interface. In object-oriented terminology, a class describes a group of objects that establishes an introduction to each object's properties. A **class** is simply a blueprint or a template for creating objects by defining its properties. An **object** is a specific, concrete instance of a class. When you create an object, you instantiate it. When you **instantiate**, you create an instance of the object by defining one particular variation of the object within a class, giving it a name, and locating it in the memory of the computer. Each class needs its own copy of an object. Later in this chapter, Java code is added to the Main class to recognize the action of tapping the Button control to open the recipe screen. Recall that each screen represents an Activity. In addition, each Activity must have a matching Java class file. The recipe.xml file that was designed as shown in Figure 2-15 must have a corresponding Java class file. It is a Java standard to begin a class name with an uppercase letter, include no spaces, and emphasize each new word with an initial uppercase letter. To add a second Java class to the application, follow these steps:

1. In the Package Explorer, expand the src folder and the net.androidbootcamp. healthyrecipes package to view the Main.java existing class. To create a second class, right-click the net.androidbootcamp.healthyrecipes folder, point to New on the shortcut menu, and then click Class.

   The New Java Class dialog box opens (Figure 2-16).

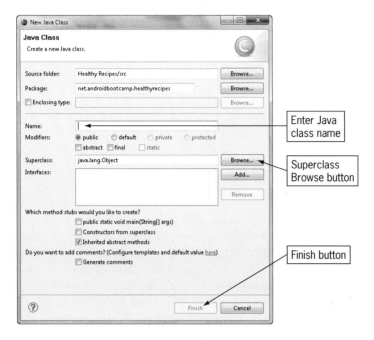

Figure 2-16   New Java Class dialog box

2. Type **Recipe** in the Name text box to create a second class for the recipe Activity. Click the Superclass Browse button. Type **Activity** in the Choose a type text box. As you type, matching items are displayed. Click Activity – android.app and then click the OK button to extend the Activity class.

    A new class named Recipe is created with the Superclass set to android.app.Activity (Figure 2-17).

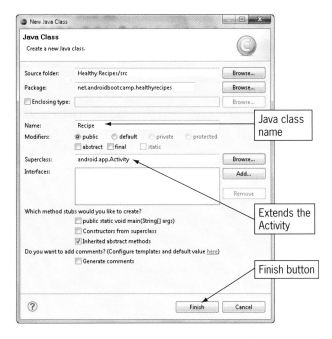

Figure 2-17 Creating the Recipe class

3. Click the Finish button to finish creating the Recipe class. Display line numbers in the code window by clicking Window on the menu bar and then clicking Preferences. In the Preferences dialog box, click General in the left pane, click Editors, and then click Text Editors. Click the Show line numbers check box to select it, and then click the OK button.

If you are using a Mac, click Eclipse on the menu bar, and then click Preferences to open the Preferences dialog box. Double-click General, double-click Editors, and then click Text Editors.

The Recipe.java class is created and line numbers are displayed (Figure 2-18).

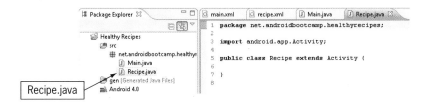

Figure 2-18 New Recipe class in the Healthy Recipes project

GTK

Using an uppercase letter to begin a Java class name and starting each new word with an uppercase letter is known as Pascal case.

The Android Manifest File

An Android project is made up of far more than the XML layout files that create the user interface. The other important components of any Android project are the Android Manifest file and the Java code in the Java classes. The **Android Manifest** file is necessary in every Android application and must have the filename AndroidManifest.xml. The Android Manifest file provides all the essential information to the Android device, such as the name of your Java application, a listing of each Activity, any permissions needed to access other Android functions such as the use of the Internet, and the minimum level of the Android API.

Adding an Activity to the Android Manifest

Eclipse automatically creates the initial Android Manifest file, but this file must be updated to include every Activity in the app. When an application has more than one Activity, the Android Manifest file must have an **intent** to navigate among multiple activities. To see which Activities an application contains, double-click the AndroidManifest.xml file in the Package Explorer, and then click the AndroidManifest.xml tab as shown in Figure 2-19. Notice that Line 14 calls an Activity named .Main. The intent in Lines 16–19 launches the opening screen.

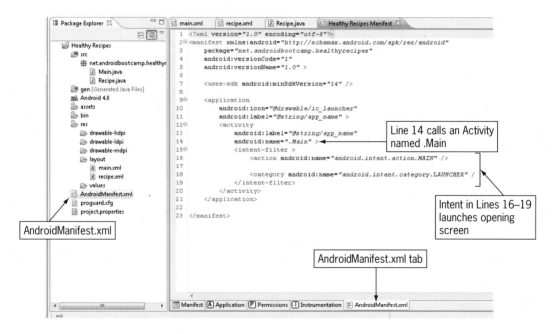

Figure 2-19   Displaying the Activities in an application

The AndroidManifest.xml file must contain an entry for each Activity. To add the second Activity to the Android Manifest file, follow these steps:

1. In the Package Explorer, double-click the AndroidManifest.xml file. To add the Recipe class to the Android Manifest, click the Application tab at the bottom of the Healthy Recipes Manifest page. Scroll down to display the Application Nodes section.

    The AndroidManifest.xml file is opened to the Application tab (Figure 2-20).

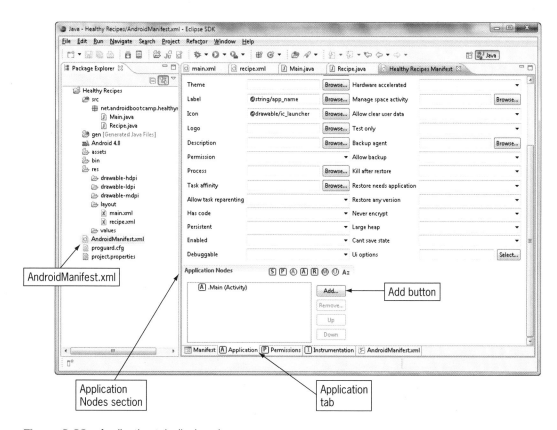

Figure 2-20 Application tab displayed

2. In the Application Nodes section, click the Add button. Select Activity in the Create a new element at the top level, in Application dialog box.

    The Create a new element at the top level, in Application dialog box opens and Activity is selected (Figure 2-21).

52

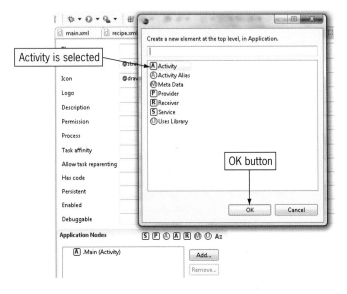

Figure 2-21   Creating an element

3.   Click the OK button. The Attributes for Activity section opens in the Application tab. In the Name text box, type the class name preceded by a period (**.Recipe**) to add the Recipe Activity to the AndroidManifest.xml file.

The class .Recipe is entered in the Name text box of the Attributes for Activity section (Figure 2-22).

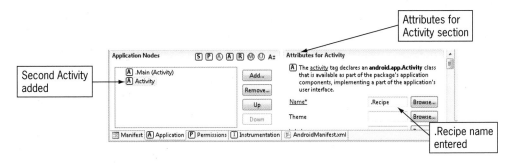

Figure 2-22   Adding the Recipe Activity

4.   To view the Main and Recipe Activities in the code, click the AndroidManifest.xml tab at the bottom of the window.

The AndroidManifest.xml code includes the .Recipe Activity in Line 21 (Figure 2-23).

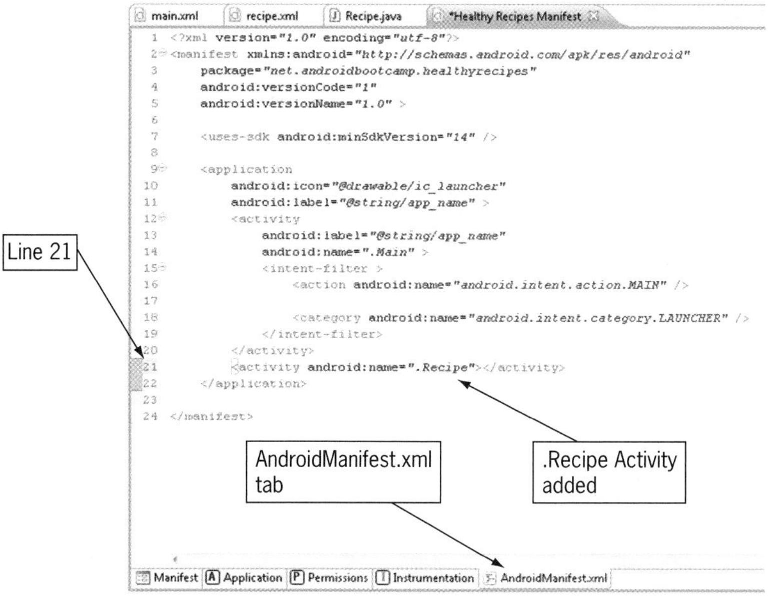

Figure 2-23 AndroidManifest.xml code

Coding the Java Activity

When the user taps an application icon on his or her Android phone or tablet, the Main.java code is read by the phone processor. The entry point of the Activity class is the onCreate( ) event handler, which is called a method. A **method** is a set of Java statements that can be included inside a Java class. The onCreate method is where you initialize the Activity. Imagine a large stack of papers on your desk. The paper on top of the stack is what you are reading right now. The Android also has a stack of Activities. The onCreate method places this new Activity on top of the stack.

Coding an onCreate Method

In the chapter project, the first Activity displayed in the title screen layout designed in main.xml is the currently running Activity. When the user presses the View Recipe button, the main.xml screen closes and a new Activity that displays the actual recipe (recipe.xml) is placed on top of the stack and becomes the running Activity. The syntax for the onCreate method is:

Code Syntax

```
public void onCreate(Bundle savedInstanceState) {
    super.onCreate(savedInstanceState);

}
```

Notice that the syntax of a method begins and ends with a curly brace.

Inside this onCreate method, the first user interface must be opened. Activities have no clue which user interface should be displayed on the screen. For a particular user interface to open on the screen, code must be added inside the onCreate method to place that specific activity on top of the stack. The Java code necessary to display the content of a specific screen is called **setContentView**.

Code Syntax

```
setContentView(R.layout.main);
```

In the code syntax, R.layout.main represents the user interface of main.xml layout, which displays the opening title, salsa image, and View Recipe button. The R represents the term Resource as the layout folder resides in the res folder.

Displaying the User Interface

The Main.java file was created automatically by Eclipse and already contains the onCreate method and setContentView(R.layout.main) code, as shown in Lines 10 and 11 in Figure 2-24. Line 10 starts the Activity and Line 11 displays the main.xml layout when the application begins.

```
  1  package net.androidbootcamp.healthyrecipes;
  2
  3⊕ import android.app.Activity;
  5
  6  public class Main extends Activity {
  7        /** Called when the activity is first created. */
  8⊝      @Override
  9        public void onCreate(Bundle savedInstanceState)         onCreate
 10            super.onCreate(savedInstanceState);                 method
 11            setContentView(R.layout.main);
 12        }                                                       setContentView(R.layout.main)
 13  }                                                            code
```

Figure 2-24   Main.java code

To display the second screen (recipe.xml), the onCreate method is necessary to place the second Activity on top of the Activity stack. Next, the setContentView command displays the recipe.xml layout. To add the onCreate and setContentView code to the Recipe.java file, follow these steps:

1. Close the Healthy Recipes Manifest tab, and then click the Yes button to save your changes. Click the Recipe.java tab to display its code. Notice that the Recipe file extends the Activity, as indicated in Line 5 of the code. Click Line 6 to move the insertion point between the two curly braces that open and close the method. Press Tab to indent the line, type **oncreate**, and then press Ctrl+spacebar (simultaneously). When you press Ctrl+spacebar, Eclipse displays an auto-complete listing with all the

possibilities that are valid at that point in the code. A yellow Help window may also appear to the left.

The onCreate method is entered in the Recipe class. A list of possible onCreate methods is displayed after pressing Ctrl+spacebar (Figure 2-25).

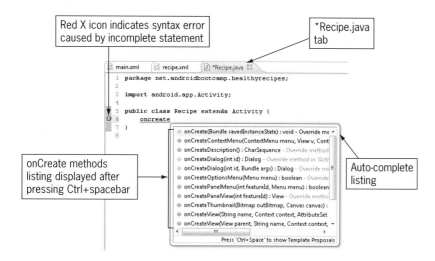

Figure 2-25 onCreate methods

2. Double-click the first onCreate method in the auto-complete listing to generate the method structure.

The onCreate method is generated in the Recipe class (Figure 2-26).

```
 main.xml      recipe.xml      *Recipe.java 
 1  package net.androidbootcamp.healthyrecipes;
 2
 3  import android.app.Activity;
 4  import android.os.Bundle;
 5
 6  public class Recipe extends Activity {
 7     @Override
 8     protected void onCreate(Bundle savedInstanceState) {
 9        // TODO Auto-generated method stub
10        super.onCreate(savedInstanceState);
11     }
12  }
13
```

onCreate method added

Figure 2-26 Inserting the onCreate method

3. Click at the end of Line 10 and then press the Enter key to insert a blank line. Type **setContentView(R.** to display an auto-complete listing. Double-click layout. Type a period. Another auto-complete listing requests the XML layout file you intend to display. Double-click recipe : int. Type **)** (a right closing parenthesis) if one does not

appear automatically. Type a semicolon after the parenthesis to complete the statement.

The setContentView command is entered to display the recipe.xml file (Figure 2-27).

```
Main.java    recipe.xml    Recipe.java ✕
1  package net.androidbootcamp.healthyrecipes;
2
3  import android.app.Activity;
4  import android.os.Bundle;
5
6  public class Recipe extends Activity {
7    @Override
8    protected void onCreate(Bundle savedInstanceState) {
9        // TODO Auto-generated method stub
10       super.onCreate(savedInstanceState);
11       setContentView(R.layout.recipe);    ◄   setContentView
12   }                                            command displays
13 }                                              recipe layout file
```

Figure 2-27   Code for displaying the recipe layout file

Creating a Button Event Handler

Android phones and tablets have touchscreens that create endless possibilities for user interaction, allowing the user to tap, swipe, and pinch in or out to change the size of the screen. As you program with this event-driven language, users typically see an interface containing controls, buttons, menus, and other graphical elements. After displaying the interface, the program waits until the user touches the device. When the user reacts, the app initiates an event, which executes code in an **event handler**, which is a part of the program coded to respond to the specific event. In the Healthy Recipes app, users have only one interaction—they can tap the Button control to start an event that displays the salsa recipe. When the user taps the Button control, code for an event listener is necessary to begin the event that displays the recipe.xml file on the Android screen. This tap event is actually known as a click event in Java code. In the Healthy Recipes application, the Main.java code must first contain the following sections:

- Class property to hold a reference to the Button object
- OnClickListener( ) method to await the button click action
- onClick( ) method to respond to the click event

The Healthy Recipes application opens with a Button control on the screen. To use that button, a reference is required in the Main.java file. To reference a Button control, use the following syntax to create a Button property:

Code Syntax

```
Button b=(Button)findViewById(R.id.btnRecipe);
```

The syntax for the Button property includes the findViewById( ) method, which is used by any Android Activity. This method finds a layout view created in the XML files that you created when designing the user interface. The variable b in the code contains the reference to the Button control. After the code is entered to reference the Button control, you can press Ctrl+spacebar to import the Button type as an Android widget. When you **import** the Button type as an Android widget, you make the classes from the Android Button package available throughout the application. An import statement is automatically placed at the top of the Java code. An **import statement** is a way of making more Java functions available to your specific program. Java can perform almost endless actions, and not every program needs to do everything. So, to limit the size of the code, Java has its classes divided into packages that can be imported at the top of your code.

After the Button property is referenced in Main.java, an OnClickListener( ) method is necessary to detect when the user taps an onscreen button. Event listeners wait for user interaction, which is when the user taps the button to view the recipe in the case of the chapter project. When an OnClickListener is placed in the code window, Java creates an onClick auto-generated stub. A **stub** is a piece of code that actually serves as a placeholder to declare itself, and it has just enough code to link to the rest of the program. The syntax needed for an OnClickListener method that listens for the Button control is shown in the following Code Syntax:

Code Syntax

```
b.setOnClickListener(new OnClickListener() {

public void onClick(View v) {
// TODO Auto-generated method stub

}
});
```

The last step to code is to call the startActivity( ) method, which opens the second Activity displaying the recipe.xml user interface. The startActivity( ) method creates an intent to start another Activity such as to start the recipe Activity class. The intent needs two parts known as parameters: a context and the name of the Activity that is being opened. A context in Android coding means that any time you request that program to launch another Activity, a context is sent to the Android system to show which initiating Activity class is making the request. The context of the chapter project is Main.this, which references the Main.java class. The following syntax line launches the Recipe Java class:

Code Syntax

```
startActivity(new Intent(Main.this, Recipe.class));
```

Coding a Button Event Handler

When the main.xml layout is initially launched by the Main.java class, it is necessary to code how the Button control interacts with the user. When this View Recipe button is tapped, the Main.java class must contain code to launch the Recipe.xml layout (Activity) and to begin the second Java class called Recipe.java. To initialize the Button control and code the Button handler to launch the second Activity class, follow these steps:

1. In the Package Explorer, double-click Main.java to open its code window. Click to the right of the setContentView(R.layout.main); line. Press the Enter key. To initialize and reference the Button control with the Id name of btnRecipe, type **Button b = (Button) findViewById(R.id.btnRecipe);**

    After the code is entered to reference the Button control, point to the red curly line below the first Button command and select Import 'Button' (android widget). Click the Save All button on the Standard toolbar to save your work.

    If you are using a Mac, error indicators in the code are red dashed lines.

    The Button control named btnRecipe is referenced in Main.java. In this case, the onCreate method is created for you in Line 11. A curly line appears below the b variable to indicate that this local variable has not been used in the code yet (Figure 2-28).

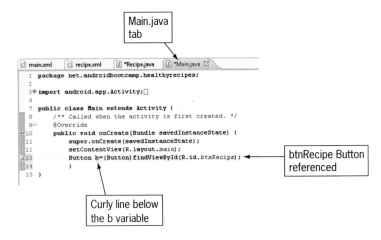

Figure 2-28   Main.java code

2. Press the Enter key. To code the button listener that awaits user interaction, type **b.seton** and then wait for a code listing to open. Double-click the first setOnClickListener to select it.

    In the parentheses, type **new on** and press Ctrl+spacebar to display an auto-complete listing. Double-click the first choice, which lists an OnClickListener with an

Anonymous Inner Type event handler. Point to the red curly line below OnClickListener. Select Import 'OnClickListener' (android.View.view).

Type **;** (semicolon) after the closing parenthesis to complete the auto-generated stub.

An OnClickListener auto-generated stub appears in the code (Figure 2-29).

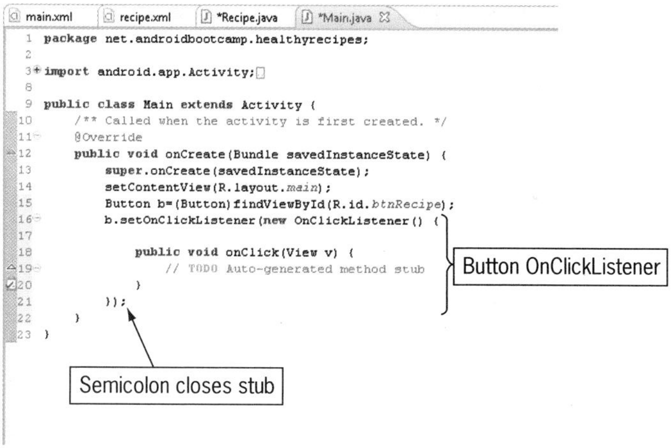

```
main.xml    recipe.xml    *Recipe.java    *Main.java ⌧
 1  package net.androidbootcamp.healthyrecipes;
 2
 3+ import android.app.Activity;▯
 8
 9  public class Main extends Activity {
10      /** Called when the activity is first created. */
11      @Override
12      public void onCreate(Bundle savedInstanceState) {
13          super.onCreate(savedInstanceState);
14          setContentView(R.layout.main);
15          Button b=(Button)findViewById(R.id.btnRecipe);
16          b.setOnClickListener(new OnClickListener() {
17
18              public void onClick(View v) {
19                  // TODO Auto-generated method stub
20              }
21          });
22      }
23  }
```

Button OnClickListener

Semicolon closes stub

Figure 2-29 Inserting the Button OnClickListener stub

3. To launch the Recipe.java class when the Button control is clicked, click inside the public void onClick(View v) braces on the line after the "TODO" comment. Type **startactivity** and press Ctrl+spacebar. Select the first option, startActivity(Intent intent): void – Activity.

    In the parentheses, change the intent text by typing **new int** and then pressing Ctrl+spacebar. In the auto-complete listing, select Intent(Context packageContext, Class<?> cls).

    In the next set of parentheses, change packageContext to **Main.this** and change cls to **Recipe.class**. Place a semicolon at the end of the line after the parenthesis. Click the Save All button on the toolbar.

    The startActivity code launches the intent to open Recipe.class (Figure 2-30).

```
main.xml    recipe.xml    *Recipe.java    *Main.java
 1  package net.androidbootcamp.healthyrecipes;
 2
 3  import android.app.Activity;
 9
10  public class Main extends Activity {
11      /** Called when the activity is first created. */
12      @Override
13      public void onCreate(Bundle savedInstanceState) {
14          super.onCreate(savedInstanceState);
15          setContentView(R.layout.main);
16          Button b= (Button) findViewById(R.id.btnRecipe);
17          b.setOnClickListener(new OnClickListener() {
18
19              public void onClick(View v) {
20                  // TODO Auto-generated method stub
21                  startActivity(new Intent(Main.this, Recipe.class));
22              }
23          });
24      }
25  }
```

startActivity code

Figure 2-30   Complete code

GTK
In Step 3, the packageContext is replaced with Main because it is the name of the Activity. The term *this* refers to the present Activity.

IN THE TRENCHES
In years past, a software developer would have to wait many months for his or her software to be published and placed in stores for sale. In today's mobile market, app stores have become the de facto app delivery channel by reducing time-to-shelf and time-to-payment and by providing developers with unprecedented reach to consumers.

Correcting Errors in Code

Using the built-in auto-complete listing to assist you when entering code considerably reduces the likelihood of coding errors. Nevertheless, because you could create one or more errors when entering code, you should understand what to do when a coding error occurs. One possible error you could commit would be to forget a semicolon at the end of a statement. In Figure 2-31, when the application is run, a dialog box opens stating your project contains error(s), please fix them before running your application. A red curly line identifies the error location. When you point to the red curly line, Java suggests the possible correction to the syntax error in the code. Also notice that Line 15 has an error icon (a red X) at the beginning of the line to identify the location of the error. After a semicolon is placed at the end of the line, the application is run again and the program functions properly.

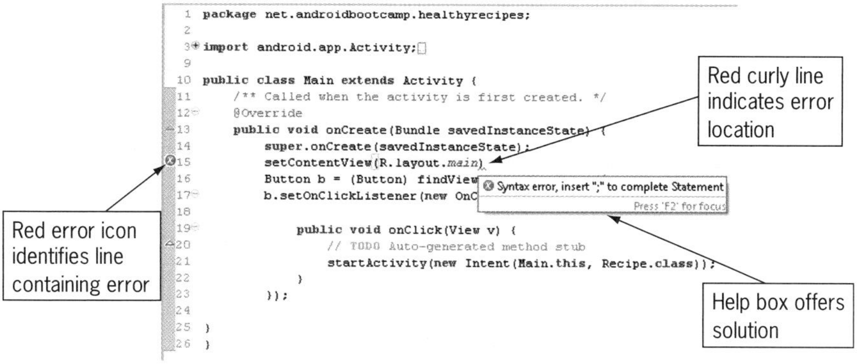

```
1   package net.androidbootcamp.healthyrecipes;
2
3   import android.app.Activity;
9
10  public class Main extends Activity {
11      /** Called when the activity is first created. */
12      @Override
13      public void onCreate(Bundle savedInstanceState) {
14          super.onCreate(savedInstanceState);
15          setContentView(R.layout.main)
16          Button b = (Button) findView
17          b.setOnClickListener(new OnC
18
19          public void onClick(View v) {
20              // TODO Auto-generated method stub
21              startActivity(new Intent(Main.this, Recipe.class));
22          }
23      ));
24
25  }
26  }
```

Red curly line indicates error location

Red error icon identifies line containing error

Syntax error, insert ";" to complete Statement
Press 'F2' for focus

Help box offers solution

Figure 2-31   Syntax error

Saving and Running the Application

Each time an Android application is tested in the emulator, the programming design and code are automatically saved. If you start your project and need to save it before completion, click the Save All button on the toolbar or click File on the menu bar and then select Save All. As shown in Chapter 1, click Run on the menu bar, and then select Run to save and test the application in the emulator. A dialog box opens the first time the application is executed that requests how you would like to run the application. Select Android Application and click the OK button. When the emulated Android main screen appears, unlock the emulator. The application opens in the emulator window, where you can click the View Recipe button to view the salsa recipe.

Wrap It Up—Chapter Summary

This chapter described the steps to create the graphical user interface for the Healthy Recipes program. As you can see, many of the steps required are somewhat repetitive in the design; that is, the same technique is used repeatedly to accomplish similar tasks. When you master these techniques, together with the principles of user interface design, you will be able to design user interfaces for a variety of different programs.

- Linear layouts arrange screen components in a vertical column or horizontal row. Relative layouts arrange screen components freely on the screen.

- Popular text properties for controls include the Text property, which specifies the text displayed in the control, and the Text size property, which specifies the size of the text.

- To display graphics such as pictures and icons in an Android app, you use an ImageView control. Before you can place an ImageView control in the emulator window, you must place a graphics file in the resources folder.

- An Activity is the point at which the application makes contact with your users and is one of the core components of the Android application. The chapter project has two Activities, one for each screen.

- Each screen represents an Activity and each Activity must have a matching Java class file. To create a Java class file, you can extend the built-in Activity class.

- Every Android application has an Android Manifest file (named AndroidManifest.xml), which provides essential information to the Android device, such as the name of your Java application and a listing of each Activity. Eclipse automatically creates the initial Android Manifest file, but this file must be updated to include every Activity in the app.

- When an application has more than one Activity, the Android Manifest file must have an intent so the application can navigate among multiple Activities.

- A method is a set of Java statements that can be included inside a Java class. The onCreate method is where you initialize an Activity. You use the setContentView command to display the content of a specific screen.

- When the user taps a Button control in an Android app, the code for an event listener, or click event, begins the event associated with the Button control. Event listeners such as the OnClickListener method wait for user interaction before executing the remaining code.

- In an Android app that contains more than one Activity, or screen, you use the startActivity( ) method to create an intent to start another Activity. The intent should contain two parameters: a context and the name of the Activity being opened. A context shows which initiating Activity class is making the request.

- When you run an Android application, a dialog box opens if your project contains any errors. Look for red error icons and red curly lines, which identify the location of the errors. Point to a red curly line to have Java suggest a correction to a syntax error in the code.

Key Terms

Activity—An Android component that represents a single screen with a user interface.

Android Manifest—A file with the filename AndroidManifest.xml that is required in every Android application. This file provides essential information to the Android device, such as the name of your Java application and a listing of each Activity.

class—A group of objects that establishes an introduction to each object's properties.

event handler—A part of a program coded to respond to the specific event.

ImageView control—A control that displays an icon or a graphic from a picture file.

import—To make the classes from a particular Android package available throughout the application.

import statement—A statement that makes more Java functions available to a program.

instantiate—To create an object of a specific class.

intent—Code in the Android Manifest file that allows an Android application with more than one Activity to navigate among Activities.

Linear layout—A layout that arranges components in a vertical column or horizontal row.

method—A set of Java statements that can be included inside a Java class.

object—A specific, concrete instance of a class.

Relative layout—A layout that arranges components in relation to each other.

setContentView—The Java code necessary to display the content of a specific screen.

sp—A unit of measurement that stands for scaled-independent pixels.

stub—A piece of code that serves as a placeholder to declare itself, containing just enough code to link to the rest of the program.

Text property—A property that changes the text written within a control.

Text size property—A property that sets the size of text in a control.

Developer FAQs

1. If you were creating an app in many different languages, would you have to write the entire program from scratch for each language?

2. What part of the program in question 1 would stay the same? What part of the program would be different?

3. In which subfolder in the Package Explorer are the XML files stored?

4. Which three controls were used in the chapter project?

5. What is the difference between Linear layout and Relative layout?

6. Is the default layout for an Android screen Linear or Relative?

7. Which measurement is most preferred for text size? Why?

8. What does px stand for?

9. What does sp stand for?

10. What does dpi stand for?

11. Which picture file types are accepted for an ImageView control?

12. Which picture file type is preferred?

13. In the Palette in the layout folder, in which category is the ImageView control found?

14. Which three properties were changed in the chapter project for the Button control?

15. What is the property that defines the name of a Button control?

16. Write one line of code that would launch a second class named Rental from the present Main class.

17. Write one line of code that declares a Button control with the variable bt that references a button in the XML layout with the Id property of btnReserve.

18. Write one line of code that opens the XML layout named medical.

19. Which two keys are pressed to auto-complete a line of Java code?

20. What symbol is placed at the end of most lines of Java code?

Beyond the Book

Using the Internet, search the Web for the following answers to further your Android knowledge.

1. Linear and Relative layouts are not the only types of Android layouts. Name three other types of layouts and write a paragraph describing each type.

2. Why are .png files the preferred type of image resource for the Android device? Write a paragraph that gives at least three reasons.

3. How much does an average Android app developer profit from his or her apps? Research this topic and write 150–200 words on your findings.

4. Research the most expensive Android apps currently available. Name three expensive apps, their price, and the purpose of each.

Case Programming Projects

Complete one or more of the following case programming projects. Use the same steps and techniques taught within the chapter. Submit the program you create to your instructor. The level of difficulty is indicated for each case programming project.

Easiest: ★

Intermediate: ★ ★

Challenging: ★ ★ ★

Case Project 2–1: Rental Property App ⋆

Requirements Document

Application title: Rental Property App

Purpose: In an apartment finder app, an apartment is selected and an address and other information are displayed.

Algorithms:
1. The opening screen displays the name of an apartment, an image, and a Button control (Figure 2-32).
2. When the user selects this apartment, an address and a cost range are displayed in a second screen (Figure 2-33).

Note: The apartment image is provided with your student files.

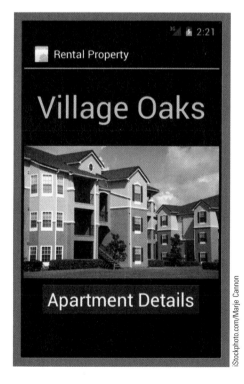

Figure 2-32

Figure 2-33

Case Project 2–2: Star Constellation App ⋆

Requirements Document

Application title:	Star Constellation App
Purpose:	In a star constellation app, the name of a constellation is selected and the constellation image is displayed with information.
Algorithms:	1. The opening screen displays the name of a constellation, a translation name, and a Button control (Figure 2-34).
	2. When the user selects this constellation, an image displaying the sky chart, position, month range, and declination is shown (Figure 2-35).
Note:	The pegasus image is provided with your student files.

Figure 2-34

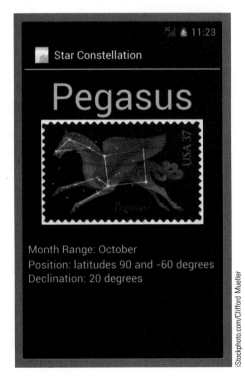

Figure 2-35

Case Project 2–3: Your School App ★ ★

Requirements Document

Application title:	Your School App
Purpose:	This large app contains every school in your country. Create two screens for your school for the app. In a school app, the name of a school is selected and the school address and logo are displayed.
Algorithms:	1. The opening screen displays the name of your school, a picture of your school, and a Button control. Create your own layout.
	2. The second screen displays the name of your school, a picture of your logo, the school address, and the phone number. Create your own layout.

Case Project 2–4: Hostel App for Travel ★ ★

Requirements Document

Application title:	Hostel App for Travel
Purpose:	This large app contains every hostel (small youth hotel) in Italy. Create two screens for the hostel app. In the hostel app, the name of a hostel is selected and the hostel room image is displayed with detailed information.
Algorithms:	1. The opening screen displays the name of the Italian hostel, an exterior image of the hostel, and a Button control. Create your own layout.
	2. The second screen displays the name of the hostel, a picture of the interior room, the street address, the Web address, and the rate. Create your own layout.

Case Project 2–5: Your Contacts App – Address Book ★ ★ ★

Requirements Document

Application title:	Your Contacts App – Address Book
Purpose:	This large app contains every business contact in an address book. Create two screens for contacts for the app. In the contacts app, you can select a particular contact and that person's info is displayed with his or her picture.
Algorithms:	1. The opening screen displays two names of contacts with the last name starting with the letter *J*. Each contact has a separate Button control below the name. Create your own layout.
	2. The second screen displays the name, address, phone number, and picture of the contact. Create your own layout.
Conditions:	Three Java classes and three XML layouts are needed.

Case Project 2–6: Latest News App ★ ★ ★

Requirements Document

Application title:	The Latest Pulse
Purpose:	This large app called The Latest Pulse contains the latest news. Create two screens for two news stories for the app. In the news app, you can select a particular news story title and an image and a paragraph about the news story is displayed.
Algorithms:	1. The opening screen displays two news story titles that you can create based on the news stories during this week. Each news story has a separate Button control below the name and displays a small image. Create your own layout.
	2. The second screen displays the name of the story and a paragraph detailing the news. Create your own layout.
Conditions:	Three Java classes and three XML layouts are needed.

CHAPTER 3

Engage! Android User Input, Variables, and Operations

In this chapter, you learn to:

- ◎ Use an Android theme
- ◎ Add a theme to the Android Manifest file
- ◎ Develop the user interface using Text Fields
- ◎ State the role of different Text Fields
- ◎ Display a hint using the Hint property
- ◎ Develop the user interface using a Spinner control
- ◎ Add text to the String table
- ◎ Add a prompt to a Spinner control
- ◎ Declare variables to hold data
- ◎ Code the GetText( ) method
- ◎ Understand arithmetic operations
- ◎ Convert numeric data
- ◎ Format numeric data
- ◎ Code the SetText( ) method
- ◎ Run the completed app in the emulator

In the Healthy Recipes app developed in Chapter 2, when the user clicked the button in the user interface, events were triggered, but the user did not enter data. In many applications, users enter data and then the program uses the data in its processing. Engaging the user by requesting input customizes the user experience each time the application is executed. When processing data entered by a user, a common requirement is to perform arithmetic operations on the data in order to generate useful output information. Arithmetic operations include adding, subtracting, multiplying, and dividing numeric data.

To illustrate the use of user data input and arithmetic operations, the application in this chapter allows the user to enter the number of concert tickets to be purchased from a concert Android app. The application then calculates the total cost to purchase the concert tickets. The user interface for the app named Concert Tickets is shown in Figure 3-1 with the company name Ticket Vault displayed at the top of the screen.

In Figure 3-2, the user entered 4 as the number of tickets purchased. When the user clicked the Find Ticket Cost button, the program multiplied 4 times the concert ticket cost ($59.99) and then displayed the result as the total cost of the concert tickets, as shown in Figure 3-2. To create this application, the developer must understand how to perform the following processes, among others:

1. Apply a theme to the design of the Android screen.

2. Define a Text Field for data entry. For this app, a number is expected for the quantity of tickets. Using a specific Text Field for positive integers, an incorrect value cannot be entered.

Figure 3-1   Concert Tickets Android app

3. Define a Spinner control to allow users to select the performance group.

4. Convert data so it can be used for arithmetic operations.

5. Perform arithmetic operations with the data the user enters.

6. Display formatted results.

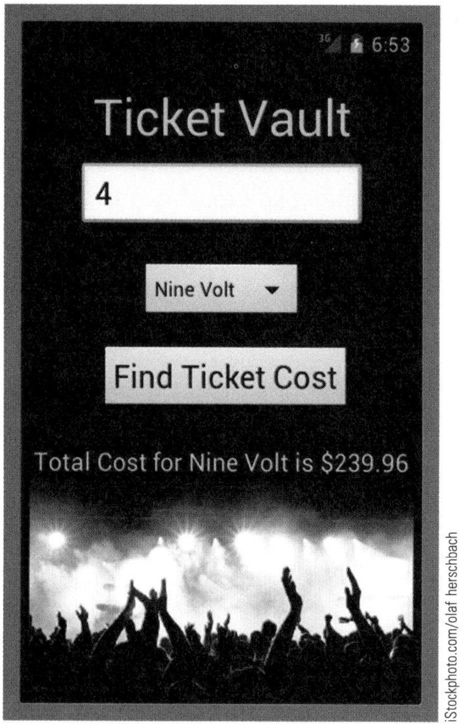

Android Themes

To prevent each Android app from looking too similar, the Android SDK includes multiple themes that provide individual flair to each application. A **theme** is a style applied to an Activity or an entire application. Some themes change the background wallpaper of the Activity, while others hide the title bar or display an action bar. Some themes display a background depending on the size of the mobile device. Themes can be previewed in the emulator window displayed in main.xml. The default theme shows the title bar (often gray) with a black background, as shown in Figure 3-3. Figure 3-4 displays a glowing holographic border

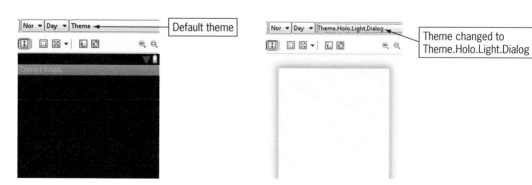

Figure 3-2 Four tickets purchased for a concert

with a light translucent background and no title bar. The light and transparent themes are sheer and allow you to see the initial home screen through the background. Figure 3-5 displays the default black background with the default Android icon and an action bar.

Figure 3-3 Default theme

Figure 3-4 Holographic theme

Previewing a Theme

By changing the theme in the emulator window in the main.xml file, you can preview what the new theme looks like, but to permanently change it in the application, you must define the themes in the Android Manifest for each Activity. You can code a predefined system theme or a customized theme of your own design. The Concert Tickets chapter project uses the predefined system theme named Theme.Black.NoTitleBar. To initiate the Concert Tickets application and preview the Theme.Black.NoTitleBar theme, follow these steps:

Theme changed to Theme.WithActionBar

Figure 3-5   Action bar theme

1. Open the Eclipse program. Click the New button on the Standard toolbar. Expand the Android folder, if necessary, and select Android Project. Click the Next button. In the New Android Project dialog box, enter the Project Name **Concert Tickets**. To save the project on your USB drive, click to remove the check mark from the Use default location check box. Type **E:\Workspace** (if necessary, enter a different drive letter that identifies the USB drive). Click Next. For the Build Target, select Android 4.0, if necessary. Click Next. Type the Package Name **net.androidbootcamp.concerttickets**. Enter **Main** in the Create Activity text box.

   The new Android Concert Tickets project has an application name, a package name, and a Main Activity (Figure 3-6).

New Android
Project dialog box

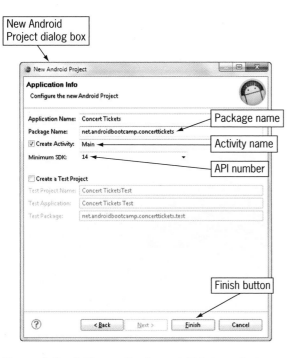

Figure 3-6   Setting up the Concert Tickets project

2. Click the Finish button. Expand the Concert Tickets project in the Package
    Explorer. Expand the res folder to display its subfolders. Expand the layout
    subfolder. Double-click the main.xml file. Click the Hello World, Main! TextView
    widget (displayed by default). Press the Delete key. On the main.xml tab, right-click
    the emulator window, and then click Change Layout on the shortcut menu. In
    the Change Layout dialog box, click the New Layout Type button, and then click
    RelativeLayout. Click the OK button.

    *The main.xml tab is displayed in the project window on the right and the Hello
    World TextView widget is deleted (Figure 3-7).*

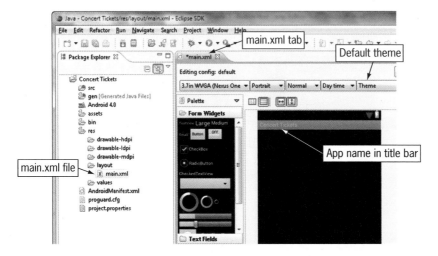

Figure 3-7   main.xml for the Concert Tickets project

3. Click the Theme button to display the list of built-in themes. Select Theme.Black.NoTitleBar.

   The theme is changed to Theme.Black.NoTitleBar. The title bar in the emulator is removed (Figure 3-8).

Coding a Theme in the Android Manifest File

Figure 3-8   New theme applied

At this point, the theme is only displayed in the main.xml graphical layout, but to actually display the theme in the application, code must be inserted in the AndroidManifest.xml file, as shown in the following example:

Code Syntax

```
android:theme="@android:style/Theme.Black.NoTitleBar"
```

Enter the theme code in the Activity section of the Android Manifest file. The code syntax shown above displays the default theme without a title bar. To code the theme within the AndroidManifest.xml file, follow these steps:

1. In the Package Explorer, double-click the AndroidManifest.xml file. Click the AndroidManifest.xml tab at the bottom of the window.

   The AndroidManifest.xml code is displayed (Figure 3-9).

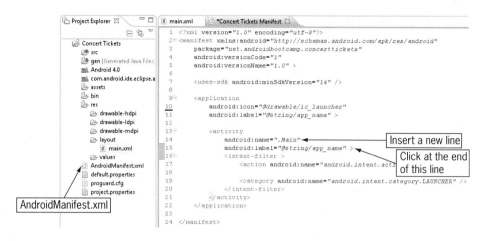

Figure 3-9 Android Manifest file for the Concert Tickets project

2. Inside the activity code, click at the end of the code that states android: name=".Main" (Line 13). Press the Enter key to insert a new blank line. Type **android:theme="@android:style/Theme.Black.NoTitleBar"**.

The Android theme is coded within the Activity in the Android Manifest file (Figure 3-10).

```
X main.xml    *Concert Tickets Manifest

 1  <?xml version="1.0" encoding="utf-8"?>
 2  <manifest xmlns:android="http://schemas.android.com/apk/res/androi
 3      package="net.androidbootcamp.concerttickets"
 4      android:versionCode="1"
 5      android:versionName="1.0" >
 6
 7      <uses-sdk android:minSdkVersion="14" />
 8
 9      <application
10          android:icon="@drawable/ic_launcher"
11          android:label="@string/app_name" >
12
13          <activity
14              android:name=".Main"
15              android:theme="@android:style/Theme.Black.NoTitleBar"
16              android:label="@string/app_name" >
17              <intent-filter >
```

Theme added in Line 14

Figure 3-10 Adding the theme to the Android Manifest file

3. Close the Concert Tickets Manifest tab and save your work.

Simplifying User Input

On the Android phone, users can enter text in multiple ways that include entering input through an onscreen soft keyboard, an attached flip button hard keyboard, and even voice-to-text capabilities on most phone models. The onscreen keyboard is called a **soft keyboard**, which is positioned at the bottom of the screen over the application window. Touch input can vary from tapping the screen to using gestures. Gestures are multitouch interactions such as pressing two fingers to pan, rotate, or zoom. The primary design challenge for mobile Web applications is how do you simplify user experiences for an application that appears on screens measuring from a few inches square to much larger tablets? You need to use legible fonts, simplify input, and optimize each device's capabilities to maximize the user experience. Certain Android Form Widgets such as those in the Text Fields category allow specific data types for user input, which simplifies data entry. For example, a numeric Text Field only allows numbers to be entered from the onscreen keyboard, limiting accidental user input, such as by touching the wrong location on a small touchscreen.

IN THE TRENCHES

A decade ago, nearly every mobile phone offered an alphanumeric keypad as part of the device. Today a touchscreen full QWERTY keyboard is available to allow users to enter information, engage in social networking, surf the Internet, and view multimedia.

Android Text Fields

In the Concert Tickets application shown in Figure 3-1, the user enters the quantity of tickets that he or she intends to purchase to attend the concert event. The most common type of mobile input is text entered from the soft keyboard or the attached keyboard. User keyboard input can be requested with the Text Fields in the Eclipse Palette (Figure 3-11). With Text Fields, the input can be received on the mobile device with an onscreen keyboard or the user can elect to use the physical keyboard if the device provides one to enter input.

A mobile application's Text Field controls can request different input types, such as free-form plain text; numbers; a person's name, password, e-mail address, and phone number; a date; and multiline text. You

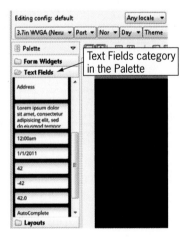

Figure 3-11   Text Fields category

need to select the correct Text Field for the specific type of data you are requesting. As shown in Figure 3-12, each Text Field control allows you to enter a specific data type from the keyboard. For example, if you select the Phone Number Text Field, Android deactivates the letters on the keyboard because letters are not part of a phone number.

GTK
The AutoComplete TextView control can suggest the completion of a word after the user begins typing the first few letters. For example, if the input control is requesting the name of a city where the user wants to book a hotel, you could suggest the completed name from a coded listing of city names that match the prefix entered by the user.

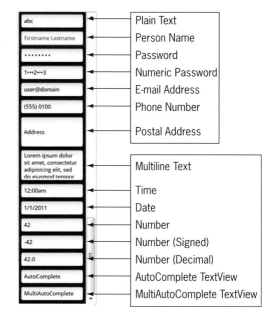

Figure 3-12 Types of Text Field controls

In the chapter project, the Concert Tickets application requests the number of concert tickets. This quantity is an integer value because you cannot purchase part of a ticket. By selecting the Number Text Field, only positive integers can be entered from the keyboard. Letters and symbols from the keyboard are not accepted, which saves you time as the developer because you do not have to write lengthy data validation code. When the app opens in the emulator and you click the Number Text Field control, the soft keyboard opens, as shown in Figure 3-13.

Onscreen numeric keyboard

Figure 3-13 Onscreen keyboard

IN THE TRENCHES
An application with appealing graphical design is preferred over applications that are textual in nature. Good graphic design communicates simplicity and engages the user.

Adding a Text Field

In the Concert Tickets application, a single screen opens when the application runs, requesting the number of concert tickets desired in a Number Text Field. To name a Text Field, use the Id property in the Properties pane to enter a name that begins with the prefix txt, which represents a text field in the code. The Id property of any widget is used in the Java code to refer to the widget. A descriptive variable name such as txtTickets can turn an unreadable piece of code into one that is well documented and easy to debug. To begin the design of the emulator screen and to add a Text Field, follow these steps:

1. With main.xml open and displaying the emulator screen, click the Form Widgets category in the Palette. Select the form widget named TextView. Drag and drop the TextView control onto the top part of the emulator user interface. To center the TextView control, drag the control to the center of the screen until a green dashed vertical line identifying the screen's center is displayed. To open the Properties pane, right-click the emulator window, point to Show In on the shortcut menu, and then select Properties. To view the properties of the TextView control, click the TextView control that you placed on the emulator. Scroll the Properties pane, and then click the Text property. Change the Text property to **Ticket Vault**. In the Properties pane, scroll to the Text size property, type **40sp**, and then press the Enter key.

   A TextView control is added to the emulator to represent the company name with the text Ticket Vault and size of 40sp (Figure 3-14).

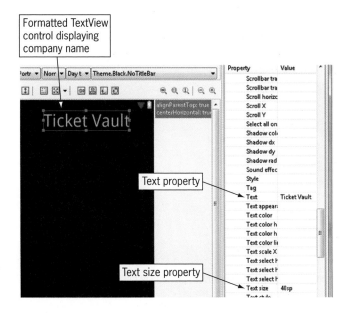

Figure 3-14   TextView control added and formatted

2. Click the Text Fields category in the Palette. Scroll down to the Number (example shows a 42) Text Field. Drag and drop the Number Text Field control onto the emulator's user interface below the Ticket Vault text. Drag the control to the center of the screen until a green dashed vertical line identifying the screen's center is displayed. Change the Id property of the Text Field to **@+id/txtTickets**. Set the Text size property to **25sp**.

A Number Text Field control named txtTickets with the size of 25sp is added to the emulator to allow the user to enter the number of tickets (Figure 3-15).

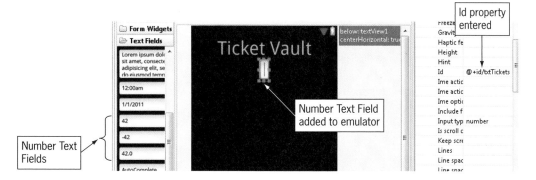

Figure 3-15 Number Text Field control

GTK
You might need to click controls in the emulator to select them before assigning properties.

IN THE TRENCHES
Iris, a popular Android app, provides a voice-recognition system for user input. Siri is a similar voice-recognition system on the iOS platform. "Iris," which is the reverse of "Siri," stands for "Intelligent Rival Imitator of Siri."

Setting the Hint Property for the Text Field

When the Concert Tickets program is executed, the user needs guidelines about the input expected in the Text Field control. These guidelines can be included in the Hint property of the Text Field control. A **hint** is a short description of a field that is visible as light-colored text (also called a watermark) inside a Text Field control. When the user clicks the control, the hint is removed and the user is free to type the requested input. The purpose of the hint in Figure 3-16

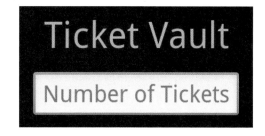

Figure 3-16 Hint in a Text Field control

is to request what is expected in this field, without the user having to select and delete default text.

To set the Hint property for the Text Field control, follow this step:

1. With the txtTickets Text Field control selected on the emulator screen, click the Hint property in the Properties pane and type **Number of Tickets**. Press the Enter key.

    A watermark hint indicates that the number of tickets is needed as input in the Text Field control (Figure 3-17).

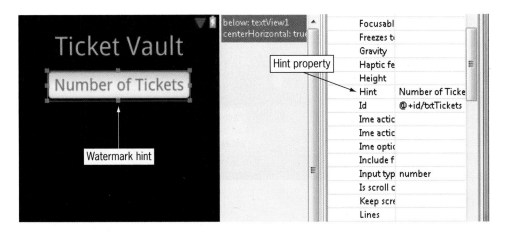

Figure 3-17   Hint added to Text Field control

Coding the EditText Class for the Text Field

To handle the input that the user enters into the numeric Text Field control in the chapter project, you use the EditText class, which extracts the text and converts it for use in the Java code. The extracted text must be assigned to a variable. A **variable** is used in a Java program to contain data that changes during the execution of the program. In the chapter project, a variable named tickets holds the text entered in the Text Field for the number of tickets. The following code syntax declares (or initializes) the variable named tickets, which contains the extracted EditText class text from the user's input. Notice the code syntax begins with the word **final**, indicating that tickets is a final variable. A final variable can only be initialized once and any attempt to reassign the value results in a compile error when the application is executed.

Code Syntax

```
final EditText tickets=(EditText) findViewById(R.id.txtTickets);
```

Recall that if you want to refer to a control in the Java code, you need to name the control when you add it to the interface using the Id property. For example, the Text Field control was assigned the id txtTickets. Now you can access the control in the code using the findViewById( ) method. In the parentheses, the R refers to resources available to the app, such as a layout control, the id indicates that the resource is identified by the Id property, and txtTickets is the assigned id.

Next, the txtTickets Text Field control should be assigned to the variable named tickets. To collect the ticket input from the user, code the EditText class for the Text Field by following these steps:

1. Close the Properties pane. In the Package Explorer, expand src and net.androidbootcamp. concerttickets, and then double-click Main.java to open the code window. Click to the right of the line setContentView(R.layout.*main*);. Press the Enter key to insert a blank line. To initialize and reference the EditText class with the Id name of txtTickets, type **final EditText tickets=(EditText) findViewById(R.id.txtTickets);**. Point to the red curly line under EditText and select Import 'EditText' (android widget) on the pop-up menu.

The EditText class extracts the value from the user's input for the number of tickets and assigns the value to the variable named tickets (Figure 3-18).

```
  main.xml        Main.java ⊠
   1  package net.androidbootcamp.concerttickets;
   2
   3⊕ import android.app.Activity;☐
   6
   7  public class Main extends Activity {
   8        /** Called when the activity is first created. */
   9
  10⊖        @Override
  11        public void onCreate(Bundle savedInstanceState) {
  12              super.onCreate(savedInstanceState);
  13              setContentView(R.layout.main);
  14              final EditText tickets = (EditText) findViewById(R.id.txtTickets);
  15        }
  16  }
```

EditText code assigns input value in the txtTickets control to a variable named tickets

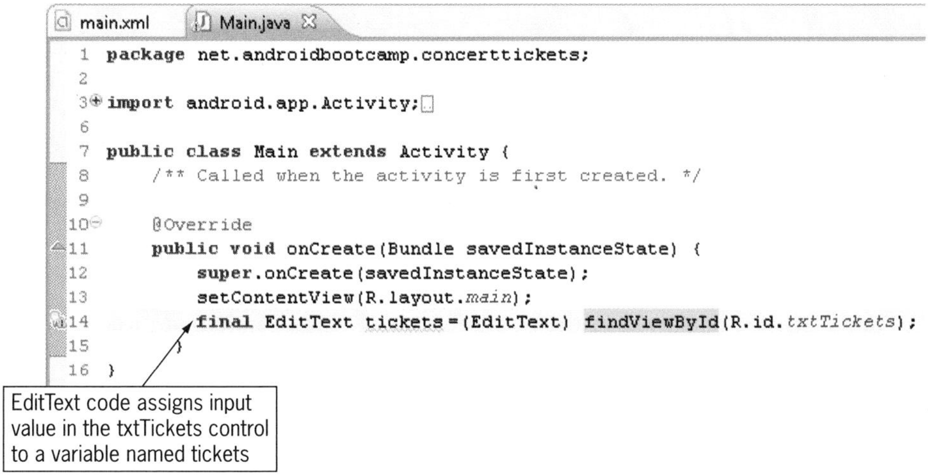

Figure 3-18 Coding the EditText class for the Text Field

2. Close the Main.java tab and save your work.

Android Spinner Control

After the user enters the number of tickets, the next step is to select which concert to attend. Three musical groups are performing next month: Dragonfly, Nine Volt, and Red Road. Due to possible user error on a small mobile keyboard, it is much easier for a user to use a Spinner control instead of actually typing in the group names. A **Spinner control** is a widget similar to a drop-down list for selecting a single item from a fixed listing, as shown in Figure 3-19. The Spinner control displays a prompt with a list of strings called **items** in a pop-up window without taking up multiple lines on the initial display. A **string** is a series of alphanumeric characters that can include spaces.

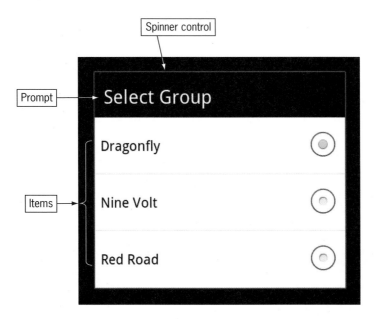

Figure 3-19   Spinner control and items

Using the String table

The string items that are displayed in the Spinner control cannot be typed directly in the Properties pane, but instead are created in a values string array in the res/values folder. A file named **strings.xml** is a default file that is part of every Android application and contains commonly used strings for an application. The String Array is part of the String table, which is best to use for text displayed in the application because it can easily be changed without changing code. Android loads text resources from the project's String table. The String table can also be used for localization. **Localization** is the use of the String table to change text based on the user's preferred language. For example, Android can select text in Spanish from the String table, based on the current device configuration and locale. The developer can add multiple translations in the String table.

In the Concert Tickets app, a String Array for the Spinner control is necessary to hold the three concert group names as individual string resources in the strings.xml resource file. The strings.xml file already has two default string variables named hello and app_name. The string resources file provides an easy way to update commonly used strings throughout your project, instead of searching through code and properties to alter string names within the application. For example, each month the concert planners can simply change the text in the strings.xml file to reflect their new concert events. A **prompt**, which can be used to display instructions at the top of the Spinner control, can also be stored in strings.xml. To add a String Array for the three musical groups and to add a prompt to display in the Spinner control, follow these steps:

1. Expand the values folder in the Package Explorer. Double-click strings.xml. Click the Add button in the Android Resources strings.xml tab.

   A dialog box opens to create a new element at the top level, in Resources (Figure 3-20).

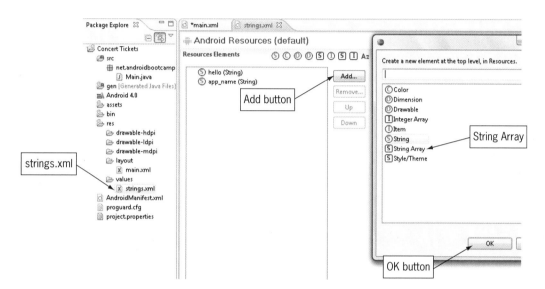

Figure 3-20 Adding a string resource

2. In the dialog box, select String Array and then click the OK button. Type **Groups** in the Name text box to name the String Array.

   The String Array is named Groups (Figure 3-21).

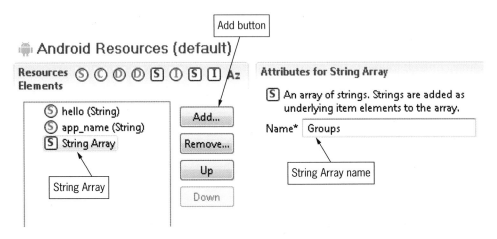

Figure 3-21   Naming the String Array

3. Click the Add button. Select Item, and then click the OK button. In the Value box, type **Dragonfly** as the name of the first item, and then click the Add button. Select Item, and then click the OK button. In the Value box, type **Nine Volt** as the name of the second item. Click the Add button again. Select Item, and then click the OK button. In the Value box, type **Red Road** as the name of the last item.

    Three items are added to the String Array named Groups (Figure 3-22).

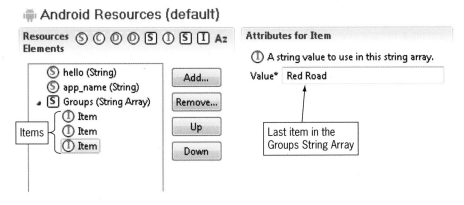

Figure 3-22   Adding items to the Groups String Array

4. To add a prompt represented as a String at the top of the Spinner, click the Add button. At the top of the dialog box, select the Create a new element at the top level, in Resources option button to create a new element at the top level, in Resources. Select String, and then click the OK button. In the Name box, type **Title**. In the Value box, type **Select Group**.

A String named Title is added to strings.xml that contains the text Select Group for the Spinner prompt (Figure 3-23).

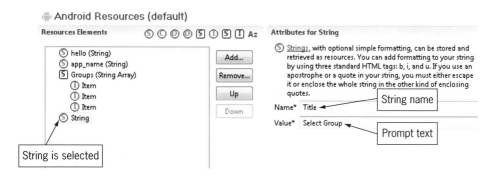

Figure 3-23 Adding a prompt

5. Close the strings.xml tab and save your work.

GTK

If your main.xml emulator window fails to update, try saving your project to update it. You can also refresh your Android project by clicking Project on the menu bar and then clicking Clean.

Adding a Spinner Control with String Array Entries

After entering the items in an array, the Spinner property called **Entries** connects the String Array to the Spinner control for display in the application. The Spinner control is located in the Form Widgets category. The following steps add the Spinner control to the Android application:

1. With the main.xml tab open, click the Form Widgets category in the Palette. Drag and drop the Spinner control below the Text Field and center it horizontally. Change the Id property of the Spinner control to **@+id/txtGroup**.

   The Spinner control is added to the emulator window and named txtGroup (Figure 3-24).

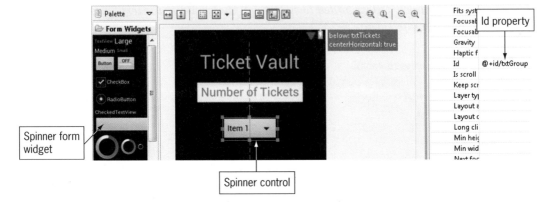

Spinner form widget

Spinner control

Figure 3-24   Spinner control

2. Click File on the menu bar and then click Save All to update all resources. In the Properties pane, click the Prompt property, and then click the ellipsis (…) button. In the Reference Chooser dialog box, click the expand arrow for String. Select Title and click the OK button. To display the String Array, click to the right of the Entries property. Click the ellipsis button. In the Reference Chooser dialog box, click the expand arrow for Array. Select Groups and click the OK button.

The Prompt property connects to the resource named @string/Title. The Entries property connects to the resources of the String Array @array/Groups. The actual groups are displayed when the app is executed in the emulator (Figure 3-25).

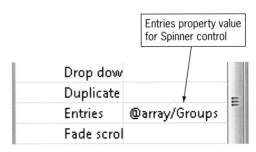

Entries property value for Spinner control

Figure 3-25   Entries property for the Spinner control

Coding the Spinner Control

The user's selection of the concert group must be assigned to a variable and stored in the computer's memory. For this application, the selection made from the Spinner control (txtGroup) is assigned to a variable named group using the following code:

Code Syntax

```
final Spinner group = (Spinner) findViewById(R.id.txtGroup);
```

To collect the input from the user's group selection, code the Spinner control by following these steps:

1. Close the Properties pane. In the Package Explorer, double-click Main.java. After the EditText line, press the Enter key to create a new line. To initialize and reference the Spinner control with the Id name of txtGroup, type **final Spinner group = (Spinner) findViewById(R.id.txtGroup);**. Point to the red curly line under Spinner and select Import 'Spinner' (android widget) on the pop-up menu.

   The Spinner control assigns the value from the user's input to the variable named group. Notice variables that have not been used in the program have a curly underline. This underline is removed when a value is assigned later in the program (Figure 3-26).

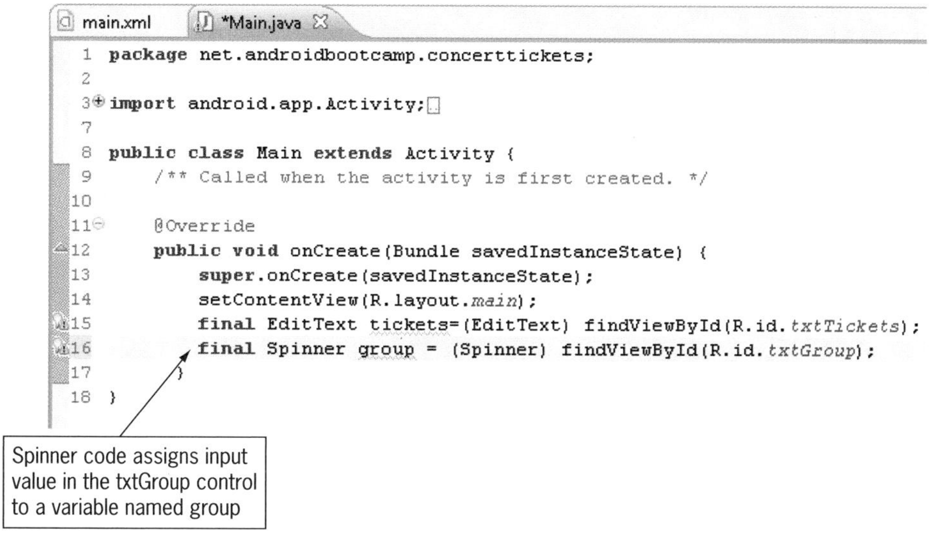

```
 main.xml       *Main.java

 1  package net.androidbootcamp.concerttickets;
 2
 3  import android.app.Activity;
 7
 8  public class Main extends Activity {
 9      /** Called when the activity is first created. */
10
11      @Override
12      public void onCreate(Bundle savedInstanceState) {
13          super.onCreate(savedInstanceState);
14          setContentView(R.layout.main);
15          final EditText tickets=(EditText) findViewById(R.id.txtTickets);
16          final Spinner group = (Spinner) findViewById(R.id.txtGroup);
17      }
18  }
```

Spinner code assigns input value in the txtGroup control to a variable named group

Figure 3-26 Coding the Spinner control

2. Close the Main.java tab and save your work.

Adding the Button, TextView, and ImageView Controls

After the user inputs the number of tickets and the concert group name, the user taps the Find Ticket Cost button to calculate the cost in a Button event. After the total cost is calculated by multiplying the number of tickets by the cost of each ticket ($59.99), the name of the group and total cost of the tickets are displayed in a TextView control. The TextView control is assigned to the variable named result using the following code:

Code Syntax

```
final TextView result = ((TextView) findViewById (R.id.txtResult));
```

You need an image file named concert.png, provided with your student files, to display in an ImageView control for the Concert Tickets app. You should already have the student files for this text that your instructor gave you or that you downloaded from the Web page for this book (*www.cengagebrain.com*). To add the Button, TextView, and ImageView controls to the emulator window, follow these steps:

1.   In the main.xml tab, drag the Button control from the Form Widgets category in the Palette to the emulator and center it below the Spinner control. Release the mouse button. Open the Properties pane, click the new Button control, and then change its Id property to **@+id/btnCost**. Scroll to the Text property, and then change the text to **Find Ticket Cost**. Change the Text size property to **25sp**. Save your work.

The Button control named btnCost displays the text Find Ticket Cost and the size is changed to 25sp (Figure 3-27).

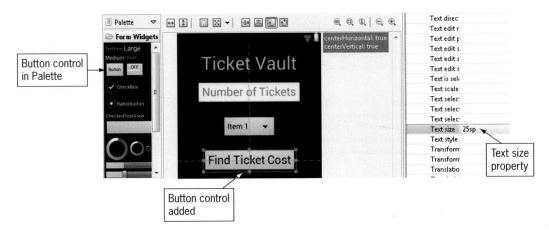

Figure 3-27   Adding a Button control

2.   To code the button, open the Main.java file from the Package Explorer. Click to the right of the code line that assigned the Spinner control to the variable named group. Press the Enter key. To initialize the Button control with the Id name of btnCost, type **Button cost = (Button) findViewById(R.id.btnCost);**. Point to Button and import the Button type as an Android widget. Press the Enter key. To code the button listener that awaits user interaction, type **cost.setOn** and wait as a code listing opens. Double-click the first setOnClickListener displayed in the auto-complete listing. Inside the parentheses, type **new on** and press Ctrl+spacebar to display an auto-complete listing. Double-click the first choice, which lists an OnClickListener with an Anonymous Inner Type event handler. Point to OnClickListener and import 'OnClickListener' (android.view.View). Place a semicolon at the end of the auto-generated stub closing brace and parenthesis.

The Button control is initialized and an OnClickListener auto-generated stub appears in the code window (Figure 3-28).

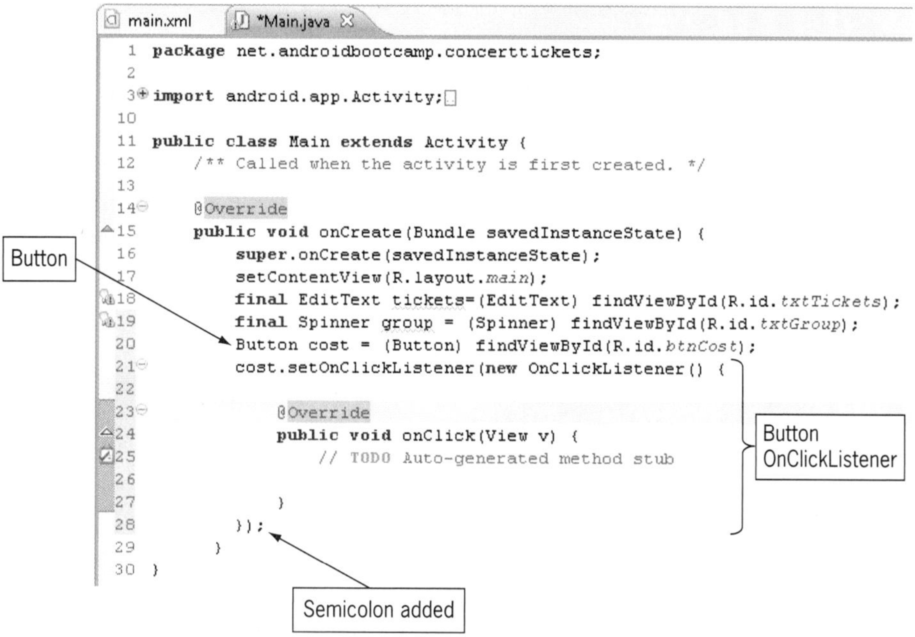

Figure 3-28   Coding the button

3.   To add a TextView control to display the final cost of the tickets, click the main.xml tab. From the Form Widgets category in the Palette, drag the TextView control to the emulator and center it below the Button control. Release the mouse button. In the Properties pane, change the Id property of the TextView control to **@+id/txtResult**. Change the Text size property to **20sp**. Click to the right of the Text property and delete the text.

The txtResult TextView control is added to the emulator window (Figure 3-29).

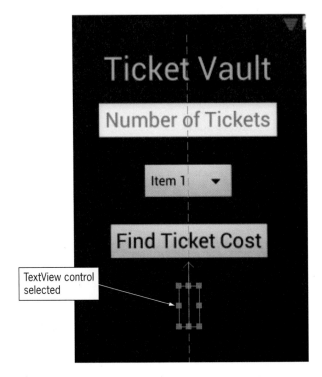

Figure 3-29   Adding a TextView control to display results

4. To code the TextView control, save your work and then click the Main.java tab. After the line of code referring to the Button cost, type **final TextView result = ((TextView) findViewById (R.id.txtResult));**. Import the 'TextView' (android. widget).

The TextView control txtResult is assigned to the variable named result (Figure 3-30).

```
  main.xml    *Main.java ⊠
   1  package net.androidbootcamp.concerttickets;
   2
   3⊕ import android.app.Activity;⬚
  11
  12  public class Main extends Activity {
  13       /** Called when the activity is first created. */
  14
  15⊖      @Override
  16      public void onCreate(Bundle savedInstanceState) {
  17          super.onCreate(savedInstanceState);
  18          setContentView(R.layout.main);
  19          final EditText tickets=(EditText) findViewById(R.id.txtTickets);
  20          final Spinner group = (Spinner) findViewById(R.id.txtGroup);
  21          Button cost = (Button) findViewById(R.id.btnCost);
  22          final TextView result = ((TextView) findViewById(R.id.txtResult));
  23⊖          cost.setOnClickListener(new OnClickListener() {
  24
  25⊖              @Override
  26              public void onClick(View v) {
  27                  // TODO Auto-generated method stub
  28
  29              }
  30          });
  31      }
  32  }
```

TextView code assigns the value displayed in the txtResult control to a variable named result

Figure 3-30   Assigning the TextView control to a variable

5. To add the ImageView control, first copy the student files to your USB drive (if necessary). Open the USB folder containing the student files. In the Package Explorer, expand the drawable-hdpi folder. Drag the concert.png file to the drawable-hdpi folder until a plus sign pointer appears. Release the mouse button. Click the OK button in the File Operation dialog box. In the main.xml tab, click the Images & Media category in the Palette. Drag the ImageView control to the emulator and center it below the TextView control at the bottom of the emulator window. Click concert in the Resource Chooser dialog box, and then click the OK button. With the image selected, click to the right of the Layout margin bottom property in the Properties pane and type **0dp**. Click a blank area on the emulator to deselect the image.

The concert image is displayed at the bottom of the emulator window (Figure 3-31).

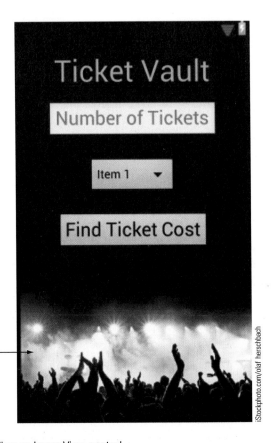

Figure 3-31 Adding an ImageView control

GTK
Variable names are case sensitive and should be mixed case (camel case) when they include more than one word, as in costPerItem. Java variables cannot start with a number or special symbol. Subsequent characters in the variable name may be letters, digits, dollar signs, or underscore characters.

Declaring Variables

As you have seen, the user can enter data in the program through the use of a Text Field control. In the Concert Tickets app, a mathematical equation multiplying the number of tickets and the cost of the tickets is calculated to find the total cost. When writing programs, it is convenient to use variables instead of the actual data such as the cost of a ticket ($59.99). Two steps are necessary in order to use a variable:

1. Declare the variable.

2. Assign a value to the variable.

The declared type of a value determines which operations are allowed. At the core of Java code are eight built-in primitive (simple) types of data.

Primitive Data Types

Java requires all variables to have a data type. Table 3-1 displays the primitive data types that are supported across all computer platforms, including the Android SDK.

Type	Meaning	Range	Default Value
byte	Often used with arrays	−128 to 127	0
short	Often used with arrays	−32,768 to 32,767	0
int	Most commonly used number value	−2,147,483,648 to 2,147,483,647	0
long	Used for numbers that exceed int	−9,223,372,036,854,775,808 to 9,223,372,036,854,775,807	0
float	A single precision 32-bit floating-point number	$+/-3.40282347\text{^}38$	0
double	Most common for decimal values	$+/-1.79769313486231570\text{^}308$	0
char	Single character	Characters	0
boolean	Used for conditional statement	True or false	False

Table 3-1 Primitive data types in Java

In the Concert Tickets program, the tickets cost $59.99 each. This cost is best declared as a double data type, which is appropriate for decimal values. The variable costPerTicket both declares the variable and assigns a value, as shown in the following code syntax. The requested quantity of tickets is assigned to a variable named numberOfTickets, which represents an integer. To multiply two values, the values must be stored in one of the numeric data types. When the total cost of the tickets is computed, the value is assigned to a variable named totalCost, also a double data type, as shown in the following code:

Code Syntax

```
double costPerTicket=59.99;
int numberOfTickets;
double totalCost;
```

String Data Type

In addition to the primitive data types, Java has another data type for working with strings of text. The String type is a class and not a primitive data type. Most strings that you use in the Java language are an object of type String. A string can be a character, word, or phrase. If you assign a phrase to a String variable, place the phrase between double quotation marks. In the Concert Tickets app, after the user selects a musical group from the Spinner control, that group is assigned to a String type variable named groupChoice, as shown in the following code:

Code Syntax

```
String groupChoice;
```

GTK
When defining variables, good programming practice dictates that the variable names you use should reflect the actual values to be placed in the variable. That way, anyone reading the program code can easily understand the use of the variable.

Declaring the Variables

Variables in an Android application are typically declared at the beginning of an Activity. A variable must first be declared before the variable can be used in the application. To initialize, or declare, the variables, follow this step:

1. In Main.java, below the comment /** Called when the activity is first created */, insert the following four lines of code to initialize the variables in this Activity:

    double costPerTicket=59.99;

    int numberOfTickets;

    double totalCost;

    String groupChoice;

    The variables are declared at the beginning of the Activity (Figure 3-32).

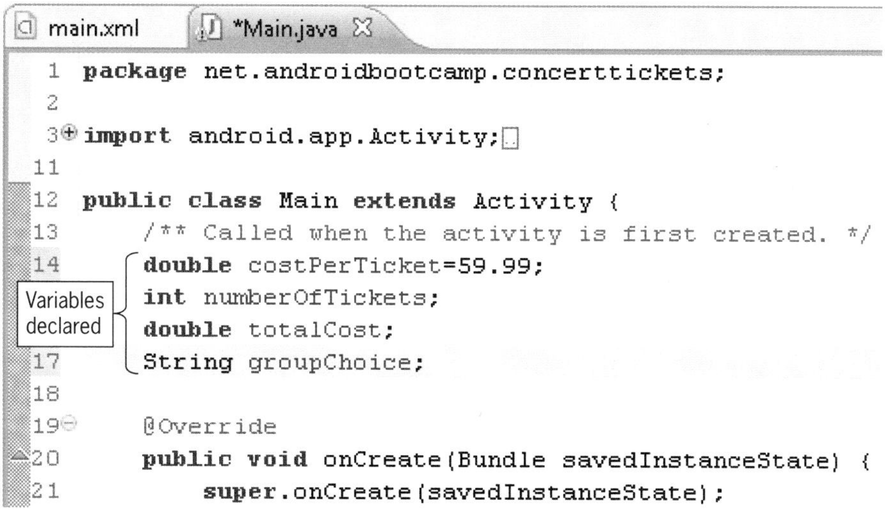

```
  main.xml     *Main.java
  1  package net.androidbootcamp.concerttickets;
  2
  3  import android.app.Activity;
 11
 12  public class Main extends Activity {
 13      /** Called when the activity is first created. */
 14      double costPerTicket=59.99;
        int numberOfTickets;
        double totalCost;
 17      String groupChoice;
 18
 19      @Override
 20      public void onCreate(Bundle savedInstanceState) {
 21          super.onCreate(savedInstanceState);
```

Variables declared

Figure 3-32   Declaring variables for the Activity

GetText( ) Method

At this point in the application development, all the controls have been assigned variables to hold their values. The next step is to convert the values in the assigned variables to the correct data type for calculation purposes. After the user enters the number of tickets and the concert group name, the Find Ticket Cost button is clicked. Inside the OnClickListener code for the button control, the text stored in the EditText control named tickets can be read with the **GetText( )** method. By default, the text in the EditText control is read as a String type. A String type cannot be used in a mathematical function. To convert a string into a numerical data type, a **Parse** class is needed to convert strings to a number data type. Table 3-2 displays the Parse types that convert a string to a common numerical data type.

Numerical Data Type	Parse Types
Integer	Integer.parseInt( )
Float	Float.parseFloat( )
Double	Double.parseDouble( )
Long	Long.parseLong( )

Table 3-2   Parse type conversions

To extract the string of text typed into the EditText control and convert the string representing the number of tickets to an integer data type, the following syntax is necessary:

Code Syntax

```
numberOfTickets = Integer.parseInt(tickets.getText().toString());
```

To code the GetText( ) method and convert the value in the tickets variable into an integer data type named numberOfTickets, follow this step:

1. In Main.java, inside the OnClickListener onClick method stub, type **numberOfTickets = Integer.parseInt(tickets.getText().toString());**.

    The GetText( ) method extracts the text from tickets, converts the string to an integer, and assigns the value to numberOfTickets (Figure 3-33).

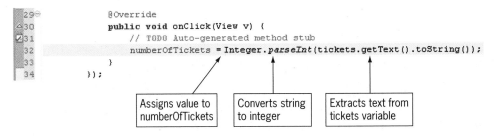

Figure 3-33   Converting a string to an integer

Working with Mathematical Operations

The ability to perform arithmetic operations on numeric data is fundamental to many applications. Many programs require arithmetic operations to add, subtract, multiply, and divide numeric data. For example, in the Concert Tickets app in this chapter, the cost of each ticket must be multiplied by the number of tickets in order to calculate the total cost of the concert tickets.

Arithmetic Operators

Table 3-3 shows a listing of the Java arithmetic operators, along with their use and an example of an arithmetic expression showing their use.

Arithmetic Operator	Use	Assignment Statement
+	Addition	value = itemPrice + itemTax;
−	Subtraction	score = previousScore − 2;
*	Multiplication	totalCost = costPerTicket * numberOfTickets;
/	Division	average = totalGrade / 5.0;
%	Remainder	leftover = widgetAmount % 3; If widgetAmount = 11 the remainder = 2
++	Increment (adds 1)	golfScore ++
--	Decrement (subtracts 1)	points --

Table 3-3   Java arithmetic operators

When multiple operations are included in a single assignment statement, the sequence of performing the calculations is determined by the rules shown in Table 3-4, which is called the order of operations.

Order of Operations Highest to Lowest Precedence	Description
( )	Parentheses
++ --	Left to right
* / %	Left to right
+ −	Left to right

Table 3-4   Order of operations

For example, the result of 2 + 3 * 4 is 14 because the multiplication is of higher precedence than the addition operation.

Formatting Numbers

After the total ticket cost is computed, the result is displayed in currency format, which includes a dollar sign and commas if needed in larger values, and rounds off to two places past the decimal point. Java includes a class called **DecimalFormat** that provides patterns for formatting numbers for output on the Android device. For example, the pattern "$###,###.##" establishes that a number begins with a dollar sign character, displays a comma if the number has more than three digits, and rounds off to the nearest penny. If the pattern "###.#%" is used, the number is multiplied by 100 and rounded to the first digit past the decimal. To establish a currency decimal format for the result of the ticket cost, the following code syntax is assigned to currency and later applied to the variable totalCost to display a currency value:

Code Syntax

```
DecimalFormat currency = new DecimalFormat("$###,###.##");
```

To code the calculation computing the cost of the tickets and to create a currency decimal format, follow this step:

1. In Main.java, after the last line entered, insert a new line, type **totalCost = costPerTicket * numberOfTickets;** and then press Enter. To establish a currency format, type **DecimalFormat currency = new DecimalFormat("$###,###.##");**. Import the 'DecimalFormat' (java.text) class.

   The equation computes the total cost of the tickets and DecimalFormat creates a currency format that is used when the total cost is displayed (Figure 3-34).

Equation calculates ticket cost

Pattern formats result as currency

Figure 3-34   Calculating and formatting the ticket cost

Displaying Android Output

In Java, computing the results does not mean displaying the results. To display the results that include the name of the group and the final cost of the tickets, first the name of the group must be assigned to a String variable.

GetSelectedItem( ) Method

To obtain the text name of the concert group that was selected by the user in the Spinner control, you use a method named GetSelectedItem( ). The **GetSelectedItem( )** method returns the text label of the currently selected Spinner item. For example, if the user selects Nine Volt, the GetSelectedItem( ) method assigns this group to a String variable named groupChoice that was declared at the beginning of the Activity, as shown in the following code:

Code Syntax

```
groupChoice = group.getSelectedItem().toString();
```

GTK

A method named GetSelectedIndex( ) can be used with a Spinner control to determine if the user selected the first, second, or subsequent choice. For example, if GetSelectedIndex( ) is equal to the integer 0, the user selected the first choice.

SetText( ) Method

Earlier in the Android project, the method GetText( ) extracted the text from the Text Field control. In an opposite manner, the method SetText( ) displays text in a TextView control. SetText( ) accepts a string of data for display. To join variable names and text, you can concatenate the string text with a plus sign (+). In the following example, the variable completeSentence is assigned *Android is the best phone platform.* This sentence is displayed in a TextView object named result.

Example:

```
String mobile = "Android";
String completeSentence = mobile + " is the best phone platform";
result.setText(completeSentence);
```

The syntax for the SetText( ) method is shown in the following code. In this example, the result is displayed in the result TextView control and includes the string that uses the concatenating operator, the plus sign connecting variables to the string text.

Code Syntax

```
result.setText("Total Cost for " + groupChoice + " is " +
currency.format(totalCost));
```

The currency.format portion of the code displays the variable totalCost with a dollar sign and rounds off to the nearest penny. The output for result is displayed in Figure 3-2: Total Cost for Nine Volt is $239.96. To code the GetSelectedItem( ) method and the SetText( ) method, follow these steps to complete the application:

1. In Main.java after the last line of code entered, insert a new line and type **groupChoice = group.getSelectedItem().toString();** to assign the concert group to the String variable groupChoice. On the next line, type **result.setText("Total Cost for " + groupChoice + " is " + currency.format(totalCost));** to display the output.

   The getSelectedItem( ) method identifies the selected group and setText( ) displays the selected group with the total cost of the tickets (Figure 3-35).

```
  1  package net.androidbootcamp.concerttickets;
  2
  3⊕ import java.text.DecimalFormat;□
 13
 14  public class Main extends Activity {
 15      /** Called when the activity is first created. */
 16      double costPerTicket=59.99;
 17      int numberOfTickets;
 18      double totalCost;
 19      String groupChoice;
 20
 21⊝     @Override
▲22      public void onCreate(Bundle savedInstanceState) {
 23          super.onCreate(savedInstanceState);
 24          setContentView(R.layout.main);
 25          final EditText tickets =(EditText) findViewById(R.id.txtTickets);
 26          final Spinner group = (Spinner) findViewById(R.id.txtGroup);
 27
 28          Button cost = (Button) findViewById(R.id.btnCost);
 29          final TextView result = ((TextView) findViewById (R.id.txtResult));
 30⊝         cost.setOnClickListener(new OnClickListener() {
 31
 32⊝             @Override
▲33              public void onClick(View v) {
▲34                  // TODO Auto-generated method stub
 35                  numberOfTickets = Integer.parseInt(tickets.getText().toString());
 36                  totalCost= costPerTicket * numberOfTickets;
 37                  DecimalFormat currency = new DecimalFormat("$###,###.##");
 38                  groupChoice = group.getSelectedItem().toString();
 39                  result.setText("Total Cost for " + groupChoice + " is " + currency.format(totalCost));
 40              }
 41          });
 42      }
 43  }
```

Figure 3-35   Completed code

2. To view the finished application, click Run on the menu bar, and select Run to save and test the application in the emulator. A dialog box opens the first time the application is executed to request how to run the application. Select Android Application and click the OK button. Save all the files in the next dialog box and unlock the emulator. When the application opens in the emulator, enter the number of tickets and select a group from the Spinner control. To view the results, click the Find Ticket Cost button.

    The Concert Tickets Android app is executed (Figures 3-1 and 3-2).

Wrap It Up—Chapter Summary

In this chapter, you have learned to declare variables and write arithmetic operations. New controls such as the Text Field to enter text and the Spinner control to select from multiple items were used in the chapter project. GetText( ) and SetText( ) methods were used to extract and display data, respectively. An Android theme was also applied to the application.

- You can assign a theme to an Activity or entire application to define its appearance and style and to prevent each Android app you develop from looking too similar.

- Preview a theme by clicking the Theme button in the emulator window and then selecting a theme. To permanently change the theme in the application, define the theme in the Android Manifest file for each Activity.

- Use Text Fields to request input from users, who can enter characters using an onscreen keyboard or a physical keyboard. You need to select the correct type of Text Field control for the type of data you are requesting.

- To provide guidelines so users enter the correct data in a Text Field control, use the control's Hint property to display light-colored text describing what to enter. The user clicks the control to remove the hint and type the requested input.

- To handle the input that users enter into a Text Field control, you use the EditText class, which extracts the text and converts it for use in the Java code. The extracted text must be assigned to a variable, which holds data that changes during the execution of the program. To extract the string of text entered in an EditText control, use the GetText( ) method. To display the extracted text in a TextView control, use the SetText( ) method.

- The strings.xml file is part of every Android application by default and contains strings used in the application, such as text displayed in a Spinner control. You can edit a string in strings.xml to update the text wherever it is used in the application. In strings.xml, you can also include prompt text that provides instructions in a Spinner control. In the Java code, use the GetSelectedItem( ) method to return the text of the selected Spinner item.

- To use a variable, you must first declare the variable and then assign a value to it. The declared type of a value determines which mathematical operations are allowed. Variables in an Android application are typically declared at the beginning of an Activity.

- After assigning variables to hold the values entered in controls, you often need to convert the values in the assigned variables to the correct data type so the values can be used in calculations. To use string data in a mathematical function, you use the Parse class to convert the string into a numerical data type.

Key Terms

DecimalFormat—A class that provides patterns for formatting numbers in program output.

Entries—A Spinner property that connects a string array to the Spinner control for display.

final—A type of variable that can only be initialized once; any attempt to reassign the value results in a compile error when the application is executed.

GetSelectedItem( )—A method that returns the text of the selected Spinner item.

GetText( )—A method that reads text stored in an EditText control.

hint—A short description of a field that appears as light text in a Text Field control.

item—In a Spinner control, a string of text that appears in a list for user selection.

localization—The use of the String table to change text based on the user's preferred language.

Parse—A class that converts a string into a number data type.

prompt—Text that displays instructions at the top of the Spinner control.

soft keyboard—An onscreen keyboard positioned over the lower part of an application's window.

Spinner control—A widget similar to a drop-down list for selecting a single item from a fixed listing.

string—A series of alphanumeric characters that can include spaces.

strings.xml—A default file that is part of every Android application and holds commonly used strings in an application.

theme—A style applied to an Activity or an entire application.

variable—A name used in a Java program to contain data that changes during the execution of the program.

Developer FAQs

1. What is an Android theme?

2. Which theme was used in the chapter project?

3. In an app, suppose you want to use the theme named Theme.Translucent. What code is needed in the AndroidManifest.xml file to support this theme?

4. What is a soft keyboard? Be sure to include its location in your answer.

5. Which five controls were used in the chapter project?

6. Which Text Field control is best for entering an amount that contains a paycheck amount?

7. Which property of the Spinner control adds text at the top of the control such as instructions?

8. What is the name of the file that holds commonly used phrases (arrays) of text in an application?

9. What is a single string of information called in a string array?

10. Which property do you assign to the string array that you create for a Spinner?

11. Write the following variable in camel case: NUMBEROFCOMPUTERJOBS.

12. Write a declaration statement for each of the following variables using the variable type and variable name that would be best for each value. Assign values if directed.

    a. The population of the state of Alaska

    b. Your weekly pay using the most common type for this type number

    c. The smallest data type you can use for your age

    d. Assign the first initial of your first name

    e. Assign the present minimum wage using the most common type for this type of number

    f. Assign the name of the city in which you live

    g. The answer to a true/false question

13. Name two numeric data types that can contain a decimal point.

14. What is the solution to each of the following arithmetic expressions?

    a. 3 + 4 * 2 + 6

    b. 16 / 2 * 4 - 3

    c. 40 - (6 + 2) / 2

    d. 3 + 68 % 9

15. Write a GetText( ) statement that converts a variable named deficit to a double data type and assigns the value to the variable named financeDeficit.

16. Assign the text of the user's choice of a Spinner control named collegeName to the variable named topCollege.

17. If a variable named amount is assigned to the value 47199.266, what would these statements display in the variable called price?

```
DecimalFormat money = new DecimalFormat("$###,###.##");
price.setText("Salary = " + money.format(amount));
```

18. Write a line of Java code that assigns the variable jellyBeans to a decimal format with six digits and a comma if needed, but no dollar sign or decimal places.

19. Write a line of Java code to use concatenation to join the phrase "Welcome to the ", versionNumber (an int variable), and the phrase "th version" to the variable combineStatement.

20. Write a line of Java code that assigns a number to the variable numberChoice, which indicates the user's selection. If the user selects the first group, the number 0 is assigned; if the user selects the second group, the number 1 is assigned; and if the user selects the third group, the number 2 is assigned with the same variables used in the chapter project.

Beyond the Book

Using the Internet, search the Web for the answers to the following questions to further your Android knowledge.

1. Name 10 themes used in your Android SDK not mentioned in this chapter.

2. Search the Internet for three real Android apps that sell any type of tickets. Name five features of each of the three apps.

3. A good Android developer always keeps up with the present market. Open the page *https://market.android.com*. Find this week's featured tablet apps and write about the top five. Write a paragraph on the purpose and cost of each for a total of five paragraphs.

4. Open the search engine Bing.com and then click the News tab. Search for an article about Androids with this week's date. Insert the URL link at the top of a new document. Write a 150–200–word summary of the article in your own words.

Case Programming Projects

Complete one or more of the following case programming projects. Use the same steps and techniques taught within the chapter. Submit the program you create to your instructor. The level of difficulty is indicated for each case programming project.

Easiest: ★

Intermediate: ★★

Challenging: ★★★

Case Project 3–1: Study Abroad App ★

Requirements Document

Application title:	Study Abroad App
Purpose:	Your school is offering a summer study abroad program. A simple app determines how many tickets are needed for a group and lets a user select the location lets a user study abroad. The app displays the location and the total price for the group's airfare.
Algorithms:	1. The app displays a title; an image; and a Text Field, Spinner, and Button control (Figure 3-36). The three cities in the Spinner control include Rome, Dublin, and Tokyo. Each round trip plane fare is $1,288.00 per person.
	2. When the user clicks the Button control, the location and the cost of the group airfare are displayed for the flight in a TextView control (Figure 3-37).
Conditions:	Use a theme, Spinner prompt, string array, and Hint property.

Figure 3-36

Figure 3-37

Case Project 3–2: Tuition App ★

Requirements Document

Application title: Tuition App

Purpose: A college tuition app allows a student to compute the tuition for a semester.

Algorithms: 1. The college tuition app has two Text Fields: One requests the cost of each credit, and the other requests the number of credits a student intends to take during the semester. A Spinner control allows the student to select one of the three possible semesters: Fall, Spring, and Summer. The app also displays a title, an image, and a Button control (Figure 3-38).

  2. After the user clicks the Button control, the selected semester and the total cost of tuition with an added student technology fee of $125.00 are displayed in a TextView control (Figure 3-39).

Conditions: Use a theme, a title, an image, a Spinner prompt, a string array, and a Hint property.

Figure 3-38

Figure 3-39

Case Project 3–3: New York City Cab Fare App ★★

Requirements Document

Application title:	NYC Cab Fare App
Purpose:	Create an app that estimates the cost for cab fare in New York City. The app calculates the cost of the trip and requests a reservation for a smart car, traditional sedan, or minivan.
Algorithms:	1. The app requests the distance in miles for the cab ride and your preference for the requested cab: a smart car, traditional sedan, or minivan. The cab company has an initial rate of $3.00. The mileage rate of $3.25 per mile is charged.
	2. The app displays the name of a cab company, a picture of a logo, and the results of the requested type of cab with the cost of the fare. Create your own layout.
Conditions:	Use a theme, Spinner prompt, string array, and Hint property. Decimal mileage is possible.

Case Project 3–4: Paint Calculator App ★★

Requirements Document

Application title: Paint Calculator App

Purpose: The paint calculator app is needed in the paint section of a large home store to calculate the number of gallons needed to paint a room. The amount of paint in gallons is displayed.

Algorithms: 1. The app displays a title; an image; two Text Fields; and a Spinner, Button, and TextView control. The Spinner control allows five colors of paint to be selected. The room's height in feet and the distance in feet around the room are entered.

  2. The color and the exact number of gallons in decimal form are displayed.

Conditions: A gallon is needed for every 250 square feet for a single coat of paint. Display the result rounded to two decimal places. Select five names for paint for the Spinner control. Use a theme, Spinner prompt, string array, and Hint property.

Case Project 3–5: Split the Bill App ★★★

Requirements Document

Application title: Split the Bill App

Purpose: You are out with friends at a nice restaurant and the bill comes! This app splits the bill, including the tip, among the members of your party.

Algorithms: 1. A welcome screen displays the title, image, and button that takes the user to a second screen. The input/output screen requests the restaurant bill and the number of people in your group. The Spinner control asks about the quality of service: Excellent, Average, or Poor.

  2. Calculate an 18% tip and divide the restaurant bill with the tip included among the members of your party. Display the service and the individual share of the bill.

Conditions: Use a theme, Spinner prompt, string array, and Hint property.

Case Project 3–6: Piggy Bank Children's App ★★★

Requirements Document

Application title: Piggy Bank Children's App

Purpose: A piggy bank app allows children to enter the number of quarters, dimes, nickels, and pennies that they have. The child can select whether to save the money or spend it. Calculate the amount of money and display the amount that the child is saving or spending. Create two screens: a welcome screen and an input/output screen.

Algorithms: 1. A welcome screen displays the title, image, and button that takes the user to a second screen. The input/output screen requests the number of quarters, dimes, nickels, and pennies. A Spinner control should indicate whether the children are saving or spending their coins. Create your own layout.

2. The results display how much the child is saving or spending.

Conditions: Use a theme, Spinner prompt, string array, and Hint property.

4

Explore! Icons and Decision-Making Controls

Unless otherwise noted in the chapter, all screenshots are provided courtesy of Eclipse.

In this chapter, you learn to:

- ◎ Create an Android project with a custom icon
- ◎ Change the text color in controls using hexadecimal colors
- ◎ Align controls using the Change Gravity tool
- ◎ Determine layout with the Change Margins tool
- ◎ Place a RadioGroup and RadioButtons in Android applications
- ◎ Write code for a RadioGroup control
- ◎ Make decisions using an If statement
- ◎ Make decisions using an If Else statement
- ◎ Make decisions using logical operators
- ◎ Display an Android toast notification
- ◎ Test the isChecked property
- ◎ Make decisions using nested If statements

Developers can code Android applications to make decisions based on the input of users or other conditions that occur. Decision making is one of the fundamental activities of a computer application. In this chapter, you learn to write decision-making statements in Java, which allows you to test conditions and perform different operations depending on the results of that test. You can test for a condition being true or false and change the flow of what happens in a program based on the user's input.

The sample program in this chapter is designed to run on an Android phone or tablet device at a hospital. The Medical Calculator application provides nurses a mobile way to convert the weight of a patient from pounds to kilograms and kilograms to pounds. Most medication amounts are prescribed based on the weight of the patient. Most hospital scales display weight in pounds, but the prescribed medication is often based on the weight of a patient in kilograms. For safety reasons, the exact weight of the patient must be correctly converted between pounds and kilograms. The nurse enters the weight of the patient and selects a radio button, as shown in Figure 4-1, to determine whether pounds are being converted to kilograms or kilograms are being converted to pounds. The mobile application then computes the converted weight based on the conversion formulas: The conversion formulas are: kilograms = pounds * 2.2 and pounds = kilograms / 2.2. To validate that correct weights are entered, if the value is greater than 500 for the conversion from pounds to kilograms or greater than 225 for the conversion from kilograms to pounds, the user is asked for a valid entry. If the user enters a number out of the acceptable range, a warning called a toast message appears on the screen. When the app is running, a nurse enters 225 for the value of the weight of the patient and selects the Convert Pounds to Kilograms radio button shown in Figure 4-1. After tapping the Convert Weight button, the application displays 102.3 kilograms (rounded off to the nearest tenth place) in a red font, as shown in Figure 4-2. By using a mobile device, the nurse can capture patient information such as weight directly at the point of care anywhere and anytime and reduce errors made by delaying entry on a traditional computer in another location.

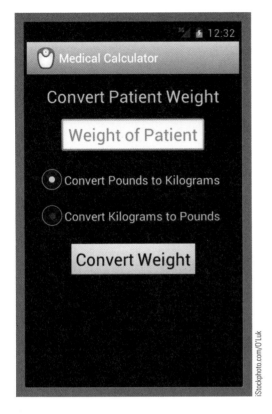

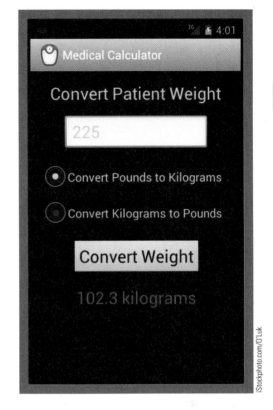

Figure 4-1 Opening screen of the Medical Calculator

Figure 4-2 Results screen of the Medical Calculator

To create this application, the developer must understand how to perform the following processes:

1. Create a customized launcher icon.

2. Define a TextField for the data entry of the weight of the patient.

3. Define a RadioGroup to select pounds to kilograms or kilograms to pounds.

4. Display a Toast message for data validation.

5. Convert data so it can be used for arithmetic operations.

6. Perform arithmetic operations on data the user enters.

7. Display formatted results.

IN THE TRENCHES

Medical phone apps are changing the entire patient point-of-care system. Apps now used in hospitals include mobile patient records, drug prescription references, medical journals, surgical checklists, dosage calculators, radiology imagery, and disease pathology.

The Launcher Icon

By default, Android places a standard Android icon, as shown in Figure 4-3, as the graphic to represent your application on the device's home screen and in the Launcher window. To view the opening icon called the **launcher icon** on the home screen, click the application listing icon at the bottom of the emulator when an application begins to execute, as shown in Figure 4-3. Instead of a default icon, each app published to the Android Market should have a custom graphic representing the contents of your application. Launcher icons form the first impression of your app on prospective users in the Android Market. With so many apps available, a high-quality launcher icon can influence users to purchase your Android app.

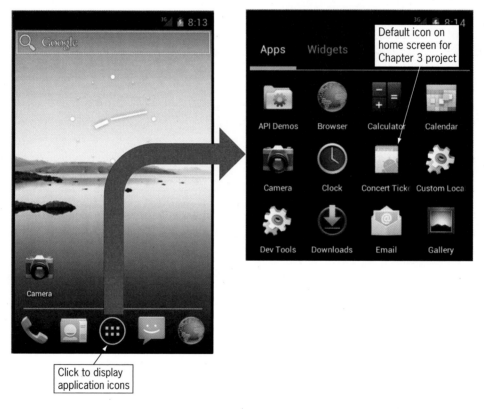

Figure 4-3   Android home screen and launcher icons

As you design a launcher icon, consider that an icon can establish brand identity. A unique image logo and program name can communicate your brand to potential customers. In the Medical Calculator app, the scale icon shown in Figure 4-4 clearly communicates that this icon launches a program about weight. A simple image with a clear visual cue like the scale has a memorable impact. It also helps users find the app in the Android Market. The Android Market suggests icons should be simple and bold in design. For example, for a paint graphics program, an icon shaped like a thin art paintbrush may be hard to distinguish from a pencil image, but a large cartoonlike paintbrush can convey its purpose easily.

The Android Market also specifies the size and format of all launcher icons for uniformity. Launcher icons should be saved in the .png file format. Based on your target device, Table 4-1 specifies the size of a finished launcher icon. You can use programs such as Microsoft Paint, Mac Paintbrush, and Adobe Photoshop to resize the icon to the correct number of pixels. In the chapter project, the icon dimension is 72 × 72 pixels for the high-density screen used by the application. If you are creating an application that can be deployed on any Android device, you can use the same name for the icon, but resize it four times and place each image in the appropriate res/drawable folder.

113

Figure 4-4 Launcher icon for the Medical Calculator app

Resolution	Dots per Inch (dpi)	Size (px)
ldpi (low-density screen)	120	36 × 36
mdpi (medium-density screen)	160	48 × 48
hdpi (high-density screen)	240	72 × 72
xhdpi (extra high-density screen)*	320	96 × 96

* Used by some tablets

Table 4-1 Launcher icon sizes

GTK
When you publish an app to the Android Market, you must provide a 512 × 512 pixel, high-resolution application icon in the developer console as you upload your program. This icon is displayed in the Android Market to provide a description of the app and does not replace your launcher icon.

The Android Market recommends a naming convention for launcher icons. Typically, the prefix ic_launcher is used to name launcher icons for Android apps. In the case of the Medical Calculator app, the launcher icon is named ic_launcher_weight.png.

GTK
Vector-based graphics are best to use for icon design because the images can be scaled without the loss of detail and are easily resized.

Customizing a Launcher Icon

To display a custom launcher icon instead of the default icon on the home screen, first the custom icon image must be placed in the res\drawable folder. In addition, the Android Manifest file must be updated to include the new filename of the image file. The application code within the Android Manifest file for the chapter project should be changed to android: icon = "ic_launcher_weight.png". To perform the following steps, you need an image file named ic_launcher_weight.png, provided with your student files, to use as the custom launcher icon for the Medical Calculator app. You should already have the student files for this text that your instructor gave you or that you downloaded from the Web page for this book (*www.cengagebrain.com*). To begin the chapter project and add a customized launcher icon, follow these steps:

1. Open the Eclipse program. Click the New button on the Standard toolbar. Expand the Android folder, if necessary, and select Android Project. Click the Next button. In the New Android Project dialog box, enter the Project name **Medical Calculator**. To save the project on your USB drive, click to remove the check mark from the Use default location check box. Type **E:\Workspace** (if necessary, enter a different drive letter that identifies the USB drive). Click the Next button. For the Build Target, select Android 4.0, if necessary. Click the Next button. Type the Package name **net. androidbootcamp.medicalcalculator**. Enter **Main** in the Create Activity text box. Click the Finish button. Expand the Medical Calculator project in the Package Explorer. Expand the res folder to display its subfolders. Expand the layout subfolder. Right-click main.xml, point to Open With, and then click Android Layout Editor. Click the Hello World, Main! TextView widget, and then press the Delete key. Click the Theme button to display the list of built-in themes, and then select Theme.WithActionBar.

    The New Android Medical Calculator project uses the Theme.WithActionBar theme, and the default icon is displayed in the action bar (Figure 4-5).

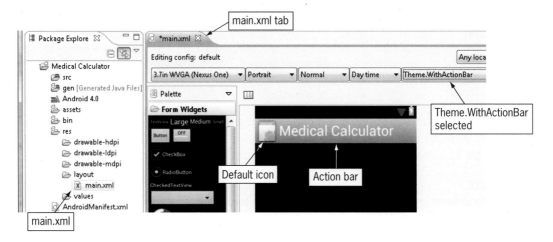

Figure 4-5   Theme with action bar

2. To add the custom launcher icon to the project, copy the student files to your USB drive (if necessary). Open the USB folder containing the student files. In the Package Explorer, expand the drawable-hdpi folder. Drag the ic_launcher_weight.png file to the drawable-hdpi folder until a plus sign pointer appears. Release the mouse button. Click the OK button in the File Operation dialog box. Click the default icon ic_launcher.png file and press the Delete key, and then click the OK button to confirm the deletion.

The custom launcher icon image is placed in the drawable-hdpi folder. The image in the emulator does not update until the Android Manifest file is changed (Figure 4-6).

Figure 4-6 New launcher icon file

3. To change the code in the Android Manifest file so the application displays the custom icon, double-click the AndroidManifest.xml file in the Package Explorer. Click the AndroidManifest.xml tab at the bottom of the window. Inside the application code, click in the line android:icon="drawable/ic_launcher". Change the filename portion from ic_launcher" to **ic_launcher_weight**".

The Android launcher icon is coded in the Android Manifest file (Figure 4-7).

```
main.xml        *Medical Calculator Manifest
 1  <?xml version="1.0" encoding="utf-8"?>
 2  <manifest xmlns:android="http://schemas.android.com/apk/res/android"
 3          package="net.androidbootcamp.medicalcalculator"
 4          android:versionCode="1"
 5          android:versionName="1.0" >
 6
 7          <uses-sdk android:minSdkVersion="14" />          Icon name
 8                                                           changed
 9          <application
10              android:icon="@drawable/ic_launcher_weight"
11              android:label="@string/app_name" >
12              <activity
13                  android:label="@string/app_name"
14                  android:name=".Main" >
15                  <intent-filter >
```

Figure 4-7 Android Manifest code with new launcher icon filename

4. To add the selected theme to the Android Manifest, inside the activity code, click at the end of the line android:label="@string/app_name". Press the Enter key to insert a blank line. Type **android:theme="@android:style/Theme.WithActionBar"**.

The Android theme is coded in the Android Manifest file (Figure 4-8).

```
    main.xml       Medical Calculator Manifest

  1  <?xml version="1.0" encoding="utf-8"?>
  2  <manifest xmlns:android="http://schemas.android.com/apk/res/and
  3      package="net.androidbootcamp.medicalcalculator"
  4      android:versionCode="1"
  5      android:versionName="1.0" >
  6
  7      <uses-sdk android:minSdkVersion="14" />
  8
  9      <application
 10          android:icon="@drawable/ic_launcher_weight"
 11          android:label="@string/app_name" >
 12          <activity
 13              android:label="@string/app_name"
 14              android:theme="@android:style/Theme.WithActionBar"
 15              android:name=".Main">
```

New Android theme referenced

Figure 4-8 Android Manifest code with new theme

5. Click the Save All button on the Standard toolbar, and then close the Medical Calculator Manifest tab.

RadioButton and RadioGroup Controls

RadioButton controls are used to select or deselect an option. In the chapter project, the user can select which mathematical conversion is needed. When a RadioButton is placed on the emulator, by default each control is arranged vertically. If you prefer the RadioButton controls to be listed horizontally, you can set the orientation property to horizontal. Each RadioButton control has a label defined by the Text property and a Checked property set to either true or false. RadioButton controls are typically used together in a **RadioGroup**. Checking one radio button unchecks the other radio buttons within the group. In other words, within a RadioGroup control, only one RadioButton control can be selected at a time. When the RadioGroup control on the Palette is placed on the emulator window, three RadioButton controls are included in the group by default. If you need additional RadioButton controls, drag them from the Palette into the group. In the case of the Medical Calculator app, only two radio buttons are needed, so the third radio button is deleted.

To make the user's input as simple as possible, offer a default selection. For example, nurses more often convert weight from pounds to kilograms, so that RadioButton option should be checked initially. The Checked property of this RadioButton control is set to true to provide a default selection.

GTK

Like RadioButton controls, a CheckBox control allows a user to check or uncheck a listing. A user may select any number of check boxes, including zero, one, or several. In other words, each check box is independent of all other check boxes in the list, so checking one box does not uncheck the others. The shape of a radio button is circular and the check box is square.

Changing the Text Color of Android Controls

Thus far, each application in this text used the default color of white for the text color for each Android control. The Android platform uses a color system called hexadecimal color codes to display different colors. A **hexadecimal color code** is a triplet of three colors. Colors are specified first by a pound sign followed by how much red (00 to FF), how much green (00 to FF), and how much blue (00 to FF) are in the final color. For example, the hexadecimal color of #FF0000 is a true red. The TextView and RadioGroup controls displayed in the chapter project have light gray text, which you designate by typing #CCCCCC as the Text color property. To look up these color codes, search for hexadecimal color codes in a search engine or refer to *http://html-color-codes.com*.

Changing the Layout Gravity

The Medical Calculator app displays controls from the Palette with a Linear layout, which is the default setting for layouts on the Android emulator. As you place controls on the emulator, each control snaps to the left edge of the screen by default. You can use a property named Layout gravity to center a control horizontally as well as position it at other places on the screen. When you place a control on the emulator, a toolbar appears above the emulator screen. You can change the gravity using the Properties pane or a button on the toolbar. The **Change Gravity** tool shown in Figure 4-9 changes the linear alignment. Layout gravity is similar to the alignment feature in Microsoft Office that allows a control to snap to the left, center, right, top, or bottom of another object or the screen.

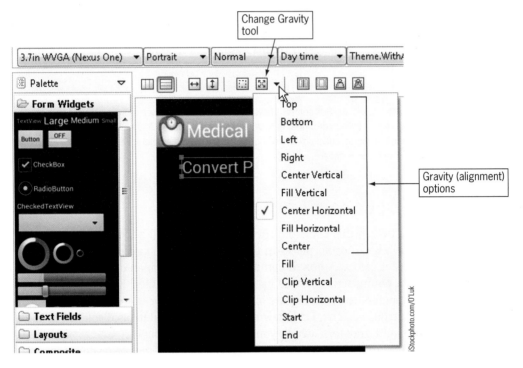

Figure 4-9   Change Gravity tool

Changing the Margins

After placing a control on the user interface, you can change the alignment by adjusting the gravity of the control. For more flexibility in controlling your layout, use **margins** to change the spacing around each object. Each control in the Medical Calculator app can use margins to add a certain amount of blank space measured in density independent pixels (dp) on each of its four sides. Instead of "eyeballing" the controls on the user interface for alignment, the Change Margins tool creates equal spacing around controls. Using the Change Margins tool helps make your user interface more organized and ultimately easier to use. The Change Margins tool is displayed when a control is selected on the user interface. For example, in Figure 4-10 a margin spacing of 15dp (pixels) specifies 15 extra pixels on the top side of the selected TextView control. As you design the user interface, use the same specified margins around each control to provide a symmetrical layout.

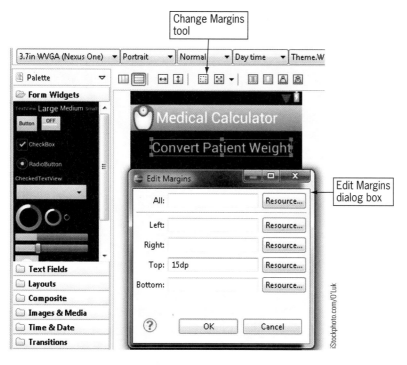

Figure 4-10 Change Margins tool

Adding the RadioButton Group

The Medical Calculator app displays a TextView control, Number Text Field, and RadioGroup control, all centered horizontally. The TextView and RadioGroup controls use the text color of gray. To name a RadioButton control, use the Id property in the Properties pane to enter a name that begins with the prefix rad, which represents a radio button in the code. To begin the design of the Android user interface and to add a RadioGroup to the Medical Calculator app, follow these steps:

1. With the main.xml tab open, click the Form Widgets category in the Palette, if necessary. Select the Form Widget named TextView. Drag and drop the TextView control onto the emulator user interface. Right-click the emulator window, point to Show In, and then select Properties to open the Properties pane, if necessary. Click the TextView control that you placed on the emulator. In the Properties pane, change the Text property to **Convert Patient Weight**. Change the Text size property to **25sp**. Click the Text color property and type **#CCCCCC** to change the text color to a light gray to match the action bar. Click the Change Gravity tool on the toolbar. Select Center Horizontal to center the control. With the control selected, click the Change Margins tool on the toolbar. In the Top text box of the Edit Margins dialog box, type **15dp** and then click the OK button to place 15 pixel spaces above the control.

The TextView control is added to the form with the text, size, text color, gravity, and margins changed (Figure 4-11).

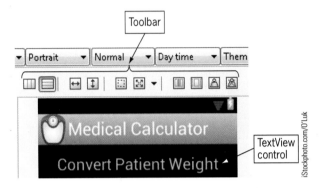

Figure 4-11   TextView control

2. To add the Number Text Field, click the Text Fields category in the Palette. Drag and drop the Number Text Field control (example shows a 42) onto the emulator's user interface below the TextView control. Change the Id property of the Number Text Field to **@+id/txtWeight**. Change the Text size property to **25sp**. Change the Hint property to **Weight of Patient**. Click the Text color property and type **#CCCCCC** as the hexadecimal color code for light gray. Resize the control to fit the hint by dragging a selection handle on the control. Select the control, click the Change Gravity tool, and select Center Horizontal to center the control. Select the control, click the Change Margins tool, and in the Top text box of the Edit Margins dialog box, type **15dp** and then click the OK button to place 15 pixel spaces between the TextView and the Number Text Field control.

    A Number Text Field control is placed on the emulator with the id, text size, text color, hint, gravity, and margins changed (Figure 4-12).

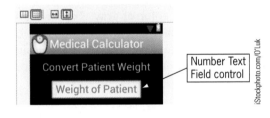

Figure 4-12   Number Text Field control

3. In the Palette, select the Form Widget named RadioGroup. Drag and drop the RadioGroup control onto the user interface below the Number Text Field. Only two radio buttons are needed for this app, so click the third RadioButton control and press the Delete key. Select the first RadioButton control. In the Properties pane, change the Id property of the RadioButton control to **@+id/radLbToKilo**. Change the Text property to **Convert Pounds to Kilograms**. Change the Text size property to **18sp**. Notice the Checked property is preset as true, indicating that the first radio button is the default selection. Click the Change Margins tool to open the Edit

Margins dialog box. In the Left text box, type **12dp** and in the Top text box, type **15dp**. Click the OK button. Select the second RadioButton control. In the Properties pane, change the Id property to **@+id/radKiloToLb**. Change the Text property to **Convert Kilograms to Pounds**. Change the Text size property to **18sp**. Click the Change Margins tool to open the Edit Margins dialog box. In the Left text box, type **12dp** and in the Top text box, type **5dp** to keep the RadioButtons close to one another within the group. Click the OK button.

The RadioGroup object is placed on the emulator with the id, text, color, and margin properties changed (Figure 4-13).

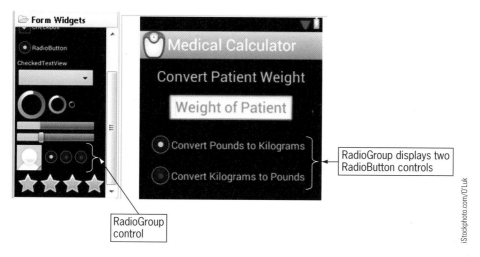

Figure 4-13 RadioGroup control

Coding a RadioButton Control

Each of the RadioButton controls placed on the emulator need to be referenced by using the findViewById Java command. In the following code syntax, lbsToKilo and kiloToLbs reference the two RadioButton controls in the Medical Calculator application:

Code Syntax

```
final RadioButton lbsToKilo = (RadioButton) findViewById(R.id.radLbToKilo);
final RadioButton kiloToLbs = (RadioButton) findViewById(R.id.radKiloToLb);
```

After the RadioButton controls have been referenced, the next priority is to determine which of the two radio buttons the user selected. If the user selected the Convert Pounds to Kilograms radio button, the weight entered is divided by 2.2, but if the user selected the Convert Kilograms to Pounds radio button, the weight is multiplied by 2.2. A variable named conversionRate is assigned the decimal value 2.2. The variables weightEntered and convertedWeight contain the patient weight and converted weight result, respectively.

To create the Java code to declare the variables used in the application and to reference the RadioButton controls, follow these steps:

1. In the Package Explorer, expand src and net.androidbootcamp.medicalcalculator, and then double-click Main.java to open the code window. Click after the comment line: /** Called when the activity is first created. */. Press the Enter key to insert a new blank line. To initialize the conversion rate value of 2.2, type **double conversionRate = 2.2;**. Press the Enter key. To initialize the weightEntered variable, type **double weightEntered;** and press the Enter key. To initialize the variable that will hold the converted weight, type **double convertedWeight;**. Press the Enter key.

Three variables are declared in the Java code (Figure 4-14).

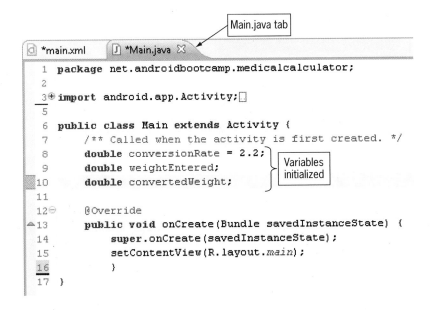

Figure 4-14   Variables declared

2. Click at the end of the line setContentView(R.layout.*main*);. Press the Enter key. To initialize and reference the EditText class with the Id name of txtWeight, type **final EditText weight = (EditText) findViewById(R.id.txtWeight);**. Point to the red curly line under EditText and select Import 'EditText' (android widget) on the pop-up menu. Press the Enter key. To initialize and reference the RadioButton class with the Id name of radLbToKilo, type **final RadioButton lbToKilo = (RadioButton) findViewById(R.id.radLbToKilo);**. Point to the red curly line under RadioButton and select Import 'RadioButton' (android widget). Press the Enter key. To initialize and reference the RadioButton class for the second radio button with the Id name of radKiloToLb, type **final RadioButton kiloToLb = (RadioButton) findViewById(R.id.radKiloToLb);**.

The EditText class extracts the value from the user's input for the patient weight and the RadioButton class extracts the checked value from the radio buttons (Figure 4-15).

```
 *main.xml      *Main.java ✕
 1  package net.androidbootcamp.medicalcalculator;
 2
 3  import android.app.Activity;
 7
 8
 9  public class Main extends Activity {
10      /** Called when the activity is first created. */
11      double conversionRate = 2.2;
12      double weightEntered;
13      double convertedWeight;
14
15      @Override
16      public void onCreate(Bundle savedInstanceState) {
17          super.onCreate(savedInstanceState);
18          setContentView(R.layout.main);
19          final EditText weight= (EditText) findViewById(R.id.txtWeight);
20          final RadioButton lbToKilo = (RadioButton) findViewById(R.id.radLbToKilo);
21          final RadioButton kiloToLb = (RadioButton) findViewById(R.id.radKiloToLb);
22
23      }
24  }
```

EditText referenced

RadioButtons referenced

Figure 4-15 EditText and RadioButtons referenced

3. Save your work.

Completing the User Interface

As you design the Android interface, it is important to have a clean layout and use the entire screen effectively. To complete the user interface by adding a Button and TextView control and code the Button and TextView controls, follow these steps:

1. In the main.xml tab, drag the Button control from the Palette to the emulator below the RadioGroup. In the Properties pane, change the Id property of the Button control to **@+id/btnConvert**. Change the Text property to **Convert Weight**. Change the Text size property to **25sp**. Click the Change Gravity tool on the toolbar, and then click Center Horizontal to center the control. Select the Button control, click the Change Margins tool, and in the Top text box of the Edit Margins dialog box, type **15dp** and then click the OK button to place 15 pixel spaces above the control.

    Drag another TextView control to the emulator below the Button. Change the Id property of the TextView control to **@+id/txtResult**. Change the Text size property to **25sp**. For the Text color property, type **#FF0000** (red). Click the Change Gravity tool on the toolbar, and then click Center Horizontal to center the control. Click the Change Margins tool, and in the Top text box of the Edit Margins dialog box, type **15dp** to place 15 pixels of space above the control, and then click the OK button. Delete the text in the Text property. Click the Save All button on the Standard toolbar.

The Button control named btnConvert displays the text Convert Weight and its id, text, text size, gravity, and margins are changed. The TextView control is placed on the emulator with an empty Text property (Figure 4-16).

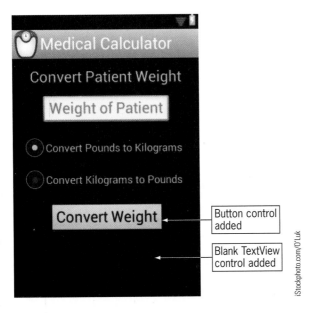

Button control added

Blank TextView control added

iStockphoto.com/O'Luk

Figure 4-16   Button and blank TextView controls

2.   To code the TextView control, click the Main.java tab. After the two lines of code referring to the RadioButton controls, type a new line with the code **final TextView result = (TextView) findViewById(R.id.txtResult);**. Import the 'TextView' (android.widget). Press the Enter key twice to insert two blank lines. To code the button, type **Button convert = (Button) findViewById(R.id.btnConvert);**. Point to Button and import the Button type as an Android widget. Press the Enter key. To code the Button listener, type **convert.setOn** and wait for a code listing to open. Double-click the first setOnClickListener displayed in the auto-complete listing. Inside the parentheses, type **new on** and press Ctrl+spacebar to display the auto-complete listing. Double-click the first choice, which lists an OnClickListener with an Anonymous Inner Type event handler. Point to OnClickListener and select Import 'OnClickListener' (android.view.View). Place a semicolon at the end of the auto-generated stub closing brace and parenthesis.

The TextView control txtResult is assigned to the variable result and the btnConvert Button control is coded (Figure 4-17).

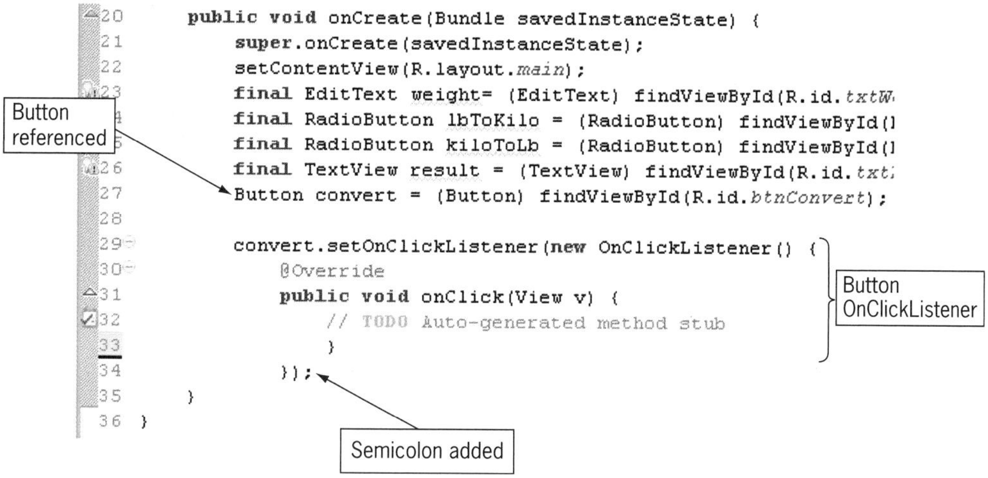

```
20    public void onCreate(Bundle savedInstanceState) {
21        super.onCreate(savedInstanceState);
22        setContentView(R.layout.main);
23        final EditText weight= (EditText) findViewById(R.id.txtW
          final RadioButton lbToKilo = (RadioButton) findViewById(]
          final RadioButton kiloToLb = (RadioButton) findViewById(]
26        final TextView result = (TextView) findViewById(R.id.txt;
27        Button convert = (Button) findViewById(R.id.btnConvert);
28
29        convert.setOnClickListener(new OnClickListener() {
30            @Override
31            public void onClick(View v) {
32                // TODO Auto-generated method stub
33            }
34        });
35    }
36 }
```

Button referenced

Button OnClickListener

Semicolon added

Figure 4-17   Button and Button OnClickListener

Making Decisions with Conditional Statements

In the Medical Calculator chapter project, which converts the weight entered to either pounds or kilograms, the user selects one of two radio buttons. Then, based on the choice, the application either divides by 2.2 or multiplies by 2.2.

Java uses decision structures to deal with the different conditions that occur based on the values entered into an application. A **decision structure** is a fundamental control structure used in computer programming. A statement that tests the radio button is called a conditional statement and the condition checked is whether the first or second radio button is selected. If the first radio button is selected, the weight is divided by 2.2. When a condition is tested in a Java program, it is either true or false. To execute a conditional statement and the statements that are executed when a condition is true, Java uses the If statement and its variety of formats.

Using an If Statement

In the chapter program, an **If statement** is used to determine which RadioButton control is selected. The simplest form of the If statement is shown in the following code:

Code Syntax

```
if (condition){
    //Statements completed if true
}
```

The statement(s) between the opening and closing braces are executed if the condition is true. If the condition is not true, no statements between the braces are executed, and program execution continues with the statement(s) that follows the closing brace.

Using If Else Statements

In many applications, the logic requires one set of instructions to be executed if a condition is true and another set of instructions to be executed if a condition is false. For example, a program requirement may specify that if a student's test score is 60 or greater, a message stating "You passed the examination" is displayed, but if the test score is less than 60, a message stating "You failed the examination" is displayed.

To execute one set of instructions if a condition is true, and another set of instructions if the condition is false, you can use the **If Else statement**, as shown in the following code:

Code Syntax

```
if (condition){
     //Statements completed if condition is true
   } else {
     //Statements completed if condition is false
   }
```

GTK

Java automatically indents statements to be executed when a condition is true or not true to indicate that the lines of code are within the conditional If structure.

Relational Operators

In the syntax of the condition portion of the If statement, a condition is tested to determine if it is true or false. The conditions that can be tested are:

- Is one value equal to another value?
- Is one value not equal to another value?
- Is one value greater than another value?
- Is one value less than another value?
- Is one value greater than or equal to another value?
- Is one value less than or equal to another value?

To test these conditions, Java provides relational operators that are used within the conditional statement to express the relationship between the numbers being tested. Table 4-2 shows these relational operators.

Relational Operator	Meaning	Example	Resulting Condition
= =	Equal to	6 = = 6	True
! =	Not equal to	4 ! = 7	False
>	Greater than	3 > 2	True
<	Less than	8 < 1	False
>=	Greater than or equal to	5 >= 5	True
<=	Less than or equal to	9 <= 6	False

Table 4-2   Relational operators

In the chapter project, an If Else statement determines if the entered weight is valid. If the nurse is converting pounds to kilograms, the weight entered must be less than or equal to 500 to be considered within a valid range of acceptable entries. If the entered weight is valid, the weight is converted by dividing it by the conversion rate of 2.2, as shown in the following code:

Code Syntax

```
if (weightEntered <=500){
   convertedWeight = weightEntered / conversionRate;
} else {
    //Statements completed if condition is false
}
```

GTK
The most common mistake made with an If statement is the use of a single equal sign to compare equality. A single equal sign (=) is used for assigning a value to a variable, not for comparison.

In addition to numbers, strings can also be compared in a conditional statement. A string value comparison compares each character in two strings, starting with the first character in each string. All characters found in strings, including letters, numbers, and special characters, are ranked in a sequence from low to high based on how the characters are coded internally on the computer. The relational operators from Table 4-2 cannot be used with string comparisons. If you are comparing equality, string characters cannot be compared with the " = =" operator. Java strings are compared with the **equals method** of the String class.

If you are comparing whether a string is alphabetically before another string, use the compareTo method to determine the order of strings. Do not use the less-than or greater-than symbols as shown in Table 4-2 to compare string data types. The compareTo method returns a negative integer if the first string precedes the second string. It returns zero if the two strings being compared are equal. It returns a positive integer if the first string follows the second string. Examples of the equals and compareTo methods are shown in Table 4-3 using the following initialized variables:

```
String name1 = "Sara";
String name2 = "Shawna";
String name3 = "Ryan";
```

If Statement	Comparison	Resulting Condition
if (name1.equals(name2))	Strings are not equal	False
if (name1.compareTo(name1) = = 0)	Strings are equal	True
if (name1.compareTo(name3) = = 0)	Strings are not equal	False
if (name1.compareTo(name2) > 0)	The first string precedes the second string; returns a negative number	False
if (name1.compareTo(name3) < 0)	The first string follows the third string; returns a negative number	True
If (name3.compareTo(name2) > 0)	The first string follows the second string; returns a positive number	True

Table 4-3   Examples of the equals and compareTo methods

Logical Operators

An If statement can test more than one condition within a single statement. In many cases, more than one condition must be true or one of several conditions must be true in order for the statements within the braces to be executed. When more than one condition is included in an If statement, the conditions are called a **compound condition**. For example, consider the following business traveling rule: "If the flight costs less than $400.00 and the hotel is less than $120.00 per night, the business trip is approved." In this case, both conditions (flight less than $400.00 and hotel less than $120.00 per night) must be true for the trip to be approved. If either condition is not true, then the business trip is not approved.

To create an If statement that processes the business traveling rule, you must use a logical operator. The most common set of logical operators is listed in Table 4-4.

Logical Operator	Meaning	Example
&&	And—all conditions must be true	if (flight < 400 && hotel < 120)
||	Or—at least one condition must be true	if (stamp < 0.49 || rate = = 2)
!	Not—reverses the meaning of a condition	if (! (grade > 70))

Table 4-4   Common logical operators

Data Validation

In the chapter project, it is important to confirm that the number entered by the user is not a typo or other type of mistake. If a value greater than 500 is entered for the conversion from pounds to kilograms or greater than 225 for the conversion from kilograms to pounds, the user should be notified and asked for a valid entry. To alert the user that an incorrect value was entered, a message called a toast notification (or toast message) can appear on the screen temporarily.

Toast Notification

A **toast notification** communicates messages to the user. These messages pop up as an overlay onto the user's current screen, often displaying a validation warning message. For example, a weather application may display a toast notification if a town is under a tornado warning. An instant messaging app might display a toast notification stating that a text message has been sent. In the chapter project, a toast notification displays a message warning the user that an invalid number was entered. A toast message only fills the amount of space required for the message to be displayed while the user's current activity remains visible and interactive. The notification automatically fades in and out on the screen.

The toast notification code uses a Toast object and the MakeText( ) method with three parameters: the context (displays the activity name), the text message, and the duration of the interval that the toast is displayed (LENGTH_SHORT or LENGTH_LONG). To display the toast notification, a show( ) method displays the Toast object.

Code Syntax

```
Toast toast = Toast.makeText(context, text, duration).show();
```

The toast message is best used for short messages. If the user enters an invalid number into the Medical Calculator, a warning toast notification fades in and then out on the screen. Notice in the following syntax that the text notification message displays *Pounds must be less than 500.*

Code Syntax

```
Toast.makeText(Main.this,"Pounds must be less than 500", Toast.LENGTH_LONG).show();
```

GTK

An ex-Microsoft employee of Google is credited with coining the term *toast,* which is a small notification window that slides upward into view, like toast popping out of a toaster.

Using the isChecked( ) Method of RadioButton Controls

You will recall that the RadioButton controls in the Medical Calculator Android application allow the user to select one conversion option. When the user selects the second radio button, a shaded small circle is displayed in that radio button. When a RadioButton is selected, the Checked property of the second RadioButton control changes from False (unselected) to True (selected). The Java code must check each RadioButton to determine if that RadioButton has been selected by the user. This checked property can be tested in an If statement using the **isChecked( ) method** to determine if the RadioButton object has been selected.

Code Syntax

```
if (lbToKilo.isChecked){
        //Statements completed if condition is true
    } else {
        //Statements completed if condition is false
    }
```

If the user selects the lbToKilo RadioButton control, the statements within the If portion between the braces are completed. If the user selects the kiloToLb RadioButton control, the statements within the Else portion are completed.

Nested If Statements

At times, more than one decision must be made to determine what processing must occur. For example, if one condition is true, a second condition might need to be tested before the correct code is executed. To test a second condition only after determining that a first condition is true (or false), you must place an If statement within another If statement. When you do this, the inner If statement is said to be **nested** within the outer If statement. In the chapter Android app, if the user checks the first radio button to convert pounds to kilograms and if the entered weight is equal to 500 pounds or less, then the weight can be converted. If the weight is above 500 pounds, a toast notification appears with a warning. A second nested If statement evaluates whether the second radio button is checked and if the user entered 225 kilograms or less as part of the final code.

Code Syntax

```
if (lbToKilo.isChecked()){
    if (weightEntered <=500){
        convertedWeight = weightEntered / conversionRate;
    } else {
        Toast.makeText(Main.this,"Pounds must be less than 500", Toast.LENGTH_LONG).show();
    }
}
```

Coding the Button Event

After the user enters the weight and selects the desired RadioButton, the Button control is tapped. The OnClickListener event is triggered and the conversion of the weight entered occurs. Within the onClick method, the weight entered must be converted to double data. A DecimalFormat layout is necessary to format the result to one place past the decimal point ("#.#"). To convert the weight to a double data type and establish the format for the output, follow these steps:

1. On a new line inside the OnClickListener onClick method stub of the Main.java code, type **weightEntered=Double.parseDouble(weight.getText().toString());** to convert the weight entered to a double data type.

   The weight entered by the user is converted to a double data type (Figure 4-18).

```
29      convert.setOnClickListener(new OnClickListener() {
30          @Override
31          public void onClick(View v) {
32              // TODO Auto-generated method stub
33              weightEntered=Double.parseDouble(weight.getText().toString());
34          }
```

Text entered for weight is converted to a double data type

Figure 4-18 Weight converted to a double data type

2. Press the Enter key. To create a decimal layout that changes the weight to a decimal rounded to the nearest tenth for use in the result later in the code, type **DecimalFormat tenth = new DecimalFormat("#.#");**. Point to the red curly line below DecimalFormat and select Import 'DecimalFormat' (java.text).

   The DecimalFormat code rounds off to the nearest tenth (Figure 4-19).

```
31      convert.setOnClickListener(new OnClickListener() {
32          @Override
33          public void onClick(View v) {
34              // TODO Auto-generated method stub
35              weightEntered=Double.parseDouble(weight.getText().toString());
36              DecimalFormat tenth = new DecimalFormat("#.#");
37          }
38      });
```

DecimalFormat rounds off to one place past the decimal point

Figure 4-19 Rounding off a number

Coding the Nested If Statements

After the weight entered is converted to a double and a format is set, code is necessary to determine which RadioButton was selected by using the isChecked property. Within each RadioButton If statement, the weight entered is converted to the appropriate weight unit and displayed, only if that weight is within the valid weight ranges (500 pounds or 225 kilograms). If the weight is not within the valid range, a toast notification appears warning the user to enter a value within the acceptable range. To code a nested If statement to display the result, follow these steps:

1. After the DecimalFormat line of code, to determine if the first RadioButton control is selected, type **if(lbToKilo.isChecked())** { and press the Enter key. Java automatically adds the closing brace.

   An If statement determines if the lbToKilo RadioButton control is checked (Figure 4-20).

```
33   public void onClick(View v) {
34       // TODO Auto-generated method stub
35       weightEntered=Double.parseDouble(weight.getText().toString());
36       DecimalFormat tenth = new DecimalFormat("#.#");
37       if(lbToKilo.isChecked()){
38
39       }
40       }
41   }};
```
If statement determines if the first RadioButton is checked

Figure 4-20   If statement

2. Within the first If statements, braces create a nested If Else statement that determines if the weight entered for pounds is less than or equal to 500. Type **if (weightEntered <=500)** { and press the Enter key. Java automatically adds the closing brace. After the closing brace, type **else** { and press the Enter key. Java automatically adds the closing brace.

   A nested If Else statement determines if the number of pounds entered is valid (Figure 4-21).

```
33   public void onClick(View v) {
34       // TODO Auto-generated method stub
35       weightEntered=Double.parseDouble(weight.getText
36       DecimalFormat tenth = new DecimalFormat("#.#");
37       if(lbToKilo.isChecked()){
38           if (weightEntered <=500){
39
40           }else {
41
```
Nested If Else statement determines if weight is valid

Figure 4-21   Nested If Else statement

3. After the pounds variable is validated, the weight must be converted. To divide the weight by the conversion rate of 2.2, inside the nested If statement, type **convertedWeight = weightEntered / conversionRate;** and press the Enter key. To display the result of the equation rounded to one place past the decimal point, type **result.setText(tenth.format(convertedWeight) + " kilograms");**.

   The number of pounds is converted to kilograms and displayed in the result TextView control (Figure 4-22).

```
33    public void onClick(View v) {
34        // TODO Auto-generated method stub
35        weightEntered=Double.parseDouble(weight.getText().toString());
36        DecimalFormat tenth = new DecimalFormat("#.#");
37        if(lbToKilo.isChecked()){
38            if (weightEntered <=500){
39                convertedWeight = weightEntered / conversionRate;
40                result.setText(tenth.format(convertedWeight) + " kilograms");
41            }else {
```

Equation to convert pounds to kilograms

Displays converted weight

Figure 4-22   Equation for weight conversion and displayed results

4. If the weight is not within the valid range, a toast message requesting that the user enter a valid weight is displayed briefly. Click the line after the Else statement and type **Toast.makeText(Main.this,"Pounds must be less than 500", Toast. LENGTH_LONG).show();** and then point to Toast and select Import 'Toast' (android.widget).

A toast message displays a reminder to enter a valid weight (Figure 4-23).

```
public void onClick(View v) {
    // TODO Auto-generated method stub
    weightEntered=Double.parseDouble(weight.getText().toString());
    DecimalFormat tenth = new DecimalFormat("#.#");
    if(lbToKilo.isChecked()){
        if (weightEntered <=500){
            convertedWeight = weightEntered / conversionRate;
            result.setText(tenth.format(convertedWeight) + " kilograms");
        }else {
            Toast.makeText(Main.this,"Pounds must be less than 500", Toast.LENGTH_LONG).show();
        }
    }
    }
});
```

Toast message

Figure 4-23   Toast message added to enter a valid weight

5. For when the user selects the Convert the Kilograms to Pounds RadioButton control, type the following lines of code, as shown in Figure 4-24:

```
if(kiloToLb.isChecked()) {
    if (weightEntered <=225) {
        convertedWeight = weightEntered * conversionRate;
        result.setText(tenth.format(convertedWeight) + " pounds");
    }else {
      Toast.makeText(Main.this, "Kilos must be less than 225",
Toast.LENGTH_LONG).show();
        }
    }
```

The nested If statement is executed if the second RadioButton control is selected (Figure 4-24).

```
  main.xml      Main.java
  1  package net.androidbootcamp.medicalcalculator;
  2
  3⊕ import java.text.DecimalFormat;□
 14
 15
 16  public class Main extends Activity {
 17      /** Called when the activity is first created. */
 18      double conversionRate = 2.2;
 19      double weightEntered;
 20      double convertedWeight;
 21
 22⊝     @Override
 23      public void onCreate(Bundle savedInstanceState) {
 24          super.onCreate(savedInstanceState);
 25          setContentView(R.layout.main);
 26          final EditText weight= (EditText) findViewById(R.id.txtWeight);
 27          final RadioButton lbToKilo = (RadioButton) findViewById(R.id.radLbToKilo);
 28          final RadioButton kiloToLb = (RadioButton) findViewById(R.id.radKiloToLb);
 29          final TextView result = (TextView) findViewById(R.id.txtResult);
 30          Button convert = (Button)findViewById(R.id.btnConvert);
 31
 32⊝         convert.setOnClickListener(new OnClickListener() {
 33⊝             @Override
 34              public void onClick(View v) {
 35                  // TODO Auto-generated method stub
 36                  weightEntered=Double.parseDouble(weight.getText().toString());
 37                  DecimalFormat tenth = new DecimalFormat("#.#");
 38                  if(lbToKilo.isChecked()){
 39                      if (weightEntered <=500){
 40                          convertedWeight = weightEntered / conversionRate;
 41                          result.setText(tenth.format(convertedWeight) + " kilograms");
 42                      }else{
 43                          Toast.makeText(Main.this,"Pounds must be less than 500", Toast.LENGTH_LONG).show();
 44                      }
 45                  }
 46                  if(kiloToLb.isChecked()){
 47                      if (weightEntered <=225){
 48                          convertedWeight = weightEntered * conversionRate;
 49                          result.setText(tenth.format(convertedWeight) + " pounds");
 50                      }else {
 51                          Toast.makeText(Main.this, "Kilos must be less than 225", Toast.LENGTH_LONG).show();
 52                      }
 53                  }
 54              }
 55          });
 56      }
 57  }
```

Second nested
If statement

Figure 4-24 Completed code

6. To view the finished application, click Run on the menu bar, and then select Run
    to save and test the application in the emulator. The first time the application is
    executed, a dialog box opens asking how to run the application. Select Android
    Application and click the OK button. Save all the files in the next dialog box and
    unlock the emulator. The application opens in the emulator where you enter a
    weight and select a radio button. To view the results, click the Convert Weight
    button.

    The Medical Calculator Android app is executed (see Figures 4-1 and 4-2).

Wrap It Up—Chapter Summary

Beginning with a customized icon, this chapter has completed the steps to create the graphical user interface including a RadioGroup control for the Medical Calculator program. The decision structure including a nested If Else statement determines different outcomes based on user input. If necessary, a toast message reminds the user of the expected input. You have learned to customize feedback and make decisions based on any user's input.

- To display a custom launcher icon instead of the default icon on the home screen of an Android device, copy the custom icon image to the res/drawable folder for the project, and then update the Android Manifest file to include the filename of the image file.

- Include RadioButton controls to allow users to select or deselect an option. Each RadioButton control has a label defined by the Text property and a Checked property set to either true or false. In a RadioGroup control, only one RadioButton control can be selected at a time.

- Android apps use hexadecimal color codes to set the color displayed in controls.

- Use the Layout gravity property to position a control precisely on the screen. You can change this property using the Properties pane or the Change Gravity tool on the toolbar. For more flexibility in controlling your layout, use the Change Margins tool to change the spacing between objects.

- A decision structure includes a conditional statement that checks whether the condition is true or false. To execute a conditional statement and the statements that are executed when a condition is true, Java uses the If statement and its variety of formats, including the If Else statement. An If statement executes one set of instructions if a specified condition is true and takes no action if the condition is not true. An If Else statement executes one set of instructions if a specified condition is true and another set of instructions if the condition is false.

- To test the conditions in a conditional statement such as an If statement, Java provides relational operators that are used within the conditional statement to express the relationship between the numbers being tested. For example, you can use a relational operator to test whether one value is greater than another.

- If more than one condition is tested in a conditional statement, the conditions are called a compound condition. To create an If statement that processes a compound condition, you must use a logical operator such as && (And).

- After including code that validates data, you can code a toast notification (also called a toast message) to display a brief message indicating that an incorrect value was entered.

- To test a second condition only after determining that a first condition is true or false, you nest one If statement within another If statement.

Key Terms

Change Gravity—A tool that changes the linear alignment of a control, so that it is aligned to the left, center, right, top, or bottom of an object or the screen.

compound condition—More than one condition included in an If statement.

decision structure—A fundamental control structure used in computer programming that deals with the different conditions that occur based on the values entered into an application.

equals method—A method of the String class that Java uses to compare strings.

hexadecimal color code—A triplet of three colors using hexadecimal numbers, where colors are specified first by a pound sign followed by how much red (00 to FF), how much green (00 to FF), and how much blue (00 to FF) are in the final color.

If Else statement—A statement that executes one set of instructions if a specified condition is true and another set of instructions if the condition is false.

If statement—A statement that executes one set of instructions if a specified condition is true and takes no action if the condition is not true.

isChecked( ) method—A method that tests a checked property to determine if a RadioButton object has been selected.

launcher icon—An icon that appears on the home screen to represent the application.

margin—Blank space that offsets a control by a certain amount of density independent pixels (dp) on each of its four sides.

nest—To place one statement, such as an If statement, within another statement.

RadioGroup—A group of RadioButton controls; only one RadioButton control can be selected at a time.

toast notification—A message that appears as an overlay on a user's screen, often displaying a validation warning.

Developer FAQs

1. What is the icon found on the Android home screen that opens an app?
2. What is the preferred prefix for a filename and file extension of the icon described in question 1?
3. What is the pixel size for the icon described in question 1 for a high-density pixel image?
4. To display a custom icon, you must perform two steps. First, add the icon image file to the drawable-hdpi folder. What is the second step?
5. Which TextView property is changed to identify the color of the control?

6. Which primary color is represented by the hexadecimal code of #00FF00?

7. What is the name of the tool used to center a TextView control horizontally?

8. Using the Change Margins tool, in which text box would you type 22dp to move a control 22 density pixels down from the upper edge of the emulator?

9. When a RadioGroup control is placed on the emulator, the first RadioButton control is selected by default. Which property is set as true by default?

10. Write an If statement that tests if the value in the variable age is between 18 and 21 years of age, inclusive, with empty braces.

11. Write an If statement that tests if the radio button named *gender* is selected with empty braces.

12. Rewrite the following line of code without a Not logical operator but keeping the same logical processing: if (! (waist <= 36) {

13. Write an If statement to compare if a string variable named *company* is equal to *Verizon* with empty braces.

14. Fix this statement: if (hours < 1 | | > 8) {

15. How many radio buttons can be selected at one time in a RadioGroup control?

16. Write an If statement that compares if wage is equal to 7.25 with empty braces.

17. If you compare two strings and the result is a positive number, what is the order of the two strings?

18. Using a relational operator, write an If statement that evaluates if a variable named *tipPercent* is not equal to .15 with empty braces.

19. Write a warning message that would display the comment "The maximum credits allowed is 18" with a long interval.

20. Write a quick reminder message that would display the comment "File saved" with a short interval.

Beyond the Book

Using the Internet, search the Web for the answers to the following questions to further your Android knowledge.

1. You have developed an application on music downloads. Search using Google Images to locate an appropriate icon and resize the icon using a paint-type program for use as a phone app launcher icon.

2. Search the Android Market site for a popular app that has a Sudoku puzzle. Take a screen shot of one Sudoku puzzle's launcher icon and another screen shot of the larger graphic used for the description of the app.

3. An Android toast message can also be coded to appear at an exact location on the screen. Explain how this works and give an example of the code that would do this.

4. Research the average price of an individual paid app. Write 75–100 words on the average selling prices of Android and iPhone apps.

Case Programming Projects

Complete one or more of the following case programming projects. Use the same steps and techniques taught within the chapter. Submit the program you create to your instructor. The level of difficulty is indicated for each case programming project.

Easiest: ★

Intermediate: ★ ★

Challenging: ★ ★ ★

Case Project 4–1: Temperature Conversion App ★

Requirements Document

Application title:	Temperature Conversion App
Purpose:	The app converts temperatures from Fahrenheit to Celsius or Celsius to Fahrenheit.
Algorithms:	1. The opening screen requests the outside temperature (Figure 4-25).
	2. The user selects a radio button labeled Fahrenheit to Celsius or Celsius to Fahrenheit and then selects the Convert Temperature button.
	3. The converted temperature is displayed (Figure 4-26).
Conditions:	1. The result is rounded off to the nearest tenth.
	2. Formulas: C = (F – 32) * 5 / 9 and F = (C * 9 / 5) + 32
	3. Do not enter more than 130 degrees Fahrenheit or 55 degrees Celsius.
	4. Use Theme with no title bar.

Figure 4-25

Figure 4-26

Case Project 4–2: Movie Time App ★

Requirements Document

Application title:	Movie Time App
Purpose:	A Movie Time app charges a monthly fee based on whether you want streaming movies, DVD movies, or combined services (three choices). The app has a customized launcher icon (Figure 4-27).
Algorithms:	1. The opening screen requests the number of months that you would like to subscribe to the movie service (Figure 4-28).
	2. The user selects which service: streaming movies for $7.99 per month, DVD movies by mail for $8.99 per month, or a combined service for $15.99 per month.
	3. When the Compute Price button is selected, the total price is displayed for the number of months subscribed (Figure 4-29).
Conditions:	1. The app allows you to subscribe for up to 24 months.
	2. Use a customized launcher icon (ic_launcher_movie.png).
	3. Use a theme with an action bar.

iStockphoto.com/Viktor Chornobay

Figure 4-27

Figure 4-28   Figure 4-29

Case Project 4–3: Floor Tiling App ★ ★

Requirements Document

Application title: Floor Tiling App

Purpose: The tiling app allows you to calculate how many tiles you need to cover a rectangular area.

Algorithms: 1. The opening screen requests the length and the width of a room in whole feet.

                                                   2. The user selects whether the tiles are 12 inches by 12 inches or 18 inches by 18 inches.

                                                   3. The number of tiles needed to cover the area in square feet is displayed.

Case Project 4–4: Math Flash Cards App ★ ★

Requirements Document

Application Title: Math Flash Cards App

Purpose: The Math Flash Cards App is designed for children to practice their basic math skills.

Algorithms: 1. The opening screen requests two integer values.

2. The user can select addition, subtraction, or multiplication.

3. The entire math problem is displayed with the result.

Conditions: 1. The integer values must be between 1 and 20.

2. Use a customized launcher icon.

Case Project 4–5: Currency Conversion App ★ ★ ★

Requirements Document

Application title: Currency Conversion App

Purpose: The Currency Conversion app converts U.S. dollars into euros, Mexican pesos, or Canadian dollars.

Algorithms: 1. The opening screen requests the amount of U.S. dollars to be converted.

2. The user selects euros, Mexican pesos, or Canadian dollars.

3. The conversion of U.S. dollars to the selected currency is displayed.

Conditions: 1. Use *http://xe.com* to locate current conversion rates.

2. The program only converts values below $100,000 U.S. dollars.

3. Use a customized launcher icon.

Case Project 4–6: Average Income Tax by Country App ★ ★ ★

Requirements Document

Application title:	Average Income Tax by Country App
Purpose:	The Average Income Tax by Country app allows the user to enter the amount of taxable income earned in the past year. The user selects his or her country of residence and the yearly income tax is displayed.
Algorithms:	1. The opening screen requests two integer values.
	2. The user can select addition, subtraction, or multiplication.
	3. The entire math problem is displayed with the result.
Conditions:	The following table displays the annual income tax percentages.

Country	Average Income Tax
China	25%
Germany	32%
Sweden	34%
USA	18%

Investigate! Android Lists, Arrays, and Web Browsers

Unless otherwise noted in the chapter, all screenshots are provided courtesy of Eclipse.

In this chapter, you learn to:

◎ Create an Android project using a list

◎ Develop a user interface that uses ListView

◎ Extend the ListActivity class

◎ Use an array to create a list

◎ Code a setListAdapter to display an array

◎ Design a custom ListView layout with XML code

◎ Display an image with the ListView control

◎ Change the default title bar text

◎ Code a custom setListAdapter for a custom layout

◎ Call the onListItemClick method when a list item is selected

◎ Write code using the Switch decision structure

◎ Call an intent to work with an outside app

◎ Open an Android Web browser

◎ Launch a Web site through the use of a URI using an Android browser

◎ Test an application with multiple decisions

Displaying a list is one of the most common design patterns used in mobile applications. This morning you likely read the news designed as a listing of articles on a phone or tablet. You scrolled down the list of news articles and selected one by tapping the screen to display a full story with text, images, and hyperlinks. As you walked to class today, you probably scrolled a list of songs on a mobile device and listened to your favorite tunes.

From a list, you can open an article, play a song, open a Web site, or even launch a video. A list created with a ListView control may be one of the most important Android design elements because it is used so frequently. To select a list item, a design structure is necessary to route your request to the intended content. In Chapter 4, you learned about the decision structure called an If statement, one of the major control structures used in computer programming. In this chapter, you learn about another decision structure called the Switch statement.

To demonstrate the process of using a list to navigate to different content, you design a travel city guide for San Francisco, California, highlighting the best attractions the city has to offer. The City Guide application shown in Figure 5-1 provides a list of city attractions. A city guide for a large city can provide easy access to all its sights, activities, and restaurants in one handy guide for your phone.

Figure 5-1   The San Francisco City Guide Android app

The Android app in Figure 5-1 could be part of a larger app that displays city maps, detailed site information, and restaurant recommendations. This mobile app provides information about popular places tourists visit in San Francisco. The City Guide app displays five San Francisco attractions. When the user taps one of the attractions, a second window opens displaying either an image or a Web site providing more information about the site or activity. The first two items on the list link to Web sites, as shown in Figure 5-2. A browser opens to display a Web site for Alcatraz Island or Ferry Marketplace. If the user selects Golden Gate Bridge, Cable Car Trolley, or Fisherman's Wharf, an image appears on a second screen, as shown in Figure 5-3.

Figure 5-2 Alcatraz and Ferry Marketplace Web sites

iStockphoto.com/DNY59

Erik Patton/Shutterstock.com

Erik Patton/Shutterstock.com

Figure 5-3   San Francisco attractions

IN THE TRENCHES
To see a professional city guide app in action, download a free app created by Trip Advisor, Triposo, or Gowalla.

To create this application, the developer must understand how to perform the following processes, among others:

1. Create a list using a ListView control.

2. Define an array to establish the items of the list.

3. Add the images used in the project.

4. Define an XML file to design the custom list with a leading image.

5. Code a Switch decision structure to handle the selection of items.

6. Open an Android Web browser to display a specified Uniform Resource Identifier (URI).

7. Create multiple classes and XML layout files to display pictures of attractions.

Creating a List

The San Francisco City Guide app begins with a vertical list of attractions on the opening screen, as shown in Figure 5-1. The Java View class creates the list and makes it scrollable if it exceeds the length of the screen. Lists can be used to display a to-do list, your personal contacts, recipe names, shopping items, weekly weather, Twitter messages, and Facebook postings, for example. You use a ListView control to contain the list attraction items. Android also has a TableLayout view that looks similar to a ListView, but a ListView allows you to select each row in the list for further action. Selecting an item opens a Web browser to a related Web page or displays an image of the attraction. You can directly use the ListView control in the Composite category of the Palette in the layout of the emulator (Figure 5-4) as you can with any other user interface component, but coding the list in Java is the preferred method and is used in the chapter project.

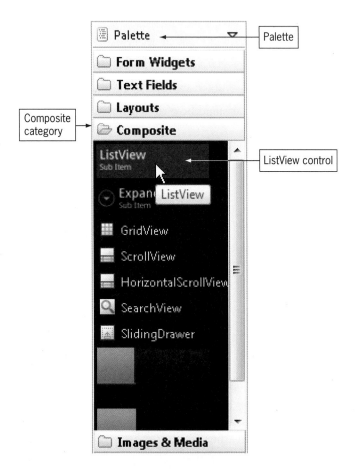

Composite category

Palette

ListView control

Figure 5-4 ListView control on the Palette

Extending a ListActivity

You begin creating a list by opening Main.java and changing the type of Activity in the code. In the previous chapters, each opening class statement (`public class Main extends Activity`) extended the basic Activity class. If the primary purpose of a class is to display a ListView control, use a class named **ListActivity** instead, which makes it simple to display a list of items within the app. To extend the ListActivity class of Main.java of the City Guide app, follow these steps to begin the application:

1.   Open the Eclipse program. Click the New button on the Standard toolbar. Expand the Android folder and select Android Project. Click the Next button. In the New Android Project dialog box, enter the Project Name **City Guide**. To save the project on your USB drive, click to remove the check mark from the Use default location check box. Type **E:\Workspace** (if necessary, enter a different drive letter that identifies the USB drive). Click the Next button. For the Build Target, select Android 4.0, if necessary. Click the Next button. For the Package Name, type **net.androidbootcamp.cityguide**. Enter **Main** in the Create Activity text box.

*The new Android City Guide project has a Project Name, a Package Name, and an
Activity named Main (Figure 5-5).*

New Android Project
dialog box

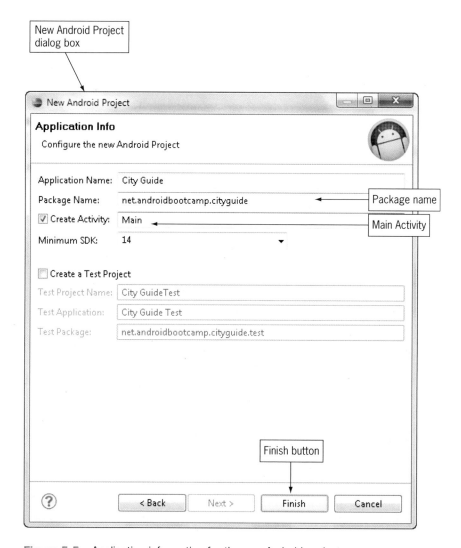

Package name

Main Activity

Finish button

Figure 5-5 Application information for the new Android project

2. Click the Finish button. Expand the City Guide project in the Package Explorer,
    expand the src and net.androidbootcamp.cityguide folders, and then double-click
    Main.java to open its code window. Click to the left of *Activity* in the public class
    Main extends Activity { line, and change Activity to **ListActivity**. Point to ListActivity
    and click Import 'ListActivity' (android.app). Delete the line import android.app.Activity;
    and then delete the line *setContentView(R.layout.main);*.

Main extends ListActivity, which contains predefined methods for the use of lists (Figure 5-6).

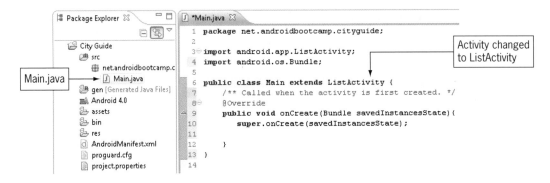

Figure 5-6   Main extends ListActivity

IN THE TRENCHES
Another type of a ListView control is the ExpandableListView, which provides a two-level list. For example, if you were renting a car, a list of all the compact cars would be listed in one category on the top half of your phone and the economy cars in a separate category at the bottom. ExpandableListView provides two separate listings.

Creating an Array

Before the list of attractions can be displayed, the string of attraction names must be declared. By using an **array variable**, which can store more than one value, you can avoid assigning a separate variable for each item in the list. Every application developed thus far involved a limited number of variables. Professional programming applications commonly require much larger sets of data using multiple variables. You learned that data type variables can store only one value at a time. If you changed a variable's value, the previous value was deleted because a typical variable can store only one value at a time. Each individual item in an array that contains a value is called an **element**.

Arrays provide access to data by using a numeric index, or subscript, to identify each element in the array. Using an array, you can store a collection of values of similar data types. For example, you can store five string values without having to declare five different variables. Instead, each value is stored in an individual element of the array, and you refer to each element by its index within the array. The index used to reference a value in the first element within an array is zero. Each subsequent element is referenced by an increasing index value, as shown in Table 5-1.

Element	Value
Attraction[0]	Alcatraz Island
Attraction[1]	Ferry Marketplace
Attraction[2]	Golden Gate Bridge
Attraction[3]	Cable Car Trolley
Attraction[4]	Fisherman's Wharf

Table 5-1 Attraction array with index values

In Table 5-1, an array named Attraction holds five attractions. Each attraction is stored in an array element, and each element is assigned a unique index. The first string is stored in the element with the index of 0. The element is identified by the term attraction [0], pronounced "attraction sub zero."

Declaring an Array

Like declarations for variables of other types, an array declaration has two components: the array's data type and the array's name. You can declare an array containing numeric values as in the following coding example:

```
double[ ] weather={72.3, 65.0, 25.7, 99.5};
```

Declare a String array containing the text values used in the chapter project with the following code:

Code Syntax

```
String[] attraction={"Alcatraz Island", "Ferry Marketplace",
    "Golden Gate Bridge", "Cable Car Trolley", "Fisherman's Wharf"};
```

The attraction list initialized in the array can easily be expanded to include more items at any time. To assign the listing of attractions to the String data type in an array named attraction, follow these steps:

1. After the super.onCreate(savedInstanceState); statement in Main.java, insert a new line and type **String[] attraction={"Alcatraz Island", "Ferry Marketplace", "Golden Gate Bridge", "Cable Car Trolley", "Fisherman's Wharf"};**.

   The String array named attraction is assigned the five attraction locations (Figure 5-7).

```
J *Main.java ✕
  1  package net.androidbootcamp.cityguide;
  2
  3⊕ import android.app.ListActivity;▯
  5
  6  public class Main extends ListActivity {
  7      /** Called when the activity is first created. */
  8⊖     @Override
  9      public void onCreate(Bundle savedInstancesState){
 10          super.onCreate(savedInstancesState);
 11          String[] attraction={"Alcatraz Island","Ferry Marketplace",
 12              "Golden Gate Bridge","Cable Car Trolley","Fisherman's Wharf");
 13      }
 14  }
```

> Press the Enter key after typing the comma to place statement on two lines

> String array initialized

Figure 5-7   String array initialized with attractions

2. Save your work.

GTK

To declare an array without assigning actual values, allocate the size of the array in the brackets to reserve the room needed in memory, as in int[ ] ages = new int[100];. The first number assigned to the ages array is placed in ages [0]. This array holds 101 elements in the array, one more than the maximum index.

Using a setListAdapter and Array Adapter

In the City Guide application, once the array is assigned, you can display an array listing using adapters. An **adapter** provides a data model for the layout of the list and for converting the data from the array into list items. The ListView and adapter work together to display a list. For example, if you want to share an iPad screen with a group, you need an adapter to connect to a projector to display the image on a large screen. Similarly, a **setListAdapter** projects your data to the onscreen list on your device by connecting the ListActivity's ListView object to the array data. A setListAdapter contains the information to connect the onscreen list with the attraction array in the chapter project. Calling a setListAdapter in the Java code binds the elements of the array to a ListView layout. In the next portion of the statement, a ListAdapter called an **ArrayAdapter<String> i** supplies the String array data to the ListView. The three parameters that follow ArrayAdapter refer to the *this* class, a generic layout called simple_list_item_1, and the array named attraction. The following code syntax shows the complete statement:

Code Syntax

```
setListAdapter(new ArrayAdapter<String>(this,
        android.R.layout.simple_list_item_1, attraction));
```

Later in the chapter, instead of using the generic layout called simple_list_item_1, you design an XML layout to customize the layout to include the City Guide's logo. You can change the setListAdapter statement to reference the custom layout when you finish designing it.

Follow these steps to add the setListAdapter that displays the array as a list:

1. After the second line of code initializing the String array, press the Enter key, type **setListAdapter(new ArrayAdapter<String>(this, android.R.layout. simple_list_item_1, attraction));**, and then press the Enter key. Point to ArrayAdapter and click Import 'ArrayAdapter' (android.widget).

   If you are using a Mac, press the Return key instead of the Enter key.

   The setListAdapter displays the attraction array in a generic ListView layout (Figure 5-8).

```
J *Main.java ⊠
 1  package net.androidbootcamp.cityguide;
 2
 3⊕ import android.app.ListActivity;▢
 6
 7  public class Main extends ListActivity {
 8      /** Called when the activity is first created. */
 9⊖     @Override
10      public void onCreate(Bundle savedInstancesState){
11          super.onCreate(savedInstancesState);
12          String[] attraction={"Alcatraz Island","Ferry Marketplace",
13              "Golden Gate Bridge","Cable Car Trolley","Fisherman's Wharf"};
14          setListAdapter(new ArrayAdapter<String>(this,
15              android.R.layout.simple_list_item_1, attraction));
16
17      }
18  }
```

Your statement might appear on one line

setListAdapter command

Generic built-in layout

Figure 5-8 setListAdapter displays an array

2. To display the attraction list in the generic ListView layout, click Run on the menu bar, and then select Run. Select Android Application and click the OK button. Save Main.java in the next dialog box, if necessary, and unlock the emulator when the app starts.

   The application opens in the emulator window (Figure 5-9).

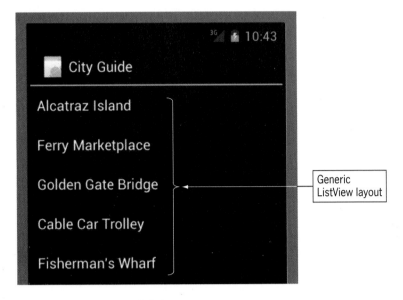

Figure 5-9 ListView built-in layout

3. Close the emulated application window.

GTK
Other generic layouts that you might want to try with ListView include simple_list_item_2, simple_list_item_
checked (displays check boxes), and simple_list_item_multiple_choice.

Adding the Images to the Resources Folder

The City Guide application uses several images throughout the app. An icon logo called
ic_launcher_sf.png displays the skyline of San Francisco and is used multiple times on the
opening screen. Images of the Golden Gate Bridge, Cable Car Trolley, and Fisherman's
Wharf appear when the user selects those items from the opening list. To place a copy of
the images from the USB drive into the res/drawable-hdpi folder, follow these steps:

1. If necessary, copy the student files to your USB drive. Open the USB folder containing
the student files. In the Package Explorer, expand the drawable-hdpi folder in the res
folder. Delete the file named ic_launcher.png (the Android logo). To add the four
image files to the drawable-hdpi resource folder, drag ic_launcher_sf.png, bridge.png,
trolley.png, and wharf.png files to the drawable-hdpi folder until a plus sign pointer
appears. Release the mouse button. If necessary, click the Copy files option button,
and then click the OK button.

Copies of the four files appear in the drawable-hdpi folder (Figure 5-10).

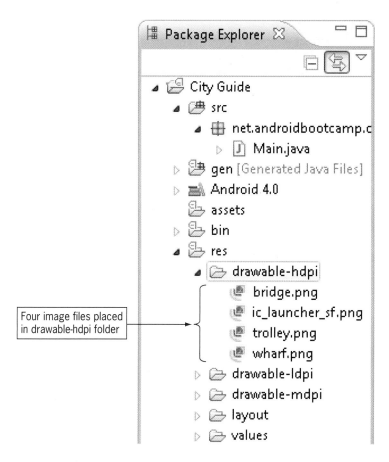

Four image files placed in drawable-hdpi folder

Figure 5-10 Images copied

2. To set the Android Manifest to use the ic_launcher_sf image as the app icon when the application is executed, in the Package Explorer, double-click the AndroidManifest.xml file. Click the AndroidManifest.xml tab at the bottom of the screen. Inside the application code, click in the line android:icon=@"drawable/ic_launcher". Change the filename portion from ic_launcher" to **ic_launcher_sf"**.

The Android launcher icon is coded in the Android Manifest file (Figure 5-11).

```
J  *Main.java      ⊂  *City Guide Manifest  ⊠                                    City Guide
                                                                                 Manifest tab
 1   <?xml version="1.0" encoding="utf-8"?>
 2⊖  <manifest xmlns:android="http://schemas.android.
 3       package="net.androidbootcamp.cityguide"
 4       android:versionCode="1"
 5       android:versionName="1.0" >
 6
 7       <uses-sdk android:minSdkVersion="14" />
 8
 9⊖      <application
10           android:icon="@drawable/ic_launcher_sf"          Launcher icon
11           android:label="@string/app_name" >              name changed
```

Figure 5-11   Android Manifest code with new Launcher Icon file

3. Click the Save All button on the Standard toolbar to save your work.

IN THE TRENCHES
When publishing apps, you must follow copyright laws relative to copyrighted images used within your
Android apps. Copyright is the legal protection extended to the authors or owners of original published
and unpublished artistic and intellectual works, and you must seek copyright permissions. However, if the
image is accompanied by the statement "This work is dedicated to the public domain," the image is
available for fair use in your app.

Creating a Custom XML Layout for ListView

You can design a layout by using the emulator window on the Graphical Layout tab and then
drag and drop controls from the Palette, or you can code the main.xml file using XML code.
It is easier to use the Palette for a simple layout. However, the opening screen for the City
Guide chapter project shown in Figure 5-1 requires a custom layout for the list that includes a
San Francisco City Guide logo and unique size and spacing of the attraction names. In the
XML code, you must first add an ImageView control to display the ic_launcher_sf image file.
The ImageView is named with the id property in the code and resized with the layout_width
and layout_height properties, margins are set, and the location source of the file is entered.
Next, the code for the TextView control is named, the layout is identified, and the textSize
property is set. The text property of android:text="@+id/travel" is used in the setListAdapter
and the actual items in the array display instead of the text object named travel. To create a
custom XML layout for main.xml, follow these steps:

1. Close the City Guide Manifest tab. In the res\layout folder, double-click main.xml.
   Delete the Hello World, Main! TextView control, and then click the main.xml tab
   at the bottom of the window to display the XML code. By default, LinearLayout is
   already set. Delete the android:orientation property statement but *not* the closing

angle bracket (>), and then type **<ImageView** after the closing angle bracket. Press the Enter key. Type the following code using auto-completion as much as possible:

```
android:id="@+id/ic_launcher_sf"
android:layout_width="50px"
android:layout_height="50px"
android:layout_marginLeft="4px"
android:layout_marginRight="10px"
android:layout_marginTop="2px"
android:src="@drawable/ic_launcher_sf" >
</ImageView>
```

The ImageView control is customized in the main.xml file (Figure 5-12).

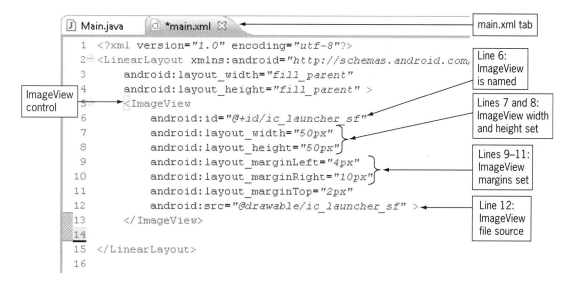

Figure 5-12   ImageView XML code

2.   Insert a blank line after the ImageView code and type **<TextView**. Press the Enter key. Type the following code using auto-completion as much as possible:

```
android:id="@+id/travel"
android:layout_width="wrap_content"
android:layout_height="wrap_content"
android:text="@+id/travel"
android:textSize="25sp" >
</TextView>
```

The TextView control is customized in the main.xml file (Figure 5-13).

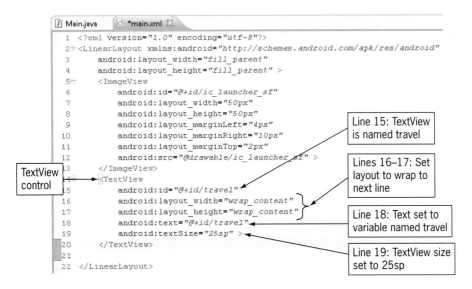

Figure 5-13   TextView XML code

Changing the Title Bar Text

Developers often want a custom title to appear on the title bar at the top of the window instead of the actual application name. A string named app_name in the strings.xml file by default displays the project name. To change the title bar on the opening screen of the City Guide app to *San Francisco City Guide*, follow these steps:

1.   Save your work and then close the main.xml window. Expand the res\values folder and double-click the strings.xml file. Click app_name (String) in the Android Resources window. Change the text in the Value text box to **San Francisco City Guide**.

The app_name value is changed (Figure 5-14).

Figure 5-14   Title bar text is changed from default

2.   Save your work.

Coding a setListAdapter with a Custom XML Layout

When the setListAdapter was coded and executed as shown in Figure 5-9, the attractions list was displayed within a built-in layout called simple_list_item_1 in the following statement:

```
setListAdapter(new ArrayAdapter<String>(this,
android.R.layout.simple_list_item_1, attraction));
```

Instead of using a standard layout in the setListAdapter, the custom XML layout you designed in main.xml adds the San Francisco City Guide logo and updates the TextView properties. The syntax changes from the default in two significant ways:

1. The second parameter in the default statement (android.R.layout.*simple_list_item_1*) is changed to R.layout.*main*. The android reference is removed because the Android library default layout is not being used. Instead R.layout.*main* references the main.xml custom layout design for the ImageView and TextView controls.

2. A third parameter is added before the attraction array name to reference the variable travel, which identifies the TextView control created in the main.xml file. The variable is substituted for the actual attraction locations initialized in the attraction array.

The following code syntax shows the code for a custom XML layout:

Code Syntax

```
setListAdapter(new ArrayAdapter<String>(this,
        R.layout.main, R.id.travel, attraction));
```

To edit the setListAdapter to use the custom XML layout, follow these steps:

1. Close the strings.xml window. In the setListAdapter statement of Main.java, click after the comma following the *this* command. Change the android.R.layout.simple_list_item_1, text to **R.layout.main, R.id.travel,** to add the custom layout named main.xml.

    The default setListAdapter is edited to include the custom layout (Figure 5-15).

```
1  package net.androidbootcamp.cityguide;
2
3+ import android.app.ListActivity;
6
7  public class Main extends ListActivity {
8      /** Called when the activity is first created. */
9-     @Override
10     public void onCreate(Bundle savedInstancesState){
11         super.onCreate(savedInstancesState);
12         String[] attraction={"Alcatraz Island","Ferry Marketplace",
13             "Golden Gate Bridge","Cable Car Trolley","Fisherma
14         setListAdapter(new ArrayAdapter<String>(this,
15             R.layout.main, R.id.travel, attraction));
16     }
17  }
```

Custom layout formatted by main.xml; yours might appear on one line

Figure 5-15 setListAdapter with custom layout for list

2. Run and save the application to view the custom layout of the ListView.

The emulator displays the opening screen with a custom ListView (Figure 5-16).

Figure 5-16   ListView custom layout in emulator

3. Close the emulated application window.

Using the onListItemClick Method

The City Guide opening screen has a custom list shown in Figure 5-16. Each of the attractions displayed in the list can be selected by tapping the attraction name on the mobile device. The method **onListItemClick( )** is called when an item in the list is selected. When an attraction in the list is selected, the **position** of the item is passed from the onListItemClick and evaluated with a decision structure, as shown in the following code syntax. If the user selects the first attraction, the position parameter is assigned an integer value of 0. The second item is assigned the position of 1, and so forth.

Code Syntax

```
protected void onListItemClick(ListView l, View v, int position, long id){
 }
```

To code the onListItemClick method to respond to the event of the user's selection, follow these steps:

1. In Main.java, press the Enter key after the closing brace of the onCreate method to insert a new line. To respond to the user's selection, type **protected void onListItemClick(ListView l, View v, int position, long id)**. (Be sure to type a lowercase l after ListView, not the number 1.) Type an opening brace after the statement and press the Enter key. A closing brace is automatically placed in the code. After the code is entered to reference the ListView and View, point to the red error line below ListView and select 'Import ListView' (android.widget), and then point to the red error line below View and select 'Import View' (android.view).

The onListItemClick method detects the selection's position (Figure 5-17).

```
🗋 *Main.java ⊠
  1  package net.androidbootcamp.cityguide;
  2
  3⊕ import android.app.ListActivity;
  8
  9  public class Main extends ListActivity {
 10      /** Called when the activity is first created. */
 11⊖     @Override
▲12      public void onCreate(Bundle savedInstancesState){
 13          super.onCreate(savedInstancesState);
 14          String[] attraction={"Alcatraz Island","Ferry Marketplace",
 15              "Golden Gate Bridge","Cable Car Trolley","Fisherman's Wharf"};
 16          setListAdapter(new ArrayAdapter<String>(this,
 17              R.layout.main, R.id.travel, attraction));
 18      }
▲19⊖     protected void onListItemClick(ListView l, View v, int position, long id) {
 20
 21      }
 22  }
```

Lowercase l, not number 1

onListItemClick method

Figure 5-17   onListItemClick method

2.   Save your work.

Decision Structure—Switch Statement

Each item in the list produces a different result when selected, such as opening a Web browser or displaying a picture of the attraction on a second screen. In Chapter 4, If statements evaluated the user's selection and the decision structure determined the results. You can use another decision structure called a Switch statement with a list or menu. The **Switch** statement allows you to choose from many statements based on an integer or char (single character) input. The switch keyword is followed by an integer expression in parentheses, which is followed by the cases, all enclosed in braces, as shown in the following code syntax:

Code Syntax

```
switch(position){
    case 0:
        //statements that are executed if position == 0
    break;
    case 1:
        //statements that are executed if position == 1
    break;
    default:
        //statements that are executed if position != any of the cases
}
```

The integer named *position* is evaluated in the Switch statement and executes the corresponding case. The **case** keyword is followed by a value and a colon. Typically the statement within a case ends with a **break** statement, which exits the Switch decision structure and continues with the next statement. Be careful not to omit the break statement or the subsequent case statement is executed as well. If there is no matching case value, the default option is executed. A default statement is optional. In the chapter project, a default statement is not necessary because the user must select one of the items in the list for an action to occur.

In the City Guide app, five attractions make up the list, so the following positions are possible for the Switch statement: case 0, case 1, case 2, case 3, and case 4. To code the Switch decision structure, follow these steps:

1. Within the braces of the onListItemClick method, type **switch(position){** and press the Enter key.

   The Switch decision structure is coded within the onListItemClick method (Figure 5-18).

```
19  protected void onListItemClick(ListView l, View v, int position, long id) {     Beginning of Switch
20      switch(position){ ←                                                          statement decision
21                                                                                   structure
22          }
23      }
```

Figure 5-18 Switch statement

2. Within the braces of the Switch statement, add the case integer options. Type the following code, inserting a blank line after each case statement:

   case 0:

        break;
   case 1:

        break;
   case 2:

        break;
   case 3:

        break;
   case 4:

        break;

   The case statements for the five selections from the attractions list each are coded (Figure 5-19).

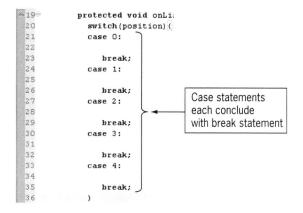

```
△ 19~    protected void onLi:
  20        switch(position){
  21          case 0:
  22
  23            break;
  24          case 1:
  25
  26            break;
  27          case 2:
  28
  29            break;
  30          case 3:
  31
  32            break;
  33          case 4:
  34
  35            break;
  36        }
```

Case statements each conclude with break statement

Figure 5-19 Case statements

3. Save your work.

GTK
Switch statements do not allow ranges such as 10–50. Use If statements when evaluating a range or strings.

Android Intents

When the user selects one of the first two list items in the project, Alcatraz Island or Ferry Marketplace, a built-in Android browser launches a Web site about each attraction. A browser is launched with Android code using an intent. Android intents send and receive activities and services that include opening a Web page in a browser, calling a phone number, locating a GPS position on a map, posting your notes to a note-taking program such as Evernote, opening your contacts list, sending a photo, or even posting to your social network. Additional Android intents are explored throughout the rest of this book. Android intents are powerful features that allow apps to talk to each other in a very simple way.

To better understand an intent, imagine a student sitting in a classroom. To ask a question or make a request, the student raises a hand. The teacher is alerted to the hand and responds to the student. An intent works the same way. Your app raises its hand and the other apps state that they are ready to handle your request. When the chapter project sends an intent, the browser app handles the request and opens the Web site.

IN THE TRENCHES
Android platform devices have many options for supported browsers. Popular Android browsers include Opera Mini Web, Dolphin, Skyfire, Mozilla Firefox, and Miren.

Launching the Browser from an Android Device

Android phones have a built-in browser with an intent filter that accepts intent requests from other apps. The intent sends the browser a **URI** (Uniform Resource Identifier), a string that identifies the resources of the Web. You might already be familiar with the term **URL** (Uniform Resource Locator), which means a Web site address. A URI is a URL with additional information necessary for gaining access to the resources required for posting the page. Depending on the lists of browsers installed on an Android device, Android selects a suitable browser (usually a user-set preferred browser), which accepts the action called ACTION_VIEW (must be in caps) and displays the site. **ACTION_VIEW** is the most common action performed on data. It is a generic action you can use to send any request to get the most reasonable action to occur. As shown in the following code syntax, a startActivity statement informs the present Activity that a new Activity is being started and the browser opens the Web site:

Code Syntax

```
startActivity(new Intent(Intent.ACTION_VIEW,
     Uri.parse("http://alcatrazcruises.com/")));
```

When the user selects the Alcatraz Island item from the attractions list, the Switch statement sends a zero integer value to the case statements. The case 0: statement is true, so the program executes the startActivity statement, which sends the browser a parsed string containing the URI Web address. The browser application then launches the Alcatraz Web site. When you click the Back button in some browser windows or the left arrow to the right of the menu button on the right side of the emulator, the previous Activity opens. In the chapter project, the attractions list ListView activity is displayed again. To code the startActivity that launches a Web site in an Android browser, follow these steps:

1. In Main.java, click the blank line after the line containing case 0: inside the Switch decision structure. Type **startActivity(new Intent(Intent.ACTION_VIEW, Uri.parse("http://alcatrazcruises.com/")));**. Point to Intent and click Import 'Intent' (android content). Point to Uri and Import 'Uri' (android.net).

   The startActivity code launches the Alcatraz Web site when the user selects the first list item (Figure 5-20).

```
switch(position){
case 0:
    startActivity(new Intent(Intent.ACTION_VIEW,
            Uri.parse("http://alcatrazcruises.com/")));
  break;
case 1:
```

Opens Web browser to display Alcatraz site

Figure 5-20 Code for launching the Alcatraz Web site

2. In Main.java, click the blank line after the line containing case 1:. Type **startActivity(new Intent(Intent.ACTION_VIEW, Uri.parse("http://ferrybuildingmarketplace.com")));**.

The startActivity code launches the Ferry Marketplace Web site when the user selects the second list item (Figure 5-21).

```
23      case 0:
24          startActivity(new Intent(Intent.ACTION_VIEW,
25                  Uri.parse("http://alcatrazcruises.com/")));
26          break;
27      case 1:
28          startActivity(new Intent(Intent.ACTION_VIEW,
29                  Uri.parse("http://ferrybuildingmarketplace.com")));
30          break;
```

Opens Web browser to display Ferry Marketplace site

Figure 5-21   Code for launching the Ferry Marketplace Web site

3. To display the Alcatraz Island Web site in the browser, click Run on the menu bar, and then select Run. Select Android Application and click the OK button. Save all the files in the next dialog box, if necessary, and unlock the emulator. Select the Alcatraz Island list item.

    The first item is selected from the list in the emulator and the Android browser displays the Alcatraz Island Web site. The site loads slowly in the emulator. Some Web sites are especially designed for mobile devices (Figure 5-22).

Android browser displays Alcatraz Web site in emulator

Figure 5-22   Browser opens in the emulator

4. Close the emulated application window.

IN THE TRENCHES

Be sure to test any links within your Android apps often. If you have hundreds of links, verifying Web links can be simple in concept but very time consuming in practice. A good place to start is with the World Wide Web Consortium's free Web Site Validation Service (*http://validator.w3.org*).

Designing XML Layout Files

The last three case statements open a second screen that displays a picture of the selected attraction. Three XML layout files must be designed to display an ImageView control with an image source file. To create an XML layout file, follow these steps:

1. In the Package Explorer, right-click the layout folder. On the shortcut menu, point to New and then click Other. In the New dialog box, click Android XML Layout File, and then click the Next button. In the New Android Layout XML File dialog box, type **bridge.xml** in the File text box to name the layout file. In the Root Element list, select LinearLayout. Click the Finish button. The emulator window opens. In the Images & Media category in the Palette, drag the ImageView control to the emulator. The Resource Chooser dialog box opens. Select bridge, and then click the OK button. Resize the image to fill the entire window.

The bridge XML file is designed with an image of the Golden Gate Bridge (Figure 5-23).

Figure 5-23   bridge.xml layout file

2. Close the bridge.xml file tab and save your work. Right-click the layout folder, point to New on the shortcut menu, and then click Other. In the New dialog box, click Android XML Layout File, and then click the Next button. In the New Android Layout XML File dialog box, type **trolley.xml** in the File text box to name the layout file. In the Root Element list, select LinearLayout. Click the Finish button. The emulator window opens. In the Images & Media category in the Palette, drag the ImageView control to the emulator. The Resource Chooser dialog box opens. Select trolley, and then click the OK button. Resize the image to fill the entire window.

The trolley XML file is designed with an image of the cable car trolley (Figure 5-24).

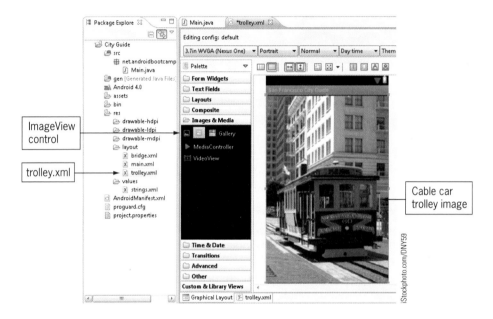

ImageView control

trolley.xml

Cable car trolley image

iStockphoto.com/DNY59

Figure 5-24 trolley.xml layout file

3. Close the trolley.xml file tab and save your work. Right-click the layout folder, point to New on the shortcut menu, and then click Other. In the New dialog box, click Android XML Layout File, and then click the Next button. In the New Android Layout XML File dialog box, type **wharf.xml** in the File text box to name the layout file. In the Root Element list, select LinearLayout. Click the Finish button. The emulator window opens. In the Images & Media category in the Palette, drag the ImageView control to the emulator. The Resource Chooser dialog box opens. Select wharf, and then click the OK button. Resize the image to fill the entire window.

The wharf XML file is designed with an image of the Fisherman's Wharf (Figure 5-25).

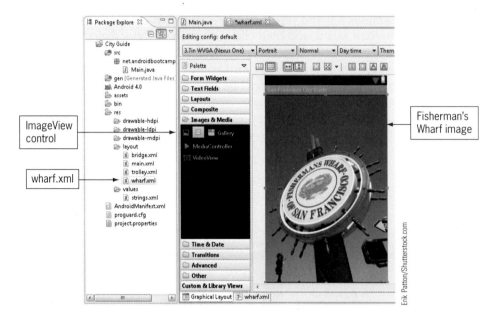

ImageView
control

wharf.xml

Fisherman's
Wharf image

Erik Patton/Shutterstock.com

Figure 5-25   wharf.xml layout file

Adding Multiple Class Files

The three XML files are displayed in three Java class files. Multiple classes are needed to launch the XML layout files that each display an image when the user selects Golden Gate Bridge, Cable Car Trolley, or Fisherman's Wharf. An onCreate method requests that the user interface opens to display an image of the attraction. Remember, each time you add a class to an application, the class must be referenced in the Android Manifest file. To add a class file to launch the XML layout file and add those files to the Android Manifest file, follow these steps:

1. Close the wharf.xml file tab and save your work. To create a second class, right-click the src\net.androidbootcamp.cityguide folder, point to New on the shortcut menu, and then click Class. Type **Bridge** in the Name text box to create a second class that will define the bridge Activity. Click the Superclass Browse button. Type **Activity** in the Choose a type text box. As you type, matching items are displayed. Click Activity – android.app and then click the OK button to extend the Activity class. Click the Finish button. To launch the Activity, in the Bridge.java file, click inside the braces and type **oncreate** and then press Ctrl+spacebar to display an auto-complete listing. Double-click the first onCreate method in the auto-complete listing. Click at the end of Line 10 and then press the Enter key to insert a blank line. Type **setContentView(R.** to display an auto-complete listing. Double-click layout. Type a period. Another auto-complete listing requests the XML layout file you intend to display. Double-click bridge : int. Type a right closing parenthesis if one does not appear automatically. Type a semicolon after the parenthesis to complete the statement.

A new class named Bridge that launches bridge.xml is created (Figure 5-26).

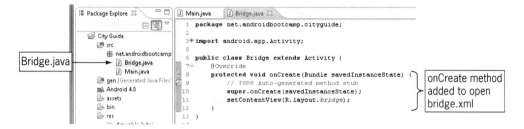

Figure 5-26 Complete code for Bridge.java class

2. Close the Bridge.java file tab and save your work. To create a third class, right-click the src\net.androidbootcamp.cityguide folder, point to New on the shortcut menu, and then click Class. Type **Trolley** in the Name text box to create a third class that will define the trolley Activity. Click the Superclass Browse button. Type **Activity** in the Choose a type text box. As you type, matching items are displayed. Click Activity – android.app and then click the OK button to extend the Activity class. Click the Finish button. To launch the Activity, click inside the braces in the Trolley.java file, type **oncreate** and then press Ctrl+spacebar. Double-click the first onCreate method in the auto-complete listing. Click at the end of the line containing *super.onCreate(savedInstanceState);* and then press the Enter key to insert a blank line. Type **setContentView(R.** to display an auto-complete listing. Double-click layout. Type a period. Another auto-complete listing requests the XML layout file you intend to display. Double-click trolley : int. A right closing parenthesis appears. Type a semicolon after the parenthesis to complete the statement.

A new class named Trolley is created that launches trolley.xml (Figure 5-27).

Figure 5-27 Complete code for Trolley.java class

3. Close the Trolley.java file tab and save your work. To create a fourth class, right-click the src\net.androidbootcamp.cityguide folder, point to New on the shortcut menu, and then click Class. Type **Wharf** in the Name text box to create a fourth class that

will define the wharf Activity. Click the Superclass Browse button. Type **Activity** in the Choose a type text box. Click Activity – android.app in the matching items, and then click the OK button to extend the Activity class. Click the Finish button. To launch the Activity, in the Wharf.java file click inside the braces, type **oncreate** and then press Ctrl+spacebar. Double-click the first onCreate method in the auto-complete listing. Click at the end of Line 10 and then press the Enter key to insert a blank line. Type **setContentView(R.** to display an auto-complete listing. Double-click layout. Type a period. Another auto-complete listing requests the XML layout file you intend to display. Double-click wharf : int. A right closing parenthesis appears. Type a semicolon after the parenthesis to complete the statement.

A new class named Wharf is created that launches wharf.xml (Figure 5-28).

Figure 5-28   Complete code for Wharf.java class

4. Close the Wharf.java file tab and save your work. To add the reference to these Java class files in the Android Manifest file, in the Package Explorer, double-click the AndroidManifest.xml file. Click the Application tab at the bottom of the City Guide Manifest page. Scroll down to display the Application Nodes section. Click the Add button. Select Activity in the Create a new element at the top level, in Application dialog box. Click the OK button. The Attributes for Activity section opens in the Application tab. In the Name text box, type the class name preceded by a period (**.Bridge**) to add the Bridge Activity. Click the Add button again. Click the first radio button (Create a new element at the top level, in Application) and select Activity. Click the OK button. In the Name text box, type the class name preceded by a period (**.Trolley**) to add the Trolley Activity. Click the Add button again. Click the first radio button (Create a new element at the top level, in Application) and select Activity. Click the OK button. In the Name text box, type the class name preceded by a period (**.Wharf**) to add the Wharf Activity. Save your work.

The AndroidManifest.xml file includes the three Activities (Figure 5-29).

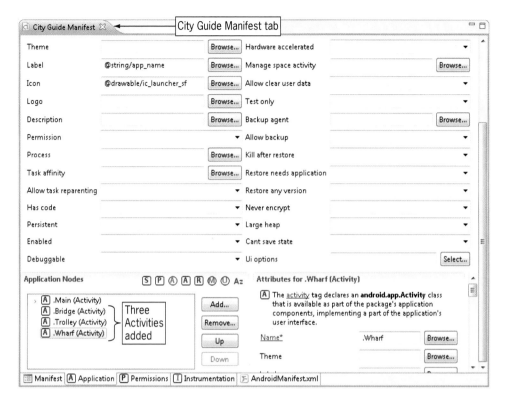

Figure 5-29 City Guide Android Manifest

Opening the Class Files

The last step in the development of the San Francisco City Guide app is to open the class files when the user selects Golden Gate Bridge (case 2), Cable Car Trolley (case 3), or Fisherman's Wharf (case 4). A startActivity method opens the next Activity, which in turn launches the appropriate XML layout displaying an image of the attraction. To code the remaining case statement within the Switch decision structure that starts each of the Activities, follow these steps:

1. Close the City Guide Manifest tab. In Main.java, click the blank line below the one containing case 2: and type **startActivity(new Intent(Main.this, Bridge.class));**. Click the blank line below the one containing case 3: and type **startActivity(new Intent(Main.this, Trolley.class));**. Click the blank line below the one containing case 4: and type **startActivity(new Intent(Main.this, Wharf.class));**.

   The case statements 2 through 4 are coded with a startActivity that executes the appropriate class (Figure 5-30).

```
 J Main.java ⊠
 1 package net.androidbootcamp.cityguide;
 2
 3⊕ import android.app.ListActivity;☐
10
11 public class Main extends ListActivity {
12      /** Called when the activity is first created. */
13⊖     @Override
14      public void onCreate(Bundle savedInstancesState){
15          super.onCreate(savedInstancesState);
16          String[] attraction={"Alcatraz Island","Ferry Marketplace",
17                  "Golden Gate Bridge","Cable Car Trolley","Fisherman's Wharf"};
18          setListAdapter(new ArrayAdapter<String>(this,
19                  R.layout.main, R.id.travel, attraction));
20      }
21⊖      protected void onListItemClick(ListView l, View v, int position, long id) {
22          switch(position){
23          case 0:
24              startActivity(new Intent(Intent.ACTION_VIEW,
25                      Uri.parse("http://alcatrazcruises.com/")));
26              break;
27          case 1:
28              startActivity(new Intent(Intent.ACTION_VIEW,
29                      Uri.parse("http://ferrybuildingmarketplace.com")));
30              break;
31          case 2:
32              startActivity(new Intent(Main.this, Bridge.class));
33              break;
34          case 3:
35              startActivity(new Intent(Main.this, Trolley.class));
36              break;
37          case 4:
38              startActivity(new Intent(Main.this, Wharf.class));
39              break;
40          }
41      }
42 }
```

Figure 5-30   Complete code for Main.java

2. Compare your code to Figure 5-30, make changes as necessary to match the code in the figure, and then save your work.

Running and Testing the Application

As you save and run the San Francisco City Guide application, be sure you test every option of this app. Before publishing to the Android Market, it is critical to make sure all the fields can gracefully handle any click or any value entered in any Android app. Click Run on the menu bar, and then select Run to save and test the application in the emulator. A dialog box requesting how you would like to run the application opens the first time the application is executed. Select Android Application and click the OK button. Save all the files in the next dialog box, if necessary, and unlock the emulator. The application opens in the emulator window where you can test each list item in the San Francisco City Guide app, as shown in Figure 5-1, Figure 5-2, and Figure 5-3.

IN THE TRENCHES
Testing an Android app is called usability testing. In addition to the traditional navigation and ease of use, Section 508 compliance is a third component to be tested. The 1998 Amendment to Section 508 of the Rehabilitation Act spells out accessibility requirements for individuals with certain disabilities. For more details, refer to *www.section508.gov.*

Wrap It Up—Chapter Summary

This chapter described the steps to create a list with items users select to launch Web sites and XML layouts through the use of a Switch decision structure in the City Guide program. The introduction of intents to outside services such as a Web browser begins our adventure of many other intent options used throughout the rest of this book.

- The Java View class creates a list and makes it scrollable if it exceeds the length of the screen. To contain the list items, use a ListView control, which allows you to select each row in the list for further action, such as displaying an image or Web page.

- Instead of extending the basic Activity class in Main.java by using the `public class Main extends Activity` opening class statement, when you want to display a ListView control, extend the ListActivity class in Main.java with the statement `public class Main extends ListActivity`.

- Before you can specify the items in a list, declare the item names using an array variable, which can store more than one value of similar data types. For example, you can store five string values in an array without having to declare five variables.

- Arrays provide access to data by using a numeric index to identify each element in the array. Each value is stored in an element of the array, which you refer to by its index. The index for the first element in an array is zero. For example, attraction [0] is the first element in the Attraction array.

- To declare an array, specify the array's data type and name followed by the values in braces, as in String[ ] attraction={"Alcatraz Island", "Ferry Marketplace", "Golden Gate Bridge", "Cable Car Trolley", "Fisherman's Wharf"};.

- You can display the values in an array using an adapter, which provides a data model for the layout of the list and for converting the array data into list items. A ListView control is the container for the list items, and an adapter such as the setListAdapter command connects the array data to the ListView control so the items are displayed on the device screen. In other words, calling a setListAdapter in the Java code binds the elements of an array to a ListView layout.

- To design a simple layout, you drag controls from the Palette to the emulator on the Graphical Layout tab. To design a custom layout, you add code to the main XML file for the application, such as main.xml.

- By default, the application name is displayed in an app's title bar. To display text other than the application name, change the app_name value in the strings.xml file.

- A setListAdapter statement has three parameters: One refers to the *this* class, the second refers to the layout used to display the list, and the third refers to the array containing the list values to display. For the second parameter, setListAdapter can use a standard layout, as in android.R.layout.*simple_list_item_1*, which specifies the built-in simple_list_item_1 layout to display the list. To use a custom layout instead, replace the name of the standard layout with the name of the custom layout, as in R.layout.*main*, which references a custom layout named main.xml. You also remove the *android* reference because you are no longer using an Android library default layout.

- To have an app take action when a user selects an item in a list, you code the onListItemClick method to respond to the event of the user's selection.

- You can use the Switch decision structure with a list or menu. In a Switch statement, an integer or character variable is evaluated and the corresponding case is executed. Each case is specified using the *case* keyword followed by a value and a colon. For example, if a list contains five items, the Switch statement will have five cases, such as case 0, case 1, case 2, case 3, and case 4. End each case with a break statement to exit the Switch decision structure and continue with the next statement.

- Android intents send and receive activities and services, including opening a Web page in a browser. An intent can use the ACTION_VIEW action to send a URI to a built-in Android browser and display the specified Web site.

- As you develop an application, you must test every option and possible user action, including incorrect values and selections. Thoroughly test an Android app before publishing to the Android Market.

Key Terms

ACTION_VIEW—A generic action you can use to send any request to get the most reasonable action to occur.

adapter—Provides a data model for the layout of a list and for converting the data from the array into list items.

array variable—A variable that can store more than one value.

ArrayAdapter<String> i—A ListAdapter that supplies string array data to a ListView object.

break—A statement that ends a case within a Switch statement and continues with the statement following the Switch decision structure.

case—A keyword used in a Switch statement to indicate a condition. In a Switch statement, the case keyword is followed by a value and a colon.

element—A single individual item that contains a value in an array.

ListActivity—A class that displays a list of items within an app.

onListItemClick( )—A method called when an item in a list is selected.

position—The placement of an item in a list. When an item in a list is selected, the position of the item is passed from the onListItemClick method and evaluated with a decision structure. The first item is assigned the position of 0, the second item is assigned the position of 1, and so forth.

177

setListAdapter—A command that projects your data to the onscreen list on your device by connecting the ListActivity's ListView object to array data.

Switch—A type of decision statement that allows you to choose from many statements based on an integer or char input.

URI—An acronym for Uniform Resource Identifier, a URI is a string that identifies the resources of the Web. Similar to a URL, a URI includes additional information necessary for gaining access to the resources required for posting the page.

URL—An acronym for Uniform Resource Locator, a URL is a Web site address.

Developer FAQs

1. Which Android control displays a vertical listing of items?

2. When does a scroll bar appear in a list?

3. Typically in an Android .java file, the class extends Activity. When the primary purpose of the class is to display a list, what is the opening Main class statement?

4. Initialize an array named lotteryNumbers with the integers 22, 6, 38, 30, and 17.

5. Answer the following questions about the following initialized array:

   ```
   String[] toppings = new String[12];
   ```

   a. What is the statement to assign pepperoni to the first array location?

   b. What is the statement to assign green peppers to the fourth location in the array?

   c. How many toppings can this array hold?

   d. Rewrite this statement to initially be assigned the following four toppings only: extra cheese, black olives, mushrooms, and bacon.

6. Write a line of code that assigns the values Samsung, Creative, Sony, Motorola, and Asus to the elements in the array phoneBrands.

7. Fix this array statement:

   ```
   doubles { } driveSize = ["32.0", "64.0", "128.0"]
   ```

8. Write two lines of code that assign an array named languages with the items Java, C#, Python, Visual Basic, and Ruby and display this array as a generic list.

CHAPTER 5   Investigate! Android Lists, Arrays, and Web Browsers

178

9. Which type of pictures can be used for free fair use without copyright?

10. What does URI stand for?

11. Write a statement that opens the Android Help Site: *http://developer.android.com.*

12. Write a single line of XML code that changes the size of the text of a TextView control to 35 scaled-independent pixels.

13. Write a single line of XML code that changes the height of an image to 100 pixels.

14. Write a Switch decision structure that tests the user's age in an integer variable named teenAge and assigns the variable schoolYear as in Table 5-2.

Age	High School Year
14	Freshman
15	Sophomore
16	Junior
17	Senior
Any other age	Not in High School

Table 5-2

15. Change the following If decision structure to a Switch decision structure:

```
if (count == 3) {
      result = "Password incorrect";
} else {
      result = "Request password";
}
```

16. What is the purpose of a default statement in a decision structure?

17. Name two decision structures.

18. What happens when the Web page opens in the emulator and the Back button is clicked in the chapter project?

19. What does the "R" in R.id.travel stand for?

20. Write a startActivity statement that launches a class named Car.

Beyond the Book

Using the Internet, search the Web for the answers to the following questions to further your Android knowledge.

1. Create a five-item list array program of your own favorite hobby and test out three types of built-in Android list formats. Take a screen shot comparing the three layouts identified by the layout format.

2. Compare four different Android browsers. Write a paragraph about each browser.

3. Research the 508 standards for Android app design. Create a list of 10 standards that should be met while designing Android applications.

4. Besides the 508 standards, research the topic of Android usability testing. Write one page on testing guidelines that assist in the design and testing process.

Case Programming Projects

Complete one or more of the following case programming projects. Use the same steps and techniques taught within the chapter. Submit the program you create to your instructor. The level of difficulty is indicated for each case programming project.

Easiest: ⋆

Intermediate: ⋆⋆

Challenging: ⋆⋆⋆

Case Project 5–1: Italian Restaurant App ⋆

Requirements Document

Application title:	Italian Restaurant App
Purpose:	An Italian restaurant named La Scala would like an app that displays the specials of the day on a list. As each special is selected, an image is displayed.
Algorithms:	1. The opening screen displays a list of today's specials (Figure 5-31):

       Appetizer Special – Antipasto

       Main Course – Spaghetti and Clams

       Dessert Special – Tiramisu

       La Scala Full Web Site

    2. When the user selects an item from the list, a full-screen image of the item is displayed (Figure 5-32). The fourth option opens the Web site *http://www.lascaladining.com*.

Conditions:	1. The pictures of the three specials are provided with your student files (antipasto.png, clams.png, and tiramisu.png).

    2. Use the built-in layout *simple_list_item_1*.

    3. Use the Switch decision structure.

Figure 5-31

Igor Dutina/Shutterstock.com

Francesco83/Shutterstock.com

erwinova/Shutterstock.com

Figure 5-32

Case Project 5–2: Box Office App ★

Requirements Document

Application title: Box Office App

Purpose: The top 10 grossing movies of all time are placed on a list in the Box Office App. As each movie is clicked, the list link opens the Internet Movie Database site for that movie.

Algorithms:
1. The opening screen displays the top 10 movie apps on a custom layout with a movie icon (Figure 5-33).

2. When the user selects one of the top 10 box office hits, the Web site that corresponds to each movie on *www.imdb.com* opens.

Conditions:
1. The movie icon is provided with your student files.

2. Design a custom layout similar to Figure 5-33.

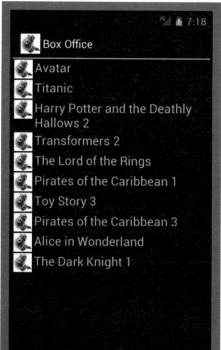

Figure 5-33

Case Project 5–3: Rent a Car App ★★

Requirements Document

Application title:	Rent a Car App
Purpose:	A rental car app provides a listing of six nationally known car rental companies. By selecting a car company, a car rental site opens.
Algorithms:	1. An opening screen displays an image of a car and a button.
	2. The second screen displays a listing of six car rental companies. This screen also contains a custom icon and layout.
	3. Each car rental agency can be selected to view a Web site of the corresponding company.
Conditions:	1. Select your own images.
	2. Create a custom layout for the list.

Case Project 5–4: Coffee Finder App ★★

Requirements Document

Application title:	Coffee Finder App
Purpose:	This Coffee Finder App locates four places in your town or city to get a great cup of joe.
Algorithms:	1. The opening screen displays the name of four coffee shops.
	2. When the user selects a coffee shop, a second screen displays the name and address of the selected coffee shop with a picture or logo for the coffee shop.
Conditions:	1. Select your own images.
	2. Create a custom layout for the list.

Case Project 5–5: Tech Gadgets App ★★★

Requirements Document

Application title:	Tech Gadgets App
Purpose:	The Tech Gadgets app shows the top five technology gifts on your wish list.
Algorithms:	1. The opening screen displays names of five technology gadgets of your own choosing.
	2. If you select any of the gadgets, a second screen opens that has an image and a button. If the user clicks the button, a Web page opens that displays more information about the tech gadget.
Conditions:	1. Select your own images.
	2. Create a custom layout for the list.

Case Project 5–6: Create Your Own App ★★★

Requirements Document

Application title:	Create Your Own App
Purpose:	Get creative! Create an app with five to eight list items with a custom layout and a custom icon that links to Web pages and other XML layout screens.
Algorithms:	1. Create an app on a topic of your own choice. Create a list.
	2. Display XML layout pages as well as Web pages on different list items.
Conditions:	1. Select your own images.
	2. Use a custom layout and icon.

Jam! Implementing Audio in Android Apps

In this chapter, you learn to:

- ◎ Create an Android project using a splash screen
- ◎ Design a TextView control with a background image
- ◎ Pause the execution of an Activity with a timer
- ◎ Understand the Activity life cycle
- ◎ Open an Activity with onCreate( )
- ◎ End an Activity with finish( )
- ◎ Assign class variables
- ◎ Create a raw folder for music files
- ◎ Play music with a MediaPlayer method
- ◎ Start and resume music playback using the start and pause methods
- ◎ Change the Text property of a control
- ◎ Change the visibility of a control

Playing music on a smartphone is one of the primary uses of a mobile device, especially as MP3 players are losing popularity. The most common phone activities include texting, talking, gaming, and playing music. Talking and texting continue to be mainstream communication channels, but the proportion of users taking advantage of apps, games, and multimedia on their phones is growing. The principal specification when purchasing a smartphone is typically the amount of memory it has. Consumers often purchase a phone with more memory so they can store music.

To demonstrate playing music through an Android built-in media player, the Chapter 6 project is named Eastern Music and opens with an image and the text "Sounds of the East." This opening screen (Figure 6-1), also called a splash screen, is displayed for approximately five seconds, and then the program automatically opens the second window. The Eastern Music application (Figure 6-2) plays two songs: Bamboo, a Far East song from the ancient Orient, and Palace, a Turkish folk song. If the user selects the first button, the Bamboo song plays until the user selects the first button again to pause the Bamboo song. If the user selects the second button, the Palace song plays until the user selects the second button again. The emulator plays the music through your computer's speakers.

turtix/Shutterstock.com

Figure 6-1   Eastern Music Android app

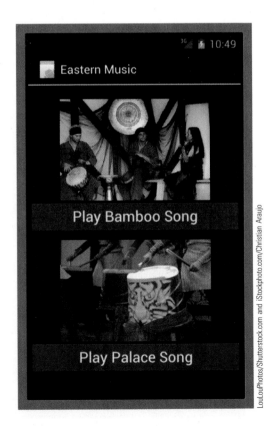

LouLouPhotos/Shutterstock.com and iStockphoto.com/Christian Araujo

Figure 6-2   Music played in the Android app

IN THE TRENCHES
Android music apps can play music on the memory card, download music available for purchase or free from music-sharing sites, tune into Internet-based radio stations, or connect to music saved in a cloud service.

To create this application, the developer must understand how to perform the following processes, among others:

1. Create a splash screen with a timer.

2. Design a TextView control with a background image.

3. Initialize a TimerTask and a timer.

4. Launch a second Activity.

5. Design a second XML layout.

6. Add music files to the raw folder.

7. Initialize the MediaPlayer class.

8. Play and pause music with a Button control.

Creating a Splash Screen

The Eastern Music app opens with a window that is displayed for approximately five seconds before automatically launching the next window. Unlike the project in Chapter 2 (Healthy Recipes), which required a button to be tapped to begin a click event that opened a second screen, this program does not require user interaction to open the second Activity class. Many Android applications on the market show splash screens that often include the name of the program, display a brand logo for the application, or identify the author. A splash screen opens as you launch your app, providing time for Android to initialize its resources. Extending the length of time that your splash screen is displayed enables your app to load necessary files.

In the Eastern Music app, instead of using Main as the name of the initial Activity, the opening Activity shown in Figure 6-3 is named Splash. A second .java file named Main.java is added later in the chapter. The Main Activity is responsible for playing the two songs. To start the Eastern Music application with a splash screen, complete the following step:

1. Open the Eclipse program. Click the New button on the Standard toolbar. Expand the Android folder, if necessary, and select Android Project. Click the Next button. In the New Android Project dialog box, enter the Project Name **Eastern Music**. To save the project on your USB drive, click to remove the check mark from the Use default location check box. Type **E:\Workspace** (if necessary, enter a different drive letter that identifies the USB drive). Click the Next button. For the Build Target, select Android 4.0, if necessary. Click the Next button. For the Package Name, type **net.androidbootcamp.easternmusic**. Enter **Splash** in the Create Activity text box.

The new Android Eastern Music project has an application name, a package name, and a Splash Activity (Figure 6-3).

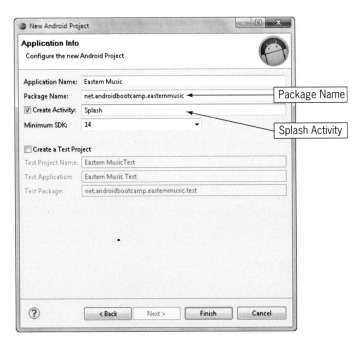

Figure 6-3   Setting up the Splash Activity in the Eastern Music project

Adding a Background Image to a TextView Widget

On the splash screen in Figure 6-1, an image with the text "Sounds of the East" is displayed. This image is not an ImageView widget, but instead a TextView widget with a background image. You use a TextView property named background to specify the image. The image is first placed in the drawable-hdpi folder and then referenced in the TextView background. The TextView background can display an image or a solid-color fill such as the hexadecimal color #0000FF for blue. The margins and gravity properties are used to place the text in the location of your choice. To add the images for this project and a splash.xml file with a TextView widget that contains a background image, follow these steps:

1. Click the Finish button in the New Android Project dialog box. Expand the Eastern Music project in the Package Explorer. Open the USB folder containing the student files. In the Package Explorer pane, expand the res folder. To add the three image files to the drawable-hdpi resource folder, drag band.png, bell.png, and drums.png to the drawable-hdpi folder until a plus sign pointer appears. Release the mouse button. If necessary, click the Copy files option button, and then click the OK button.

   Copies of the three image files appear in the drawable-hdpi folder (Figure 6-4).

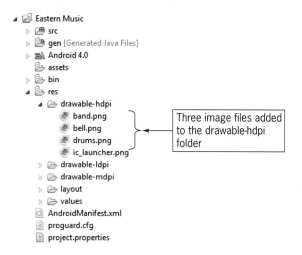

Three image files added to the drawable-hdpi folder

Figure 6-4   Image files in the drawable-hdpi folder

2. To add a splash.xml file, right-click the layout folder. On the shortcut menu, point to New and then click Other. In the New dialog box, click Android XML Layout File, and then click the Next button. In the New Android Layout XML File dialog box, type **splash.xml** in the File text box to name the layout file. In the Root Element list, select LinearLayout. Click the Finish button. The emulator window opens. In the Form Widgets category in the Palette, drag the TextView control to the emulator. To open the Properties pane, right-click the emulator window, point to Show In on the shortcut menu, and then click Properties. With the TextView control selected, change the Text property to **Sounds of the East** and type **#000000** for the Text color property. Set the Text size property to **20sp**. Click to the right of the Text style property, click the ellipsis button, and then select bold. Click the OK button. Click to the right of the Gravity property, click the ellipsis button, and then select center_horizontal. Click the OK button. In the Background property, click the ellipsis button. In the Reference Chooser dialog box, expand the Drawable folder and then click bell. Click the OK button. Resize the image to fit the emulator window.

A TextView image with an image background is displayed in the splash.xml file (Figure 6-5).

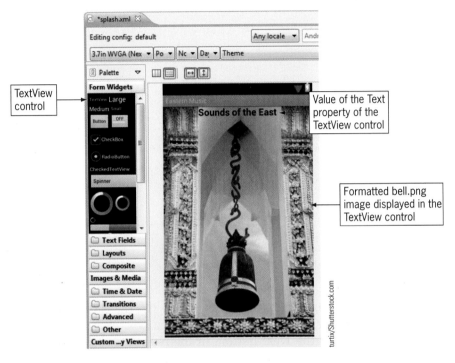

Figure 6-5   splash.xml displays a TextView control

3.   Close the splash.xml tab and save your work.

Creating a Timer

When most Android apps open, a splash screen is displayed for a few seconds, often preloading database files and information behind the scenes in large-scale applications. In the Eastern Music app, a timer is necessary to display the splash.xml file for approximately five seconds before the Main Activity intent is called. A **timer** in Java executes a one-time task, such as displaying an opening splash screen, or performs a continuous process, such as a morning wake-up call set to run at regular intervals.

Timers can be used to pause an action temporarily or to time dependent or repeated activities such as animation in a cartoon application. The timer object uses milliseconds as the unit of time. On an Android device, 1,000 milliseconds is equivalent to about one second. This fixed period of time is supported by two Java classes, namely **TimerTask** and **Timer**. To create a timer, the first step is to create a TimerTask object, as shown in the following syntax:

Code Syntax

```
TimerTask task = new TimerTask() {

}
```

GTK

Each time a timer runs its tasks, it executes within a single thread. A **thread** is a single sequential flow of control within a program. Java allows an application to have multiple threads of execution running concurrently. You can assign multiple threads so they occur simultaneously, completing several tasks at the same time. For example, a program could display a splash screen, download files needed for the application, and even play an opening sound at the same time.

A TimerTask invokes a scheduled timer. A timer may remind you of a childhood game called hide-and-seek. Do you remember covering your eyes and counting to 50 while your friends found a hiding spot before you began searching for everyone? A timer might only count to five seconds (5,000 milliseconds), but in a similar fashion, the application pauses while the timer counts to the established time limit. After the timed interval is completed, the program resumes and continues with the next task.

After entering the TimerTask code, point to the red error line under the TimerTask( ) to add the run( ) method, an auto-generated method stub, as shown in the following code syntax. Any statements within the braces of the run( ) method are executed after the TimerTask class is invoked.

Code Syntax

```
TimerTask task = new TimerTask() {
        @Override
        public void run() {
        // TODO Auto-generated method stub
}
```

The TimerTask must implement a run method that is called by the timer when the task is scheduled for execution. To add a TimerTask class to the Splash Activity, follow these steps:

1. In the Package Explorer, expand the src folder, expand net.androidbootcamp.easternmusic, and then double-click Splash.java to open the code window. To set the splash.xml layout as the opening window, change setContentView (R.layout.*main*) to **setContentView(R.layout.*splash*);**. Press the Enter key to insert a new line, and then type **TimerTask task = new TimerTask( ) {** to add the TimerTask. Point to the red error line below TimerTask( ).

    The setContentView method is updated to display the splash.xml file and the TimerTask class is initiated (Figure 6-6).

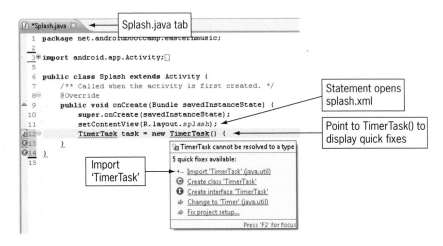

Figure 6-6   setContentView and TimerTask statements

2. First add the import statement by clicking Import 'TimerTask' (java util). Point to TimerTask( ) again to view the quick fix. Select Add unimplemented methods to add the auto-generated method stub for the run method. To complete the stub, click to right of } at the end of the stub, press the Enter key, and then type }; to close the class.

    The auto-generated stub for the run method is created automatically (Figure 6-7).

```
 1  package net.androidbootcamp.easternmusic;
 2
 3⊕ import java.util.TimerTask;□
 7
 8  public class Splash extends Activity {
 9      /** Called when the activity is first created. */
10⊖     @Override
11      public void onCreate(Bundle savedInstanceState) {
12          super.onCreate(savedInstanceState);
13          setContentView(R.layout.splash);
14⊖         TimerTask task = new TimerTask() {
15
16⊖             @Override
17              public void run() {
18                  // TODO Auto-generated method stub
19
20              }
21          };
22      }
23  }
```

run( ) method stub

Semicolon ends stub

Figure 6-7   run( ) method

IN THE TRENCHES

Timers can also be used to display updates of how long an installation is taking by displaying a countdown, monitor what a user is doing, or execute other routines while an Activity is running.

Scheduling a Timer

After including a reference to the TimerTask class, a timer must be scheduled for the amount of time that the splash screen is displayed. The Timer class shown in the following code syntax creates a timed event when the schedule method is called. A delay timer is scheduled in milliseconds using the Timer class. Delay schedules simply prompt an event to occur once at a specified time.

Code Syntax

```
Timer opening = new Timer();
opening.schedule(task,5000);
```

In the first line of the code syntax, the object named opening initializes a new instance of the Timer class. When the schedule method of the Timer class is called in the second line, two arguments are required. The first parameter (task) is the name of the variable that was initialized for the Timer class. The second parameter represents the number of milliseconds (5,000 milliseconds = 5 seconds). Follow these steps to add the scheduled timer:

1. In the code on the Splash.java tab, after the closing braces for the TimerTask class and the semicolon, insert a new line and then type **Timer opening = new Timer();**. Point to Timer and click Import 'Timer' (java.util).

   An instance of the Timer class is created named opening (Figure 6-8).

```
🗋 *Splash.java ⊠
  1  package net.androidbootcamp.easternmusic;
  2
  3⊕ import java.util.Timer;▯
  7
  8  public class Splash extends Activity {
  9      /** Called when the activity is first created. */
 10⊖     @Override
⚠11      public void onCreate(Bundle savedInstanceState) {
 12          super.onCreate(savedInstanceState);
 13          setContentView(R.layout.splash);
 14⊖         TimerTask task = new TimerTask() {
 15
 16⊖             @Override
⚠17             public void run() {
 18                 // TODO Auto-generated method stub
 19
 20             }
 21          };
 22          Timer opening = new Timer();  ◄─────────  Instance of Timer
 23      }
 24  }
```

Figure 6-8   Timer class

2. To schedule a timer using the schedule method from the Timer class to pause for five seconds, press the Enter key to insert a new line, and then type **opening.schedule (task,5000);**.

The timer lasting five seconds is scheduled (Figure 6-9).

```java
Splash.java

 1  package net.androidbootcamp.easternmusic;
 2
 3  import java.util.Timer;
 7
 8  public class Splash extends Activity {
 9      /** Called when the activity is first created. */
10      @Override
11      public void onCreate(Bundle savedInstanceState) {
12          super.onCreate(savedInstanceState);
13          setContentView(R.layout.splash);
14          TimerTask task = new TimerTask() {
15
16              @Override
17              public void run() {
18                  // TODO Auto-generated method stub
19
20              }
21          };
22          Timer opening = new Timer();
23          opening.schedule(task,5000);
24      }
25  }
```

Timer scheduled for 5 seconds

Figure 6-9   Timer scheduled

IN THE TRENCHES
Be careful not to code excessively long timers that waste the time of the user. A user-friendly program runs smoothly without long delays.

Life and Death of an Activity

In Line 12 of the Eastern Music app, as shown in Figure 6-9, the Splash Activity begins its life in the Activity life cycle with the onCreate( ) method. Each Activity has a **life cycle**, which is the series of actions from the beginning of an Activity to its end. Actions that occur during the life cycle provide ways to manage how users interact with your app. Each Activity in this book begins with an onCreate( ) method. The onCreate( ) method initializes the user interface with an XML layout; the life of the Activity is started. As in any life cycle, the opposite of birth is death. In this case, an **onDestroy( ) method** is the end of the Activity. The onCreate( ) method sets up all the resources required to perform the Activity, and onDestroy( ) releases those same resources to free up memory on your mobile device. The life cycle of the Splash Activity also begins with onCreate( ) and ends with onDestroy( ). Other actions can take place during the life of the Activity. For example, when the scheduled timer starts (Line 23 in Figure 6-9), the Splash Activity is paused. If you open multiple apps on a smartphone and receive a phone call, you must either pause or terminate the other apps to secure enough available memory to respond to the incoming call. To handle the life cycle actions between onCreate( ) and onDestroy( ), you use methods such as onRestart( ), onStart( ), onResume( ), onPause( ), and onStop( ). Each of these methods changes the state of the Activity. The four **states** of an Activity determine whether the activity is active, paused, stopped, or dead. The life cycle of an application affects how an app works and how the different parts are being orchestrated. Table 6-1 shows the development of an Activity throughout its life cycle.

Method	Description
onCreate( )	The onCreate( ) method begins each Activity. This method also provides a Bundle containing the Activity's previously frozen state, if it had one.
onRestart( )	If the Activity is stopped, onRestart( ) begins the Activity again. If this method is called, it indicates your Activity is being redisplayed to the user from a stopped state. The onRestart( ) method is always followed by onStart( ).
onStart( )	If the Activity is hidden, onStart( ) makes the Activity visible.
onResume( )	The onResume( ) method is called when the user begins interacting with the Activity. The onResume( ) method is always followed by onPause( ).
onPause( )	This method is called when an Activity is about to resume.
onStop( )	This method hides the Activity.
onDestroy( )	This method destroys the Activity. Typically, the finish( ) method (part of onDestroy( )) is used to declare that the Activity is finished; when the next Activity is called, it releases all the resources from the first Activity.

Table 6-1   Methods used in the life cycle of an Activity

When an Activity is launched using onCreate( ), the app performs the actions in the Activity. In other words, the Activity becomes the top sheet of paper on a stack of papers. When the methods shown in Table 6-1 are used between the onCreate( ) and onDestroy( ) methods, they shuffle the order of the papers in that stack. When onDestroy( ) is called, imagine that the pile of papers is thrown away. The finish( ) method is part of the onDestroy( ) method and is called when the Activity is completed and should be closed. Typically, the finish( ) method occurs directly before another Activity is launched. As an Android developer, you should be well acquainted with the life cycle of Activities because an app that you publish in the Android market must "play" well with all the other apps on a mobile device. For example, your Android app must pause when a text message, phone call, or other event occurs.

The diagram in Figure 6-10 shows the life cycle of an Activity. The rectangles represent methods you can implement to perform operations when the Activity moves between states. The colored ovals are the possible major states of the Activity.

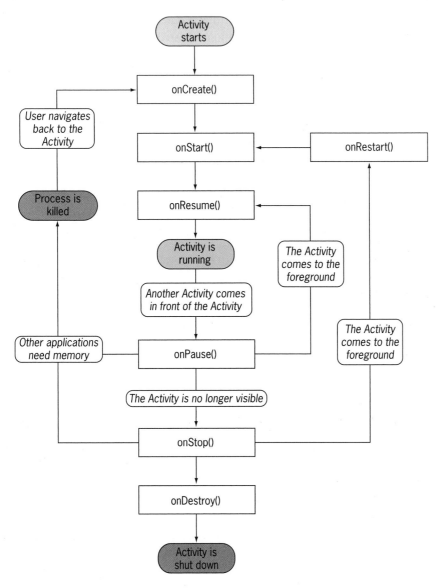

Figure 6-10   Activity life cycle

As an example of the Activity life cycle, the native Android application designed for taking a picture using the built-in camera transitions through each stage in the life cycle. When the user launches the camera app, the camera Activity executes the onCreate( ) method to display the opening screen and the image captured through the camera lens. The user taps a Button control to take a picture. The onStop( ) method is called to hide the live image displayed after the picture is taken. The onRestart( ) method is called after the picture is taken to restart the rest of the app. The onStart( ) method is called to display the picture that was just taken. If the user taps the screen to upload the image to Facebook, the onPause( ) method is called to pause operations of the camera app while the image is uploaded. The onResume( ) method is launched after the picture is uploaded to reactivate the camera. The user can choose to take another image, which repeats the process, or to exit the camera app. If the user selects the exit option, onDestroy( ) or finish( ) frees the saved resources from the temporary memory of the device and closes the camera application.

In the Eastern Music application, after the timer pauses the program temporarily, the Splash Activity should be destroyed with onDestroy( ) before launching the second Activity. The app should call the onDestroy( ) method from within the run method of the timer task that was invoked by TimerTask. Doing so guarantees that the ongoing task execution is the last task this timer performs. To close the Splash Activity, follow these steps:

1. In Splash.java, click inside the run( ) auto-generated method stub in the blank line under the comment // TODO Auto-generated method stub and type **finish( );**.

    The finish( ) statement releases the resources that were created for the Splash Activity and closes the Activity (Figure 6-11).

```
 Splash.java
 1  package net.androidbootcamp.easternmusic;
 2
 3  import java.util.Timer;
 7
 8  public class Splash extends Activity {
 9      /** Called when the activity is first created.
10      @Override
11      public void onCreate(Bundle savedInstanceState)
12          super.onCreate(savedInstanceState);
13          setContentView(R.layout.splash);
14          TimerTask task = new TimerTask(){
15
16              @Override
17              public void run() {
18                  // TODO Auto-generated method stub
19                  finish();                            ← finish( ) method
20              }
21          };
22          Timer opening = new Timer();
23          opening.schedule(task,5000);
24      }
25  }
26
```

Figure 6-11   finish( ) method called

2. Save your work.

Launching the Next Activity

After the Activity for the splash screen is destroyed, an intent must request that the next Activity is launched. An XML layout named main.xml already exists as the default layout. A second class named Main must be created before the code can launch this Java class. You must update the Android Manifest file to include the Main Activity. The Main Activity is responsible for playing music. To create a second class and launch the Main Activity, follow these steps:

1. In the Package Explorer, right-click the net.androidbootcamp.easternmusic folder, point to New on the shortcut menu, and then click Class. Type **Main** in the Name text box. Click the Superclass Browse button. Type **Activity** in the Choose a type text box. Click Activity – android.app and then click the OK button to extend the Activity class. Click the Finish button to finish creating the Main class.

A second class named Main is created (Figure 6-12).

Figure 6-12   Main class created

2. In the Package Explorer, double-click the AndroidManifest.xml file. To add the Main class to the Android Manifest, click the Application tab at the bottom of the Eastern Music Manifest page. Scroll down to display the Application Nodes section. Click the Add button. Select Activity in the Create a new element at the top level, in Application dialog box. Click the OK button. The Attributes for Activity section opens in the Application tab. In the Name text box in this section, type **.Main**.

The .Main class is added to the Android Manifest file (Figure 6-13).

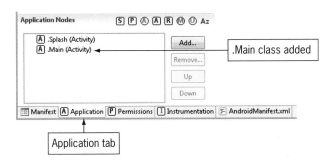

Figure 6-13   Adding the Main Activity

3. Close the Eastern Music Manifest tab and save the changes. To launch the second Activity, display Splash.java, insert a new line in the run( ) auto-generated method stub after the finish( ); statement, and then type **startActivity(new Intent(Splash.**

this, Main.class));. Point to the red error line below Intent and select 'Import Intent' (android.content). Save your work.

The second Activity named Main is launched with an Intent statement (Figure 6-14).

```
Splash.java
 1  package net.androidbootcamp.easternmusic;
 2
 3  import java.util.Timer;
 8
 9  public class Splash extends Activity {
10      /** Called when the activity is first created. */
11      @Override
12      public void onCreate(Bundle savedInstanceState) {
13          super.onCreate(savedInstanceState);
14          setContentView(R.layout.splash);
15          TimerTask task = new TimerTask(){
16
17              @Override
18              public void run() {
19                  // TODO Auto-generated method stub
20                  finish();
21                  startActivity(new Intent(Splash.this, Main.class));    Opens the
22              }                                                           Main Activity
23          };
24          Timer opening = new Timer();
25          opening.schedule(task,5000);
26      }
27  }
```

Figure 6-14 Intent statement

Designing the main.xml File

In the Eastern Music app, after the first Activity displaying the splash screen finishes and the second Activity named Main is launched, a second XML layout file is displayed when the onCreate( ) method is called within the Main.java file. The Main.java file uses the default Linear layout with two ImageView and Button controls. To design the XML layout for main.xml, follow these steps:

1. Close the Splash.java tab. In the res/layout folder, right-click main.xml, point to Open With on the shortcut menu, and then click Android Layout Editor. Delete the default Hello World, Splash! control. Drag an ImageView control from the Images & Media category of the Palette to the emulator window. In the Resource Chooser dialog box, click the first option button if necessary, click band, and then click the OK button. With the band.png image selected, change the Layout height in the Properties pane to **150dp**, the Layout margin top to **20dp**, and the Layout width to **320dp**. Drag a Button from the Form Widgets category of the Palette and place it below the image. Set the Button Id property to **@+id/btnBamboo**. Change the Text property to **Play Bamboo Song**. Set the Text size to **22sp** and the Layout margin bottom to **10dp**. Set the Layout width to **320dp**. Save your work.

    The image and button to select the first song named Bamboo are designed in main.xml (Figure 6-15).

202

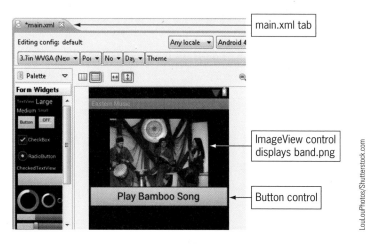

LouLouPhotos/Shutterstock.com

Figure 6-15   ImageView and Button controls in main.xml

2. Drag another ImageView control to the emulator window. In the Resource Chooser dialog box, click drums, and then click the OK button. With the drums.png image selected, change the Layout height in the Properties pane to **150dp**, the Layout margin top to **20dp**, and the Layout width to **320dp**. Drag a Button from the Form Widgets category of the Palette and place it below the image. Set the Button Id property to **@+id/btnPalace**. Change the Text property to **Play Palace Song**. Set the Text size to **22sp** and the Layout margin bottom to **10dp**. Set the Layout width to **320dp**. Save your work.

The image and button to select the second song named Palace are designed in main.xml (Figure 6-16).

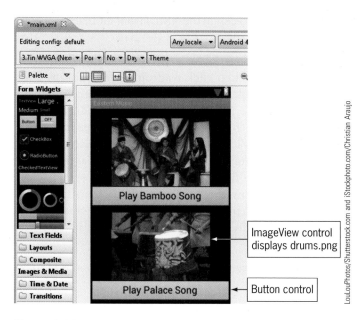

LouLouPhotos/Shutterstock.com and iStockphoto.com/Christian Araujo

Figure 6-16   main.xml layout complete

Class Variables

In the coding examples used thus far in this book, variables have been local variables. **Local variables** are declared by variable declaration statements within a method, such as a primitive integer variable within an onCreate( ) method. The local variable effectively ceases to exist when the execution of the method is complete. The **scope** of a variable refers to the variable's visibility within a class. Variables that are accessible only to a restricted portion of a program such as a single method are said to have local scope. Variables that are accessible from anywhere in a class, however, are said to have global scope. If a variable is needed in multiple methods within a class, the global variable is assigned at the beginning of a class, not within a method. This global scope variable is called a **class variable** in Java, and can be accessed by multiple methods throughout the program. In the chapter project, the Button, MediaPlayer (necessary for playing sound), and an integer variable named playing are needed in the onCreate( ) method and within both onClick( ) methods for each Button control. To keep the value of these variables throughout multiple classes, the variables are defined as class variables that cease to exist when their class or activity is unloaded.

After class variables are defined in Main.java, the onCreate( ) method opens the main.xml layout and defines the two Button controls. The Activity waits for the user to select one of the two buttons, each of which plays a song. If a button is clicked twice, the music pauses. Each button must have a setOnClickListener that awaits the user's click. After the user taps a button, the setOnClickListener method implements the Button.OnClickListener, creating an instance of the OnClickListener and calling the onClick method. The onClick method responds to the user's action. For example, in the chapter project, the response is to play a song. The onClick method is where you place the code to handle playing the song. To code the class variables, display the main.xml layout, reference the two Button controls, and set an onClickListener, follow these steps:

1. Close the main.xml window and save your work. In Main.java, after the public class Main extends Activity statement, create two blank lines. On the second line, type **Button btBamboo, btPalace;** to create a class variable reference. Point to Button and click 'Import Button' (android widget). Insert a new line, and then type **MediaPlayer mpBamboo, mpPalace;** to create a class variable reference for the media player. Point to MediaPlayer and click 'Import MediaPlayer' (android.media). Insert a new line, and then type **int playing;** to create a primitive class variable named playing, which keeps track of whether a song is playing.

   Class variables that can be accessed by the rest of the program are initialized (Figure 6-17).

```
J *Main.java ⌛
  1  package net.androidbootcamp.easternmusic;
  2
  3⊖ import android.app.Activity;
  4  import android.media.MediaPlayer;
  5  import android.widget.Button;
  6
  7  public class Main extends Activity {
  8
  9  Button btBamboo, btPalace;
 10  MediaPlayer mpBamboo, mpPalace;
 11  int playing;
 12
 13  }
```

Button, MediaPlayer, and primitive class variables

Figure 6-17   Class variables

2. Press the Enter key twice, type **oncreate**, and then press Ctrl+spacebar. Double-click the first onCreate method in the auto-complete listing to generate the method structure. Click after the semicolon, press the Enter key, and then type **setContentView(R.** to display an auto-complete listing. Double-click layout. Type a period. Double-click main: int—R layout. Type **);** to complete the statement.

   The onCreate method displays the main.xml file (Figure 6-18).

```
J Main.java ⌛
  1  package net.androidbootcamp.easternmusic;
  2
  3⊕ import android.app.Activity;▯
  7
  8  public class Main extends Activity {
  9
 10  Button btBamboo, btPalace;
 11  MediaPlayer mpBamboo, mpPalace;
 12  int playing;
 13
 14      /** Called when the activity is first created. */
 15⊖     @Override
 16     public void onCreate(Bundle savedInstanceState) {
 17         super.onCreate(savedInstanceState);
 18         setContentView(R.layout.main);
 19         }
 20
 21  }
```

onCreate method opens main.xml

Figure 6-18   onCreate method

3. Both Button references were made as class variables. To create an instance of each Button control, press the Enter key and type **btBamboo = (Button)findViewById(R.id.btnBamboo);**. Press the Enter key and then type **btPalace = (Button)findViewById(R.id.btnPalace);**.

   The Button controls named btnBamboo and btnPalace are referenced in Main.java (Figure 6-19).

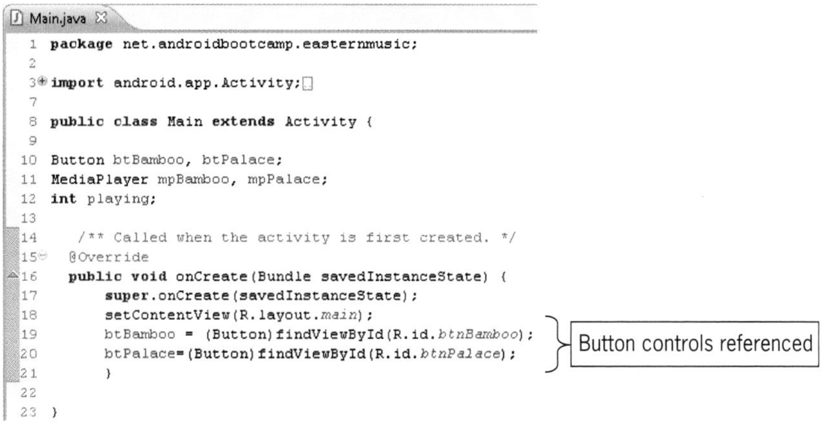

```
J Main.java ⌧
 1  package net.androidbootcamp.easternmusic;
 2
 3⊕ import android.app.Activity;☐
 7
 8  public class Main extends Activity {
 9
10  Button btBamboo, btPalace;
11  MediaPlayer mpBamboo, mpPalace;
12  int playing;
13
14     /** Called when the activity is first created. */
15◯    @Override
16     public void onCreate(Bundle savedInstanceState) {
17         super.onCreate(savedInstanceState);
18         setContentView(R.layout.main);
19         btBamboo = (Button)findViewById(R.id.btnBamboo);
20         btPalace=(Button)findViewById(R.id.btnPalace);
21         }
22
23  )
```

Button controls referenced

Figure 6-19 Button controls referenced

4. To create a setOnClickListener method so the btBamboo Button waits for the user's click, press the Enter key and type **btBamboo.setOnClickListener(bBamboo);**. To create an instance of the Button OnClickListener, click between the two ending braces and type **Button.OnClickListener bBamboo = new Button.OnClickListener() {** and then press the Enter key. Place a semicolon after the closing brace. This onClickListener is designed for a class variable for a Button. Point to the red error line below Button.OnClickListener and select Add unimplemented methods to add the quick fix.

An OnClickListener auto-generated stub appears in the code for the first button (Figure 6-20).

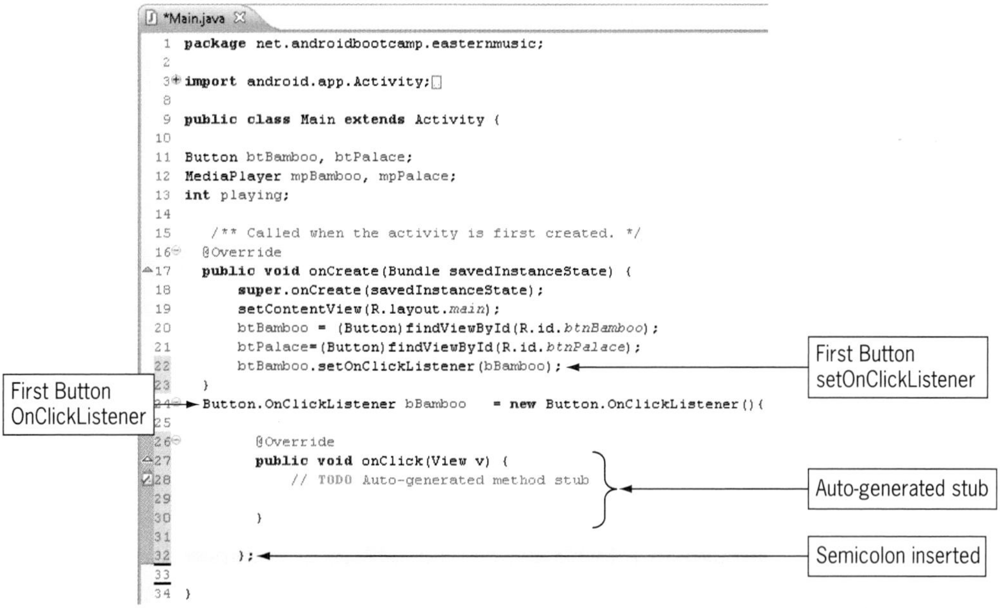

```
J *Main.java ⌧
 1  package net.androidbootcamp.easternmusic;
 2
 3⊕ import android.app.Activity;☐
 8
 9  public class Main extends Activity {
10
11  Button btBamboo, btPalace;
12  MediaPlayer mpBamboo, mpPalace;
13  int playing;
14
15     /** Called when the activity is first created. */
16◯    @Override
17     public void onCreate(Bundle savedInstanceState) {
18         super.onCreate(savedInstanceState);
19         setContentView(R.layout.main);
20         btBamboo = (Button)findViewById(R.id.btnBamboo);
21         btPalace=(Button)findViewById(R.id.btnPalace);
22         btBamboo.setOnClickListener(bBamboo);
23         }
24  Button.OnClickListener bBamboo    = new Button.OnClickListener(){
25
26◯        @Override
27         public void onClick(View v) {
28             // TODO Auto-generated method stub
29
30         }
31
32         };
33
34  )
```

First Button setOnClickListener

First Button OnClickListener

Auto-generated stub

Semicolon inserted

Figure 6-20 Inserting the first Button OnClickListener stub

5. To create a setOnClickListener method so the btPalace Button waits for the user's click, click after the btBamboo.setOnClickListener(bBamboo); statement, press the Enter key, and then type **btPalace.setOnClickListener(bPalace);**. To create an instance of the btnPalace button OnClickListener, click after the brace with the semicolon at the end of the code, press the Enter key, type **Button.OnClickListener bPalace = new Button.OnClickListener() {** and then press the Enter key to create the closing brace. Place a semicolon after this closing brace. Point to the red error line below Button.OnClickListener and select Add unimplemented methods to add the quick fix. Save your work.

An OnClickListener auto-generated stub appears in the code for the second button (Figure 6-21).

Figure 6-21   Inserting the second Button OnClickListener stub

Playing Music

Every Android phone and tablet includes a built-in music player where you can store your favorite music. You can also write your own applications that offer music playback capabilities. To enable the Eastern Music chapter project to play two songs, Android includes a MediaPlayer class that can play both audio and music files. Android lets you play audio and video from several types of data sources. You can play audio or video from media files stored in the application's resources (a folder named raw), from stand-alone files in the Android file system of the device, from an SD (Secure Digital) memory card in the phone itself, or from a data stream provided through an Internet connection. The most common file type of media supported for audio playback with the MediaPlayer class is .mp3, but other audio file types such as .wav, .ogg, and .midi are typically supported by most Android hardware. The Android device platform supports a wide variety of media types based on the codecs included in the device by the manufacturer. A **codec** is a computer technology used to compress and decompress audio and video files.

IN THE TRENCHES
The Android platform provides a class to record audio and video, where supported by the mobile device hardware. To record audio or video, use the MediaRecorder class. The emulator does not provide the capability to capture audio or video, but an actual mobile device can record media input, accessible through the MediaRecorder class.

Creating a Raw Folder for Music Files

In an Android project, music files are typically stored in a subfolder of the res folder called raw. In newer versions of Android, the raw folder must be created before music files can be placed in that folder. The two .mp3 files played in the Eastern Music app are named bamboo.mp3 and palace.mp3, and should be placed in the raw folder. To create a raw folder that contains music files, follow these steps:

1. In the Package Explorer, right-click the res folder. Point to New on the shortcut menu, and then click Folder. The New Folder dialog box opens. In the Folder name text box, type **raw**.

   A folder named raw is created using the New Folder dialog box (Figure 6-22).

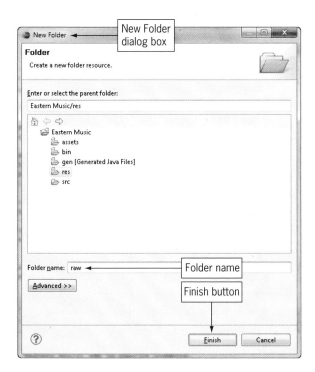

Figure 6-22   New Folder dialog box

2. Click the Finish button. To add the project music files to the raw folder, open the USB folder containing your student files. To add the two music files to the raw resource folder, select bamboo.mp3 and palace.mp3, and then drag the files to the raw folder until a plus sign pointer appears. Release the mouse button. If necessary, click the Copy files option button, and then click the OK button. Expand the raw folder.

Copies of the music files appear in the raw folder (Figure 6-23).

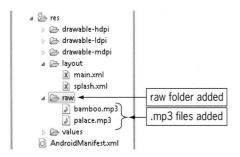

Figure 6-23   Music files in the raw folder

Using the MediaPlayer Class

The **MediaPlayer class** provides the methods to control audio playback on an Android device. At the beginning of the Main.java code, two MediaPlayer class variables are declared. After the variables are declared, an instance of the MediaPlayer class is assigned to each variable. In the following code syntax, mpBamboo is assigned to an instance of the MediaPlayer class that accesses the bamboo music file in the raw folder.

Code Syntax

```
MediaPlayer mpBamboo = MediaPlayer.create(this, R.raw.bamboo);
```

The class variables mpBamboo and mpPalace are assigned the music files from the raw folder. To declare an instance of the MediaPlayer class, follow this step:

1. In Main.java, press the Enter key after the btPalace.setOnClickListener(bPalace); statement to create a new line. Type **mpBamboo = new MediaPlayer();** to create a new instance of MediaPlayer. Insert a new line and type **mpBamboo = MediaPlayer.create(this, R.raw.bamboo);** to assign the first song to mpBamboo. Press the Enter key. Type **mpPalace = new MediaPlayer();** to add an instance for the second MediaPlayer variable. Insert a new line and type **mpPalace = MediaPlayer. create(this, R.raw.palace);** to assign the second song to mpPalace.

The two class variables are assigned an instance of the MediaPlayer class (Figure 6-24).

```
J *Main.java ⌧
 1  package net.androidbootcamp.easternmusic;
 2
 3⊕ import android.app.Activity;
 8
 9  public class Main extends Activity {
10
11  Button btBamboo, btPalace;
12  MediaPlayer mpBamboo, mpPalace;
13  int playing;
14
15     /** Called when the activity is first created. */
16⁻    @Override
▲17    public void onCreate(Bundle savedInstanceState) {
18         super.onCreate(savedInstanceState);
19         setContentView(R.layout.main);
20         btBamboo = (Button)findViewById(R.id.btnBamboo);
21         btPalace = (Button)findViewById(R.id.btnPalace);
22         btBamboo.setOnClickListener(bBamboo);
23         btPalace.setOnClickListener(bPalace);
24         mpBamboo = new  MediaPlayer();
25         mpBamboo = MediaPlayer.create(this, R.raw.bamboo);
26         mpPalace = new MediaPlayer();
27         mpPalace = MediaPlayer.create(this, R.raw.palace);
28
29     }
30⁻    Button.OnClickListener bBamboo   = new Button.OnClickListener(){
31
```

MediaPlayer
statements

Figure 6-24   MediaPlayer instance statements

GTK

Music can be used in many ways throughout Android apps. Music can provide sound effects to inform the user of a recent e-mail or to praise you when you reach the winning level on your favorite game. Background music is often used as a soundtrack to create a theme in an adventure game.

The MediaPlayer State

Android uses the MediaPlayer class to control the playing of the audio file. Whether the music file is playing is called the state of the MediaPlayer. The three common states of the audio file include when the music starts, when the music pauses, and when the music stops. The state of the music is established by the MediaPlayer's temporary behavior. Table 6-2 provides an example of the most common MediaPlayer states.

Method	Purpose
start( )	Starts media playback
pause( )	Pauses media playback
stop( )	Stops media playback

Table 6-2   Common MediaPlayer states

In the Eastern Music project, the user first taps a button to start the music playing. The start( ) method is used to begin the playback of the selected music file. When the user taps the same button again, the music temporarily pauses the music file by calling the pause( ) method. To restart the song, the start( ) method must be called again. To determine the state of MediaPlayer, the code must assess if this is the first time the user is tapping the button to start the song or if the user is tapping the same button twice to pause the song. The user can tap the button a third time to start the song again. This cycle continues until the user exits the project. In the chapter project, an integer variable named playing is initially set to zero. Each time the user taps the button, the playing variable changes value. The first time the user taps the button, the variable is changed to the value of 1 to assist the program in determining the state of the MediaPlayer. If the user taps the same button again to pause the song, the variable changes to the value of 0. Android does not have a method for determining the present state of the MediaPlayer, but by using this simple primitive variable, you can keep track of the state of the music. A Switch decision structure uses the variable named playing to change the state of the music. The onClick( ) method is called every time the user selects a button. To initiate the variable used to determine the state of MediaPlayer and to code a Switch decision structure to determine the state, follow these steps:

1.   In Main.java, press the Enter key after the mpPalace = MediaPlayer.create(this, R.raw.palace); statement to create a new line. Type **playing = 0;** to initialize the variable named playing as the value 0. When the user clicks a button, the Switch statement follows the path of case 0, which begins the audio playback of one of the songs.

The variable named playing is initialized as the value 0 (Figure 6-25).

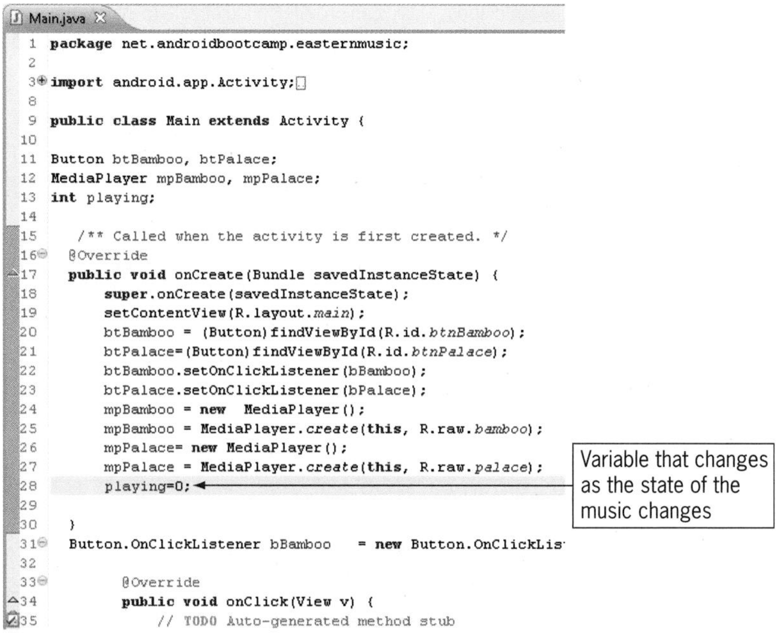

Figure 6-25   The *playing* variable is set to 0

2.   Inside the braces of the first onClick method (after the // TODO comment), type the following Switch decision structure that is used to determine the state of the music:

```
switch(playing) {
        case 0:
                mpBamboo.start();
                playing = 1;
                break;
        case 1:
                mpBamboo.pause();
                playing = 0;
                break;
    }
```

The Switch decision structure that determines the state of the music is coded for the first onClick method (Figure 6-26).

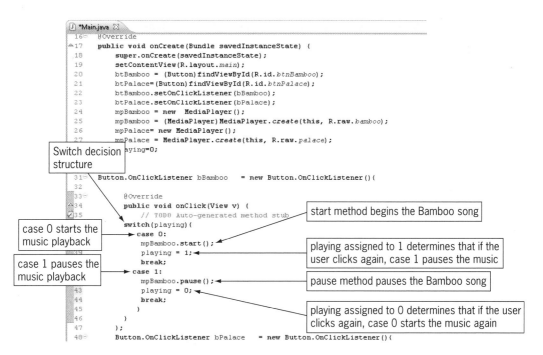

Figure 6-26 Switch statements for both onClick methods

IN THE TRENCHES

Music playback control operation may fail due to various reasons, such as unsupported audio/video format, poorly interleaved audio/video, file size overwhelming memory capabilities, or a streaming timeout on the Internet.

Changing the Text Property Using Code

When the user selects a song to play, the Button control with the text "Play Bamboo Song" is tapped. To pause the song, the user must tap the same button, but the text should be changed to a more fitting action, such as "Pause Bamboo Song." A property can initially be entered in the XML layout or coded in Java. In Chapter 4, the setText( ) method displays text in the TextView control. To change the Text property for a Button control using Java code, the control name and the SetText( ) method are separated by a period that precedes a string of text within parentheses, as shown in the following code syntax:

Code Syntax

```
btBamboo.setText("Pause Bamboo Song");
```

The btBamboo Button control displays the text "Pause Bamboo Song." If the user wants to restart the song, a second setText( ) method changes the text back to "Play Bamboo Song." To change the text on the Button control for the first button, follow these steps:

1. In Main.java in the first onClick( ) method, press the Enter key after the statement playing = 1; in case 0. Type **btBamboo.setText("Pause Bamboo Song");** to change the text displayed on the Button control. To change the text back to the original text if the user restarts the music, in case 1 of the Switch decision structure, press the Enter key after the statement playing = 0;. Type **btBamboo.setText("Play Bamboo Song");** to change the text displayed on the Button control.

The first button changes text while the music is paused or restarted (Figure 6-27).

```
 *Main.java
19      setContentView(R.layout.main);
20      btBamboo = (Button)findViewById(R.id.btnBamb
21      btPalace=(Button)findViewById(R.id.btnPalace
22      btBamboo.setOnClickListener(bBamboo);
23      btPalace.setOnClickListener(bPalace);
24      mpBamboo = new  MediaPlayer();
25      mpBamboo = (MediaPlayer)MediaPlayer.create(tl
26      mpPalace= new MediaPlayer();
27      mpPalace = MediaPlayer.create(this, R.raw.pa.
28      playing=0;
29
30   }
31   Button.OnClickListener bBamboo   = new Button.On(
32
33       @Override
34       public void onClick(View v) {
35           // TODO Auto-generated method stub
36           switch(playing){
37             case 0:
38               mpBamboo.start();
39               playing = 1;
40               btBamboo.setText("Pause Bamboo Song");
41               break;
42             case 1:
43               mpBamboo.pause();
44               playing = 0;
45               btBamboo.setText("Play Bamboo Song");
46               break;
47           }
48       }
```

Each setText( ) statement changes the Button text

Figure 6-27 The setText( ) method changes the button control in both case statements

2. To test the music and text on the first Button control, save and run the program. The second Button control has not been coded yet.

When you tap the first Button control, the Bamboo song plays and the Button text is changed. You can restart or pause the music by pressing the button again (Figure 6-28).

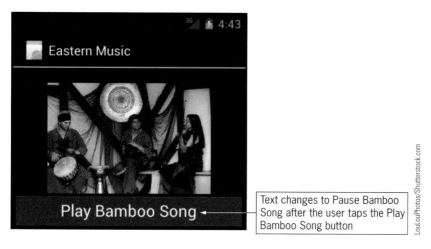

Text changes to Pause Bamboo Song after the user taps the Play Bamboo Song button

Figure 6-28   Music plays and the button text is changed

Changing the Visibility Property Using Code

When the program is complete, the user can select the button that plays the Bamboo song or the Palace song. One issue that must be resolved is that it is possible to tap the Bamboo song button and then tap the Palace button, playing both songs at once. To resolve this problem, when the user selects one of the songs, the button to the other song can be coded to disappear until the user has paused the current song from playing. The Java property that controls whether a control is displayed on the emulator is the **Visibility property**. By default, the Visibility property is set to display any control you place on the emulator when the program runs. To cause the control not to appear, you must code the setVisibility property to change the view to invisible. To change the visibility of the button to reappear, the setVisibility property is changed to visible, as shown in the following code syntax:

Code Syntax

```
To hide the control:    btBamboo.setVisibility(View.INVISIBLE);
To display the control: btBamboo.setVisibility(View.VISIBLE);
```

To set the setVisibility property for the Bamboo button control to change the view to invisible and to copy and paste the code for the first onClick code to create a Switch decision structure for the second button, you can complete the following steps:

1. In Main.java in the first onClick( ) method in the case 0 option, press the Enter key after the statement btBamboo.setText("Pause Bamboo Song");. Type **btPalace.setVisibility(View.INVISIBLE);** to hide the Palace button when the Bamboo song is playing. When the music is paused, the Palace button should be visible again. In the case 1 option, press the Enter key after the statement btBamboo.setText("Play Bamboo Song");. Type **btPalace.setVisibility(View.VISIBLE);** to change the visibility of the Palace button.

The Palace button hides when the music plays and displays when the music stops (Figure 6-29).

```
Main.java

20        btBamboo = (Button)findViewById(R.id.btnBamboo
21        btPalace=(Button)findViewById(R.id.btnPalace);
22        btBamboo.setOnClickListener(bBamboo);
23        btPalace.setOnClickListener(bPalace);
24        mpBamboo = new MediaPlayer();
25        mpBamboo = MediaPlayer.create(this, R.raw.bamb
26        mpPalace= new MediaPlayer();
27        mpPalace = MediaPlayer.create(this, R.raw.pala
28        playing=0;
29
30    }
31    Button.OnClickListener bBamboo    = new Button.OnCl
32
33        @Override
34        public void onClick(View v) {
35            // TODO Auto-generated method stub
36        switch(playing){
37            case 0:
38            mpBamboo.start();
39            playing = 1;
40            btBamboo.setText("Pause Bamboo Song");
41            btPalace.setVisibility(View.INVISIBLE);      ← setVisibility( ) method hides Palace button
42            break;
43            case 1:
44            mpBamboo.pause();
45            playing = 0;
46            btBamboo.setText("Play Bamboo Song");
47            btPalace.setVisibility(View.VISIBLE);         ← setVisibility( ) method displays Palace button
48            break;
49            }
50        }
51    };
52    Button.OnClickListener bPalace    = new Button.
```

Figure 6-29   The setVisibility( ) method changes the visibility of the Button control

2. To code the second onClick( ) method for Palace button, select and copy Lines 36–48 in Figure 6-29 by clicking Edit on the menu bar and then clicking Copy. Click Line 57 inside the second onClick( ) method, click Edit on the menu bar, and then click Paste. Change every reference of mpBamboo to **mpPalace**. Change every reference of btBamboo to **btPalace** or vice versa. Change the setText messages to read **Pause Palace Song** and **Play Palace Song**. You might need to add **};** as the second-to-last line of code. Compare your code with the complete code, making changes as necessary.

The second onClick( ) method is coded using a Switch decision structure (Figure 6-30).

```java
1  package net.androidbootcamp.easternmusic;
2
3  import android.app.Activity;
8
9  public class Main extends Activity {
10
11 Button btBamboo, btPalace;
12 MediaPlayer mpBamboo, mpPalace;
13 int playing;
14
15    /** Called when the activity is first created. */
16    @Override
17    public void onCreate(Bundle savedInstanceState) {
18        super.onCreate(savedInstanceState);
19        setContentView(R.layout.main);
20        btBamboo = (Button)findViewById(R.id.btnBamboo);
21        btPalace=(Button)findViewById(R.id.btnPalace);
22        btBamboo.setOnClickListener(bBamboo);
23        btPalace.setOnClickListener(bPalace);
24        mpBamboo = new MediaPlayer();
25        mpBamboo = MediaPlayer.create(this, R.raw.bamboo);
26        mpPalace= new MediaPlayer();
27        mpPalace = MediaPlayer.create(this, R.raw.palace);
28        playing=0;
29
30    }
31    Button.OnClickListener bBamboo   = new Button.OnClickListener(){
32
33        @Override
34        public void onClick(View v) {
35            // TODO Auto-generated method stub
36        switch(playing){
37          case 0:
38            mpBamboo.start();
39            playing = 1;
40            btBamboo.setText("Pause Bamboo Song");
41            btPalace.setVisibility(View.INVISIBLE);
42            break;
43          case 1:
44            mpBamboo.pause();
45            playing = 0;
46            btBamboo.setText("Play Bamboo Song");
47            btPalace.setVisibility(View.VISIBLE);
48            break;
49          }
50        }
51    };
52    Button.OnClickListener bPalace   = new Button.OnClickListener(){
53
54        @Override
55        public void onClick(View v) {
56            // TODO Auto-generated method stub
57        switch(playing){
58        case 0:
59          mpPalace.start();
60          btPalace.setText("Pause Palace Song");
61          btBamboo.setVisibility(View.INVISIBLE);
62          playing = 1;
63          break;
64        case 1:
65          mpPalace.pause();
66          btPalace.setText("Play Palace Song");
67          btBamboo.setVisibility(View.VISIBLE);
68          playing = 0;
69          break;
70        }
71    };
72    };
73 }
74
75
```

Bamboo button is coded

Palace button is coded

Semicolon ends the second onClickListener

Figure 6-30   Complete code for Main.java

Running and Testing the Application

Your first experience with media in an Android application is complete. Click Run on the menu bar, and then select Run to save and test the application in the emulator. Select Android Application and click the OK button. Save all the files in the next dialog box, if necessary, and unlock the emulator. The application opens in the emulator window, as shown in Figure 6-1 and Figure 6-2. The splash screen opens for five seconds. The main screen opens next, requesting your button selection to play each of the songs. Test both buttons and make sure your speakers are on so you can hear the Eastern music play.

Wrap It Up—Chapter Summary

In this chapter, the Android platform created a memorable multimedia experience with the sounds of Eastern music. A splash screen provided time to load extra files if needed and displayed an initial logo for brand recognition. Methods such as setText( ) and setVisibility( ) helped to create an easy-to-use Android application that was clear to the user. The state of music using the start and pause methods of MediaPlayer filled your classroom or home with the enjoyment of music.

- An Android application can show a splash screen that displays the name of the program, a brand logo for the application, or the name of the author. The splash screen opens as you launch your app, providing time for Android to initialize its resources.

- A TextView widget can display a background color or image stored in one of the project's drawable folders.

- A timer in Java executes a one-time task such as displaying an opening splash screen, or it performs a continuous process such as a wake-up call that rings each morning at the same time. Timers can be used to pause an action temporarily or to time dependent or repeated activities. The timer object uses milliseconds as the unit of time.

- After including a reference to the TimerTask class in your code, schedule a timer for the amount of time that an event occurs, such as a splash screen being displayed.

- Each Activity has a life cycle, which is the series of actions from the beginning of an Activity to its end. An Activity usually starts with the onCreate( ) method, which sets up all the resources required to perform the Activity. An Activity usually ends with the onDestroy( ) method, which releases those same resources to free up memory on the mobile device. Other actions can take place during the life of the Activity, including onRestart( ), onStart( ), onResume( ), onPause( ), and onStop( ).

- Local variables are declared by variable declaration statements within a method. The local variable effectively ceases to exist when the execution of the method is complete.

- The scope of a variable refers to the variable's visibility within a class. Variables that are accessible only to a restricted portion of a program such as a single method have local scope. Variables that are accessible from anywhere in a class, however, have global scope. If a variable is needed in multiple methods within a class, the global variable is assigned at the beginning of a class, not within a method. This global scope variable is called a class variable in Java and can be accessed by multiple methods throughout the program.

- Every Android phone and tablet includes a built-in music player where you can store music. You can also write applications that offer music playback capabilities. The media types an Android device platform supports are determined by the codecs the manufacturer included in the device. A codec is a computer technology used to compress and decompress audio and video files.

- In an Android project, music files are typically stored in the res\raw subfolder. In newer versions of Android, you must create the raw subfolder before storing music files.

- The MediaPlayer class provides the methods to control audio playback on an Android device. First declare the MediaPlayer class variables, and then assign an instance of the MediaPlayer class to each variable. Whether the music file is playing is called the state of the MediaPlayer. The three common states of the audio file include when the music starts, when the music pauses, and when the music stops.

- The Java property that controls whether a control is displayed on the emulator is the Visibility property. By default, the Visibility property is set to display any control you place on the emulator when the program runs. To cause the control not to appear, you must code the setVisibility property in Java to change the view to invisible. To change the visibility of the button to reappear, change the setVisibility property to visible.

Key Terms

class variable—A variable with global scope; it can be accessed by multiple methods throughout the program.

codec—A computer technology used to compress and decompress audio and video files.

life cycle—The series of actions from the beginning, or birth, of an Activity to its end, or destruction.

local variable—A variable declared by a variable declaration statement within a method.

MediaPlayer class—The Java class that provides the methods to control audio playback on an Android device.

onDestroy( ) method—A method used to end an Activity. Whereas the onCreate( ) method sets up required resources, the onDestroy( ) method releases those same resources to free up memory.

scope—The scope of a variable refers to the variable's visibility within a class.

state—A stage in an Activity's life cycle that determines whether the Activity is active, paused, stopped, or dead.

thread—A single sequential flow of control within a program.

Timer—A Java class that creates a timed event when the schedule method is called.

timer—A tool that performs a one-time task such as displaying an opening splash screen, or performs a continuous process such as a morning wake-up call set to run at regular intervals.

TimerTask—A Java class that invokes a scheduled timer.

Visibility property—The Java property that controls whether a control is displayed on the emulator.

Developer FAQs

1. What is the name of the initial window that typically displays a company logo for a few seconds?

2. Which property of TextView displays a solid color behind the text?

3. Which property of TextView displays an image as a backdrop behind the text?

4. Write a line of code that creates an instance of the TimerTask class with the object named welcome.

5. Write a line of code that creates an instance of the Timer class with the object named stopwatch.

6. Write a line of code that would hold the initial opening screen for four seconds. The Timer object is named stopwatch and the TimerTask object is named welcome.

7. How long (identify units) does this statement schedule a pause in the execution?

   ```
   logo.schedule(trial, 3);
   ```

8. Write a line of code that closes the resources of the existing Activity.

9. Typically, which method begins an Activity?

10. Typically, which method releases the resources used within an Activity and ends the Activity?

11. What are the four states of an Activity?

12. Which method follows an onPause( ) method?

13. Write two statements that initialize the media player necessary to create an instance of a file named blues residing in your raw folder. Name the variable mpJazz.

14. Write a statement that is needed to begin the song playing from question 13.

15. Write a statement that is needed to pause the song playing from question 14.

16. Write a statement that is needed to change the text on a button named btJazz to the text Pause Unforgettable.

17. Write a statement that hides the button in question 16.

18. What is the name of the folder that typically holds media files in the Android project?

19. Why are class variables sometimes used instead of local variables?

20. What is the most common extension for a song played on an Android device?

Beyond the Book

Using the Internet, search the Web for the answers to the following questions to further your Android knowledge.

1. Research the four most common music file types played on an Android device. Write a paragraph about each music file type. Compare the file size, music quality, and usage of each file type.

2. Using a typical weather app as an example, describe the Android life cycle using each of the methods and a process that happens within the weather app. (*Hint*: See the example using the camera app in the chapter.)

3. At the Android Market, research five music apps. Write a paragraph on the name, features, and purpose of each app.

4. The MediaPlayer class has a method named seekTo( ). Research the purpose of this method.

Case Programming Projects

Complete one or more of the following case programming projects. Use the same steps and techniques taught within the chapter. Submit the program you create to your instructor. The level of difficulty is indicated for each case programming project.

Easiest: ★

Intermediate: ★★

Challenging: ★★★

Case Project 6–1: Rhythm of the Strings App ⋆

Requirements Document

Application title: Rhythm of the Strings App

Purpose: A music app compares the music types of different string instruments.

Algorithms: 1. A splash screen opens displaying the strings.png image with the title "Rhythm of the Strings" for four seconds (Figure 6-31).

   2. Two types of string music are available in this app. A country song named country.mp3 can be played while displaying an image of a banjo. A second selection of a violin plays sonata.mp3 while displaying an image of a violin (Figure 6-32).

Conditions: 1. The pictures of the two string instruments (banjo and violin) and the two music files are provided with your student files.

   2. The music should be played and paused by a button control. When a song is playing, the other button should not be displayed.

Figure 6-31

Figure 6-32

Case Project 6–2: Guitar Solo App ★

Requirements Document

Application title:	Guitar Solo App
Purpose:	A new guitar performance artist needs an Android app to demo her talent.
Algorithms:	1. The opening screen displays the text "Solo Guitar Demo" and an image of a guitar (Figure 6-33).
	2. A second screen displays the guitar image and a button. When the user selects the Play Guitar Solo button, a guitar solo plays.
Conditions:	1. The opening screen is displayed for three seconds.
	2. Design a layout similar to Figure 6-34.
	3. The song can be paused by the user and restarted.

Figure 6-33

Figure 6-34

Case Project 6–3: Serenity Sounds App ★★

Requirements Document

Application title:	Serenity Sounds App
Purpose:	A relaxation app provides songs to allow you to breathe deeply and meditate.
Algorithms:	1. An opening screen displays an image of a relaxing location.
	2. The second screen displays two song names with a description about each song. A button is available that plays each song or pauses each song.
Conditions:	1. An opening image is provided named relax.png in the student files.
	2. Listen to each song and create your own description of each song.
	3. When a song is playing, the other button should not be displayed. Each song can play and pause on the user's selection.

Case Project 6–4: Sleep Machine App ★★

Requirements Document

Application title:	Sleep Machine App
Purpose:	The Sleep Machine app plays sounds of the ocean and a babbling brook to help you sleep.
Algorithms:	1. The opening screen displays an image and the title Sleep Machine for four seconds.
	2. The second screen displays two buttons with two images that allow the user to select ocean sounds or babbling brook sounds for restful sleeping.
Conditions:	1. Select your own images and sound effects located on free audio Web sites.
	2. When a sound effect is playing, the other button should not be displayed. Each sound effect can play and pause on the user's selection.

Case Project 6–5: Ring Tones App ★★★

Requirements Document

Application title:	Ring Tones App
Purpose:	The Ring Tones app allows you to listen to three different ring tones available using RadioButton controls for selection.
Algorithms:	1. Create an app that opens with a mobile phone picture and a title for three seconds.
	2. The second screen shows three RadioButton controls displaying different ring tone titles and a description of each ring tone.
Conditions:	1. Select your own images and free ring tones available by searching the Web.
	2. When a ring tone is playing, the other buttons should not be displayed. Each ring tone can play and pause on the user's selection.

Case Project 6–6: Your Personal Playlist App ★★★

Requirements Document

Application title:	Your Personal Playlist App
Purpose:	Get creative! Play your favorite three songs on your own personal playlist app.
Algorithms:	1. Create an app that opens with your own picture and a title for six seconds.
	2. The second screen shows three buttons displaying different song titles and an image of the artist or group.
Conditions:	1. Select your own images and music files.
	2. When a song is playing, the other buttons should not be displayed. Each song can play and pause on the user's selection.

Reveal! Displaying Pictures in a Gallery

In this chapter, you learn to:

◎ Create an Android project using a Gallery control

◎ Add a Gallery to display a horizontal list of images

◎ Reference images through an array

◎ Create an ImageAdapter class

◎ Code an OnItemClickListener

◎ Display a custom toast message

◎ Define a Context resource

◎ Understand the use of constructors

◎ Return a value from a method

◎ Determine the length of an array

◎ Assign an ImageView control using setImageResource

◎ Change the scale and layout size of the Gallery

Using multimedia within an Android program brings personality and imagery to your app. Images are a powerful marketing tool and add visual appeal to any Android application, but it is essential to create a clean, professional effect with those images. To meet this goal, Android provides a layout tool called a Gallery view that shows items in a center-locked, horizontally scrolling list.

To demonstrate the visual appeal of a Gallery, you will design a Gallery control displaying animals on the endangered species list. The Endangered Species application shown in Figure 7-1 allows users to select the animal they want to symbolically adopt and contribute funds for support groups that work to protect these iconic animals. Users can then scroll the image Gallery by flicking their fingers across a horizontal listing of thumbnail-sized pictures of the endangered animals. To view a larger image, users can tap a thumbnail to display a full-size image below the horizontal list.

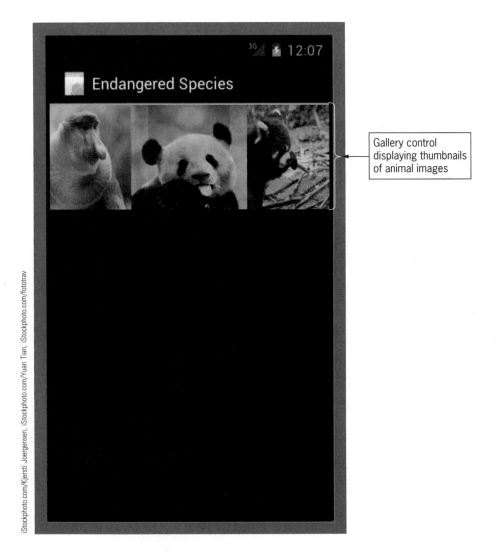

Gallery control displaying thumbnails of animal images

Figure 7-1   Endangered Species Android app

The Android app in Figure 7-1 is more visually appealing than one that simply displays images of the six endangered species in a tiled layout or grid view. The Endangered Species app also provides an easy way for a donor to select an animal to symbolically adopt. The app displays six different animals on the endangered species list, or animals at risk of becoming extinct. The images include an Asian elephant, mountain gorilla, snow leopard, proboscis monkey, giant panda, and red panda. When a user scrolls through the Gallery and selects the snow leopard, for example, a larger image is displayed with a toast message stating "You have selected picture 3 of the endangered species," as shown in Figure 7-2. A different image is displayed each time the user selects another thumbnail in the Gallery.

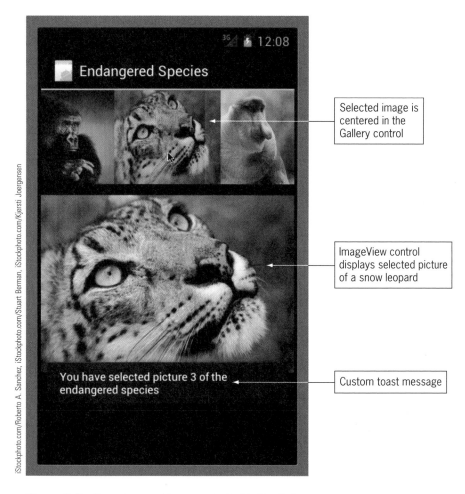

Figure 7-2 Snow Leopard image selected in the Gallery

GTK
A Gallery of images is typically used to select a wallpaper image for the background of an Android device.

To create this application, the developer must understand how to perform the following processes, among others:

1. Add a Gallery control to the emulator.

2. Add XML code for an ImageView control not linked to a particular image.

3. Place six images in a drawable folder.

4. Define an array to hold the image files.

5. Instantiate the Gallery and ImageView controls.

6. Create an ImageAdapter class.

7. Display a custom toast message.

8. Display the selected image.

9. Customize the ImageAdapter class.

10. Define the layout using the getView( ) method.

Adding a Gallery Control

The Endangered Species app opens with a horizontal scrolling list of animal pictures in a View container called a Gallery, as shown in Figure 7-1. A **View** container is a rectangular area of the screen that displays an image or text object. A View container can include layouts such as Gallery, GridView, ScrollView, ImageSwitcher, TabHost, and ListView. In Chapter 5, you used the ListView layout to create a vertical list of San Francisco attractions. In the Endangered Species project, the **Gallery** View container displays a horizontal list of objects with the center item displaying the current image. The user can move through the horizontal list by scrolling either to the left or the right. The Gallery of photos can be sized as small as thumbnail images or as large as full-screen images. The photos can be stored in the drawable folders, in your phone's storage, or even on a Web site such as Picasa.

The Gallery control is a widget in the Images & Media category of the Palette. The default id for the Gallery widget is gallery1. To add a Gallery control to main.xml, follow these steps to begin the application:

1. Open the Eclipse program. Click the New button on the Standard toolbar. Expand the Android folder and select Android Project. Click the Next button. In the New Android Project dialog box, enter the Project Name **Endangered Species**. To save the project on your USB drive, click to remove the check mark from the Use default location check box. Type **E:\Workspace** (if necessary, enter a different drive letter

that identifies the USB drive). Click the Next button. For the Build Target, select Android 4.0, if necessary. Click the Next button. For the Package Name, type **net.androidbootcamp.endangeredspecies**. Enter **Main** in the Create Activity text box.

The new Android Endangered Species project has an Application Name, a Package Name, and an Activity named Main (Figure 7-3).

Figure 7-3 Application information for the Endangered Species project

2. Click the Finish button. Expand the Endangered Species project in the Package Explorer. In the res\layout folder, double-click main.xml. Delete the Hello World, Main! TextView control from the emulator. In the Images & Media category of the Palette, drag the Gallery control to the emulator.

The Gallery control appears at the top of the emulator (Figure 7-4).

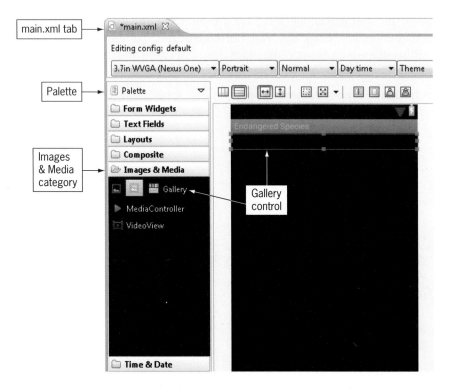

Figure 7-4   Gallery control

Adding the ImageView Control and Image Files

In the Endangered Species chapter project, the Gallery control displays a horizontal list of six thumbnail-sized animal photos stored in the drawable-hdpi folder. When the user taps one of these images, a full-size image appears in an ImageView control below the Gallery control, as shown in Figure 7-2. Typically, you add an ImageView control by dragging the control onto the emulator. A dialog box automatically opens requesting which image file in the drawable folders should be displayed. In the case of the chapter project, an image appears in the ImageView only if the user taps the thumbnail image in the Gallery. Otherwise, no image should appear in the ImageView control. To prevent an image from being assigned to (and displayed in) the ImageView control, you must enter the XML code for the ImageView control in the main.xml file. To add the XML code for the ImageView control named imgAnimal and add the six image files to the drawable folder, follow these steps:

1. Click the main.xml tab at the bottom of the window to display the XML code. By default, LinearLayout is set, followed by the code for the Gallery control. On the line below the last line of the Gallery XML code, press the Enter key to insert a blank line and type the following custom XML code on Line 12 using auto-completion as much as possible:

\<ImageView

   android:id="@+id/imgAnimal"

   android:layout_width="wrap_content"

   android:layout_height="wrap_content" />

The ImageView control is coded in the main.xml file (Figure 7-5).

```
 1  <?xml version="1.0" encoding="utf-8"?>
 2  <LinearLayout xmlns:android="http://schemas.android
 3      android:layout_width="fill_parent"
 4      android:layout_height="fill_parent"
 5      android:orientation="vertical" >
 6
 7      <Gallery
 8          android:id="@+id/gallery1"
 9          android:layout_width="match_parent"
10          android:layout_height="wrap_content" />
11
12      <ImageView
13          android:id="@+id/imgAnimal"
14          android:layout_width="wrap_content"
15          android:layout_height="wrap_content" />
16
17
18  </LinearLayout>
```

ImageView
XML code

Figure 7-5   ImageView XML code

2.   To add the six image files to the drawable folder, if necessary, copy the student files to your USB drive. Open the USB folder containing the student files. In the Package Explorer, expand the drawable-hdpi folder in the res folder. Delete the file named ic_launcher.png (the Android logo). To add the six image files to the drawable-hdpi resource folder, drag the elephant.png, gorilla.png, leopard.png, monkey.png, panda.png, and redpanda.png files to the drawable-hdpi folder until a plus sign pointer appears. Release the mouse button. If necessary, click the Copy files option button, and then click the OK button.

Copies of the six files appear in the drawable-hdpi folder (Figure 7-6).

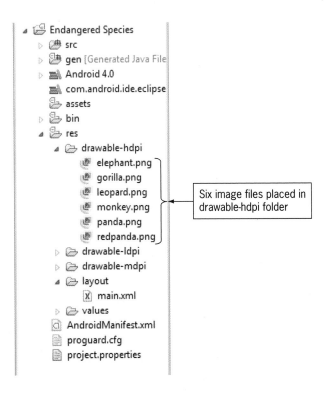

Figure 7-6   Images copied

IN THE TRENCHES
If you are creating an Android application that can be installed on a variety of Android platforms, it is best to create high-, medium-, and low-density photos. Typically, you should provide alternative layouts for some of the different screen sizes and alternative bitmap images for different screen densities. At runtime, the system uses the appropriate resources for your application based on the generalized size or density of the current device screen.

Creating an Array for the Images

Before the images can be displayed in the Gallery control, the images in the drawable folder must be referenced in the code and assigned to an array. By using an array variable, which can store more than one value, you can avoid assigning a separate variable for each image in the folder. Arrays provide access to data by using a numeric index, or subscript, to identify each element in the array. In the chapter project, the images are assigned to an integer array named Animals and each image is associated with an integer value. For example, the first image of the elephant is assigned to the subscript of 0, as shown in Table 7-1. Typically an array is used to assign values to a Gallery control that has multiple items.

Element of Array	Image File
Animals[0]	elephant.png
Animals[1]	gorilla.png
Animals[2]	leopard.png
Animals[3]	monkey.png
Animals[4]	panda.png
Animals[5]	redpanda.png

Table 7-1 Animals array

233

In Main.java, the Animals array and ImageView control are declared as class-level variables because they are referenced in multiple methods throughout the application. Recall that class-level variables are accessed from anywhere within a Java class. The array is available throughout the entire Activity. To declare the Animals array and ImageView control in Main.java, follow these steps:

1. Save your work and then close the main.xml tab. Expand the src and net.androidbootcamp.endangeredspecies folders, and then double-click Main.java to open its code window. Click at the end of the public class Main extends Activity { line, press the Enter key, and type the following code to create the Animals array using auto-completion as much as possible:

   Integer[] Animals = { R.drawable.elephant, R.drawable.gorilla, R.drawable.leopard, R.drawable.monkey, R.drawable.panda, R.drawable.redpanda };

   The Animals array references the images stored in the drawable folder (Figure 7-7).

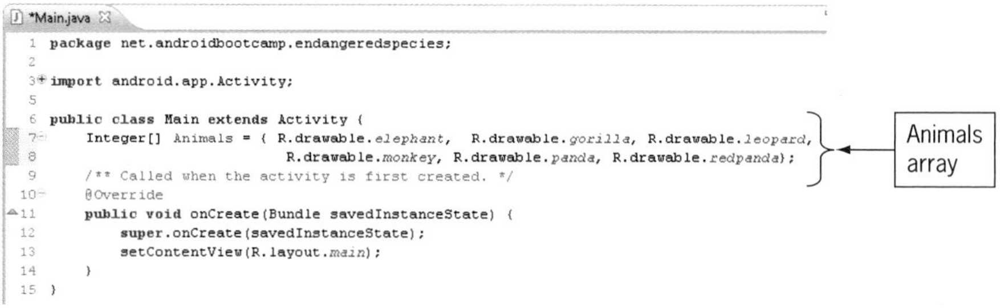

Figure 7-7 Animals array declared

2. Press the Enter key. To declare ImageView as a class variable, type **ImageView imageView;**, point to ImageView, and then click Import 'ImageView' (android.widget). Press the Enter key.

ImageView is referenced as a class variable (Figure 7-8).

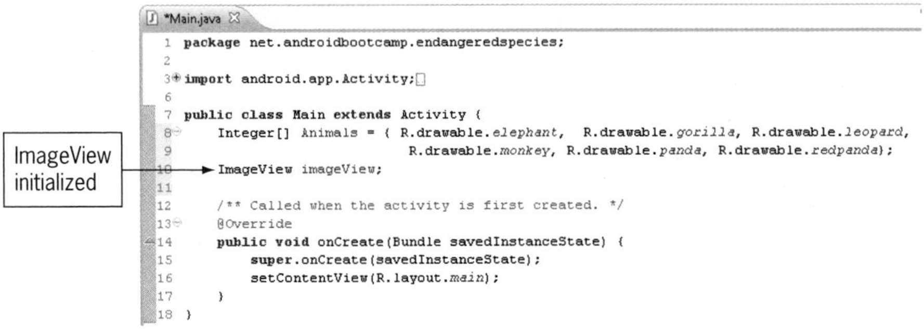

```
*Main.java ⊠
  1  package net.androidbootcamp.endangeredspecies;
  2
  3⊕ import android.app.Activity;☐
  6
  7  public class Main extends Activity {
  8⊝     Integer[] Animals = { R.drawable.elephant,   R.drawable.gorilla, R.drawable.leopard,
  9                          R.drawable.monkey, R.drawable.panda, R.drawable.redpanda);
 10     ImageView imageView;
 11
 12     /** Called when the activity is first created. */
 13⊝     @Override
⊸14     public void onCreate(Bundle savedInstanceState) {
 15         super.onCreate(savedInstanceState);
 16         setContentView(R.layout.main);
 17     }
 18  }
```

ImageView initialized →

Figure 7-8   ImageView referenced

Instantiating the Gallery and ImageView Controls

The Gallery and ImageView controls in main.xml must be instantiated in the onCreate( ) method of Main.java. The first Gallery control in a project is named gallery1 by default. The code to instantiate the Gallery assigns the control created in main.xml the name gallery1, as shown in the following code syntax:

Code Syntax

```
Gallery ga = (Gallery)findViewById(R.id.gallery1);
```

To instantiate the Gallery and ImageView controls, follow these steps:

1. To instantiate the Gallery, in the onCreate( ) method of Main.java, click at the end of the setContentView(R.layout.main); line, press the Enter key, type **Gallery ga = (Gallery)findViewById(R.id.gallery1);**, point to Gallery, and then click Import 'Gallery' (android.widget).

   The Gallery control is instantiated (Figure 7-9).

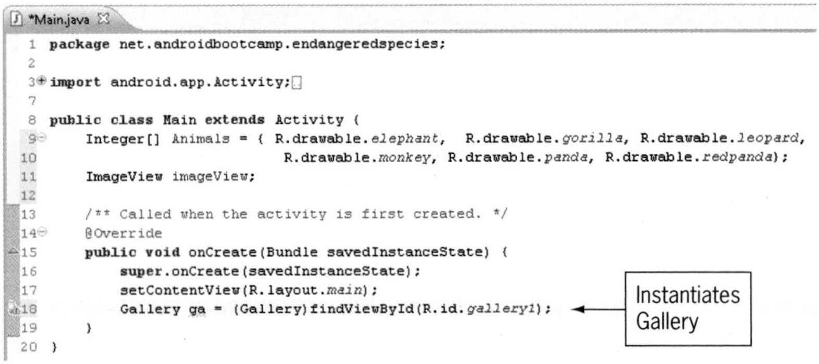

```
*Main.java ⊠
  1  package net.androidbootcamp.endangeredspecies;
  2
  3⊕ import android.app.Activity;☐
  7
  8  public class Main extends Activity {
  9⊝     Integer[] Animals = { R.drawable.elephant,   R.drawable.gorilla, R.drawable.leopard,
 10                          R.drawable.monkey, R.drawable.panda, R.drawable.redpanda);
 11     ImageView imageView;
 12
 13     /** Called when the activity is first created. */
 14⊝     @Override
⊸15     public void onCreate(Bundle savedInstanceState) {
 16         super.onCreate(savedInstanceState);
 17         setContentView(R.layout.main);
 18         Gallery ga = (Gallery)findViewById(R.id.gallery1);
 19     }
 20  }
```

Instantiates Gallery ←

Figure 7-9   Gallery control is instantiated

2. Press the Enter key. To instantiate the ImageView that is assigned as a class variable, type **imageView = (ImageView)findViewById(R.id.imgAnimal);**.

The ImageView control is instantiated (Figure 7-10).

```
*Main.java
 1  package net.androidbootcamp.endangeredspecies;
 2
 3 +import android.app.Activity;
 7
 8  public class Main extends Activity {
 9      Integer[] Animals = { R.drawable.elephant, R.drawable.gorilla, R.drawable.leopard,
10                            R.drawable.monkey, R.drawable.panda, R.drawable.redpanda};
11      ImageView imageView;
12
13      /** Called when the activity is first created. */
14      @Override
15      public void onCreate(Bundle savedInstanceState) {
16          super.onCreate(savedInstanceState);
17          setContentView(R.layout.main);
18          Gallery ga = (Gallery)findViewById(R.id.gallery1);
19          imageView = (ImageView)findViewById(R.id.imgAnimal);        Instantiates
20      }                                                                ImageView
21  }
22
```

Figure 7-10 ImageView control is instantiated

IN THE TRENCHES

Another type of View control called GridView displays items in a two-dimensional, scrollable grid. For example, an app can display three rows of four images each in a grid to represent the top 12 selling Android phones on the market, and then users can scroll over the grid to select an image of their favorite phone. If more phone images are added to the grid, the GridView control automatically becomes scrollable, allowing users to view every image in the grid.

Using a setAdapter with an ImageAdapter

In Chapter 5, an adapter was used to display a ListView control. Similarly, a **setAdapter** provides a data model for the Gallery layout. The Gallery data model functions as a photo gallery in touch mode. The following code syntax shows how to instantiate a custom BaseAdapter class called ImageAdapter and apply it to the Gallery using setAdapter( ):

Code Syntax

```
ga.setAdapter(new ImageAdapter(this));
```

After the ImageAdapter is instantiated, the ImageAdapter class must be added to extend the custom BaseAdapter class. Using controls such as the Gallery, ListView, and Spinner, the adapter binds specific types of data and displays that data in a particular layout. To instantiate the ImageAdapter class for the Gallery control, follow these steps:

1. Press the Enter key and type **ga.setAdapter(new ImageAdapter(this));**. A red error line appears under ImageAdapter. Instead of automatically creating the class, a custom ImageAdapter class is added in the next step.

    The ImageAdapter is coded for the Gallery control. A red error line appears below ImageAdapter (Figure 7-11).

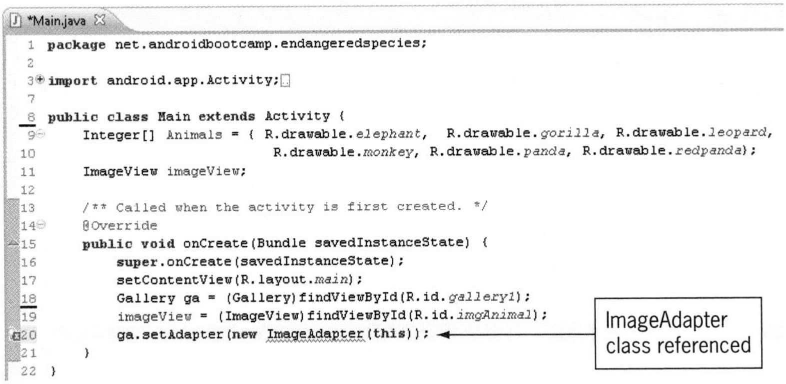

```
*Main.java

 1   package net.androidbootcamp.endangeredspecies;
 2
 3⊕  import android.app.Activity;
 7
 8   public class Main extends Activity {
 9⊖      Integer[] Animals = { R.drawable.elephant,  R.drawable.gorilla, R.drawable.leopard,
10                            R.drawable.monkey, R.drawable.panda,  R.drawable.redpanda};
11       ImageView imageView;
12
13       /** Called when the activity is first created. */
14⊖      @Override
15       public void onCreate(Bundle savedInstanceState) {
16           super.onCreate(savedInstanceState);
17           setContentView(R.layout.main);
18           Gallery ga = (Gallery)findViewById(R.id.gallery1);
19           imageView = (ImageView)findViewById(R.id.imgAnimal);
20           ga.setAdapter(new ImageAdapter(this));          ImageAdapter
21       }                                                   class referenced
22   }
```

Figure 7-11   Instance of the ImageAdapter class

2. To add an ImageAdapter class that extends the BaseAdapter custom class, click after the first closing brace at the end of the code. Press the Enter key and type **public class ImageAdapter extends BaseAdapter {** . Press the Enter key, and a closing brace appears. Point to BaseAdapter and click Import 'BaseAdapter' (android.widget). Point to ImageAdapter in the same line and click Add unimplemented methods. Point to ImageAdapter in the ga.setAdapter(new ImageAdapter (this)); line and select Create constructor 'ImageAdapter(Main)'.

    The ImageAdapter class is coded (Figure 7-12). The methods within the ImageAdapter are auto-generated.

```
⌐ Main.java ⌐
   1  package net.androidbootcamp.endangeredspecies;
   2
   3⊕ import android.app.Activity;☐
  10
  11  public class Main extends Activity {
  12      Integer[] Animals = { R.drawable.elephant,  R.drawable.gorilla, R.drawable.leopard,
  13                            R.drawable.monkey, R.drawable.panda, R.drawable.redpanda);
  14      ImageView imageView;
  15
  16      /** Called when the activity is first created. */
  17      @Override
▲ 18      public void onCreate(Bundle savedInstanceState) {
  19          super.onCreate(savedInstanceState);
  20          setContentView(R.layout.main);
  21          Gallery ga = (Gallery)findViewById(R.id.gallery1);
  22          imageView = (ImageView)findViewById(R.id.imgAnimal);
  23          ga.setAdapter(new ImageAdapter(this));
  24      }
  25      public class ImageAdapter extends BaseAdapter{
  26
  27          public ImageAdapter(Main main) {
  28              // TODO Auto-generated constructor stub
  29          }
  30
  31          @Override
  32          public int getCount() {
  33              // TODO Auto-generated method stub
  34              return 0;
  35          }
  36
  37          @Override
  38          public Object getItem(int arg0) {
  39              // TODO Auto-generated method stub
  40              return null;
  41          }
  42
  43          @Override
  44          public long getItemId(int arg0) {
  45              // TODO Auto-generated method stub
  46              return 0;
  47          }
  48
  49          @Override
  50          public View getView(int arg0, View arg1, ViewGroup arg2) {
  51              // TODO Auto-generated method stub
  52              return null;
  53          }
  54      }
  55  }
```

ImageAdapter class added

Auto-generated methods

Figure 7-12 ImageAdapter class

Coding the OnItemClickListener

Like the OnClickListener used for a Button control in previous chapter projects, the OnItemClickListener awaits user interaction within the Gallery control. When the user touches the Gallery display layout, the OnItemClickListener processes an event called onItemClick. The **onItemClick** method defined by OnItemClickListener provides a number of arguments, which are listed in the parentheses included in the line of code. All three controls—ListView, GridView, and Gallery—enable the Android device to monitor for click events using the OnItemClickListener and onItemClick commands. The following code syntax shows how to use onItemClick in the chapter project.

Code Syntax

```
ga.setOnItemClickListener(new OnItemClickListener() {
  @Override
    public void onItemClick(AdapterView<?> arg0,
      View arg1, int arg2, long arg3) {

   }
}
```

In this code syntax example, ga is the instance of the Gallery control. The OnItemClickListener executes the onItemClick method as soon as the user touches the Gallery control. The onItemClick method has four arguments. Table 7-2 describes the role of the four arguments in the onItemClick method.

Argument	Purpose
AdapterView<?> arg0	The AdapterView records "where" the user actually touched the screen in the argument variable arg0. In other words, if the app has more than one View control, the AdapterView determines if the user touched this Gallery control or another control in the application.
View arg1	The View parameter is the specific View within the item that the user touched. This is the View provided by the adapter.
int arg2	This is one of the most important portions of this statement in the chapter project. The arg2 argument is an integer value that holds the position of the View in the adapter. For example, if the user taps the gorilla picture, the integer value of 2 is stored in arg2 because the gorilla picture is the second image in the Animals array.
long arg3	The Gallery control is displayed across one row of the Android device. The argument arg3 determines the row id of the item that was selected by the user. This is especially useful for a GridView control that has multiple rows in the layout.

Table 7-2   Arguments in the onItemClick method

Users can change their minds more than once when selecting picture images in the Gallery. The onItemClick method responds an unlimited number of times throughout the life of the class based on the user's interaction with the Gallery control. To code the OnItemClickListener and onItemClick method, follow these steps:

1. In Main.java, press the Enter key after the ga.setAdapter command line. To set up the OnItemClickListener, type **ga.setOnItemClickListener(new OnItemClickListener() {**. Press the Enter key, and a closing brace appears. A red error line appears under OnItemClickListener. Point to OnItemClickListener and import the 'OnItemClickListener' (android.widget.AdapterView). After the closing brace, type a closing parenthesis and a semicolon to complete the statement.

The Gallery OnItemClickListener awaits user interaction. A red error line appears below OnItemClickListener (Figure 7-13).

```
*Main.java ⊠
 1  package net.androidbootcamp.endangeredspecies;
 2
 3⊕ import android.app.Activity;☐
11
12  public class Main extends Activity {
13⊖     Integer[] Animals = { R.drawable.elephant,  R.drawable.gorilla, R.drawable.leopard,
14                           R.drawable.monkey, R.drawable.panda, R.drawable.redpanda};
15      ImageView imageView;
16
17      /** Called when the activity is first created. */
18⊖     @Override
19      public void onCreate(Bundle savedInstanceState) {
20          super.onCreate(savedInstanceState);
21          setContentView(R.layout.main);
22          Gallery ga = (Gallery)findViewById(R.id.gallery1);
23          imageView = (ImageView)findViewById(R.id.imgAnimal);
24          ga.setAdapter(new ImageAdapter(this));
25⊖         ga.setOnItemClickListener(new OnItemClickListener() {
26
27          });
28      }
29⊖     public class ImageAdapter extends BaseAdapter{
30
```

Closing brace, parenthesis, and semicolon

OnItemClickListener( )

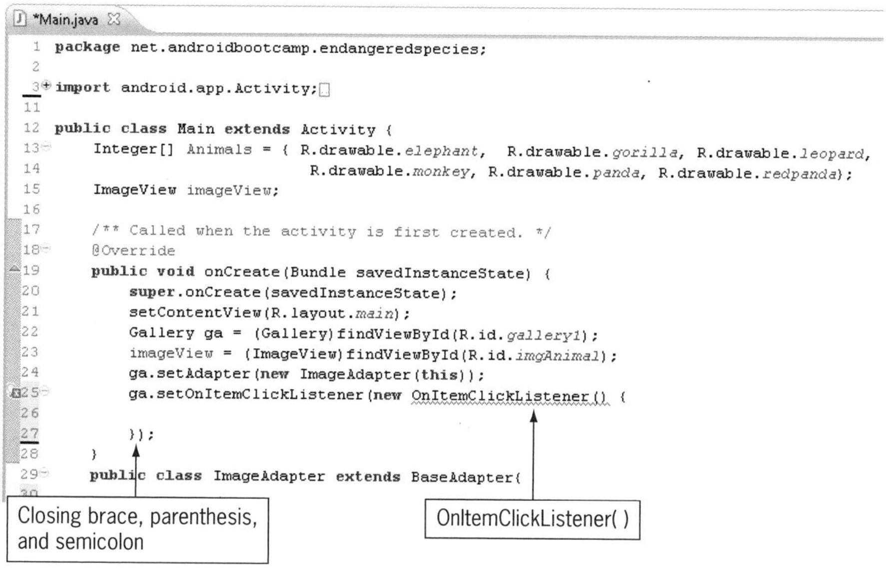

Figure 7-13 Gallery OnItemClickListener

2. To add the onItemClick method within the OnItemClickListener, point to the red error line under the OnItemClickListener and select Add unimplemented methods.

The onItemClick method stub appears automatically (Figure 7-14).

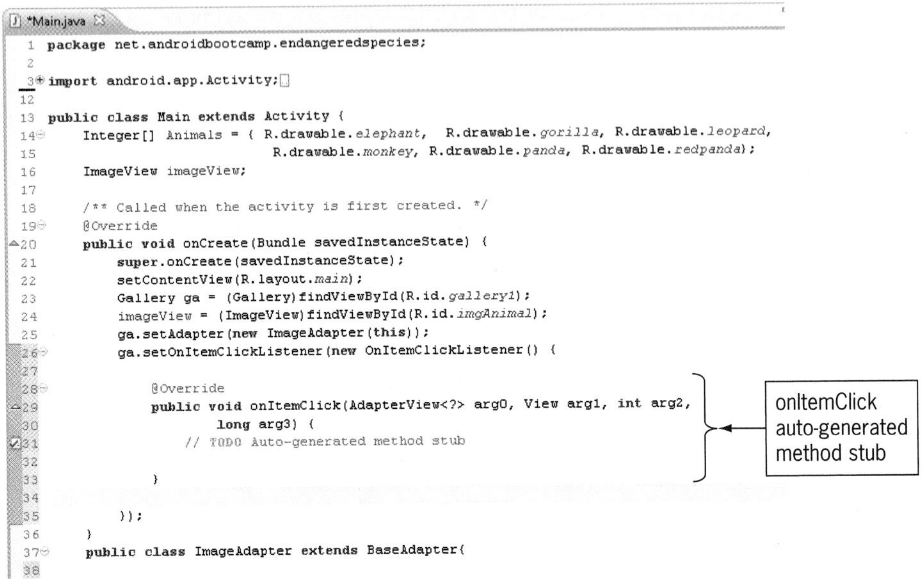

240

```
1  package net.androidbootcamp.endangeredspecies;
2
3⊕ import android.app.Activity;□
12
13  public class Main extends Activity {
14⊖     Integer[] Animals = ( R.drawable.elephant,  R.drawable.gorilla, R.drawable.leopard,
15                           R.drawable.monkey, R.drawable.panda, R.drawable.redpanda);
16      ImageView imageView;
17
18      /** Called when the activity is first created. */
19⊖     @Override
20      public void onCreate(Bundle savedInstanceState) {
21          super.onCreate(savedInstanceState);
22          setContentView(R.layout.main);
23          Gallery ga = (Gallery)findViewById(R.id.gallery1);
24          imageView = (ImageView)findViewById(R.id.imgAnimal);
25          ga.setAdapter(new ImageAdapter(this));
26⊖         ga.setOnItemClickListener(new OnItemClickListener() {
27
28⊖             @Override
29             public void onItemClick(AdapterView<?> arg0, View arg1, int arg2,
30                     long arg3) {
31                 // TODO Auto-generated method stub
32
33             }
34
35         });
36      }
37⊖     public class ImageAdapter extends BaseAdapter{
38
```

> onItemClick auto-generated method stub

Figure 7-14   The onItemClick method

Coding a Custom Toast Notification

A toast notification in the Endangered Species program provides feedback as to which animal image is selected. When the toast message is shown to the user, it floats over the application so it will never receive focus. In earlier chapters, you entered a toast notification displaying a temporary message in this form:

`Toast.makeText(Main.this, "A typical Toast message", Toast.LENGTH_SHORT).show();`

In the Endangered Species project, the toast notification message is different in two ways. First, the toast message in the Gallery control appears in the onItemClick method that is executed only when the user makes a selection. Because the toast notification is not used directly in the Main Activity, the reference to Main.this in the toast statement creates an error. To use a toast message within an onItemClick method, considered an AlertDialog class, you must replace Main.this with a Context class called getBaseContext( ). In Android programs, you can place the **getBaseContext( )** method in another method (such as onItemClick) that is triggered only when the user touches the Gallery control. If you do, the getBaseContext( ) method obtains a Context instance.

A second difference is that the toast message includes a variable. The variable indicates which image number is selected in the Animals array. Figure 7-15 shows the message when the user selects the gorilla.

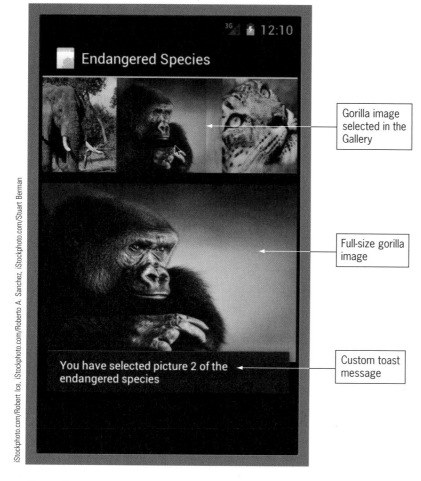

Gorilla image selected in the Gallery

Full-size gorilla image

Custom toast message

iStockphoto.com/Robert Ice, iStockphoto.com/Roberto A. Sanchez, iStockphoto.com/Stuart Berman

Figure 7-15 Toast message displayed when user selects the gorilla image

Notice that even though the gorilla is in position Animals[1], the custom toast message states "You have selected picture 2 of the endangered species". Array position 1 is really the second image because the array values begin with 0. The value of 1 is added in the toast message shown in the following code syntax to the integer position value of arg2. The arg2 argument is an integer value that holds the position number of the View in the adapter that was an argument of the onItemClick( ) method. The position identifies the image placement in the array.

Code Syntax

```
Toast.makeText(getBaseContext(), "You have selected picture " + (arg2 + 1)
                + " of the endangered species", Toast.LENGTH_SHORT).show();
```

To code the custom toast message that includes a getBaseContext( ) method and variables, follow this step:

1. Save your work. In Main.java, click the blank line after the first TODO comment in the code to add the custom toast message. Use auto-completion to type **Toast. makeText(getBaseContext(), "You have selected picture " + (arg2 + 1)** and press the Enter key. Continue typing on the next line: **+ " of the endangered species", Toast.LENGTH_SHORT).show();**. If necessary, import the 'Toast' (android.widget).

The custom toast message provides feedback to the user of his or her picture selection from the Gallery (Figure 7-16).

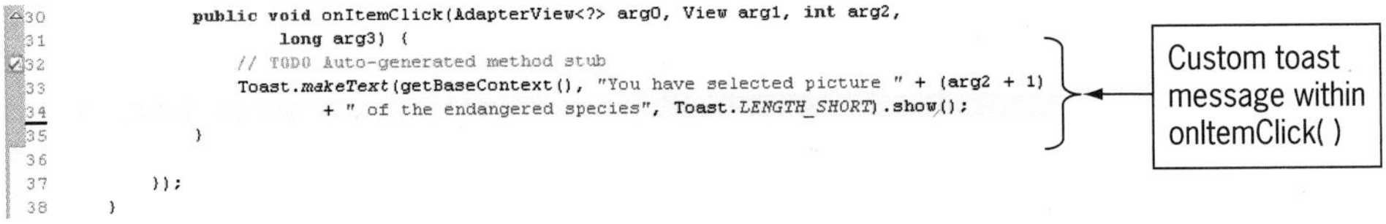

```
30  public void onItemClick(AdapterView<?> arg0, View arg1, int arg2,
31         long arg3) {
32         // TODO Auto-generated method stub
33         Toast.makeText(getBaseContext(), "You have selected picture " + (arg2 + 1)
34             + " of the endangered species", Toast.LENGTH_SHORT).show();
35     }
36
37  });
38  }
```

Custom toast message within onItemClick( )

Figure 7-16   Custom toast message

Displaying the Selected Image

When the user touches an animal picture in the Gallery, a toast message appears with an ImageView control displaying the selected image. The ImageView control was previously coded in main.xml, though a specific image was not selected in the code. Instead, the full-sized picture in the ImageView control should be displayed dynamically to the user. An ImageView control is defined either by the android:src attribute in the XML element or by the setImageResource(int) method. The setImageResource method indicates which image is selected, as shown in the following code syntax:

Code Syntax

```
imageView.setImageResource(Animals[arg2]);
```

Animals is the name of the array and arg2 represents the index of the array. The argument arg2 is defined as the position of the selected image in the Gallery. To assign a picture to the ImageView control, follow this step:

1. In Main.java, click at the end of the line you just entered, if necessary (the second line of the toast statement), and press the Enter key. To display the selected image, type **imageView.setImageResource(Animals[arg2]);**.

The selected image is displayed in the ImageView with the use of setImageResource (Figure 7-17).

```
30    public void onItemClick(AdapterView<?> arg0, View arg1, int arg2,
31         long arg3) {
32        // TODO Auto-generated method stub
33        Toast.makeText(getBaseContext(), "You have selected picture " + (arg2 + 1)
34            + " of the endangered species", Toast.LENGTH_SHORT).show();
35        imageView.setImageResource(Animals[arg2]);
36    }
```

setImageResource
displays the selected
image

Figure 7-17   ImageView control displays selected Gallery picture

IN THE TRENCHES
An image can also be placed on the surface of a Button control by the android:src attribute in the XML code
or by the setImageResource(int) method of a button.

Customizing the ImageAdapter Class

At this point in the chapter project code, the Gallery and ImageView are initialized, the
onClickListener awaits interaction, the toast message and ImageView are prepared for
display, but the ImageAdapter class is simply a set of auto-generated method stubs. The
ImageAdapter class was called with this line of code: ga.setAdapter(new ImageAdapter
(this));. Recall that the ImageAdapter class determines the layout of the Gallery. The context
and images of the Gallery need to be referenced within the ImageAdapter class. The task to
complete inside the ImageAdapter class is to manage the layout of the Gallery and connect
the data sources from the array for display within the Gallery control.

Defining the Context of the ImageAdapter Class

The ImageAdapter class must provide the information to set up the Gallery with data and
specifications necessary for the display. A Context variable is used to load and access resources
for the application. In the following code syntax, the class variable named context is initialized
so it can hold each image in the Gallery temporarily before it is displayed. The ImageAdapter
constructor is changed from Main to handle the Context resources necessary for the Gallery.
Constructors are used to initialize the instance variables of an object. This command is called a
constructor because it constructs the values of data members of the class.

Code Syntax

```
private Context context;
public ImageAdapter(Context c){
    // TODO Auto-generated constructor stub
    context=c;
}
```

This ImageAdapter class constructor is where the Context for an ImageAdapter instance is defined. To define the Context for the ImageAdapter, follow these steps:

1. Save your work. Click the blank line after the public class ImageAdapter extends BaseAdapter { line. Initialize the Context variable by typing **private Context context;**, point to Context, and select Import 'Context' (android.content).

The Context variable named context is initialized (Figure 7-18).

```
39          });
40      }
41⊖    public class ImageAdapter extends BaseAdapter{
 42         private Context context;          ◄──────    context is initialized in
43⊖        public ImageAdapter(Main main){                the ImageAdapter class
 44              // TODO Auto-generated constructor stub
45         }
46
```

Figure 7-18   Context variable

2. To change the ImageAdapter constructor to define the Context in the next statement, change public ImageAdapter(Main main){ on the next line to **public ImageAdapter (Context c) {**. At the end of the TODO comment on the next line, press the Enter key to insert a blank line. Type **context=c;**.

The ImageAdapter constructor for the ImageAdapter class holds the Context (Figure 7-19).

```
39          });
40      }
41⊖    public class ImageAdapter extends BaseAdapter{
 42         private Context context;
43⊖        public ImageAdapter(Context c){    ◄──────    ImageAdapter is
 44              // TODO Auto-generated constructor stub     customized to hold
45              context=c;                                  Context resources
46         }
47
48⊖        @Override
49         public int getCount() {
 50              // TODO Auto-generated method stub
51              return 0;
52         }
```

Figure 7-19   ImageAdapter constructor

Calculating the Length of an Array

The next method in the ImageAdapter class is the getCount( ) method. When the ImageAdapter class is called, the getCount( ) method determines how many pictures should be displayed in the Gallery control. It does so by finding the length of the Animals array, which references the pictures of the endangered species. To determine the length of an array, Java provides a method named length( ) that returns an integer value of any given string or array. For example, if a variable named phone is assigned the text Android, the integer phoneLength is assigned the integer value of 7, representing the length of the word Android.

```
String phone = "Android";
int phoneLength = phone.length( );
```

The length of an array is determined by the number of elements in the array. The length of the Animals array is an integer value of 6. The getCount( ) method must return the number of elements in the Gallery in order to create the correct layout for the Gallery control. To do so, include in the getCount( ) method a return statement as shown in the following code syntax:

Code Syntax

```
return Animals.length;
```

A Java **method** is a series of statements that perform some repeated task. In the case of the chapter project, the method is called within the ImageAdapter class. The purpose of the getCount( ) method is to return the number of elements in the array. You declare a method's return type in its method declaration. In the following syntax, the declaration statement public int getCount( ) includes int. The data type int indicates that the return data type is an integer. Within the body of the method, you use the return statement to return the value. Any method declared void does not return a value because it returns to the method normally. Therefore, no return statement is necessary. Any method that is not declared void must contain a return statement with a corresponding return value such as the length of an array.

Code Syntax

```
public int getCount() {
    // TODO Auto-generated constructor stub
    return Animals.length;
}
```

To return the length of an array from the getCount( ) method, follow this step:

1. In the return statement for public int getCount( ), change the return type from return 0; to return **Animals.length;**.

    The getCount( ) method returns the length of the Animals array (Figure 7-20).

CHAPTER 7   Reveal! Displaying Pictures in a Gallery

246

```
41    public class ImageAdapter extends BaseAdapter{
42        private Context context;
43        public ImageAdapter(Context c){
44            // TODO Auto-generated constructor stub
45            context=c;
46        }
47
48        @Override
49        public int getCount() {
50            // TODO Auto-generated method stub
51            return Animals.length;
52        }
53
```

Returns the length of the Animals array

Figure 7-20   Length of the Animals array

GTK
The length of an array is one more than the maximum subscript number.

Coding the getView Method

The most powerful method in the ImageAdapter class is the getView( ) method. The getView( ) method uses Context to create a new ImageView instance that temporarily holds each image displayed in the Gallery. In addition, the ImageView is scaled to fit the Gallery control and sized according to a custom height and width. The following code syntax shows how the chapter project uses the getView( ) method:

Code Syntax

```
public View getView(int arg0, View arg1, ViewGroup arg2){
        // TODO Auto-generated method stub
        ImageView pic = new ImageView(context);
        pic.setImageResource(Animals[arg0]);
        pic.setScaleType(ImageView.ScaleType.FIT_XY);
        pic.setLayoutParams(new Gallery.LayoutParams(200,175));
        return pic;
}
```

In the getView( ) method, notice that a return type of View is expected (in the View convertView argument). Recall that a View occupies a rectangular area on the screen and is responsible for drawing the Gallery component. When pic is returned at the end of the method, it includes a scaled, resized image, ready to display in the Gallery control.

In the getView( ) method, an instance of an ImageView control named pic is established in the ImageView pic = new ImageView(context); Java code. On the next line, pic is given an image to display in the Gallery as defined by a position in the Animals array. As each position is passed to the getView( ) method, the ImageView control changes to hold each of the images referenced in the Animals array. The setImageResource method assigns an image from the drawable folder to the ImageView control. After an animal picture is assigned to pic, the layout of the ImageView control needs to be established. In the next statement, setScaleType scales the image to the bounds of the ImageView. Scaling keeps or changes the aspect ratio of the image within the ImageView control. When an image is scaled, the aspect ratio is changed; for example, the picture may be stretched horizontally, but not vertically. Notice that the ScaleType is set to the option FIT_XY. Several ScaleType options are available, but the most popular options are listed in Table 7-3.

ScaleType option	Meaning
ImageView.ScaleType.CENTER	This option centers the image within the View type, but does not change the aspect ratio (no scaling).
ImageView.ScaleType.CENTER_CROP	This option centers the image within the View type and scales the image uniformly, maintaining the same aspect ratio.
ImageView.ScaleType.FIT_XY	This option scales the image to fit the View type. The aspect ratio is changed to fit within the control.

Table 7-3   Popular ScaleType options

After the image is scaled, the Gallery images are resized to fit the custom layout. The design of the Endangered Species app calls for small thumbnail-sized images, so the setLayoutParams are set to the Gallery.LayoutParams(200,175). The first value, 200, represents the number of pixels across the width of the image. The second value, 175, determines a height of 175 pixels. If you want to display a large Gallery, the setLayoutParams can be changed to larger dimensions. The last statement in the getView( ) method (return pic;) must return the instance of the ImageView control named pic to display in the Gallery control. To code the getView( ) method, follow these steps:

1. Scroll down to the statement beginning with public View getView. Click at the end of the TODO comment and press the Enter key to insert a blank line. To create an ImageView control that holds the images displayed in the Gallery, type **ImageView pic = new ImageView(context);**.

    An instance of ImageView named pic is created (Figure 7-21).

```
61      public long getItemId(int arg0) {
62          // TODO Auto-generated method stub
63          return 0;
64      }
65
66      @Override
67      public View getView(int arg0, View arg1, ViewGroup arg2) {
68          // TODO Auto-generated method stub
69          ImageView pic = new ImageView(context);   ◀────── pic in this statement
70          return null;                                        is an instance of
71      }                                                       ImageView
72  }
73  }
```

Figure 7-21   Code for the ImageView control

2. Press the Enter key. To assign each of the images referenced in the Animals array, type **pic.setImageResource(Animals[arg0]);**.

The instance of pic holds each of the images within the array (Figure 7-22).

```
67   public View getView(int arg0, View arg1, ViewGroup arg2) {
68       // TODO Auto-generated method stub
69       ImageView pic = new ImageView(context);
70       pic.setImageResource(Animals[arg0]);
71       return null;
72   }
```

Each image referenced in the Animals array is displayed in pic

Figure 7-22   Assigning images in the Animals array to the pic ImageView control

3. Press the Enter key. To set the scale type of the ImageView control, type **pic.setScaleType(ImageView.ScaleType.FIT_XY);**.

The scale type for the ImageView pic is set to FIT_XY (Figure 7-23).

```
67   public View getView(int arg0, View arg1, ViewGroup arg2) {
68       // TODO Auto-generated method stub
69       ImageView pic = new ImageView(context);
70       pic.setImageResource(Animals[arg0]);
71       pic.setScaleType(ImageView.ScaleType.FIT_XY);
72       return null;
73   }
```

ImageView control is scaled to fit

Figure 7-23   Setting the scale type for the ImageView control

4. Press the Enter key. To resize the images displayed in the Gallery control, type **pic.setLayoutParams(new Gallery.LayoutParams(200,175));**.

The size of the images displayed in the Gallery is set to 200 pixels wide by 175 pixels tall (Figure 7-24).

```
67   public View getView(int arg0, View arg1, ViewGroup arg2) {
68       // TODO Auto-generated method stub
69       ImageView pic = new ImageView(context);
70       pic.setImageResource(Animals[arg0]);
71       pic.setScaleType(ImageView.ScaleType.FIT_XY);
72       pic.setLayoutParams(new Gallery.LayoutParams(200,175));
73       return pic;
74   }
75   }
76 }
```

Gallery images are resized

Figure 7-24   Resizing the Gallery images

5. To return pic to the Main Activity, change the return null; statement to **return pic;**.

The pic instance is returned to the Main Activity (Figure 7-25).

```
 1  package net.androidbootcamp.endangeredspecies;
 2
 3⊕ import android.app.Activity;
14
15  public class Main extends Activity {
16⊝      Integer[] Animals = ( R.drawable.elephant,  R.drawable.gorilla, R.drawable.leopard,
17                            R.drawable.monkey, R.drawable.panda, R.drawable.redpanda);
18      ImageView imageView;
19
20      /** Called when the activity is first created. */
21⊝      @Override
△22      public void onCreate(Bundle savedInstanceState) {
23          super.onCreate(savedInstanceState);
24          setContentView(R.layout.main);
25          Gallery ga = (Gallery)findViewById(R.id.gallery1);
26          imageView = (ImageView)findViewById(R.id.imgAnimal);
27          ga.setAdapter(new ImageAdapter(this));
28⊝          ga.setOnItemClickListener(new OnItemClickListener() {
29
30⊝              @Override
△31              public void onItemClick(AdapterView<?> arg0, View arg1, int arg2,
32                      long arg3) {
33                  // TODO Auto-generated method stub
34                  Toast.makeText(getBaseContext(), "You have selected picture " + (arg2 + 1)
35                          + " of the endangered species", Toast.LENGTH_SHORT).show();
36                  imageView.setImageResource(Animals[arg2]);
37              }
38
39          });
40      }
41⊝      public class ImageAdapter extends BaseAdapter{
42          private Context context;
43⊝          public ImageAdapter(Context c){
44              // TODO Auto-generated constructor stub
45              context=c;
46          }
47
48⊝          @Override
△49          public int getCount() {
50              // TODO Auto-generated method stub
51              return Animals.length;
52          }
53
54⊝          @Override
△55          public Object getItem(int arg0) {
56              // TODO Auto-generated method stub
57              return null;
58          }
59
60⊝          @Override
△61          public long getItemId(int arg0) {
62              // TODO Auto-generated method stub
63              return 0;
64          }
65
66⊝          @Override
△67          public View getView(int arg0, View arg1, ViewGroup arg2) {
68              // TODO Auto-generated method stub
69              ImageView pic = new ImageView(context);
70              pic.setImageResource(Animals[arg0]);
71              pic.setScaleType(ImageView.ScaleType.FIT_XY);
72              pic.setLayoutParams(new Gallery.LayoutParams(200,175));
73              return pic;         ◄───────────────── Return variable pic
74          }
75      }
76  }
77
```

Figure 7-25   Complete code of Main.java

GTK

Aspect ratio is the fractional relation of the width of an image compared with its height. The two most common aspect ratios are 4:3 and 16:9 in HDTV. Keeping the aspect ratio means that an image is not distorted from its original ratio of width to height.

Running and Testing the Application

It is time to see your finished product. Click Run on the menu bar, and then select Run to save and test the application in the emulator. A dialog box requesting how you would like to run the application opens the first time the application is executed. Select Android Application and click the OK button. Save all the files in the next dialog box, if necessary, and unlock the emulator. The application opens in the emulator window where you can touch the Gallery to view the images and select an image, as shown in Figure 7-1 and Figure 7-2.

Wrap It Up—Chapter Summary

Many Android applications display a Gallery to easily accommodate viewing a large amount of pictures. Creating a Gallery in this chapter to dynamically display images from an array provided experience with using a second class, a custom toast message, methods with return variables, and the length of an array. Creating a second class called the ImageAdapter class provided the customization for the Gallery layout.

- A View container is a rectangular area of the screen that displays an image or text object. It can include various layouts, including a Gallery layout, which displays a horizontal list of objects. Users can scroll the Gallery list to select an object such as a photo and display it in another control such as an ImageView control.

- To display an image in an ImageView control only if the user selects the image in the Gallery, you must enter XML code for the ImageView control in main.xml.

- An array variable can store more than one value. Arrays provide access to data by using a numeric index, or subscript, to identify each element in the array. For example, the first element in the array is assigned to the subscript of 0. An array can assign more than one image to a Gallery control to eventually display only one image.

- A setAdapter provides a data model for the Gallery layout. With the Gallery control, the adapter binds certain types of data and displays that data in a specified layout.

- Like the OnClickListener used for a Button control, the OnItemClickListener waits for user interaction in a Gallery control. When the user selects an item in the Gallery, the OnItemClickListener processes an onItemClick event, which includes four arguments. The arg2 argument is an integer value that contains the position of the View in the adapter. For example, if the user taps the second image in the Gallery, the integer value of 2 is stored in arg2.

- By including a toast notification in the onItemClick method, you can display a message indicating which image is selected in a Gallery control. The message can include a variable to display the number of the image selected in the Gallery. The toast message can float over the other controls so it never receives focus.

- Because the toast notification is not used directly in the Main Activity, you must replace Main.this in the onItemClick method with a Context class called getBaseContext( ). In Android programs, you use the getBaseContext( ) method to obtain a Context instance. This Context instance is triggered only when the user touches the Gallery control.

- To display in an ImageView control the image selected in the Gallery, you use the setImageResource( ) method with an int argument. The setImageResource command inserts an ImageView control and the int argument specifies which image is selected for display. If you are using an array to identify the images, you can use arg2 as the int argument because it represents the position of the selected image in the Gallery.

- The ImageAdapter class must provide information to set up the Gallery so it can display the appropriate images. You use the Context class to load and access resources for the application. A class variable can hold each image in the Gallery temporarily before it is displayed. To handle the Context resources necessary for the Gallery, you use the ImageAdapter constructor. A constructor can initialize the instance variables of an object. In other words, it constructs the values of data members of the class. You define the Context for an ImageAdapter instance in the ImageAdapter class constructor.

- The chapter project uses the getCount( ) method to determine how many pictures to display in the Gallery control. It does so by referencing the array specifying the images for the Gallery. To determine the length of an array, Java provides a method named length( ) that returns an integer type value of any given string or array. The length of an array is determined by the number of its elements. The getCount( ) method uses length( ) to return the number of elements in the Gallery.

- The declaration statement public int getCount( ) indicates that the return data type (int) is an integer. Because the getCount( ) method is not declared void, it must contain a return statement with a corresponding return value such as the length of an array.

- In the chapter project, the getView( ) method uses Context to create a new ImageView instance to temporarily hold each image displayed in the Gallery. The getView( ) method also contains statements that scale the ImageView to fit the Gallery control and a specified height and width.

Key Terms

constructor—A part of the Java code used to initialize the instance variables of an object.

Gallery—A View container that displays a horizontal list of objects with the center item displaying the current image.

getBaseContext( )—A Context class method used in Android programs to obtain a Context instance. Use getBaseContext( ) in a method that is triggered only when the user touches the Gallery control.

method—In Java, a series of statements that perform some repeated task.

onItemClick—An event the OnItemClickListener processes when the user touches the Gallery display layout. The onItemClick method is defined by OnItemClickListener and sends a number of arguments in the parentheses included within the line of code.

setAdapter—A command that provides a data model for the Gallery layout, similar to an adapter, which displays a ListView control.

View—A rectangular container that displays a drawing or text object.

Developer FAQs

1. Which Android control displays a horizontal listing of images?

2. In which category on the Palette is the Gallery control located?

3. Name three locations where photos that are used in the Android environment can be stored.

4. Why was the ImageView control coded in XML code in the chapter project instead of dragging the ImageView control onto the emulator?

5. Name six View containers.

6. Write a line of code that uses an instance of a Gallery control named gaLayout in a new ImageAdapter class using setAdapter( ).

7. Write a line of code that creates a reference array named Games for the images named worldofwarcraft, nflmadden, halo, and fable.

8. What are the array name and index of halo in question 7?

9. What is the array length of the Games array in question 7?

10. Write a line of code that determines the length of the Games array from question 7 and assigns the value to an int variable named numberOfGames.

11. Write a line of code that assigns dentalLength to the length of a string named dental.

12. What is the purpose of the argument arg2 in the chapter project?

13. In the chapter project, if the user selects red panda, what is the value of arg2?

14. Write a custom toast message that resides within an onItemClick( ) method and states *You have selected picture 4 of the political photos* when arg2 is 4.

15. What do the numbers in this statement represent?

```
pic.setLayoutParams(new Gallery.LayoutParams(300,325));
```

16. What does the aspect ratio 3:2 mean?

17. In the following method, what does int (integer) represent?
    ```
    public int getCount() {
        return Soccer.length;
    }
    ```

18. What would be returned in the method in question 17 if the Soccer array has the maximum index of 22?

19. What term does the following define? *Constructs the values of data members of the class*

20. Write a statement that sets the scale type to CENTER for an ImageView instance named tower.

Beyond the Book

Using the Internet, search the Web for the answers to the following questions to further your Android knowledge.

1. Research the GridView Android image layout. Find an image from a Web site that displays a GridView with images and provide a URL of that Web site.

2. Name five types of apps not discussed in this chapter and how they would each use a Gallery control.

3. An excellent Web site that provides up-to-date information about the Android world can be found at *http://android.alltop.com*. Read an article that interests you and write a summary of that article of at least 100 words.

4. One of the major issues in the Android world is the multiple operating systems currently running on Android devices. Write a one-page report about the issue of upgrading Android devices to the newest OS available.

Case Programming Projects

Complete one or more of the following case programming projects. Use the same steps and techniques taught within the chapter. Submit the program you create to your instructor. The level of difficulty is indicated for each case programming project.

Easiest: ★

Intermediate: ★ ★

Challenging: ★ ★ ★

Case Project 7–1: Power Tools App ★

Requirements Document

Application title: Power Tools App

Purpose: A power tools company would like to display its newest line of power tools in a Gallery layout.

Algorithms:
1. The opening screen displays four new power tools in a Gallery control (Figure 7-26).
2. When the user selects a tool image in the Gallery control, a full-size image appears below the Gallery. A toast message states which tool image the user selected (Figure 7-27).

Conditions:
1. The pictures of the four power tools are provided with your student files with the names powerdrill, powersaw, powerscrewdriver, and powerwasher.
2. Display each image in the Gallery with the size 250, 190.

Figure 7-26   Figure 7-27

Case Project 7–2: S.P.C.A. Rescue Shelter App ✶

Requirements Document

Application title:	S.P.C.A. Rescue Shelter App
Purpose:	Your local S.P.C.A. needs an app to display the dogs in need of a home.
Algorithms:	1. The screen displays six dogs from the shelter in a large Gallery control (Figure 7-28).
	2. When the user selects a thumbnail image of a dog, a full-size image appears below the Gallery (Figure 7-29).
Conditions:	1. The pictures of the six dogs eligible for adoption are provided with your student files with the names dog1, dog2, dog3, dog4, dog5, and dog6.
	2. Display each image in the Gallery with the size 300, 250.

Figure 7-28   **Figure 7-29**

Case Project 7–3: Four Seasons App ★ ★

Requirements Document

Application title:	Four Seasons App
Purpose:	The Four Seasons app displays a beautiful image of each of the four seasons and allows you to select your favorite season of the year.
Algorithms:	1. The opening screen displays the four season images in a Gallery control.
	2. When the user selects a season image, a full-size image appears below the Gallery. Using If statements, a toast message states that your favorite season is [season], such as *Your favorite season is spring*.
Conditions:	1. The pictures of the four seasons are provided with your student files with the names spring, summer, fall, and winter.
	2. Display each image in the Gallery with the size 188, 220.

Case Project 7–4: Car Rental App ★ ★

Requirements Document

Application title:	Car Rental App
Purpose:	A car rental company would like to display its car rental choices in a Gallery.
Algorithms:	1. The opening screen displays images of six rental car models in a Gallery control.
	2. When the user selects a car thumbnail image, a full-size image appears below the Gallery. Using an If statement, a toast message states the types of car and cost of each rental car.
Conditions:	1. Locate six rental car images on the Internet.
	2. Create a custom layout using the CENTER scale type.

Case Project 7–5: Anthology Wedding Photography App ★ ★ ★

Requirements Document

Application title:	Anthology Wedding Photography App
Purpose:	Anthology Wedding Photography would like to display a sample of its work with 10 wedding images in a Gallery.
Algorithms:	1. Create a Gallery that displays 10 wedding photos.
	2. When the user selects a specific wedding image in the Gallery, a large image appears with a custom toast message that displays *Anthology Wedding Photo* and the image number.
	3. A text line appears at the bottom of the screen: *Contact us at anthology@wed.com*.
Conditions:	1. Select wedding images from the Internet.
	2. Use a layout of your choice.

Case Project 7–6: Personal Photo App ★ ★ ★

Requirements Document

Application title:	Personal Photo App
Purpose:	Create your own photo app with eight images of your family and friends in a Gallery control.
Algorithms:	1. Create a Gallery that displays eight images of your friends and family.
	2. When the user selects a specific thumbnail image in the Gallery, a large image appears with a custom toast message that states the first name of the pictured person.
Conditions:	1. Select your own images.
	2. Use a layout of your choice.

Design! Using a DatePicker on a Tablet

In this chapter, you learn to:

- ◎ Create an Android project on a tablet
- ◎ Understand tablet specifications
- ◎ Follow design principles for the Android tablet
- ◎ Add a second Android Virtual Device
- ◎ Add a custom launcher and tablet theme
- ◎ Understand the Calendar class
- ◎ Use date, time, and clock controls
- ◎ Determine the system date
- ◎ Display a DatePicker control
- ◎ Launch a dialog box containing a DatePicker control
- ◎ Code an onDateSetListener method to await user interaction
- ◎ Determine the date entered on a calendar control
- ◎ Test an application on a tablet emulator

The explosion of the Android market is not limited to the phone platform. Android tablet sales are successfully competing with the Apple iPad as well, proving that consumers are ready for a tablet environment. Now more than ever, mobile designers are being asked to create experiences for a variety of tablet devices. In today's post-PC world, the tablet market provides the mobility and simplicity users demand for connecting to the Internet, playing games, using Facebook, checking e-mail, and more. Lower price points and a large app marketplace are driving growth in the Android tablet market. To understand the process of designing an application on the Android tablet, you design a calendar program that books a reservation on a deep sea fishing boat in Hawaii called Marlin Adventures. The Marlin Adventures application shown in Figure 8-1 provides information about one of its fishing adventures located in Kona, Hawaii. This single-screen experience could be part of a larger app featuring fishing trips throughout the world.

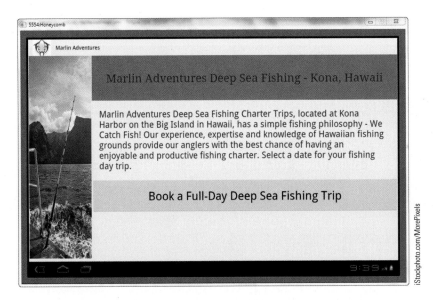

Figure 8-1   Marlin Adventures Android Tablet app

The Android tablet app in Figure 8-1 appears on a 10.1-inch display. When the user makes a reservation by touching the button control, a floating dialog box opens with a DatePicker calendar control, as shown in Figure 8-2. When the date is set by the user, a TextView control confirms the reservation for the deep sea fishing day trip, as shown in Figure 8-3.

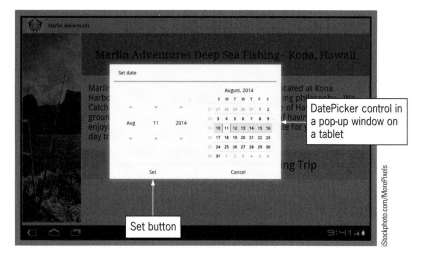

DatePicker control in a pop-up window on a tablet

Set button

Figure 8-2 DatePicker calendar control in a dialog box

Reservation date is set

Figure 8-3 TextView control displays reservation

IN THE TRENCHES
The Android platform has been ported to many kinds of devices beyond phones and tablets, such as toasters, televisions, microwaves, and laptops.

To create this application, the developer must understand how to perform the following processes, among others:

1. Add an Android Virtual Device specifically designed for tablets.

2. Add the images used in this project.

3. Change the theme and icon for the tablet display.

4. Create a custom XML file with a Table layout.

5. Add and initialize the TextView controls and the Button control.

6. Initialize a DatePickerDialog with the present date and listen for the user to select a date.

7. Return the selected date.

8. Display the selected reservation date in the TextView control.

Designing a Tablet Application

The Android market initially only included mobile phone devices, but the recent popularity of the tablet device provides a new platform for Android app programming. The growth of the Android tablet market goes hand in hand with dedicated applications designed especially for the tablet, not just enlarged versions of a phone app. **Native applications** are programs locally installed on a specific platform such as a phone or tablet. A native application is typically designed for a specific platform such as a phone on a 3-inch screen or a tablet on a 10.1-inch screen. In contrast, an **emulated application** is converted in real time to run on a variety of platforms such as a Web page, which can be displayed on various screen sizes through a browser. A native Android tablet app creates an optimal user experience based on the most common tablet screen size between approximately 7 and 10.1 inches, a 1280 × 800 pixel resolution, and a 16:9 screen ratio, as shown in Figure 8-4. In comparison, an Apple iPad has a 9.7-inch screen, a 1024 × 768 pixel resolution, and a screen ratio of 4:3. If you plan to create apps on multiple platforms, the different screen specifications will affect your design.

Figure 8-4   Android tablet displays Gallery controls

As you consider creating an Android tablet application, remember that tablets are not simply huge smartphones. Even the primary use of each device is different. A smartphone is most likely used on the go in a truly mobile fashion to quickly check e-mail, update your Facebook status, or send a text message between classes or as you run errands. Tablets are typically used for longer periods of time. This prolonged interaction on tablets is more involved, with users sitting down at a table in Starbucks, riding a train, or relaxing with the tablet positioned in their laps while watching a movie. Whereas phone app design relies on simplicity, a tablet can handle the complexity of more graphics, more text, and more interaction during longer sessions.

Design Tips for Tablets

As you begin designing an Android app, first consider how the user most likely will interact with your app. Will the tablet be in his or her lap, held with two hands (games often require this), or in a tablet stand? Will the user spend seconds, minutes, or hours using your app?

What is the optimal way to deliver the content? As you consider the answers to each of these questions, also keep these design guidelines in mind:

- Keep screens uncluttered and ensure touch controls such as buttons and radio buttons are of sufficient size. Larger controls are easier to find and enable simpler interaction for the user.

- Focus apps on the task at hand. Keep the design simple. Do not force the user to spend undue time figuring out how to use the application.

- Resist filling the large screen with "cool" interactions that distract the user without adding to the quality of the program.

- Use flexible dimension values such as dp and sp instead of px or pt.

- Provide higher resolution resources for screen densities (DPI) to ensure that your app looks great on any screen size.

- Create a unique experience for both the phone and tablet designs.

- Use larger fonts than with a phone app. Consider printing out your user interface design to see how it looks.

IN THE TRENCHES
Consumers of all ages are spending more time playing games on tablets. This trend affects the retail market sales of console-based video games and traditional children's toys. This shift leaves retailers out of the sales streams because most digital content is distributed within the different phone platform markets.

Adding an Android Virtual Device for the Tablet

To make sure your Android tablet app deploys to any device in the Android platform, use the Android Honeycomb 3.0 operating system, which is dedicated to tablet applications. You can add multiple Android Virtual Devices (AVDs) in Eclipse for your intended device and platform. Honeycomb was initially designed for the Android Xoom, the first tablet introduced, but now supports the full range of new Android tablet devices on the market. Each Android device configuration is stored in AVD.

To use the Honeycomb emulator, you first add the appropriate AVD configuration. To download the Android Development Tools for Honeycomb 3.0, follow these steps:

1. Open the Eclipse program, click Window on the menu bar, and then click AVD Manager to open the Android Virtual Device Manager dialog box. Click the New button to open the Create new Android Virtual Device (AVD) dialog box. To name the Honeycomb Android emulator, type **Honeycomb** in the Name text box. To target your Android app to appear in the Android 3.0 version, select Android 3.0 – API Level 11 in the Target list. (If you do not see Android 3.0 – API Level 11 listed as a target, install the SDK platform for Android 3.0 by clicking Window and then clicking Android SDK Manager. Select Android 3.0 and then click Install packages.)

   A new AVD named Honeycomb to support tablets using Android 3.0 – API Level 11 is added to Eclipse (Figure 8-5).

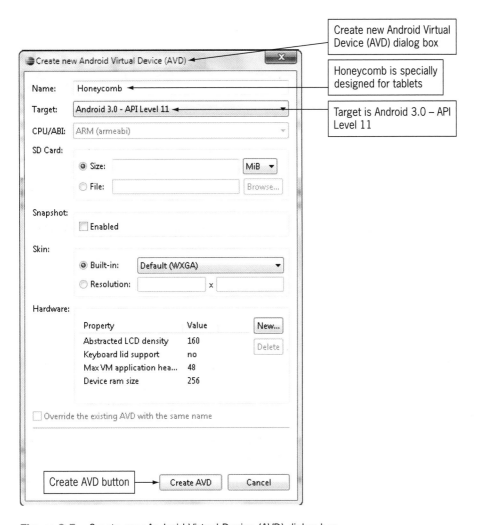

Figure 8-5   Create new Android Virtual Device (AVD) dialog box

2.   Click the Create AVD button. The Android Virtual Device Manager dialog box lists the new AVD Name (Honeycomb) for the Android 3.0 target device along with the existing IceCream Android 4.0 target device.

The Android Virtual Device Manager dialog box displays both Honeycomb and IceCream targets (Figure 8-6).

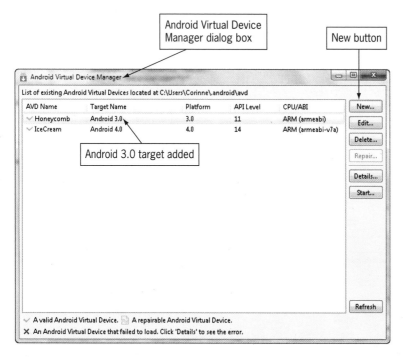

Figure 8-6   Android 3.0 AVD is added to create a tablet app

Creating a Tablet App

To create a Honeycomb 3.0 tablet application for the Marlin Adventures app, follow these steps to begin the application:

1. Close the Android Virtual Device Manager dialog box. Click the New button on the Standard toolbar. Expand the Android folder and select Android Project. Click the Next button. In the New Android Project dialog box, enter the Project Name **Marlin Adventures**. To save the project on your USB drive, click to remove the check mark from the Use default location check box. Type **E:\Workspace** (if necessary, enter a different drive letter that identifies the USB drive). Click the Next button. For the Build Target, select Android 3.0. Click the Next button. For the Package Name, type **net.androidbootcamp.marlinadventures**. Enter **Main** in the Create Activity text box.

   The new Android Marlin Adventures tablet project has a Project Name, a Package Name, and an Activity named Main (Figure 8-7).

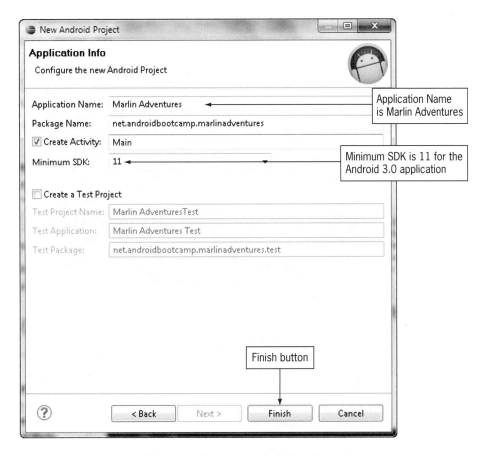

Figure 8-7   Application information for the new Android tablet project

2. Click the Finish button. Expand the Marlin Adventures tablet project in the Package Explorer. Expand the res and layout subfolders and double-click main.xml to view the Android tablet emulator. Delete the TextView control Hello World, Main!.

The Android 10.1in WXGA tablet emulator is displayed in main.xml (Figure 8-8).

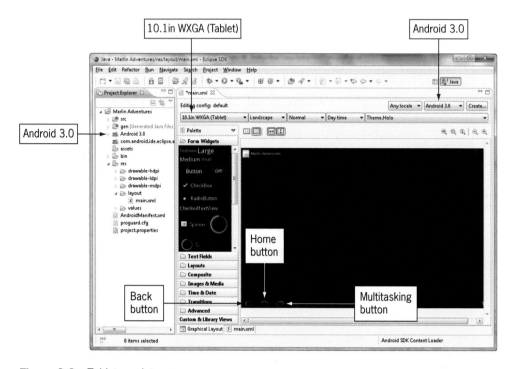

Figure 8-8   Tablet emulator

GTK

The three navigation buttons on the lower-left side of the Android tablet are Back, Home, and Multitasking. The Back button returns to the previous action. The Home button returns to the default home screen. The Multitasking button opens a list of the apps that have been used recently.

Setting the Launcher Icon of a Tablet App

The Marlin Adventures deep-sea fishing charter company has an established logo. The Marlin Adventures logo is displayed as a custom launcher icon in the tablet app. On an Android phone app, the size of the launcher icon is typically 72 × 72 pixels, but due to the larger real estate available on the tablet, the preferred launcher icon size should measure 96 × 96 pixels. Microsoft Paint provides a simple Resize button to change the pixel size of an image.

If you are using a Mac, use the Preview application to resize image files. Click Tools on the Preview menu bar and then click Adjust Size.

To add the icon and left column image to the folder and to add a customized launcher icon to the tablet app, follow these steps:

1. To add the custom launcher icon to the tablet project, copy the student files to your USB drive (if necessary). Open the USB folder containing the student files. In the Package Explorer, expand the drawable-hdpi folder. Drag the ic_launcher_marlin.png

and marlin.png file to the drawable-hdpi folder until a plus sign pointer appears. Release the mouse button. Click the OK button in the File Operation dialog box. Click the default icon ic_launcher.png and press the Delete key, and then click the OK button to confirm the deletion.

The custom launcher icon image is placed in the drawable-hdpi folder. The image in the emulator is not updated until the Android Manifest file is changed (Figure 8-9).

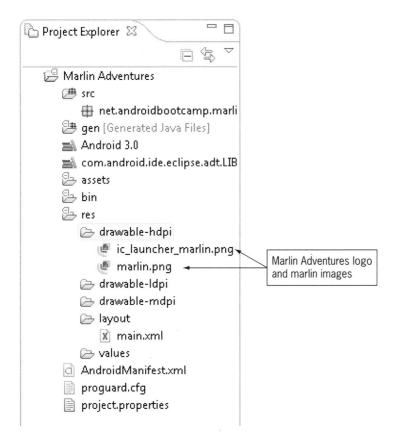

Figure 8-9   New launcher icon file

2. To change the code in the Android Manifest file so the application displays the custom icon, double-click the AndroidManifest.xml file in the Package Explorer. Click the AndroidManifest.xml tab at the bottom of the window. Inside the application code, click in the line android:icon="drawable/ic_launcher". Change the filename portion from ic_launcher" to **ic_launcher_marlin"**.

The Android launcher icon is coded in the Android Manifest file (Figure 8-10).

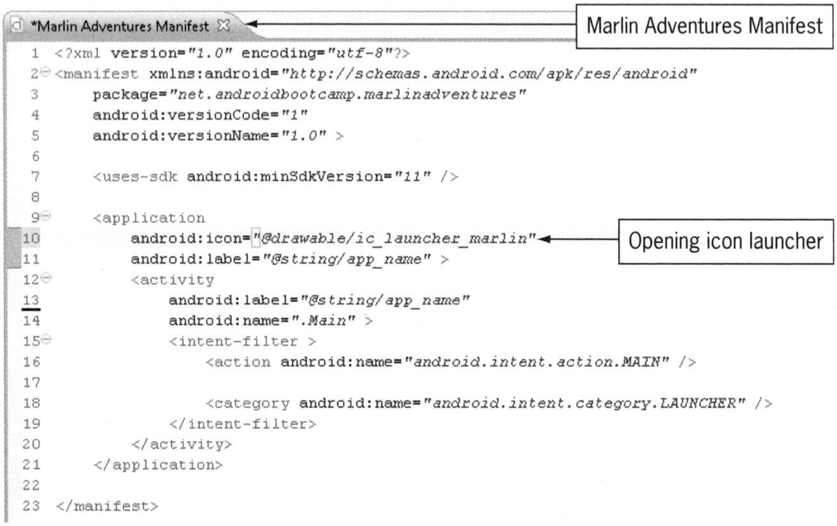

```
  *Marlin Adventures Manifest ⊠  ◄─────────────────────  Marlin Adventures Manifest
  1  <?xml version="1.0" encoding="utf-8"?>
  2  <manifest xmlns:android="http://schemas.android.com/apk/res/android"
  3      package="net.androidbootcamp.marlinadventures"
  4      android:versionCode="1"
  5      android:versionName="1.0" >
  6
  7      <uses-sdk android:minSdkVersion="11" />
  8
  9      <application
 10          android:icon="@drawable/ic_launcher_marlin"  ◄─────  Opening icon launcher
 11          android:label="@string/app_name" >
 12          <activity
 13              android:label="@string/app_name"
 14              android:name=".Main" >
 15              <intent-filter >
 16                  <action android:name="android.intent.action.MAIN" />
 17
 18                  <category android:name="android.intent.category.LAUNCHER" />
 19              </intent-filter>
 20          </activity>
 21      </application>
 22
 23  </manifest>
```

Figure 8-10   Android Manifest code with new launcher icon file

3.   Save your work.

Setting a Custom Theme of a Tablet

In the chapter project shown in Figure 8-1, the tablet app opens with a polished entrance using a Holo.Light theme, which includes a light background with a black status bar at the bottom of the tablet screen. Android themes are a mechanism for applying a consistent style to an app or activity. To change the tablet theme, follow these steps:

1.   Click the main.xml tab, click the Theme button to display the list of built-in themes, and then select Theme.Holo.Light.

The Marlin Adventures project uses the Theme.Holo.Light theme (Figure 8-11).

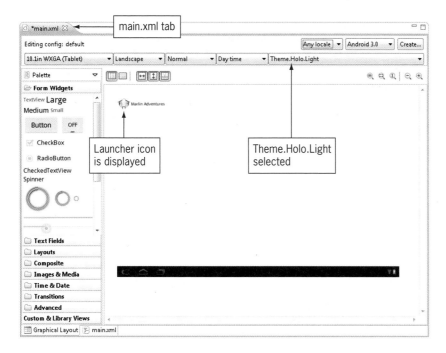

Figure 8-11 Custom theme displayed on tablet emulator

2. To add the selected theme to the Android Manifest file, click the Marlin Adventures Manifest tab. Inside the Activity code, click at the end of the line android: label="@string/app_name" (if a closing bracket > appears at the end of the line, click to the left of the bracket). Press the Enter key to insert a blank line. Type **android:theme="@android:style/Theme.Holo.Light"**.

    The Android theme is coded in the Android Manifest file (Figure 8-12).

272

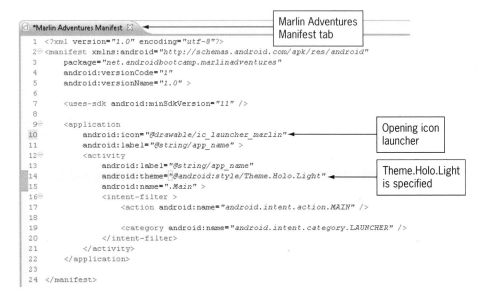

Marlin Adventures Manifest tab

```
 1  <?xml version="1.0" encoding="utf-8"?>
 2  <manifest xmlns:android="http://schemas.android.com/apk/res/android"
 3      package="net.androidbootcamp.marlinadventures"
 4      android:versionCode="1"
 5      android:versionName="1.0" >
 6
 7      <uses-sdk android:minSdkVersion="11" />
 8
 9      <application
10          android:icon="@drawable/ic_launcher_marlin"
11          android:label="@string/app_name" >
12          <activity
13              android:label="@string/app_name"
14              android:theme="@android:style/Theme.Holo.Light"
15              android:name=".Main" >
16              <intent-filter >
17                  <action android:name="android.intent.action.MAIN" />
18
19                  <category android:name="android.intent.category.LAUNCHER" />
20              </intent-filter>
21          </activity>
22      </application>
23
24  </manifest>
```

Opening icon launcher

Theme.Holo.Light is specified

Figure 8-12   Android Manifest code with new theme

GTK

Google created an Android Design Web site (*http://developer.android.com/design*) to assist in best practices and to set a uniform look and feel across the various Android platforms.

Designing a Tablet Table Layout

In the Marlin Adventures application, two layouts are combined in main.xml to organize the tablet user interface controls. The Linear layout and the Table layout create a simple, clean interface on the tablet containing both rows and columns. The left column described in Table 8-1 uses the Linear layout to display the marlin.png image. On the right side of Table 8-1, four rows are inserted in a Table layout to display the title, description, button, and reservation result. (Figure 8-3 shows this layout with all the design elements.)

marlin.png image	Title
	Day trip description
	Reservation button
	Display reservation date after selection

Table 8-1   Table layout

A user interface design layout named **TableLayout** is composed of TableRow controls—one for each row in your table in main.xml. In Table 8-1, the layout consists of four rows and one column. The contents of each TableRow are the view controls that will go in each cell of the table grid. The TableLayout shown in the following code has four TableRow controls with either a TextView or Button control within each row:

Code Syntax

```
<?xml version="1.0" encoding="utf-8"?>
<LinearLayout
xmlns:android="http://schemas.android.com/apk/res/android"
        <ImageView />
        <TableLayout
            <TableRow>
                <TextView />
            </TableRow>
            <TableRow>
                <TextView />
            </TableRow>
            <TableRow>
                <Button />
            </TableRow>
            <TableRow>
                <TextView />
            </TableRow>
        </TableLayout>
</LinearLayout>
```

To create additional columns, you add a view to a row. Adding a view in a row forms a cell, and the width of the largest view determines the width of the column.

Within the XML layout file, an Android property named padding is used to spread out the content displayed on the tablet. The **padding property** can be used to offset the content of the control by a specific number of pixels. For example, if you set a padding of 20 pixels, the content of a control is distanced from other controls by 20 pixels. Another Android property named **typeface** sets the style of the text to font families that include monospace, sans_serif, and serif. Follow these steps to code the layout of main.xml for the tablet:

1. Save and close the Android Manifest file. Click the main.xml tab at the bottom of the window to display the XML code. By default, LinearLayout is already set. In Line 5, change the android orientation property from vertical to **horizontal**. To the right of the > bracket, press the Enter key to insert a blank line and then type **<ImageView** in the new line. Press the Enter key. Type the following code to add the ImageView control using auto-completion as much as possible:

```
android:id="@+id/imgMarlin"
android:layout_width="220dp"
android:layout_height="685dp"
android:src="@drawable/marlin" />
```

The ImageView control is coded in main.xml (Figure 8-13).

```
*main.xml ⊠
 1  <?xml version="1.0" encoding="utf-8"?>
 2  <LinearLayout xmlns:android="http://schema:
 3      android:layout_width="fill_parent"
 4      android:layout_height="fill_parent"
 5      android:orientation="horizontal" >          ← Horizontal orientation
 6      <ImageView
 7          android:id="@+id/imgMarlin"
 8          android:layout_width="220dp"            ← ImageView displays marlin.png
 9          android:layout_height="685dp"
10          android:src="@drawable/marlin" />
11  </LinearLayout>
```

Figure 8-13　ImageView control coded in the LinearLayout

2. To code the TableLayout for the first two table rows to display the title and description TextView controls, press the Enter key. Type the following code using auto-completion as much as possible:

```
<TableLayout
    android:layout_width="fill_parent"
    android:layout_height="wrap_content">
    <TableRow>
        <View android:layout_height="80dp"/>
        <TextView
            android:id="@+id/txtTitle"
            android:layout_width="wrap_content"
            android:layout_gravity="left"
            android:padding="50dp"
            android:background="#666FFF"
            android:text="Marlin Adventures Deep Sea Fishing – Kona, Hawaii"
            android:typeface="serif"
            android:textSize="39sp" />
    </TableRow>
    <TableRow>
        <View android:layout_height="80dp"/>
        <TextView
            android:id="@+id/txtDescription"
            android:layout_width="wrap_content"
            android:layout_gravity="left"
            android:padding="25dp"
            android:text="Marlin Adventures Deep Sea Fishing Charter Trips,
located at Kona Harbor on the Big Island in Hawaii, has a simple fishing
philosophy – We Catch Fish! Our experience, expertise and knowledge of
Hawaiian fishing grounds provide our anglers with the best chance of having
an enjoyable and productive fishing charter. Select a date for your fishing
day trip."
            android:textSize="30sp" />
    </TableRow>
```

The first two rows of the table display the title and description of Marlin Adventures (Figure 8-14).

First TableRow

Second TableRow

Scroll to display the rest of the line

Figure 8-14 TableLayout XML code for first two TableRows

3. Next, write the XML code for the third and fourth table rows, which display a Button and TextView control. Press the Enter key after the closing </TableRow> tag, and then type the following code using auto-completion as much as possible:

```
<TableRow>
    <View android:layout_height="80dp"/>
    <Button
        android:id="@+id/btnDate"
        android:layout_width="100dp"
        android:padding="30dp"
        android:textSize="40sp"
        android:text="Book a Full-Day Deep Sea Fishing Trip" />
</TableRow>
<TableRow>
    <View android:layout_height="80dp"/>
    <TextView
        android:id="@+id/txtReservation"
        android:padding="20dp"
        android:layout_gravity="center"
        android:textSize="36sp" />
</TableRow>
</TableLayout>
```

The last two rows of the table display the button and reservation date of Marlin Adventures (Figure 8-15). To view the finished design, click the Graphical Layout tab at the bottom of the window (Figure 8-16).

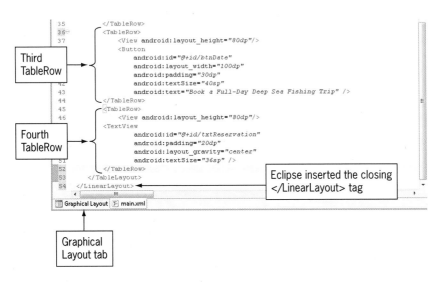

Third
TableRow

Fourth
TableRow

```
35        </TableRow>
36        <TableRow>
37            <View android:layout_height="80dp"/>
          <Button
              android:id="@+id/btnDate"
              android:layout_width="100dp"
              android:padding="30dp"
42            android:textSize="40sp"
43            android:text="Book a Full-Day Deep Sea Fishing Trip" />
44        </TableRow>
45        <TableRow>
46            <View android:layout_height="80dp"/>
          <TextView
              android:id="@+id/txtReservation"
              android:padding="20dp"
              android:layout_gravity="center"
51            android:textSize="36sp" />
52        </TableRow>
53        </TableLayout>
54    </LinearLayout>
```

Eclipse inserted the closing
</LinearLayout> tag

Graphical Layout main.xml

Graphical
Layout tab

Figure 8-15   TableLayout XML code for last two TableRows

Figure 8-16   main.xml Table layout

iStockphoto.com/MorePixels

IN THE TRENCHES
After an app is published, it is the developer's responsibility to monitor comments and reviews for the app at the Android Market. Consider conducting user surveys and doing further usability testing to create a popular application.

Date, Time, and Clocks

A common Android application topic is managing calendars and time. Whether you are a student or a businessperson, a solid scheduling app can assist in personal organization to remind you about that upcoming test or to pay that bill, and an alarm clock app can help you wake up each morning. In the chapter project, a calendar tool called a DatePicker control is displayed in a dialog box to determine the user's preferred date for a full-day fishing trip. In the Time & Date category in the Palette, many calendar controls are available: TimePicker, DatePicker, CalendarView, Chronometer, AnalogClock, and DigitalClock, as shown in Figure 8-17.

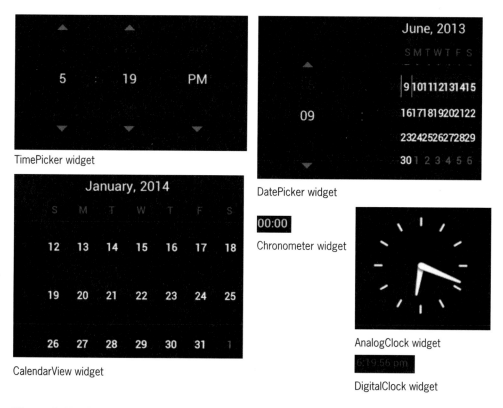

Figure 8-17   TimePicker, DatePicker, CalendarView, Chronometer, AnalogClock, and DigitalClock widgets

All Android devices keep a numeric representation of the system's current date and time. These numbers can be displayed in multiple formats based on the cultural preferences of the user's location. For example, in the United States, the format of dates looks like this: March 17th, 2015, or 03/17/2015. In Canada and Europe, the day value normally precedes the month, like this: 17 March 2015 or 17/03/2015. Similarly, some countries use the concept of AM and PM with a 12-hour clock, whereas others commonly use a 24-hour clock. Developers often program these cultural differences based on user preference and location.

Creating a control to enter the date is crucial because requiring users to type the date in a text box can lead to multiple errors, including incorrect format or typos. Web sites primarily rely on some type of calendar control for input in the same way that the Marlin Adventures app requests the reservation in a DatePicker control to streamline the process. Initially, the Marlin Adventures app does not display a DatePicker widget. The user clicks the button to launch a dialog box that includes a coded DatePicker widget displaying today's date. Date and time controls are often launched in dialog boxes to keep the user interface uncluttered.

Determining the Current Time

When the user opens the DatePicker control and touches the Button control, the Android system date is initially displayed, making it easier for the user to select a future date without having to move forward in a calendar from a date decades ago. To access the system date, the following variables are initialized and are assigned the appropriate date value later in the code.

The following code syntax shows the code for a custom XML layout:

Code Syntax

```
private int currentYear;
private int currentMonth;
private int currentDay;
static final int DATE_DIALOG_ID = 0;
```

The class variables currentYear, currentMonth, and currentDay hold the integer value of the system year, month, and day, respectively. Recall that class variables are used in multiple methods. To create a DatePickerDialog instance, you must define a unique identifier to represent the dialog box. DATE_DIALOG_ID is a static integer that identifies the dialog box displaying the calendar. A **static variable** is a program variable that does not vary and has the same value throughout execution of the application.

To code the class variables for the date, follow this step:

1. Save your work and then close the main.xml window. In the Package Explorer, expand the src folder, expand net.androidbootcamp.marlinadventures, and then double-click Main.java to open it. In Main.java, click after the public class Main

extends Activity { statement and press the Enter key to insert a blank line. To initialize the class variables, type:

```
private int currentYear;
private int currentMonth;
private int currentDay;
static final int DATE_DIALOG_ID = 0;
```

Press the Enter key to insert a blank line.

The class variables necessary for holding the system date are initialized (Figure 8-18).

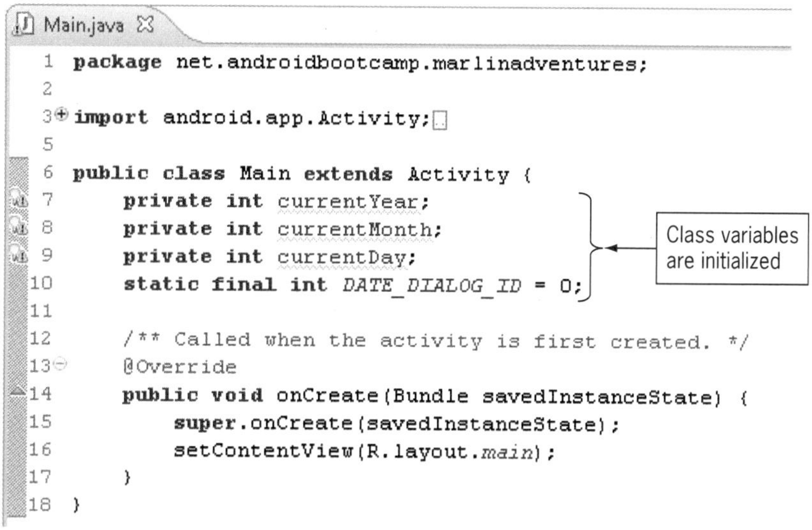

Figure 8-18   Date class variables

Initializing the Button and TextView Controls

The first two TextView controls were assigned text in main.xml, but the Button (btnDate) and reservation TextView (txtReservation) control must be initialized in the Java code and referenced with the controls in the XML layout. To initialize the controls, follow these steps:

1. In Main.java, on the new blank line, create a class variable reference for the Button by typing **private Button btDate;** and then press the Enter key. Point to Button and then click Import 'Button' (android.widget). On the next line, create a class variable reference for the TextView by typing **private TextView reservation;** and then press the Enter key. Point to TextView and then click Import 'TextView' (android.widget).

Class variables that can be accessed by the rest of the program are initialized (Figure 8-19).

```
 *Main.java ☒
 1  package net.androidbootcamp.marlinadventures;
 2
 3⊕ import android.app.Activity;▯
 7
 8  public class Main extends Activity {
 9      private int currentYear;
10      private int currentMonth;
11      private int currentDay;
12      static final int DATE_DIALOG_ID = 0;
13      private Button btDate;
14      private TextView reservation;
15
16      /** Called when the activity is first created. */
17⊝     @Override
18      public void onCreate(Bundle savedInstanceState) {
19          super.onCreate(savedInstanceState);
20          setContentView(R.layout.main);
21      }
22  }
```

Button class variable

TextView class variable

Figure 8-19   Class variables for Button and TextView controls

2. In the onCreate( ) method, click at the end of the setContentView(R.layout.main); line and press the Enter key to insert a blank line. To create an instance of the Button and TextView controls from the XML layout, type **btDate = (Button) findViewById (R.id.btnDate);** and then press the Enter key. Type **reservation = (TextView) findViewById(R.id.txtReservation);**.

The Button and TextView controls named btnDate and txtReservation are referenced in Main.java (Figure 8-20).

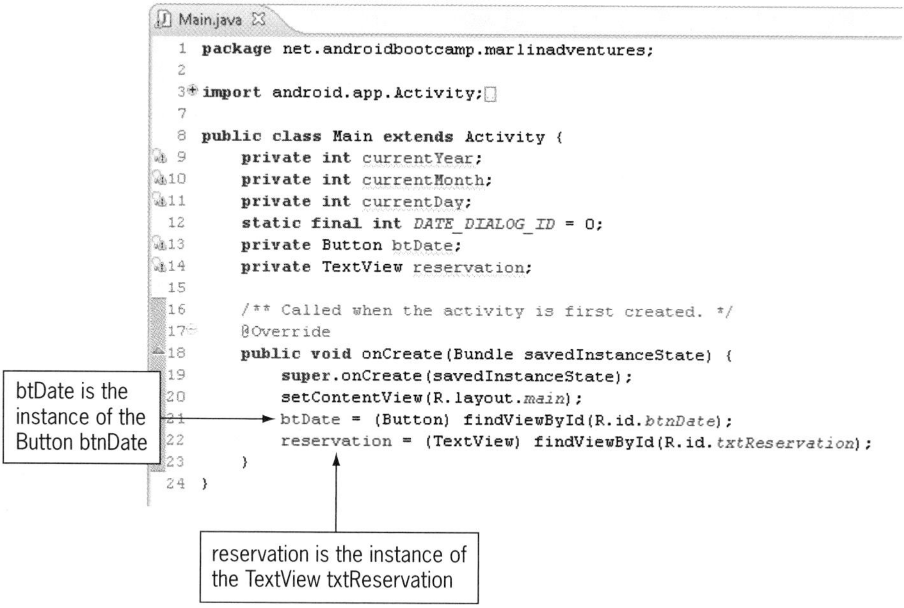

```
Main.java ⊠
1  package net.androidbootcamp.marlinadventures;
2
3⊕ import android.app.Activity;
7
8  public class Main extends Activity {
9      private int currentYear;
10     private int currentMonth;
11     private int currentDay;
12     static final int DATE_DIALOG_ID = 0;
13     private Button btDate;
14     private TextView reservation;
15
16     /** Called when the activity is first created. */
17     @Override
18     public void onCreate(Bundle savedInstanceState) {
19         super.onCreate(savedInstanceState);
20         setContentView(R.layout.main);
21         btDate = (Button) findViewById(R.id.btnDate);
22         reservation = (TextView) findViewById(R.id.txtReservation);
23     }
24 }
```

btDate is the instance of the Button btnDate

reservation is the instance of the TextView txtReservation

Figure 8-20 Instance of the Button and TextView controls

3. Save your work.

ShowDialog Method

If the user decides to make a reservation using the Marlin Adventures app and taps the Button control, the setOnClickListener method implements the Button.OnClickListener, creating an instance of the OnClickListener and calling the onClick method. The onClick method responds to the user's action. For example, in the chapter project, the response is to launch a dialog box. The onClick method is where you place the code to launch the DatePicker dialog box using the showDialog method. The Android method showDialog( ) triggers a call to the onCreateDialog method of the Activity class. The following code syntax shows the code for a showDialog method:

Code Syntax

```
showDialog(DATE_DIALOG_ID);
```

When the button is tapped, it calls showDialog( ), which passes the unique integer id for the constant DATE_DIALOG_ID to the DatePicker dialog box. To code the onClickListener and the showDialog method, follow these steps:

1. To create the btDate button setOnClickListener method necessary to wait for the user's click, insert a blank line in Main.java after the reservation statement, type **btDate.setOnClickListener(new View.OnClickListener() {** and then press the Enter key to insert the closing brace. Place a parenthesis and semicolon after this closing brace. This onClickListener is designed for a Button control's class variable. If a red error line appears below View, point to View and then click Import 'View' (android.view). Point to the red error line below View.OnClickListener and select Add unimplemented methods to add the quick fix.

An onClick auto-generated stub appears in the code for the button (Figure 8-21).

```
 *Main.java ⌗
  1  package net.androidbootcamp.marlinadventures;
  2
  3⊕ import android.app.Activity;⬚
  8
  9  public class Main extends Activity {
 10      private int currentYear;
 11      private int currentMonth;
 12      private int currentDay;
 13      static final int DATE_DIALOG_ID = 0;
 14      private Button btDate;
 15      private TextView reservation;
 16
 17      /** Called when the activity is first created. */
 18⊖     @Override
 19      public void onCreate(Bundle savedInstanceState) {
 20          super.onCreate(savedInstanceState);
 21          setContentView(R.layout.main);
 22          btDate = (Button) findViewById(R.id.btnDate);
 23          reservation = (TextView) findViewById(R.id.txtReservation);
 24⊖         btDate.setOnClickListener(new View.OnClickListener() {    ◄──  setOnClickListener
 25                                                                         awaits user
 26⊖             @Override                                                  interaction
 27              public void onClick(View v) {
 28                  // TODO Auto-generated method stub   ◄──  onClick auto-generated
 29                                                            stub
 30              }
 31
 32          });
 33      }
 34  }
```

Figure 8-21   Inserting the Button onClick stub

2. In the blank line after the // TODO comment, to launch the dialog box, type **showDialog(DATE_DIALOG_ID);**.

A showDialog method is called in the onClick event (Figure 8-22).

```
▲19      public void onCreate(Bundle savedInstanceState) {
  20          super.onCreate(savedInstanceState);
  21          setContentView(R.layout.main);
  22          btDate = (Button) findViewById(R.id.btnDate);
  23          reservation = (TextView) findViewById(R.id.txtReservation);
  24⊖        btDate.setOnClickListener(new View.OnClickListener() {
  25
  26⊖           @Override
 ▲27           public void onClick(View v) {
 ☑28               // TODO Auto-generated method stub
  29               showDialog(DATE_DIALOG_ID);  ◄──────
  30           }
  31
  32        });
  33      }
  34 }
```

> showDialog launches a dialog box

Figure 8-22 The onClick method launches a dialog box

3. Save your work.

GTK

In addition to displaying a DatePicker control, a dialog box in the Android environment can be used to alert the user, to display a progress bar, to select choices from radio buttons and check boxes, and to display a TimePicker control.

Using the Calendar Class

In the onClick method, when the int DATE_DIALOG_ID is passed, a new DatePickerDialog is passed along with the values for year, month, and day. The values for the present date must be set for the DatePicker to display today's date. The Android system date can be accessed by using the **Calendar class**, which is responsible for converting between a Date object and a set of integer fields such as YEAR, MONTH, and DAY_OF_MONTH. Typically, an Android mobile device connects to a cellphone tower or wireless network, which automatically updates the time zone and date. When using the Calendar class, a method of this class called **getInstance** returns a calendar date or time based on the system settings. The date constants in this class **YEAR**, **MONTH**, and **DAY_OF_MONTH** retrieve an integer value of the system's current year, month, and day, respectively. Another Calendar constant includes **DAY_OF_YEAR**, which displays the day number of the current year, as shown in the following code. For example, February 1 would be identified as the value 32 for the 32nd day of the year.

Code Syntax

```
final Calendar c = Calendar.getInstance();
currentYear = c.get(Calendar.YEAR);
currentMonth = c.get(Calendar.MONTH);
currentDay = c.get(Calendar.DAY_OF_MONTH);
```

In the code syntax, notice that c is an instance of the calendar class. The variable currentYear represents the system's year, currentMonth represents the system's month, and currentDay represents which day of the month is set on the system calendar. The field manipulation method called **get** accesses the system date or time, and **set** changes the current date or time. To get the current date from the system calendar within the onCreate method, follow these steps:

1. In Main.java, click to the right of the closing brace, parenthesis, and semicolon of the onClick method and press the Enter key. To create an instance of the Calendar class, type **final Calendar c = Calendar.getInstance();**. Point to Calendar and click Import 'Calendar' (java.util), if necessary.

An instance of the Calendar class named c is created (Figure 8-23).

```
20     public void onCreate(Bundle savedInstanceState) {
21         super.onCreate(savedInstanceState);
22         setContentView(R.layout.main);
23         btDate = (Button) findViewById(R.id.btnDate);
24         reservation = (TextView) findViewById(R.id.txtReservation);
25         btDate.setOnClickListener(new View.OnClickListener() {
26
27             @Override
28             public void onClick(View v) {
29                 // TODO Auto-generated method stub
30                 showDialog(DATE_DIALOG_ID);
31             }
32
33         });
34         final Calendar c = Calendar.getInstance();    ←——— c is an instance of
35     }                                                        the Calendar class
36 }
```

Figure 8-23   The getInstance method creates an instance of the Calendar class

2. Press the Enter key to insert a blank line. To get the device's system year, month, and day of the month, type:

```
currentYear = c.get(Calendar.YEAR);
currentMonth = c.get(Calendar.MONTH);
currentDay = c.get(Calendar.DAY_OF_MONTH);
```

The calendar instance named c is assigned the current system date (Figure 8-24).

```
19    @Override
20    public void onCreate(Bundle savedInstanceState) {
21        super.onCreate(savedInstanceState);
22        setContentView(R.layout.main);
23        btDate = (Button) findViewById(R.id.btnDate);
24        reservation = (TextView) findViewById(R.id.txtReservation);
25        btDate.setOnClickListener(new View.OnClickListener() {
26
27            @Override
28            public void onClick(View v) {
29                // TODO Auto-generated method stub
30                showDialog(DATE_DIALOG_ID);
31            }
32
33        });
34        final Calendar c = Calendar.getInstance();
35        currentYear = c.get(Calendar.YEAR);
36        currentMonth = c.get(Calendar.MONTH);
37        currentDay = c.get(Calendar.DAY_OF_MONTH);
38    }
39 }
```

Assigns the system year

Assigns the system month

Assigns the system day

Figure 8-24 Current system date assigned to be displayed in the DatePicker dialog box

Adding the OnCreateDialog Method

The Marlin Adventures application calls a showDialog(DATE_DIALOG_ID) method in reaction to the user tapping the reservation button. The showDialog method calls the OnCreateDialog callback method. The **OnCreateDialog** method creates a dialog box based on the argument passed by the showDialog method call. The OnCreateDialog method, called by showDialog( ), is passed the identifier DATE_DIALOG_ID, which initializes the DatePicker to the date retrieved from the Calendar instance for today's system date, as shown in Figure 8-25.

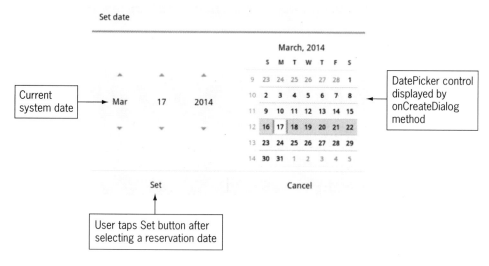

Figure 8-25 Current system date in DatePicker if today were March 17, 2014

In the following syntax, a Switch statement is passed the DATE_DIALOG_ID identifier. When the ID matches the switch case defined, the case statement returns a new DatePicker control that is displayed within a dialog box with the current year, month, and day. The return type is designated as Dialog, which returns the contents of the dialog box. The keyword **protected** signifies that the method or variable can only be accessed by elements residing in its class.

Code Syntax

```
protected Dialog onCreateDialog(int id) {
switch (id) {
case DATE_DIALOG_ID:
    return new DatePickerDialog(this, reservationDate, currentYear,
        currentMonth, currentDay);
}
    return null;
}
```

Notice the argument named reservationDate in the DatePickerDialog method. In addition to the current system date being displayed in the DatePicker calendar, the argument reservationDate is necessary to hold the date that is selected by the user for the reservation of the fishing day trip. The argument reservationDate later in code is assigned the new date selected by the user, so a red error line is displayed. The next set of steps code the onCreateDialog method that displays the dialog box with the current date:

1. In Main.java, insert a blank line before the last closing brace in the code so you can add the onCreateDialog method within the Main Activity. Type **protected Dialog onCreateDialog(int id) {**. Press the Enter key to automatically add the closing brace to this method. Point to Dialog and click Import 'Dialog' (android.app). Point to onCreateDialog and click Add return statement.

A return null statement automatically appears within onCreateDialog (Figure 8-26).

Figure 8-26   onCreateDialog is called by the showDialog method

2. Insert a blank line after the protected statement so you can enter a Switch statement. Recall that a Switch statement is a decision structure that determines how to handle the id passed into the onCreateDialog method. Type **switch (id) {** and press the Enter key to automatically insert the closing brace. Inside the Switch statement, type **case DATE_DIALOG_ID:** to specify the identifier for the dialog box.

A Switch statement handles the id passed into onCreate using a case statement (Figure 8-27).

```
37          final Calendar c = Calendar.getInstance();
38          currentYear = c.get(Calendar.YEAR);
39          currentMonth = c.get(Calendar.MONTH);
40          currentDay = c.get(Calendar.DAY_OF_MONTH);
41      }
42      protected Dialog onCreateDialog(int id) {
43          switch (id) {
44            case DATE_DIALOG_ID:          Switch decision
45          }                                structure
46          return null;
47
48      }
49
50  }
51
```

Figure 8-27 Switch and case statements

3. To return a DatePicker control within a dialog box with the current date initially displayed, press the Enter key and type **return new DatePickerDialog(this, reservationDate, currentYear, currentMonth, currentDay);**. Point to DatePickerDialog and click Import 'DatePickerDialog' (android.app). The variable named reservationDate is assigned the date the user enters as the desired date for the fishing day trip.

A DatePickerDialog method creates a dialog box displaying a DatePicker control with today's date. A red error line appears below reservationDate (Figure 8-28).

```
41      }
42      protected Dialog onCreateDialog(int id) {
43          switch (id) {                              DatePickerDialog
44            case DATE_DIALOG_ID:                     method displays the
45              return new DatePickerDialog(this, reservationDate, currentYear,   current year, month,
46                  currentMonth, currentDay);         and day
47          }
48          return null;
49
50  }
51
52  }
```

Figure 8-28 DatePickerDialog method is returned

4. Save your work.

CHAPTER 8   Design! Using a DatePicker on a Tablet

288

Coding the onDateSetListener Method

Just like the button listener that awaits user interaction, a second listener is necessary to "listen" for the user to select a date after the dialog box displays a DatePicker control. When the dialog box appears, the user selects the date and taps the Set button, as shown in Figure 8-25, and onDateSetListener is invoked in DatePickerDialog. When the user changes the date and taps the Set button, the reservation date for the fishing trip is passed to reservationDate, as shown in the following code syntax:

Code Syntax

```
private DatePickerDialog.OnDateSetListener reservationDate =
new DatePickerDialog.OnDateSetListener() {

public void onDateSet(DatePicker view, int year, int month, int day) {
        reservation.setText("Your reservation is set for " +
            month + 1)+("-") + day + ("-") + year);
    }
};
```

When a reservation date is selected, three integers from the DatePicker are passed into onDateSet representing the year, the month, and the day. The **onDateSet** event is fired after the user sets a date selection. The year, month, and day arguments are then displayed in the reservation TextView control using setText, as shown in Figure 8-2. For example, if the user selects March 17, 2014, the TextView control displays *Your reservation is set for 3-17-2014*. Notice that the setText statement in the code syntax adds 1 to the month. Android uses a zero-based month numbering system; for example, January is considered month 0. By adding 1 to the month, the correct month is displayed. If you live in Canada or Europe, you set reservation.setText to display the day first, then the month plus 1 and the year. The Marlin Adventures application at this point is one of many bookings that might be part of a larger application. Typically, the application would either e-mail the reserved date to the owners or verify the date in a connected database. Follow the steps to create an OnDateSetListener method to display the reserved date:

1. In Main.java, insert a blank line before the last closing brace in the code to add the onDateSet method within the Main Activity. Type **private DatePickerDialog.OnDateSetListener reservationDate = new DatePickerDialog.OnDateSetListener()** {. Press the Enter key to automatically add the closing brace to this method. Type **;** (semicolon) to the right of this closing brace. Point to DatePickerDialog and click Add unimplemented methods. If necessary in the method stub, change monthOfYear to **month** and change dayOfMonth to **day**.

   The onDateSet method stub appears automatically after the OnDateSetListener is typed (Figure 8-29).

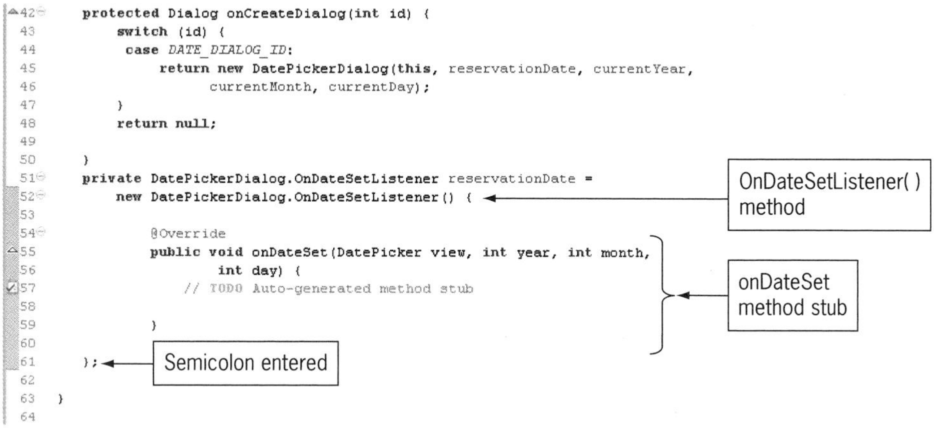

```
42   protected Dialog onCreateDialog(int id) {
43       switch (id) {
44       case DATE_DIALOG_ID:
45           return new DatePickerDialog(this, reservationDate, currentYear,
46               currentMonth, currentDay);
47       }
48       return null;

49
50   }
51   private DatePickerDialog.OnDateSetListener reservationDate =
52       new DatePickerDialog.OnDateSetListener() {
53
54       @Override
55       public void onDateSet(DatePicker view, int year, int month,
56           int day) {
57           // TODO Auto-generated method stub
58
59       }
60
61   };
62
63   }
64
```

OnDateSetListener( ) method

onDateSet method stub

Semicolon entered

Figure 8-29 The onDateSet method reacts to the date selected by the user

2. Click the blank line after the // TODO comment to enter code that will display the reservation date in the last row of the table layout, and then type **reservation.setText ("Your reservation is set for " + (month + 1)+("-") + day + ("-") + year);**.

The reservation details are displayed in the reservation TextView control (Figure 8-30).

290

```
J Main.java 

  1  package net.androidbootcamp.marlinadventures;
  2
  3⊕ import java.util.Calendar;
 12
 13  public class Main extends Activity {
 14      private int currentYear;
 15      private int currentMonth;
 16      private int currentDay;
 17      static final int DATE_DIALOG_ID = 0;
 18      private Button btDate;
 19      private TextView reservation;
 20
 21      /** Called when the activity is first created. */
 22⊖     @Override
▲23      public void onCreate(Bundle savedInstanceState) {
 24          super.onCreate(savedInstanceState);
 25          setContentView(R.layout.main);
 26          btDate = (Button) findViewById(R.id.btnDate);
 27          reservation = (TextView) findViewById(R.id.txtReservation);
 28⊖         btDate.setOnClickListener(new View.OnClickListener() {
 29
 30⊖             @Override
▲31              public void onClick(View v) {
✓32                  // TODO Auto-generated method stub
 33                  showDialog(DATE_DIALOG_ID);
 34              }
 35
 36          });
 37          final Calendar c = Calendar.getInstance();
 38          currentYear = c.get(Calendar.YEAR);
 39          currentMonth = c.get(Calendar.MONTH);
 40          currentDay = c.get(Calendar.DAY_OF_MONTH);
 41      }
▲42⊖    protected Dialog onCreateDialog(int id) {
 43          switch (id) {
 44           case DATE_DIALOG_ID:
 45              return new DatePickerDialog(this, reservationDate, currentYear,
 46                  currentMonth, currentDay);
 47          }
 48          return null;
 49
 50      }
 51⊖     private DatePickerDialog.OnDateSetListener reservationDate =
 52⊖         new DatePickerDialog.OnDateSetListener() {
 53
 54⊖             @Override
▲55              public void onDateSet(DatePicker view, int year, int month,
 56                      int day) {
✓57                  // TODO Auto-generated method stub
 58                  reservation.setText("Your reservation is set for " +
 59                      (month + 1)+("-") + day + ("-") + year);
 60              }
 61
 62          };
 63
 64  }
 65
```

Figure 8-30   Complete code for Main.java

GTK

This same program would function with a TimePicker control, showDialog(TIME_DIALOG_ID),
Calendar.HOUR_OF_DAY, Calendar.MINUTE, and TimePickerDialog method.

Running and Testing the Application

It's time to make your day trip reservation using the Marlin Adventures apps. Click Run on the menu bar, and then select Run to save and test the application in the tablet emulator. A dialog box requesting how you would like to run the application opens the first time the application is executed. Select Android Application and click the OK button. Save all the files in the next dialog box, if necessary, and unlock the tablet emulator. If necessary, click Apps and then double-click Marlin Adventures. The application opens in the tablet 10.1-inch emulator window where you can test the Button and DatePicker controls in the Marlin Adventures app, as shown in Figure 8-1 and Figure 8-2.

IN THE TRENCHES
On the Windows and Mac computer platforms, the newest operating systems are quickly replacing installed programs launched by icons with an app platform that allows full use of download markets such as the Windows Marketplace and the App Store. Desktop and laptop computer sales are dropping while tablet computer sales are rising.

Wrap It Up—Chapter Summary

This chapter described the steps to create a tablet application on a much larger screen. Creating a calendar control is a common specification on many Android applications. This same DatePicker application would work with a smaller Android phone window with a different design, but the code would work the same. Just like a well-made tool, your Android app, whether it is displayed on a phone or tablet, should strive to combine beauty, simplicity, and purpose to create a magical experience that is effortless to the end user.

- When designing apps for an Android tablet, keep your users' objectives and the size of the device in mind.

- To use an Android emulator designed for tablets, you first add AVD configurations appropriate for tablets.

- You can combine the Linear layout and the Table layout to create a simple, clean layout that takes advantage of a tablet's width. The TableLayout contains TableRow controls— one for each row in your table in main.xml. In each TableRow, you can insert a view control such as a Button or TextView.

- You can display a calendar tool called a DatePicker control in a dialog box so users can select a date from the control. The Time & Date category in the Palette contains many calendar controls, including TimePicker, DatePicker, CalendarView, Chronometer, AnalogClock, and DigitalClock.

- To display the current system date when the DatePicker control opens, you use the currentYear, currentMonth, and currentDay class variables to access the system date. These class variables hold the integer value of the system year, month, and day.

- To create a DatePickerDialog instance, you must define a unique identifier to represent the dialog box that displays the DatePicker control. The DATE_DIALOG_ID is a static integer that identifies the dialog box that will display the calendar.

- If you include a control, such as a Button, that users tap to display a calendar, use the setOnClickListener method to implement the Button.OnClickListener, which creates an instance of the OnClickListener and calls the onClick method. The onClick method responds to the user's action, so you place the code to launch the DatePicker dialog box in the onClick method. The showDialog( ) method triggers a call to the onCreateDialog method of the Activity class and passes the unique integer id for the constant DATE_DIALOG_ID to the DatePicker dialog box.

- When the integer id for the DATE_DIALOG_ID constant is passed to the DatePicker dialog box in the onClick method, a new DatePicker Dialog is passed along with the values for year, month, and day. You must set the values for the current date by using the Calendar class. Use the get field manipulation method to access the system date or time, and use set to change the current date or time.

- After an app calls a showDialog(DATE_DIALOG_ID) method in reaction to the user tapping a Button control, the showDialog method calls the OnCreateDialog callback method. The OnCreateDialog method creates a dialog box based on the argument passed by the showDialog method call, which is the value associated with DATE_DIALOG_ID. That value initializes the DatePicker to the date retrieved from the Calendar instance for today's system date.

- When a dialog box containing a DatePicker appears, users can select a date and tap a Button control. Tapping the Button invokes an onDateSetListener in DatePickerDialog, which passes integers representing the year, month, and day from the DatePicker into onDateSet. The selected date can then be displayed in a TextView control using setText.

Key Terms

Calendar class—A class you can use to access the Android system date. The Calendar class also is responsible for converting between a Date object and a set of integer fields such as YEAR, MONTH, and DAY_OF_MONTH.

DAY_OF_MONTH—A date constant of the Calendar class that retrieves an integer value of the system's current day.

DAY_OF_YEAR—A date constant of the Calendar class that retrieves the day of the current year as an integer. For example, February 1 is day 32 of the year.

emulated application—An application that is converted in real time to run on a variety of platforms such as a Web page, which can be displayed on various screen sizes through a browser.

get—The field manipulation method that accesses the system date or time.

getInstance—A method of the Calendar class that returns a calendar date or time based on the system settings.

MONTH—A date constant of the Calendar class that retrieves an integer value of the system's current month.

native application—A program locally installed on a specific platform such as a phone or tablet.

OnCreateDialog—A method that creates a dialog box based on the argument passed by the showDialog method call.

onDateSet—An event that is triggered when the DatePicker passes a value representing the year, the month, and the day. In other words, the onDateSet event is fired after the user sets a date selection.

padding property—A property that you can use to offset the content of a control by a specific number of pixels.

protected—A keyword signifying that the method or variable can only be accessed by elements residing in its class.

set—The field manipulation method that changes the system date or time.

static variable—A program variable that does not vary and has the same value throughout execution of the application.

TableLayout—A user interface design layout that includes TableRow controls to form a grid.

typeface—A property that you can use to set the style of control text to font families, including monospace, sans_serif, and serif.

YEAR—A date constant of the Calendar class that retrieves an integer value of the system's current year.

Developer FAQs

1. Explain the difference between a native app and a Web page.

2. What is the range of the diagonal measurement of tablet screens?

3. What is the diagonal size of the iPad screen?

4. Describe the three most common activities mentioned in the chapter used with an Android phone.

5. How do the activities in question 4 differ from how you would typically use a tablet?

6. Which Android AVD was designed specifically for tablets? Identify the name and version.

7. Which theme was used in the chapter project?

8. Inside of an XML Table layout, what is the XML code name of each row?

9. True or False? A LinearLayout and TableLayout cannot be used in the same XML layout file.

294

10. Write the single line of XML code to set the padding to 22 density independent pixels.

11. Write the single line of XML code to set the text to the font family of sans serif.

12. Name six calendar widgets.

13. If a date is displayed as 9/30/1995 in the United States, how would that same date be displayed in Europe?

14. Why is it best to use a pop-up dialog box for a DatePicker control?

15. Write a statement that triggers a call to onCreateDialog for a dialog box that displays a DatePicker control.

16. Name five purposes of a dialog box.

17. Write a line of code that, for the calendar instance named cal, assigns dueDay to the day of the month.

18. Why was the value of 1 added to the month in the chapter project?

19. Write a line of code that, for the calendar instance named c, assigns currentHour to the hour of the day.

20. Write a line of code that, for the calendar instance named c, assigns currentMinute to the minute within an hour.

Beyond the Book

Using the Internet, search the Web for the answers to the following questions to further your Android knowledge.

1. Research Android tablet design. Find five design tips not mentioned in the chapter and describe them using complete sentences.

2. Research five popular Android calendar apps available in the Android Market. Write a paragraph about the purpose of each one.

3. In the Information Technology (IT) field, Gartner, Inc., is considered one of the world's leading IT research and advisory companies. Research Gartner's opinion on the growth of the tablet. Locate a recent article by Gartner and write a summary of at least 150 words of the tablet trend.

4. The Android style guide online at *http://developer.android.com/design* provides a foundation in Android best practices. Create a bulleted list of 15 best practices from this site.

Case Programming Projects

Complete one or more of the following case programming projects. Use the same steps and techniques taught within the chapter. Submit the program you create to your instructor. The level of difficulty is indicated for each case programming project.

Easiest: ★

Intermediate: ★★

Challenging: ★★★

Case Project 8–1: Oasis Day Spa Tablet App ★

Requirements Document

Application title:	Oasis Day Spa Tablet App
Purpose:	The Oasis Day Spa in Dublin, Ireland, would like an Android tablet app that first displays a full-day spa treatment title and description, and then displays a calendar for reserving a day at the spa.
Algorithms:	1. The opening tablet screen displays an image, a spa icon, a title, a description, and a button to create a reservation for a day at the spa (Figure 8-31).
	2. When the user taps a button, a DatePicker is displayed in a dialog box (Figure 8-32). The dialog box displays the date of the reservation.
Conditions:	1. The pictures named spa.png and ic_launcher_spa.png are provided with your student files.
	2. Write your own description of the spa treatment.
	3. Use a European style date.
	4. Use the default theme.
	5. Use a Table layout with five rows.

Figure 8-31

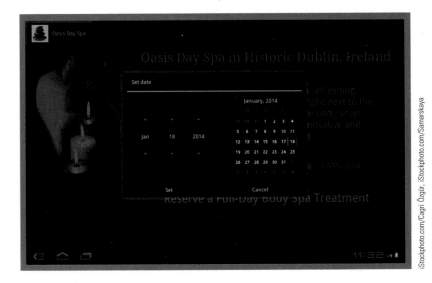

Figure 8-32

iStockphoto.com/Cagri_Özgür, iStockphoto.com/Samarskaya

Case Project 8–2: Washington D.C. Walking Tour Tablet App ⋆

Requirements Document

Application title: Washington D.C. Walking Tour Tablet App

Purpose: The Washington D.C. Walking Tour tablet app provides a reservation button to select a date to see all the Washington DC sights on this guided walking tour of the nation's capital.

Algorithms: 1. The opening screen displays an image, a tour description, and a button that launches a DatePicker dialog box (Figure 8-33).

2. When the user taps the button, a DatePicker control is displayed in a dialog box. The dialog box confirms the date of the reservation.

Conditions: 1. A picture of Washington named dc.png is provided with your student files.

2. Write your own description of the walking tour.

3. Use a theme without an action bar.

4. Use a Table layout.

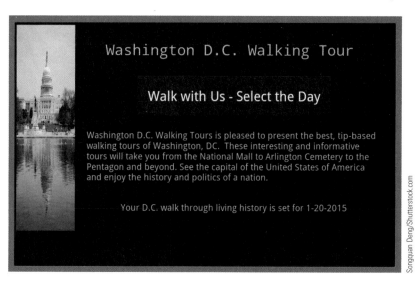

Figure 8-33

Case Project 8–3: Country Cabin Rental Tablet App ★★

Requirements Document

Application title:	Country Cabin Rental Tablet App
Purpose:	The Country Cabin Rental realty agency provides cabins for rental. Two cabins are available for a minimum three-night stay.
Algorithms:	1. The opening screen displays an image, cabin descriptions, two radio button controls with different cabin names, and a button that launches a DatePicker dialog box.
	2. When the user taps the button, a DatePicker control is displayed in a dialog box. The user selects the first night of a three-night reservation. The dialog box displays the date range of the three-night reservation with the name of the selected cabin.
Conditions:	1. A picture named cabin.png is provided with your student files.
	2. Write your own descriptions of the cabins.
	3. Do not use the default theme.
	4. Only one radio button can be selected at a time.
	5. Use a Table layout.

Case Project 8–4: Final Touch Auto Detailing Tablet App ★★

Requirements Document

Application title:	Final Touch Auto Detailing Tablet App
Purpose:	The Final Touch Auto Detailing business provides a variety of detailing services. The company wants an app to list each service and its price and display a calendar for making a service reservation.
Algorithms:	1. The opening screen displays an image, service descriptions, four check boxes offering different detailing services each with different prices, and a button that launches a DatePicker dialog box to make a reservation for the all-day auto-detailing services.
	2. When the user taps the button, a DatePicker control is displayed in a dialog box. The user selects the date for the reservation. The dialog box displays the date and final cost of the detailing services.
Conditions:	1. A picture named car.png is provided with your student files.
	2. Write your own descriptions about the car detailing services.
	3. Do not use the default theme.
	4. More than one check box can be checked at once.
	5. Use a Table layout.

Case Project 8–5: Wild Ginger Dinner Delivery Tablet App ★★★

Requirements Document

Application title:	Wild Ginger Dinner Delivery Tablet App with TimePicker
Purpose:	Wild Ginger Dinner Delivery service delivers dinners in the evening. The business wants an app that customers can use to select a dinner and reserve a delivery time.
Algorithms:	1. The opening screen displays an image, a Wild Ginger food description, and a button that launches a TimePicker dialog box to make a reservation for delivery tonight.
	2. When the user taps the button, a TimePicker control is displayed in a dialog box. The user selects the time for delivery, and the app confirms the delivery time, which is available only from 5 pm to 11 pm.
Conditions:	1. Select your own image(s).
	2. Write your own description of the great food offered at Wild Ginger.
	3. Do not use the default theme.
	4. Use a Table layout.

Case Project 8–6: Create Your Own Tablet App ★★★

Requirements Document

Application title:	Create Your Own Tablet App
Purpose:	Create an app with a DatePicker and a TimePicker to create a reservation.
Algorithms:	1. Create an app on a topic of your own choice.
	2. Use two buttons. The first button allows the user to select the date and the second button allows the user to select the time.
Conditions:	1. Select your own image(s).
	2. Use a custom layout and icon.

CHAPTER 9

Customize! Navigating with Tabs on a Tablet App

In this chapter, you learn to:

- ◎ Create an Android tablet project using a tab layout
- ◎ Code an XML layout with a TabHost control
- ◎ Display a TabWidget and FrameLayout within a TabHost
- ◎ Customize a GridView XML layout
- ◎ Develop a user interface that displays images in a GridView control
- ◎ Extend a TabActivity class
- ◎ Display multiple classes as content within a tab layout
- ◎ Customize the ImageAdapter class for a GridView layout
- ◎ Open an Android Web browser in a tablet
- ◎ Customize a tab specification with TabSpec
- ◎ Add a TabSpec to a TabHost

Creating an attractive user interface that provides simple navigation can be challenging when programming a tablet app on an Android device. Fortunately, the Android platform provides a flexible way to simplify layout and navigation using a tab interface. Tab interfaces have replaced traditional drop-down menus across many platforms from Web page browsers to newer versions of Microsoft Office. Like multiple windows, tabs can be used to show different topics within a single window in an intuitive interface.

In this chapter, you create a tab interface in an Android application designed to customize a European bike and barge cruise vacation. Bike and barge cruises combine two popular ways of exploring Europe—cycling and river cruising. On a bike and barge experience, you spend your days cycling through historic European sites and your nights cruising down scenic rivers through cities such as Amsterdam and Budapest. The Bike and Barge application shown in Figure 9-1 features three tabs for Photos, Tour, and Web Site. The first tab displays a photo grid of the bike and cruise boat tour images using a GridView control in a two-dimensional grid layout.

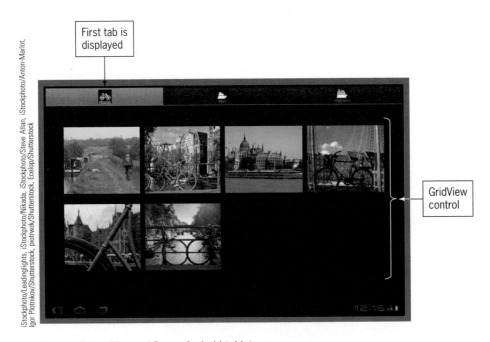

First tab is
displayed

GridView
control

iStockphoto/Leadinglights, iStockphoto/Nikada, iStockphoto/Steve Allan, iStockphoto/Anton-Marlot, Igor Plotnikov/Shutterstock, piotrwzk/Shutterstock, Ecelop/Shutterstock

Figure 9-1   Bike and Barge Android tablet app

This Android tablet Bike and Barge app provides images, text, and a link that opens a Web page within the Android browser. When the user taps the second tab, a second window opens displaying tour information, as shown in Figure 9-2. The third tab links to a browser that displays the full Bike and Barge Web site, including tour company contact information, as shown in Figure 9-3. The intuitive tabs eliminate the need for additional instructions.

Customize! Navigating with Tabs on a Tablet App

303

Figure 9-2 Second tab displays tour information

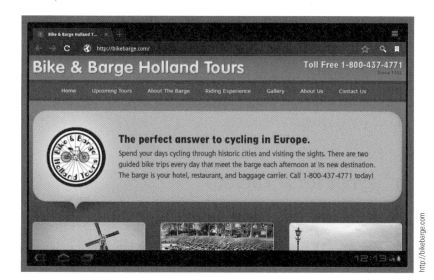

Figure 9-3 Third tab opens a Web site

IN THE TRENCHES
Cycling apps already in the Android marketplace include GPS-based biking routes, personal cycling logs, mountain biking trails, bike repair, distance tracking, and cycling fitness to use on your trip.

To create this application, the developer must understand how to perform the following processes, among others:

1. Create a TabHost within the XML code that includes the TabWidget and FrameLayout.

2. Extend the TabActivity class.

3. Add the tab and GridView images needed for the project.

4. Create three different XML layouts for each of the tabs.

    a. Create the XML layout for the first tab to display a GridView control.

    b. Create the XML layout for the second tab to display TextView information.

    c. Create the XML layout for the third tab to display a Web site in a browser.

5. Create three different Activities, one for each tab.

    a. Code the first tab to display a GridView control.

    b. Code the second tab to display TextView information.

    c. Code the third tab to display a Web site in a browser.

6. Code the Main Activity to specify the TabSpec and launch the tabs.

7. Update the Android Manifest file.

Creating a Tab Layout for a Tablet

The Bike and Barge tablet app features an opening screen with three tabs, as shown in Figure 9-1. Digital tab controls represent the tabbed manila folders used to organize information in filing cabinets. Tabs function as they do in a browser tabbed window. Each tab in a browser window displays Web page content using intuitive navigation. You can switch between tabs without opening more browser windows. An Android SDK provides a **TabHost** control so you can wrap multiple views in a single window. A tabbed window view can have two or more tabs within an Android phone or tablet interface. The TabHost contains two distinct parts: a **TabWidget** for displaying the tabs and a **FrameLayout** for displaying the tab content, as shown in Figure 9-4.

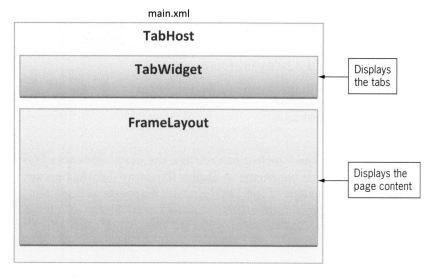

Figure 9-4   Anatomy of a TabHost control

The TabHost, the root for the layout, can be placed at the top or bottom of the Android window. In the chapter project, the TabHost is at the top of the window with individual tabs for the photos, tours, and Web site located on a tab bar called the TabWidget. Below the tab bar, the TabHost wraps the contents of each tab in the FrameLayout. The tab content can be coded in two ways:

- Each tab launches a separate Activity class.
- All tabs are launched within a single Activity class.

The Bike and Barge tablet application provides three different Activities: a GridView control to display images in the first tab, TextView controls to describe the tour in the second tab, and a Web browser to open a Web page in the third tab. Having separate Activity classes with code in each Activity is easier to manage than one extremely large class with a massive XML layout file.

The TabHost Layout

In main.xml of the chapter project, the TabHost control creates the tab layout. TabHost requires a TabWidget and a FrameLayout within the XML layout code. Use the default LinearLayout to position the TabWidget and FrameLayout vertically; that is, with the TabWidget at the top of the TabHost and the FrameLayout below the TabWidget. When coding the XML for the tabbed user interface, the TabHost, TabWidget, and FrameLayout must have ids assigned in the code, as shown in Table 9-1.

Control	Android id
TabHost	android:id="@+id/tabhost"
TabWidget	android:id="@android:id/tabs"
FrameLayout	android:id="@android:id/tabcontent"

Table 9-1   Tab control Android id

These names must be used so that the TabHost can retrieve the exact references to each control. It is best to avoid using a title bar theme to display the entire TabHost because a large title bar can change the dimensions of the TabHost, which appears at the top of the tablet window. In the chapter project, the theme is set to Theme.Black.NoTitleBar to avoid this problem. The following XML code provides the framework needed for the tab layout:

Code Syntax

```
<TabHost xmlns:android="http://schemas.android.com/apk/res/android"
    android:id="@android:id/tabhost"
    <LinearLayout
        <TabWidget
            android:id="@android:id/tabs" />
        <FrameLayout
            android:id="@android:id/tabcontent" />
    </LinearLayout>
</TabHost>
```

Notice how the TabHost is the root control of the TabWidget and FrameLayout. Each control has the standard id shown in Table 9-1. The Eclipse XML layout does not display TabHost controls properly in design mode, so you must use XML layout code to specify the tabs instead of using the widgets from the Palette. After the XML and Java code are complete later in the chapter, you can view the tab layout using the Android emulator. To begin the application, code main.xml on the tablet to create the XML code for the tabbed layout using TabHost, and to change the theme, follow these steps:

1. Open the Eclipse program. Click the New button on the Standard toolbar. Expand the Android folder and select Android Project. Click the Next button. In the New Android Project dialog box, enter the Project Name **Bike and Barge**. To save the project on your USB drive, click to remove the check mark from the Use default location check box. Type **E:\Workspace** (if necessary, enter a different drive letter that identifies the USB drive). Click the Next button. For the Build Target, select Android 3.0, if necessary. Click the Next button. For the Package Name, type **net.androidbootcamp.bikeandbarge**. Enter **Main** in the Create Activity text box. The Minimum SDK should be 11.

The new Android Bike and Barge tablet project has an Application Name, a Package Name, and an Activity named Main (Figure 9-5).

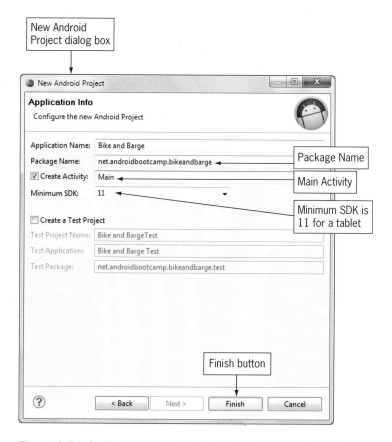

New Android
Project dialog box

Package Name

Main Activity

Minimum SDK is
11 for a tablet

Finish button

Figure 9-5 Application information for the new Android project

2. Click the Finish button. In the res\layout folder, double-click main.xml. Delete the Hello World, Main! TextView control, and then click the main.xml tab at the bottom of the window to display the XML code. Delete all the code except for the first line. On the second line, type the following code using auto-completion as much as possible:

```
<TabHost xmlns:android="http://schemas.android.com/apk/res/android"
    android:id="@android:id/tabhost"
    android:layout_width="fill_parent"
    android:layout_height="fill_parent">

</TabHost>
```

The TabHost XML code creates the root for the tabbed interface (Figure 9-6).

Figure 9-6   TabHost XML code

3. Click Line 6 (the blank line) to add the LinearLayout necessary to orient the TabWidget and FrameLayout vertically so that the FrameLayout appears below the TabWidget. Type the following code using auto-completion as much as possible:

```
<LinearLayout
        android:orientation="vertical"
        android:layout_width="fill_parent"
        android:layout_height="fill_parent">

</LinearLayout>
```

The LinearLayout XML code creates the vertical layout for the two parts of the TabHost (Figure 9-7).

```
 1  <?xml version="1.0" encoding="utf-8"?>
 2  <TabHost xmlns:android="http://schemas.android.com/apk/res/android"
 3          android:id="@android:id/tabhost"
 4          android:layout_width="fill_parent"
 5          android:layout_height="fill_parent">
 6          <LinearLayout
 7              android:orientation="vertical"
 8              android:layout_width="fill_parent"
 9              android:layout_height="fill_parent">
10
11          </LinearLayout>
12  </TabHost>
```

Blank line

LinearLayout

Figure 9-7   LinearLayout to place the TabWidget and FrameLayout vertically

4. Click Line 10 (the blank line) to place the TabWidget and FrameLayout within the LinearLayout XML code. Type the following code using auto-completion as much as possible:

```
<TabWidget
    android:id="@android:id/tabs"
    android:layout_width="fill_parent"
    android:layout_height="wrap_content" />
<FrameLayout
    android:id="@android:id/tabcontent"
    android:layout_width="fill_parent"
    android:layout_height="fill_parent"/>
```

The TabWidget creates tabs within the TabHost. The FrameLayout creates the content area of the TabHost (Figure 9-8).

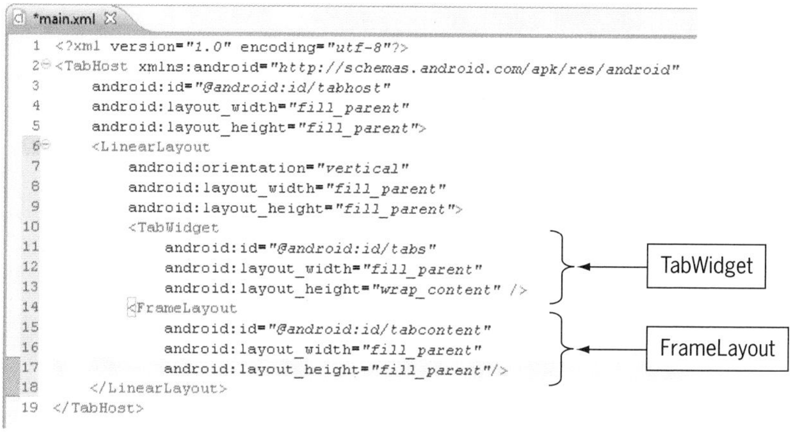

```
 1   <?xml version="1.0" encoding="utf-8"?>
 2   <TabHost xmlns:android="http://schemas.android.com/apk/res/android"
 3       android:id="@android:id/tabhost"
 4       android:layout_width="fill_parent"
 5       android:layout_height="fill_parent">
 6       <LinearLayout
 7           android:orientation="vertical"
 8           android:layout_width="fill_parent"
 9           android:layout_height="fill_parent">
10           <TabWidget
11               android:id="@android:id/tabs"
12               android:layout_width="fill_parent"
13               android:layout_height="wrap_content" />      TabWidget
14           <FrameLayout
15               android:id="@android:id/tabcontent"
16               android:layout_width="fill_parent"
17               android:layout_height="fill_parent"/>        FrameLayout
18       </LinearLayout>
19   </TabHost>
```

Figure 9-8   TabWidget and FrameLayout within the TabHost

5. To view the graphical layout created by the main.xml code, click the Graphical Layout tab at the bottom of main.xml. Click the Theme button and change the Theme to Theme.Black.NoTitleBar. Click the orange placeholder and then click the FrameLayout area to identify the two separate portions of the screen layout.

The TabHost XML code creates a placeholder in the Graphical Layout tab. Notice that the tabs are not displayed. An orange placeholder bar marks the location of the future tabs (Figure 9-9).

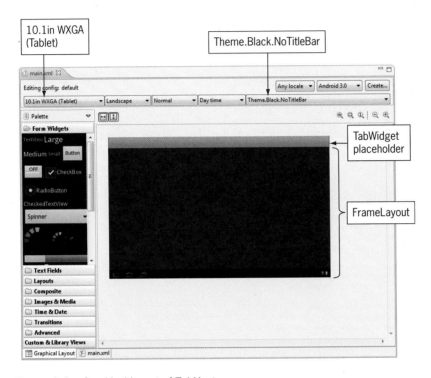

Figure 9-9 Graphical layout of TabHost

GTK
The tabs can be placed at the bottom of the Android window by inserting the FrameLayout XML code before the TabWidget code in main.xml and adding `android:layout_marginBottom="-5px"` to the TabWidget code. The TabHost is now displayed at the bottom of the screen 5 pixels from the edge.

Extending the TabActivity Class

Begin designing a tabbed control in Java by opening Main.java and changing the type of Activity in the code. In previous chapters, the opening class statement (`public class Main extends Activity`) extended the basic Activity class. If the primary purpose of a class is to display a TabHost control, use a class named **TabActivity** instead of Activity, which makes it simple to display tabs within the app. To extend the TabActivity class of Main.java of the Bike and Barge tablet app, follow this step:

1. Close and save main.xml. In src/net.androidbootcamp.bikeandbarge, double-click Main.java to open its code window. Click to the right of extends in the public class Main extends Activity { line, and change Activity to **TabActivity**. Point to TabActivity and click Import 'TabActivity' (android app). If necessary, point to Bundle in Line 8, and then click Import 'Bundle' (android.os).

Main extends TabActivity, which contains predefined methods for the use of tabs (Figure 9-10).

```
J  *Main.java  ⊠
 1  package net.androidbootcamp.bikeandbarge;
 2
 3⊕ import android.app.TabActivity;☐
 5
 6  public class Main extends TabActivity {  ◄─────────   Main extends
 7      /** Called when the activity is first created. */      TabActivity
 8⊖     @Override
▲9      public void onCreate(Bundle savedInstanceState) {
10          super.onCreate(savedInstanceState);
11          setContentView(R.layout.main);
12      }
13  }
```

Figure 9-10   Main extends TabActivity

Adding the Tab and GridView Images

Each of the three tabs in the Bike and Barge app contains an image and text. As shown in Figure 9-1, the GridView control on the first tab displays six images illustrating the bike and barge tour. To add the three tab and six GridView image files to the drawable folder, follow this step:

1. To add the nine image files to the drawable folder, if necessary, copy the student files to your USB drive. Open the USB folder containing the student files. In the Package Explorer, expand the drawable-hdpi folder in the res folder. To add the nine image files to the drawable-hdpi resource folder, drag the bike1.png, bike2.png, bike3.png, bike4.png, bike5.png, bike6.png, tab1.png, tab2.png, and tab3.png files to the drawable-hdpi folder until a plus sign pointer appears. Release the mouse button. If necessary, click the Copy files option button, and then click the OK button.

Copies of the nine files appear in the drawable-hdpi folder (Figure 9-11).

312

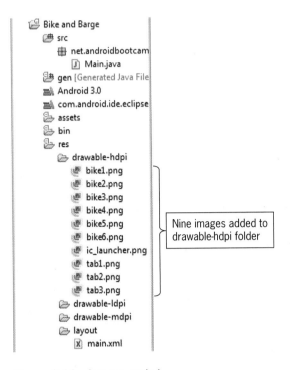

Figure 9-11   Images copied

GTK

Tab icons should be designed as simple, flat shapes rather than 3D images. Typically, tab icons are also sized as 72 x 72 pixels.

Creating a GridView XML Layout for the First Tab

The first tab in the Bike and Barge project displays a grid of images in two rows to provide a visual marketing tool for the tour company. Inviting images displayed in a photo GridView help travelers visualize their trip. The first tab uses an XML layout file named tab1.xml to display the GridView control. Similar to the Gallery control used in Chapter 7, a **GridView** control is part of the View group and displays objects in a two-dimensional, scrollable grid. To customize a GridView layout, you can specify the number of columns, the width of each column, and the space between columns. The following code shows the XML code for a GridView layout:

Code Syntax

```xml
<GridView xmlns:android="http://schemas.android.com/apk/res/android"
    android:id="@+id/photos"
    android:layout_width="fill_parent"
    android:layout_height="fill_parent"
    android:padding="40dp"
    android:verticalSpacing="30dp"
    android:horizontalSpacing="10dp"
    android:numColumns="auto_fit"
    android:columnWidth="60dp"
    android:stretchMode="columnWidth"
    android:gravity="center">
</GridView>
```

Most of the properties in the GridView control resemble earlier examples in the book, but notice a new property called numColumns. The GridView property **numColumns** can be set to an integer value or to a setting called auto_fit, which automatically defines how many columns to show based on the size of the Android screen and the image width. The **columnWidth** property specifies a fixed width for each column. Follow these steps to create an XML layout file that displays a GridView control:

1. In the Package Explorer, right-click the layout folder. On the shortcut menu, point to New and then click Other. In the New dialog box, click Android XML Layout File, and then click the Next button. In the New Android Layout XML File dialog box, type **tab1.xml** in the File text box to name the layout file. In the Root Element list, select GridView. Click the Finish button. The emulator window opens. Click the tab1.xml tab at the bottom of the window to open the XML code.

   The tab1.xml file opens with a basic GridView control automatically displayed in the code (Figure 9-12).

Figure 9-12   tab1.xml layout file

2. To customize the GridView layout, click at the end of Line 4 and delete the closing > symbol. Delete the closing </GridView> tag. On the first blank line, type the following XML code using auto-completion as much as possible:

```
android:id="@+id/photos"
android:padding="60dp"
android:verticalSpacing="20dp"
android:horizontalSpacing="20dp"
android:numColumns="auto_fit"
android:columnWidth="230dp"
android:stretchMode="columnWidth"
android:gravity="center" />
```

The GridView control is coded for a custom layout (Figure 9-13).

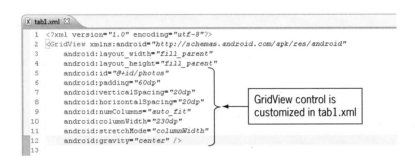

Figure 9-13   Custom GridView layout

Creating a TextView XML Layout for the Second Tab

For the content of the second tab, three TextView controls display the tour details for the Bike and Barge application within the LinearLayout. To create an XML layout file that displays three TextView controls, follow these steps:

1. Close the tab1.xml file tab and save your work. Right-click the layout folder, point to New on the shortcut menu, and then click Other. In the New dialog box, click Android XML Layout File, and then click the Next button. In the New Android Layout XML File dialog box, type **tab2.xml** in the File text box to name the layout file. In the Root Element list, select LinearLayout. Click the Finish button. The emulator window opens. Click the tab2.xml tab at the bottom of the window to open the XML code. In Line 7, type the following XML code for the first TextView control using auto-completion as much as possible:

```
<TextView
        android:id="@+id/textView1"
        android:layout_width="wrap_content"
        android:layout_height="wrap_content"
        android:layout_gravity="center_horizontal"
        android:text="Summer - Bike and Barge Europe Tour"
        android:textSize="60sp"
        android:paddingBottom="60sp" />
```

The first TextView control is coded in tab2.xml (Figure 9-14).

```
 1  <?xml version="1.0" encoding="utf-8"?>
 2  <LinearLayout xmlns:android="http://schemas.android.com/apk/res/android"
 3      android:layout_width="match_parent"
 4      android:layout_height="match_parent"
 5      android:orientation="vertical" >
 6
 7      <TextView
 8          android:id="@+id/textView1"
 9          android:layout_width="wrap_content"
10          android:layout_height="wrap_content"
11          android:layout_gravity="center_horizontal"
12          android:text="Summer - Bike and Barge Europe Tour"
13          android:textSize="60sp"
14          android:paddingBottom="60sp" />
```

First TextView control

Figure 9-14 First TextView control

2. Press the Enter key twice, and then type the following XML code for the second TextView control using auto-completion as much as possible:

```
<TextView
        android:id="@+id/textView2"
        android:layout_width="wrap_content"
        android:layout_height="wrap_content"
        android:text="The 21-speed hybrid bikes are our mode of
transportation to view the country's landscape, history, customs, and
traditions. The barge leaves beautiful Amsterdam and finishes 13 days
later in Bruges, Belgium."
        android:textSize="45sp"
        android:paddingLeft="70sp"
        android:paddingBottom="60sp" />
```

The second TextView control is coded in tab2.xml (Figure 9-15).

Figure 9-15 Second TextView control

3. Press the Enter key twice, and then type the following XML code for the third TextView control using auto-completion as much as possible:

```
<TextView
        android:id="@+id/textView3"
        android:layout_width="wrap_content"
        android:layout_height="wrap_content"
        android:layout_gravity="center_horizontal"
        android:text="June 2 - June 15  Holland Belgium Tour"
        android:gravity="center_horizontal"
        android:textSize="50sp" />
```

315

The third TextView control for tab2.xml is coded (Figure 9-16).

```
 1  <?xml version="1.0" encoding="utf-8"?>
 2  <LinearLayout xmlns:android="http://schemas.android.com/apk/res/android"
 3      android:layout_width="match_parent"
 4      android:layout_height="match_parent"
 5      android:orientation="vertical" >
 6
 7      <TextView
 8          android:id="@+id/textView1"
 9          android:layout_width="wrap_content"
10          android:layout_height="wrap_content"
11          android:layout_gravity="center_horizontal"
12          android:text="Summer - Bike and Barge Europe Tour"
13          android:textSize="60sp"
14          android:paddingBottom="60sp" />
15
16      <TextView
17          android:id="@+id/textView2"
18          android:layout_width="wrap_content"
19          android:layout_height="wrap_content"
20          android:text="The 21-speed hybrid bikes are our mode of transportation to view the co
21          android:textSize="45sp"
22          android:paddingLeft="70sp"
23          android:paddingBottom="60sp" />
24
25      <TextView
26          android:id="@+id/textView3"
27          android:layout_width="wrap_content"
28          android:layout_height="wrap_content"
29          android:layout_gravity="center_horizontal"
30          android:text="June 2 - June 15  Holland Belgium Tour"
31          android:gravity="center_horizontal"
32          android:textSize="50sp" />
    </LinearLayout>
```

Third TextView control

Graphical Layout | tab2.xml

Figure 9-16   Complete code for tab2.xml

Creating the XML Layout for the Third Tab

The third tab has the simplest XML layout and is named tab3.xml. This layout file does not contain any controls for the Java code that opens tab3.xml and launches the Web browser displaying the Bike and Barge site. To create the simple XML layout, follow this step:

1. Close the tab2.xml file tab and save your work. Right-click the layout folder, point to New on the shortcut menu, and then click Other. In the New dialog box, click Android XML Layout File, and then click the Next button. In the New Android Layout XML File dialog box, type **tab3.xml** in the File text box to name the layout file. In the Root Element list, select LinearLayout. Click the Finish button. The emulator window opens.

The tab3.xml window opens. No controls or code are necessary (Figure 9-17).

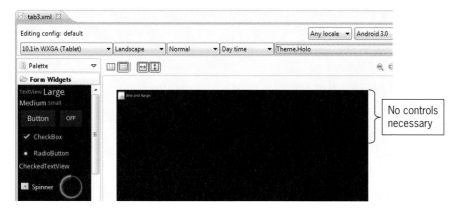

No controls necessary

Figure 9-17   tab3.xml

Coding the GridView Activity for the First Tab

When the Bike and Barge application starts, it opens to the first tab, which is a GridView control displaying six images. The other two tabs for Tour and Web Site are available in the TabHost control. To work as designed, the chapter project requires four Java code Activity files. Main.java sets up the tabs and assigns an Activity to each one. Three Activities named Tab1.java, Tab2.java, and Tab3.java are launched by Main.java according to the user's tab selection. The Java code for Tab1 creates an instance of the GridView control, which is almost identical to the Gallery control in Chapter 7. Previously, the user selected an image from the Gallery and a toast message identified that image. A GridView control can work in the same fashion, but in this chapter project, the GridView control lays out the images in a grid. The instance of the GridView control references the GridView control named with the photos id, as shown in the following code:

Code Syntax

```
GridView g = (GridView) findViewById(R.id.photos);
```

To create a Java file named Tab1.java and instantiate the GridView control, follow these steps:

1. Close the tab3.xml file tab. To create a second class, right-click the net.androidbootcamp.bikeandbarge folder, point to New on the shortcut menu, and then click Class. Type **Tab1** in the Name text box to create a second class that will define the Tab1 Activity. Click the Superclass Browse button. Type **Activity** in the Choose a type text box. As you type, matching items are displayed. Click Activity – android.app and then click the OK button to extend the Activity class. Click the Finish button. To launch the Activity, in the Tab1.java file, click Line 6, type **oncreate**, and then press Ctrl+spacebar to display an auto-complete listing. Double-click the first onCreate method in the auto-complete listing. Click at the end of Line 10 and then press the

Enter key to insert a blank line. Type **setContentView(R.** to display an auto-complete listing. Double-click layout. Type a period. Another auto-complete listing displays the requested XML layout file. Double-click tab1 : int. A right closing parenthesis appears. Type a semicolon after the parenthesis to complete the statement.

A new class named Tab1 that launches tab1.xml is created (Figure 9-18).

```
J *Tab1.java ⌧
 1  package net.androidbootcamp.bikeandbarge;
 2
 3⊕ import android.app.Activity;□
 5
 6  public class Tab1 extends Activity {          ◄————  Tab1 class
 7⊖ @Override                                             is created
 8  protected void onCreate(Bundle savedInstanceState) {
 9       // TODO Auto-generated method stub
10       super.onCreate(savedInstanceState);
11       setContentView(R.layout.tab1);       ◄————  tab1.xml layout
12  }                                                is displayed
13  }
```

Figure 9-18   Tab1.java class opens the tab1.xml layout

2. To instantiate the GridView, in Main.java in the onCreate( ) method, press the Enter key, type **GridView g = (GridView) findViewById(R.id.photos);**, point to GridView, and then click Import 'GridView' (android.widget).

The GridView control is instantiated (Figure 9-19).

```
J Tab1.java ⌧
 1  package net.androidbootcamp.bikeandbarge;
 2
 3⊕ import android.app.Activity;□
 6
 7  public class Tab1 extends Activity {
 8⊖ @Override
 9  protected void onCreate(Bundle savedInstanceState) {
10       // TODO Auto-generated method stub
11       super.onCreate(savedInstanceState);
12       setContentView(R.layout.tab1);
13       GridView g = (GridView) findViewById(R.id.photos);   ◄————  Instance of
14  }                                                               GridView
15  }
16
```

Figure 9-19   GridView control is instantiated

IN THE TRENCHES

The GridView control is commonly used on tablets to display all the images, songs, or videos stored on the device or in the cloud. Many service providers offer cloud-based storage and file-sharing options to expand your repository of media used on your Android device.

Using a setAdapter with an ImageAdapter

Previously, you used adapters to display ListView and Gallery controls. Similarly, a **setAdapter** provides a data model for the layout of the GridView control. You use setAdapter( ) to instantiate a custom BaseAdapter class called ImageAdapter and apply it to the GridView, as shown in the following code:

Code Syntax

```
g.setAdapter(new ImageAdapter(this));
```

After the ImageAdapter is instantiated, the ImageAdapter class extends the custom BaseAdapter class. The adapter used within this class binds the images to a particular layout such as a GridView control. To instantiate the ImageAdapter class for the GridView control, follow these steps:

1. Press the Enter key and type **g.setAdapter(new ImageAdapter(this));**. A red error line appears under ImageAdapter. Instead of automatically creating the class, a custom ImageAdapter class is added in the next step.

   The ImageAdapter is coded for the GridView control. A red error line appears below ImageAdapter (Figure 9-20).

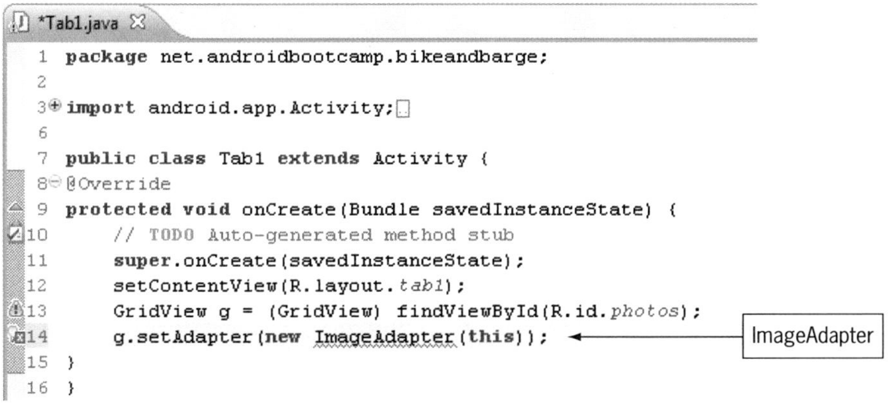

```
*Tab1.java
1  package net.androidbootcamp.bikeandbarge;
2
3  import android.app.Activity;
6
7  public class Tab1 extends Activity {
8      @Override
9      protected void onCreate(Bundle savedInstanceState) {
10         // TODO Auto-generated method stub
11         super.onCreate(savedInstanceState);
12         setContentView(R.layout.tab1);
13         GridView g = (GridView) findViewById(R.id.photos);
14         g.setAdapter(new ImageAdapter(this));     ImageAdapter
15     }
16 }
```

Figure 9-20 Instance of the ImageAdapter class

2. To add an ImageAdapter class that extends the BaseAdapter custom class, click after the first closing brace at the end of Line 15. Press the Enter key and type **public class ImageAdapter extends BaseAdapter {** . Press the Enter key and a closing brace appears. Point to BaseAdapter and then click Import 'BaseAdapter' (android.widget). Point to ImageAdapter in the same line and click Add unimplemented methods. Point to ImageAdapter in Line 17 and select Create constructor 'ImageAdapter(Tab1)'.

   The ImageAdapter class is coded. The methods within the ImageAdapter are auto-completed (Figure 9-21).

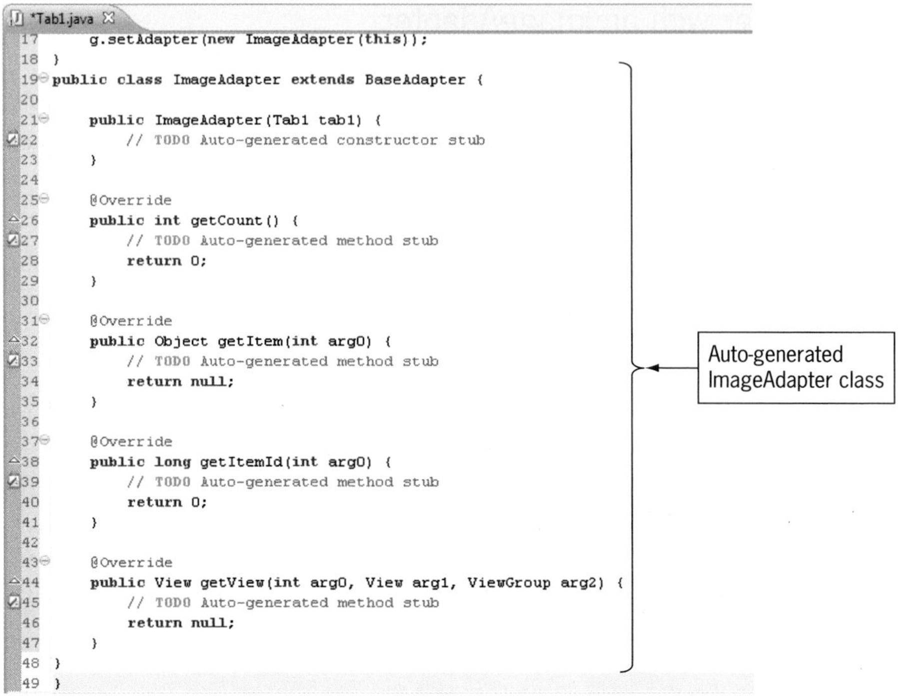

```
🗋 *Tab1.java ✕
17            g.setAdapter(new ImageAdapter(this));
18  }
19⊖ public class ImageAdapter extends BaseAdapter {
20
21⊖      public ImageAdapter(Tab1 tab1) {
22            // TODO Auto-generated constructor stub
23       }
24
25⊖       @Override
26       public int getCount() {
27            // TODO Auto-generated method stub
28            return 0;
29       }
30
31⊖       @Override
32       public Object getItem(int arg0) {
33            // TODO Auto-generated method stub
34            return null;
35       }
36
37⊖       @Override
38       public long getItemId(int arg0) {
39            // TODO Auto-generated method stub
40            return 0;
41       }
42
43⊖       @Override
44       public View getView(int arg0, View arg1, ViewGroup arg2) {
45            // TODO Auto-generated method stub
46            return null;
47       }
48  }
49  }
```

Auto-generated
ImageAdapter class

Figure 9-21   ImageAdapter class

Customizing the ImageAdapter Class

When the ImageAdapter class is called with the g.setAdapter(new ImageAdapter(this));
line of code, the ImageAdapter class controls the layout of the GridView and connects
the data sources from an array for display. The ImageAdapter class must provide
the information to set up the GridView with data and specifications necessary for the
display. Context is used to load and access resources for the application. The
ImageAdapter constructor is changed from Tab1 to handle the Context resources
necessary for the GridView. This ImageAdapter class constructor is where the Context
for an ImageAdapter instance is defined.

An array is required to hold multiple images displayed in the GridView. An array can
be adjusted to hold as many images as necessary. To define the Context for the
ImageAdapter and to establish an array to reference the images in the drawable folder,
follow these steps:

    1.   Save your work. On the blank line following public class ImageAdapter extends
           BaseAdapter {, initialize the Context variable by typing **private Context context;**,
           point to Context, and then select Import 'Context' (android.content).

           The Context variable named context is initialized (Figure 9-22).

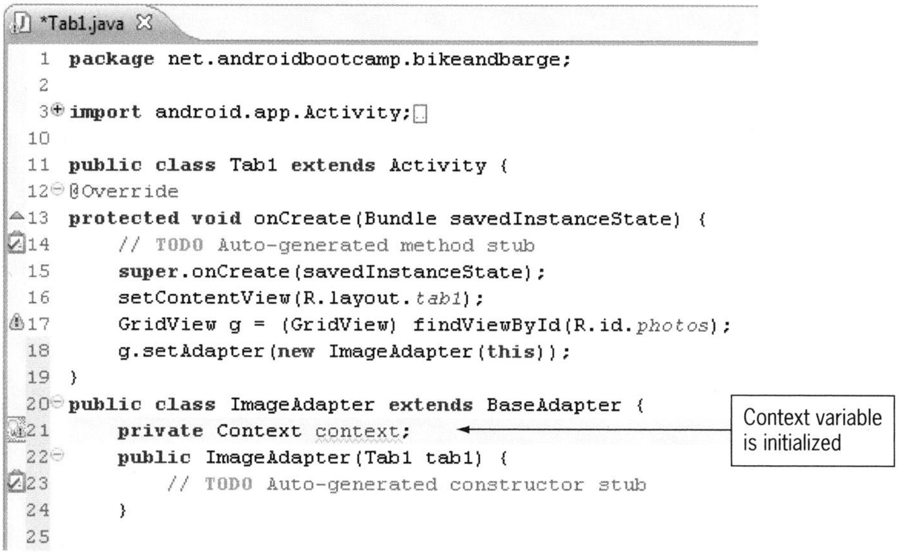

```
*Tab1.java ☒
 1  package net.androidbootcamp.bikeandbarge;
 2
 3⊕ import android.app.Activity;☐
10
11  public class Tab1 extends Activity {
12⊝ @Override
13  protected void onCreate(Bundle savedInstanceState) {
14      // TODO Auto-generated method stub
15      super.onCreate(savedInstanceState);
16      setContentView(R.layout.tab1);
17      GridView g = (GridView) findViewById(R.id.photos);
18      g.setAdapter(new ImageAdapter(this));
19  }
20⊝ public class ImageAdapter extends BaseAdapter {
21      private Context context;
22⊝      public ImageAdapter(Tab1 tab1) {
23          // TODO Auto-generated constructor stub
24      }
25
```

Context variable is initialized

Figure 9-22 Context variable

2. Press the Enter key to initialize an Integer array named Bikes that references the tour images. Type **private Integer[] Bikes = { R.drawable.bike1, R.drawable.bike2, R.drawable.bike3, R.drawable.bike4, R.drawable.bike5, R.drawable.bike6};** to initialize the Bikes array.

The Integer array named Bikes is assigned to six image files in the drawable folder (Figure 9-23).

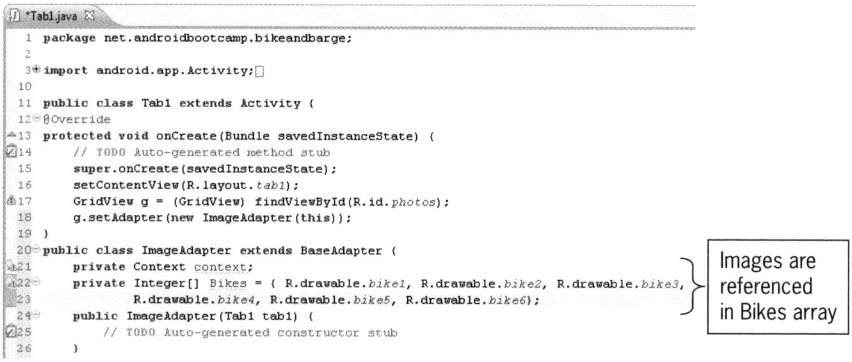

```
*Tab1.java ☒
 1  package net.androidbootcamp.bikeandbarge;
 2
 3⊕ import android.app.Activity;☐
10
11  public class Tab1 extends Activity {
12⊝ @Override
13  protected void onCreate(Bundle savedInstanceState) {
14      // TODO Auto-generated method stub
15      super.onCreate(savedInstanceState);
16      setContentView(R.layout.tab1);
17      GridView g = (GridView) findViewById(R.id.photos);
18      g.setAdapter(new ImageAdapter(this));
19  }
20⊝ public class ImageAdapter extends BaseAdapter {
21      private Context context;
22⊝      private Integer[] Bikes = ( R.drawable.bike1, R.drawable.bike2, R.drawable.bike3,
23          R.drawable.bike4, R.drawable.bike5, R.drawable.bike6);
24⊝      public ImageAdapter(Tab1 tab1) {
25          // TODO Auto-generated constructor stub
26      }
```

Images are referenced in Bikes array

Figure 9-23 Bikes array

3. To change the ImageAdapter constructor to define the Context, change public ImageAdapter(Tab1 tab1) { in the next line to public ImageAdapter(**Context c**) {. At the end of the comment in the next line, press the Enter key. Type **context = c;**.

The *ImageAdapter constructor for the ImageAdapter class holds the Context (Figure 9-24).*

```
*Tab1.java ☒
  1  package net.androidbootcamp.bikeandbarge;
  2
  3⊕ import android.app.Activity;☐
 10
 11  public class Tab1 extends Activity {
 12⊖ @Override
▲13  protected void onCreate(Bundle savedInstanceState) {
 14      // TODO Auto-generated method stub
 15      super.onCreate(savedInstanceState);
 16      setContentView(R.layout.tab1);
 17      GridView g = (GridView) findViewById(R.id.photos);
 18      g.setAdapter(new ImageAdapter(this));
 19  }
 20⊖ public class ImageAdapter extends BaseAdapter {
 21      private Context context;
 22⊖     private Integer[] Bikes = { R.drawable.bike1, R.drawable.bike2, R.drawable.bike3,
 23              R.drawable.bike4, R.drawable.bike5, R.drawable.bike6);
 24⊖     public ImageAdapter(Context c) {
 25          // TODO Auto-generated constructor stub
 26          context = c;                    ◄——  context is
 27      }                                         referenced
```

Figure 9-24   ImageAdapter constructor

4. To assign the return type of the getCount method to the number of images in the array, change the first return 0; (for the getCount method) to **return Bikes. length;**.

The length of the Bikes array is returned by the getCount method (Figure 9-25).

```
*Tab1.java ☒
  1  package net.androidbootcamp.bikeandbarge;
  2
  3⊕ import android.app.Activity;☐
 10
 11  public class Tab1 extends Activity {
 12⊖ @Override
▲13  protected void onCreate(Bundle savedInstanceState) {
 14      // TODO Auto-generated method stub
 15      super.onCreate(savedInstanceState);
 16      setContentView(R.layout.tab1);
 17      GridView g = (GridView) findViewById(R.id.photos);
 18      g.setAdapter(new ImageAdapter(this));
 19  }
 20⊖ public class ImageAdapter extends BaseAdapter {
 21      private Context context;
 22⊖     private Integer[] Bikes = { R.drawable.bike1, R.drawable.bike2, R.drawable.bike3,
 23              R.drawable.bike4, R.drawable.bike5, R.drawable.bike6);
 24⊖     public ImageAdapter(Context c) {
 25          // TODO Auto-generated constructor stub
 26          context = c;
 27      }
 28
 29⊖     @Override
 30      public int getCount() {
 31          // TODO Auto-generated method stub
 32          return Bikes.length;  ◄——         Length of the Bikes
 33      }                                      array is returned
```

Figure 9-25   getCount( ) returns length of the Bikes array

Coding the getView Method

The getView( ) method uses Context to create a new ImageView instance that is responsible for temporarily holding each image displayed in the GridView control. In addition, the ImageView is scaled to fit the GridView control and sized according to a custom height and width, as shown in the following code:

Code Syntax

```
public View getView(int position, View convertView, ViewGroup parent) {
        // TODO Auto-generated method stub
        ImageView pic = new ImageView(context);
        pic.setLayoutParams(new GridView.LayoutParams(275, 250));
        pic.setScaleType(ImageView.ScaleType.CENTER_CROP);
        pic.setPadding(8, 8, 8, 8);
        pic.setImageResource(Bikes[position]);
        return pic;

};
```

In the getView( ) method, notice that a return type of View is expected. A View occupies a rectangular area on the screen and is responsible for drawing the GridView component. When pic is returned for the View display, it includes an image that is scaled and resized, ready for display in the GridView control. Depending on your settings, Eclipse might change int position, View convertView, ViewGroup parent to int arg0, View arg1, ViewGroup arg2, or vice versa. This change does not affect the execution of the program.

An instance of an ImageView control named pic is created inside the getView( ) method using Java code. A new ImageView for each item in the Bikes array is referenced by the adapter. The display size of each GridView image is set in the LayoutParams arguments, which are the numbers representing the width in pixels and the height in pixels. This ensures that, no matter the size of the drawable file, each image is resized and cropped to fit within these dimensions. In the next statement, setScaleType scales the image to the bounds of the view. Scaling keeps or changes the aspect ratio of the image within the ImageView control. Next, setPadding defines the padding for all sides of each image. The setImageResource method assigns each image from the drawable folder to the ImageView control. The last statement within the getView( ) method must return the instance of the ImageView control named pic to be displayed in the GridView control. To code the getView( ) method, follow these steps:

1. In Tab1.java, click at the end of the // TODO comment in the getView method and press the Enter key. To create an ImageView control that holds the images displayed in the GridView control, type **ImageView pic = new ImageView(context);**. Press the Enter key. If red error lines appear, point to ImageView and then click Import 'ImageView' (android.widget). To resize the layout of the images displayed in the GridView control, type **pic.setLayoutParams(new GridView.LayoutParams (275, 250));**. Press the Enter key. To set the scale type of the ImageView control, type **pic.setScaleType(ImageView.ScaleType.CENTER_CROP);**.

An instance of ImageView named pic is created. The layout size and scale are set (Figure 9-26).

```
48⊖    @Override
△49    public View getView(int arg0, View arg1, ViewGroup arg2) {
⊘50        // TODO Auto-generated method stub
51        ImageView pic = new ImageView(context);
52        pic.setLayoutParams(new GridView.LayoutParams(275, 250));
53        pic.setScaleType(ImageView.ScaleType.CENTER_CROP);
54        return null;
55    }
56 }
57 }
```

The pic instance of ImageView is resized and scaled

Figure 9-26   The getView method creates an instance of ImageView

2. Press the Enter key. To set the padding around each image in GridView, type **pic.setPadding(8, 8, 8, 8);**. To assign each of the images referenced in the Bikes array, press the Enter key and type **pic.setImageResource(Bikes[arg0]);**. To return pic to the Main activity, change return null; in the next line to **return pic;**.

The instance of pic sets the padding of each image in the Bikes array. The instance of pic is returned (Figure 9-27).

```
🗋 Tab1.java ✕
 1  package net.androidbootcamp.bikeandbarge;
 2
 3⊕ import android.app.Activity;□
11
12  public class Tab1 extends Activity {
13⊖ @Override
△14  protected void onCreate(Bundle savedInstanceState) {
⊘15      // TODO Auto-generated method stub
16      super.onCreate(savedInstanceState);
17      setContentView(R.layout.tab1);
18      GridView g = (GridView) findViewById(R.id.photos);
19      g.setAdapter(new ImageAdapter(this));
20  }
21⊖ public class ImageAdapter extends BaseAdapter {
22      private Context context;
23⊖     private Integer[] Bikes = { R.drawable.bike1, R.drawable.bike2, R.drawable.bike3,
24          R.drawable.bike4, R.drawable.bike5, R.drawable.bike6 };
25⊖     public ImageAdapter(Context c) {
⊘26         // TODO Auto-generated constructor stub
27         context = c;
28     }
29
30⊖     @Override
△31     public int getCount() {
⊘32         // TODO Auto-generated method stub
33         return Bikes.length;
34     }
35
36⊖     @Override
△37     public Object getItem(int arg0) {
⊘38         // TODO Auto-generated method stub
39         return null;
40     }
41
42⊖     @Override
△43     public long getItemId(int arg0) {
⊘44         // TODO Auto-generated method stub
45         return 0;
46     }
47
48⊖     @Override
△49     public View getView(int arg0, View arg1, ViewGroup arg2) {
⊘50         // TODO Auto-generated method stub
51         ImageView pic = new ImageView(context);
52         pic.setLayoutParams(new GridView.LayoutParams(275, 250));
53         pic.setScaleType(ImageView.ScaleType.CENTER_CROP);
54         pic.setPadding(8, 8, 8, 8);
55         pic.setImageResource(Bikes[arg0]);
56         return pic;
57     }
58 }
59 }
60
```

pic is added and assigned the Bikes image

Figure 9-27   Complete code for Tab1.java

Coding the Second Tab Java File

When the user taps the second tab in the Bike and Barge app, the tab2.xml layout displays the current tour information. To create a Java file named Tab2.java and display tab2.xml, follow this step:

1. Close the Tab1.java file tab and save your work. To create a third class, right-click the net.androidbootcamp.bikeandbarge folder, point to New on the shortcut menu, and then click Class. Type **Tab2** in the Name text box to create a second class that will define the Tab2 Activity. Click the Superclass Browse button. Type **Activity** in the Choose a type text box. Click Activity – android.app and then click the OK button to extend the Activity class. Click the Finish button. To launch the Activity, in the Tab2.java file, click Line 6, type **oncreate**, and then press Ctrl+spacebar to display an auto-complete listing. Double-click the first onCreate method in the auto-complete listing. Click at the end of Line 10 and then press the Enter key to insert a blank line. Type **setContentView(R.** to display an auto-complete listing. Double-click layout. Type a period. Another auto-complete listing requests the XML layout file you intend to display. Double-click tab2 : int. A right closing parenthesis appears. (If it does not, type **)** to insert a right closing parenthesis.) Type a semicolon after the parenthesis to complete the statement.

    A new class named Tab2.java that launches tab2.xml is created (Figure 9-28).

```
 1  package net.androidbootcamp.bikeandbarge;
 2
 3⊕ import android.app.Activity;
 5
 6  public class Tab2 extends Activity {
 7⊖     public void onCreate(Bundle savedInstanceState) {
 8            super.onCreate(savedInstanceState);
 9            setContentView(R.layout.tab2);
10        }
11  }
12
```

Tab2.java

onCreate method added to open tab2.xml

Figure 9-28 Complete code for Tab2.java

Coding the Third Tab Java File to Display a Web Site

The Bike and Barge Web site is launched in a browser when the third tab is tapped. To launch the built-in browser, Android uses a startActivity method to open a URI (Uniform Resource Identifier) object to identify the unique location of a Web site, as shown in Chapter 5. The user taps the third tab labeled *Web site* to open the browser. To return to the tabbed interface, users press the Back button on the lower-left corner of the tablet. To create a Java file named Tab3.java, display tab3.xml, and launch an Android browser window, follow these steps:

1. Close the Tab2.java file tab and save your work. To create a fourth class, right-click the net.androidbootcamp.bikeandbarge folder, point to New on the shortcut menu, and then click Class. Type **Tab3** in the Name text box to create a second class that will define the

326

Tab3 Activity. Click the Superclass Browse button. Type **Activity** in the Choose a type text box. Click Activity – android.app and then click the OK button to extend the Activity class. Click the Finish button. To launch the Activity, in the Tab3.java file, click Line 6, type **oncreate**, and then press Ctrl+spacebar to display an auto-complete listing. Double-click the first onCreate method in the auto-complete listing. Click at the end of Line 10 and then press the Enter key to insert a blank line. Type **setContentView(R.** to display an auto-complete listing. Double-click layout. Type a period. Another auto-complete listing requests the XML layout file you intend to display. Double-click tab3 : int. A right closing parenthesis appears. (If it does not, type **)** to insert a right closing parenthesis.) Type a semicolon after the parenthesis to complete the statement.

A new class named Tab3.java that launches tab3.xml is created (Figure 9-29).

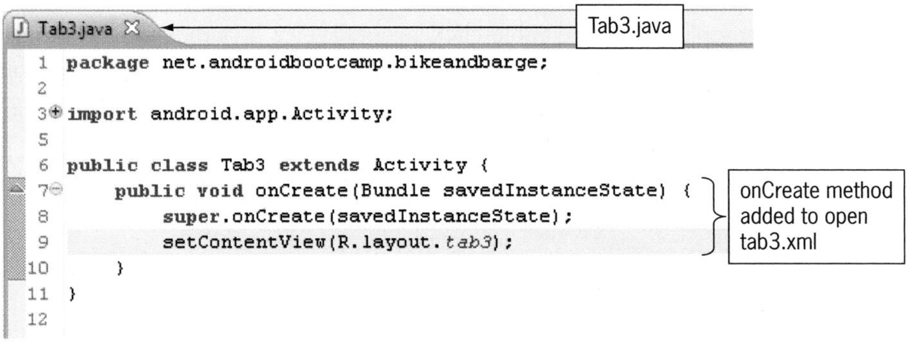

```
Tab3.java ⊠                                           ── Tab3.java
 1  package net.androidbootcamp.bikeandbarge;
 2
 3⊕ import android.app.Activity;
 5
 6  public class Tab3 extends Activity {
 7⊖     public void onCreate(Bundle savedInstanceState) {     ── onCreate method
 8         super.onCreate(savedInstanceState);                     added to open
 9         setContentView(R.layout.tab3);                          tab3.xml
10     }
11  }
12
```

Figure 9-29   Tab3.java opens the tab3.xml layout

2. Press the Enter key to add a statement to launch an intent to open the Bike and Barge Web site. Type **startActivity(new Intent(Intent.ACTION_VIEW, Uri.parse ("http://bikebarge.com/")));**. If red error lines appear in the statement, point to Intent and click Import 'Intent' (android.content), and then point to Uri and click Import 'Uri' (android.net).

The startActivity code launches the Bike and Barge Web site when the user selects the third tab (Figure 9-30).

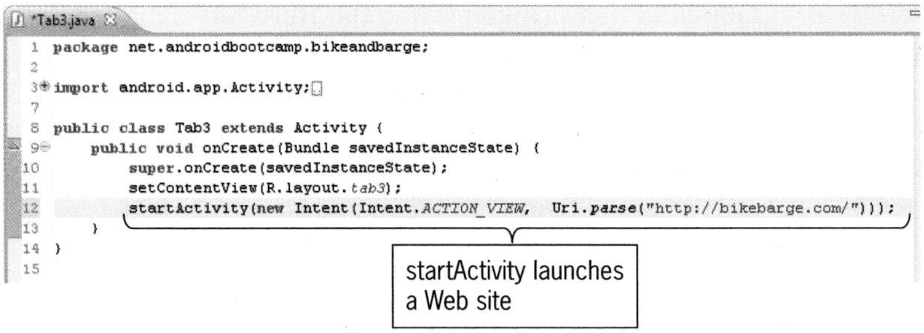

```
*Tab3.java ⊠
 1  package net.androidbootcamp.bikeandbarge;
 2
 3⊕ import android.app.Activity;⬚
 7
 8  public class Tab3 extends Activity {
 9⊖     public void onCreate(Bundle savedInstanceState) {
10         super.onCreate(savedInstanceState);
11         setContentView(R.layout.tab3);
12         startActivity(new Intent(Intent.ACTION_VIEW, Uri.parse("http://bikebarge.com/")));
13     }
14  }
15
```

startActivity launches
a Web site

Figure 9-30   Complete code for Tab3.java

Coding the TabHost

Next, you must fully code the Main.java class that extends TabActivity to display the tabbed user interface at the top of the tablet. Each XML layout file must be loaded into the appropriate FrameLayout of each tab. In the following code syntax, the first line codes the getTabHost method, which starts the Activity named TabHost and hosts the tabs in the application. The next four lines provide the specifications for the first tab.

Code Syntax

```
TabHost tabHost = getTabHost();
//First Tab
TabSpec photospec = tabHost.newTabSpec("Photos");
photospec.setIndicator("Photos", getResources().getDrawable(R.drawable.tab1));
Intent photosIntent = new Intent(this, Tab1.class);
photospec.setContent(photosIntent);
```

Each tab must have a **TabSpec**, which specifies how the tabs should actually appear. The TabSpec statement in the code syntax creates an instance named photospec, which details tab content. On the next line, the photospec instance calls the **setIndicator** method that sets the tab button caption to "Photos" and supplies an icon image named tab1.png from the drawable folder. After the tab displays the caption and image, an intent is created to launch an Activity named Tab1.class. This statement opens Tab1.java, which displays the GridView layout of the photos. Lastly, the **setContent** method indicates what is displayed in the tab content area. This method calls the instance of the intent and places the content of the Tab1 Activity within the FrameLayout (the content area of TabHost). The code is repeated for the next two tabs. Follow these steps to write the code creating the tab content:

1. Close the Tab3.java tab and save your changes. In Main.java, click at the end of the line containing setContentView and press the Enter key. Type **TabHost tabHost = getTabHost();**. Point to TabHost and select Import 'TabHost' (android.widget). If a red error line appears under getTabHost, point to the error line, and then click Create method 'getTabHost( )'. To display the content for the first tab, press the Enter key, type the comment **//First tab**, and then press the Enter key. Type **TabSpec photospec = tabHost.newTabSpec("Photos");**. Point to TabSpec and select Import 'TabSpec' (android.widget.TabHost). To display the text and icon image, press the Enter key and type **photospec.setIndicator("Photos", getResources().getDrawable (R.drawable.tab1));**. To launch Tab1.java, press the Enter key, type **Intent photosIntent = new Intent(this, Tab1.class);**, point to Intent, and then select Import 'Intent' (android.content). To display the content, press the Enter key and type **photospec.setContent(photosIntent);**.

The TabHost is provided with specifications to open the contents of the first tab (Figure 9-31).

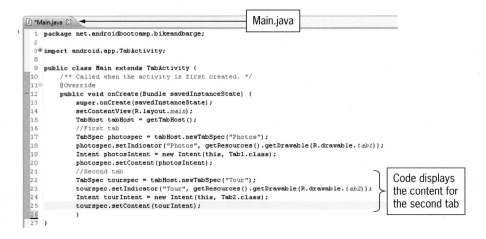

```
                                                              Main.java
*Main.java
 1  package net.androidbootcamp.bikeandbarge;
 2
 3⊕ import android.app.TabActivity;
 8
 9  public class Main extends TabActivity {
10      /** Called when the activity is first created. */
11⊝     @Override
12      public void onCreate(Bundle savedInstanceState) {
13          super.onCreate(savedInstanceState);
14          setContentView(R.layout.main);
15          TabHost tabHost = getTabHost();
16          //First tab
17          TabSpec photospec = tabHost.newTabSpec("Photos");
18          photospec.setIndicator("Photos", getResources().getDrawable(R.drawable.tab1));
19          Intent photosIntent = new Intent(this, Tab1.class);
20          photospec.setContent(photosIntent);
21          }
22  }
```

Code displays the content for the first tab

Figure 9-31   First tab is displayed with the Photos contents

2. Press the Enter key and then type the following code in Main.java to display the content for the second tab:

```
//Second tab
TabSpec tourspec = tabHost.newTabSpec("Tour");
tourspec.setIndicator("Tour",
getResources().getDrawable(R.drawable.tab2));
Intent tourIntent = new Intent(this, Tab2.class);
tourspec.setContent(tourIntent);
```

The Tour tab contents are specified for the second tab (Figure 9-32).

```
                                                              Main.java
*Main.java
 1  package net.androidbootcamp.bikeandbarge;
 2
 3⊕ import android.app.TabActivity;
 8
 9  public class Main extends TabActivity {
10      /** Called when the activity is first created. */
11⊝     @Override
12      public void onCreate(Bundle savedInstanceState) {
13          super.onCreate(savedInstanceState);
14          setContentView(R.layout.main);
15          TabHost tabHost = getTabHost();
16          //First tab
17          TabSpec photospec = tabHost.newTabSpec("Photos");
18          photospec.setIndicator("Photos", getResources().getDrawable(R.drawable.tab1));
19          Intent photosIntent = new Intent(this, Tab1.class);
20          photospec.setContent(photosIntent);
21          //Second tab
22          TabSpec tourspec = tabHost.newTabSpec("Tour");
23          tourspec.setIndicator("Tour", getResources().getDrawable(R.drawable.tab2));
24          Intent tourIntent = new Intent(this, Tab2.class);
25          tourspec.setContent(tourIntent);
26          }
27  }
```

Code displays the content for the second tab

Figure 9-32   Second tab displays the Tour contents

3. Press the Enter key and then type the following code in Main.java to display the content for the third tab:

```
// Third tab
TabSpec webspec = tabHost.newTabSpec("Web Site");
webspec.setIndicator("Web Site",
getResources().getDrawable(R.drawable.tab3));
Intent webIntent = new Intent(this, Tab3.class);
webspec.setContent(webIntent);
```

The Web site tab specifies the content for the third tab (Figure 9-33).

```
Main.java
 1  package net.androidbootcamp.bikeandbarge;
 2
 3  import android.app.TabActivity;
 8
 9  public class Main extends TabActivity {
10      /** Called when the activity is first created. */
11      @Override
12      public void onCreate(Bundle savedInstanceState) {
13          super.onCreate(savedInstanceState);
14          setContentView(R.layout.main);
15          TabHost tabHost = getTabHost();
16          //First tab
17          TabSpec photospec = tabHost.newTabSpec("Photos");
18          photospec.setIndicator("Photos", getResources().getDrawable(R.drawable.tab1));
19          Intent photosIntent = new Intent(this, Tab1.class);
20          photospec.setContent(photosIntent);
21          //Second tab
22          TabSpec tourspec = tabHost.newTabSpec("Tour");
23          tourspec.setIndicator("Tour", getResources().getDrawable(R.drawable.tab2));
24          Intent tourIntent = new Intent(this, Tab2.class);
25          tourspec.setContent(tourIntent);
26          //Third tab
27          TabSpec webspec = tabHost.newTabSpec("Web Site");
28          webspec.setIndicator("Web Site", getResources().getDrawable(R.drawable.tab3));
29          Intent webIntent = new Intent(this, Tab3.class);
30          webspec.setContent(webIntent);
31      }
32  }
```

Code displays the content for the third tab

Figure 9-33 Third tab displays the Web site contents

Adding the TabSpec to TabHost

The last step in Main.java is to add the tab specifications called TabSpec to the instance of the TabHost control. Every tab change closes the previously opened tab and opens the selected tab. To display the tab specifications (TabSpec) within the TabHost control, follow this step:

1. To display the tab specifications, press the Enter key, type the comment // **Add TabSpec to TabHost**, and then press the Enter key. Type **tabHost.addTab (photospec);**. Press the Enter key and type **tabHost.addTab(tourspec);**. Press the Enter key and type **tabHost.addTab(webspec);**.

The tabs are displayed with the appropriate specifications (Figure 9-34).

```
  Main.java
  1  package net.androidbootcamp.bikeandbarge;
  2
  3  import android.app.TabActivity;
  8
  9  public class Main extends TabActivity {
 10      /** Called when the activity is first created. */
 11      @Override
 12      public void onCreate(Bundle savedInstanceState) {
 13          super.onCreate(savedInstanceState);
 14          setContentView(R.layout.main);
 15          TabHost tabHost = getTabHost();
 16          //First tab
 17          TabSpec photospec = tabHost.newTabSpec("Photos");
 18          photospec.setIndicator("Photos", getResources().getDrawable(R.drawable.tab1));
 19          Intent photosIntent = new Intent(this, Tab1.class);
 20          photospec.setContent(photosIntent);
 21          //Second tab
 22          TabSpec tourspec = tabHost.newTabSpec("Tour");
 23          tourspec.setIndicator("Tour", getResources().getDrawable(R.drawable.tab2));
 24          Intent tourIntent = new Intent(this, Tab2.class);
 25          tourspec.setContent(tourIntent);
 26          //Third tab
 27          TabSpec webspec = tabHost.newTabSpec("Web Site");
 28          webspec.setIndicator("Web Site", getResources().getDrawable(R.drawable.tab3));
 29          Intent webIntent = new Intent(this, Tab3.class);
 30          webspec.setContent(webIntent);
 31          // Add TabSpec to TabHost
 32          tabHost.addTab(photospec);
 33          tabHost.addTab(tourspec);
 34          tabHost.addTab(webspec);
 35      }
```

> TabSpecs are displayed within the TabHost

Figure 9-34   Complete code for Main.java

Updating the Android Manifest File

Every Android application includes the AndroidManifest.xml file, which contains the information the Android system uses during runtime to display the theme, find the startup class, and stack the subsequent class Activity files. When the user selects a tab to launch a new Activity, it is pushed on the stack and becomes the running Activity. The previous Activity remains in the stack. When the user selects another tab in the TabHost, the current Activity is pushed out of the stack and the previous one resumes as the running Activity. To add the class files to the Android Manifest file and to add the custom theme, follow these steps:

1. To add the reference of Tab1, Tab2, and Tab3 Java class files to the Android Manifest, in the Package Explorer, double-click the AndroidManifest.xml file. Click the Application tab at the bottom of the Bike and Barge Manifest page. Scroll down to display the Application Nodes section. Click the Add button. Select Activity in the Create a new element at the top level, in Application dialog box. Click the OK button. The Attributes for Activity section opens in the Application tab. In the Name text box, type the class name preceded by a period (**.Tab1**) to add the Tab1 Activity. Click the Add button again. Click the first radio button (Create a new element at the top level, in Application) and select Activity. Click the OK button. In the Name text box, type the class name preceded by a period (**.Tab2**) to add the Tab2 Activity. Click the Add button again. Click the first radio button (Create a new element at the top level, in Application) and select Activity. Click the OK button. In the Name text box, type the class name preceded by a period (**.Tab3**) to add the Tab3 Activity. Save your work.

The AndroidManifest.xml file includes the three Activities (Figure 9-35).

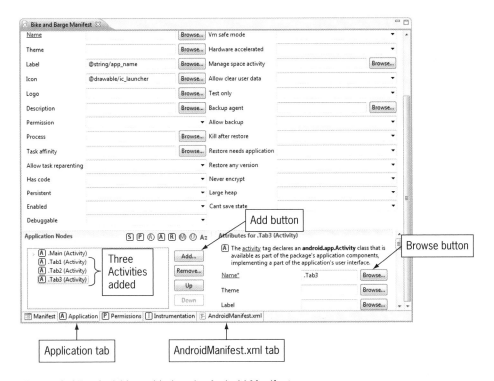

Figure 9-35 Activities added to the Android Manifest

2. To add the selected theme to the Android Manifest, click the AndroidManifest.xml tab at the bottom of the window, and then click at the end of the line android:name=".Main" inside the Activity code. Press the Enter key to insert a blank line. Type **android:theme="@android:style/Theme.NoTitleBar"**.

The Android theme is coded in the Android Manifest file (Figure 9-36).

332

```
  1  <?xml version="1.0" encoding="utf-8"?>
  2  <manifest xmlns:android="http://schemas.android.com/apk/res/android"
  3      package="net.androidbootcamp.bikeandbarge"
  4      android:versionCode="1"
  5      android:versionName="1.0" >
  6
  7      <uses-sdk android:minSdkVersion="11" />
  8
  9      <application
 10          android:icon="@drawable/ic_launcher"
 11          android:label="@string/app_name" >
 12          <activity
 13              android:label="@string/app_name"
 14              android:theme="@android:style/Theme.NoTitleBar"         Custom theme added
 15              android:name=".Main">
 16              <intent-filter >
 17                  <action android:name="android.intent.action.MAIN" />
 18
 19                  <category android:name="android.intent.category.LAUNCHER" />
 20              </intent-filter>
 21          </activity>
 22          <activity android:name=".Tab1"></activity>
 23          <activity android:name=".Tab2"></activity>
 24          <activity android:name=".Tab3"></activity>
 25      </application>
 26
 27  </manifest>
```

Manifest | Application | Permissions | Instrumentation | AndroidManifest.xml

Figure 9-36   Android Manifest code with new theme

3. Click the Save All button on the Standard toolbar, and then close the Bike and Barge Manifest tab.

Running and Testing the Application

The TabHost provides an easy-to-use navigation to display multiple windows within the tablet interface. To test the Bike and Barge Android app, click Run on the menu bar, and then select Run to save and test the application in the emulator. A dialog box requesting how you would like to run the application opens the first time the application is executed. Select Android Application and click the OK button. Save all the files in the next dialog box, if necessary, and unlock the emulator. The application opens in the tablet emulator window where you can test each tab in the Bike and Barge app, as shown in Figure 9-1, Figure 9-2, and Figure 9-3.

GTK

Another technique to display content in different portions of the tablet window is by using Fragments. A Fragment is essentially a sub-Activity hosted inside another Activity. By dividing different components of the user interface and displaying them in Fragments, it is easier for developers to reuse these components across various Activities.

Wrap It Up—Chapter Summary

A tablet provides a larger screen that allows for easier navigation using tabs. The chapter provided steps to create a TabHost that created a simple structure to display three screens of content. The GridView control was introduced for layout for images, videos, or other types of files in a grid configuration.

- To create a tabbed interface in an Android tablet app similar to one used in a browser, you use the TabHost control, which contains two parts. The TabWidget displays the tabs, including labels and icons, and the FrameLayout displays the tab content.

- You specify the layout of a tabbed interface in the XML code. The default LinearLayout positions the controls vertically, with the FrameLayout below the TabWidget. In the XML code, the TabHost, TabWidget, and FrameLayout must have the ids shown in Table 9-1.

- You begin designing a tabbed control in the main Java file, such as Main.java, by extending the TabActivity class instead of the Activity class using the statement `public class Main extends TabActivity`.

- Similar to the Gallery control, a GridView control displays objects in a two-dimensional, scrollable grid. To customize a GridView layout, you can specify the number of columns, the width of each column, and the column spacing.

- A setAdapter provides a data model for the layout of the GridView control. You use the setAdapter( ) method to instantiate the custom ImageAdapter class and apply it to the GridView, similar to the way you used adapters to display ListView and Gallery controls in previous chapters.

- When the ImageAdapter class is called, it controls the layout of the GridView and connects the data sources from an array for display. The ImageAdapter class must provide the information to set up the GridView with data and specifications necessary for the display. Context is used to load and access resources for the application.

- To display the tabbed interface, you must fully code the Main.java class that extends TabActivity. Each XML layout file must be loaded into the appropriate FrameLayout of each tab. Use the getTabHost method to start the TabHost Activity, which hosts the tabs in the application.

- Each tab in a tabbed interface must have a TabSpec statement, which specifies how the tabs should appear. The TabSpec statement creates an instance, which details tab content. The instance calls the setIndicator method that sets the tab button caption and supplies an icon image, if necessary. Next, an intent is created to launch an Activity for the first tab. Finally, the setContent method indicates what is displayed in the tab content area. This method calls the instance of the intent and places the content of the first tab's Activity within the FrameLayout (the content area of TabHost).

- The last step in Main.java is to add TabSpec to the instance of the TabHost control. Every tab change closes the previously opened tab and opens the selected tab.

Key Terms

columnWidth—A GridView property that specifies a fixed width for each column.

FrameLayout—The part of a TabHost control that displays the tab content.

GridView—A control that displays objects in a scrollable grid, similar to the Gallery control. A GridView control is part of the View group and lets you specify the number of columns, column width, and column spacing.

numColumns—A GridView property that can be set to an integer value representing the number of columns to include, or to auto fit, which determines the number of columns to show based on the size of the Android screen and the image width.

setAdapter—A method that provides a data model for the layout of the GridView control. You use the setAdapter method to instantiate a custom BaseAdapter class called ImageAdapter and then apply it to the GridView.

setContent—A method that indicates what to display in the tab content area of a TabHost control.

setIndicator—A method that sets the tab button caption and icon image in a TabHost control.

TabActivity—A class that allows you to display tabs in a TabHost control, with each tab containing an Activity or view.

TabHost—A control you use to wrap multiple views in a single window.

TabSpec—A statement that specifies how the tabs in a TabHost control should appear.

TabWidget—The part of a TabHost control that displays the tabs.

Developer FAQs

1. Which control wraps multiple views in a single window?

2. What is the minimum number of tabs typically placed on an Android device?

3. Tabs represent what physical item that was often used in an office for organization?

4. What are the two parts of a TabHost control?

5. True or False? Each tab launches a separate Activity.

6. To position the TabWidget and FrameLayout vertically in the XML layout file, the two parts should be placed in which type of layout?

7. How would you change main.xml in the chapter project if you wanted the tabs to appear at the bottom of the Android window?

8. What is the id for a TabWidget in the XML code?

9. Which control has the id of "@android:id/tabcontent"?

10. Why should you avoid using a title bar with tabs?

11. True or False? The graphical layout emulator for XML files does not display tabs properly.

12. If you tap the Web Site tab in the chapter project, how do you return to the tabbed interface without starting the application again?

13. Write a single line of XML code that sets the width of a column of a GridView control to 185 density-independent pixels.

14. To display as many pictures that can fit comfortably on the display of a GridView control, write a single line of XML code to set the number of columns.

15. What provides a data model for the layout of the GridView control?

16. Write the line of code that launches a browser and opens the *wikipedia.org* site.

17. Which methods set the text of a tab control?

18. Which layout control is similar to the GridView control?

19. Name another technique besides using tabs to display content in different portions of the tablet window.

20. Which file must be updated within your project if you add more than the Main.java file?

Beyond the Book

Using the Internet, search the Web for the answers to the following questions to further your Android knowledge.

1. Research three Android tablet devices. Write a paragraph about the cost, usage, dimensions, and posted reviews of each of these three tablets.

2. Using *cnet.com* (a popular review site), compare the newest Android, iPad, and Windows tablets and summarize their recommendations in a one-page paper.

3. Using *developer.android.com*, research the topic of GridView. After writing many Android projects, the Android help files should be easier to understand now. Explain the stretchmode property in your own words (at least 100 words).

4. A common user complaint is that it is difficult to use an onscreen keyboard to type long documents. Discuss three alternatives beyond using the traditional onscreen keyboard layout for input. Write a paragraph about each.

Case Programming Projects

Complete one or more of the following case programming projects. Use the same steps and techniques taught within the chapter. Submit the program you create to your instructor. The level of difficulty is indicated for each case programming project.

Easiest: ★

Intermediate: ★★

Challenging: ★★★

Case Project 9–1: Sushi 101 Tablet App ★

Requirements Document

Application title:	Sushi 101 Tablet App
Purpose:	This sushi tablet app explains the basics of eating sushi for those new to the Japanese fish and vegetable delicacy.
Algorithms:	1. The opening screen displays three tabs with custom icons named chopsticks.png, sushipics.png, and faq.png. The tab titles are Lesson, Images, and Web site (Figure 9-37). The first tab displays a title and an image named lesson.png that demonstrates the correct way to hold chopsticks.
	2. The second tab displays a GridView control with seven sushi images named sushi1.png–sushi7.png (Figure 9-38).
	3. The third tab opens *www.sushifaq.com* in a browser (Figure 9-39).
Conditions:	1. The pictures are provided with your student files.
	2. Use the same theme as the chapter project.
	3. The LayoutParams of the GridView control should be set to 300 pixels wide by 280 pixels tall.

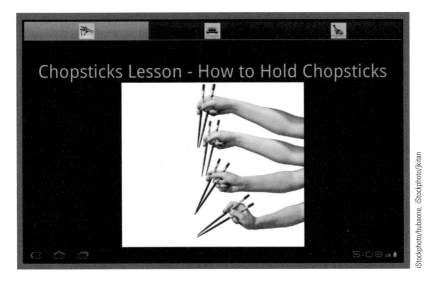

iStockphoto/bubaone, iStockphoto/jkitan

Figure 9-37

iStockphoto/bubaone, iStockphoto/ShyMan, iStockphoto/whitewish, iStockphoto/Matteo DeStefano, iStockphoto/juliichka, iStockphoto/James McD24, iStockphoto/missaigong

Figure 9-38

338

www.sushifaq.com

Figure 9-39

Case Project 9–2: Golf Course Tablet App ⋆

Requirements Document

Application title: Golf Course Tablet App

Purpose: The Myrtle Beach tourism board would like you to create a tablet app showcasing the golf course of Myrtle Beach.

Algorithms: 1. The opening screen displays two tabs with custom icons named images.png and site.png. Notice there are no titles on the tabs, just images (Figure 9-40).

2. The first tab displays a GridView control with five golf course images named golf1.png–golf5.png.

3. The second tab opens a link to a Myrtle Beach golf site such as *mbn.com*.

Conditions: 1. The pictures are provided with your student files.

2. Use the same theme as the chapter project.

339

Figure 9-40

Case Project 9–3: Famous Artist Tablet App ★★

Requirements Document

Application title: Famous Artist Tablet App

Purpose: Create one tablet screen of a large app that features information about the famous artists of the world. The artist featured in this case project is Vincent van Gogh.

Algorithms:
1. An opening screen uses a GridView to display a title (Vincent van Gogh) and two images of Van Gogh's art on the first row and two images on the second row using a GridView. The images are named art1, art2, art3, and art4. The tabs display only the following text: Art, Artist, and Site.

2. The second tab displays Van Gogh's birth date, his hometown, and names of two of his most famous paintings. Research the information needed.

3. The third tab opens this link: *http://en.wikipedia.org/wiki/Vincent_van_Gogh.*

Conditions:
1. The pictures are provided with your student files.

2. Use the same theme as the chapter project.

Case Project 9–4: Snap Fitness Tablet App ★★

Requirements Document

Application title:	Snap Fitness Tablet App
Purpose:	The local fitness gym in your area wants an app that provides information about the activities and memberships at the gym.
Algorithms:	1. An opening screen displays three tabs at the bottom of the app. The tabs display the titles Site, Info, and Photos. The tab images are named gym_icon1, gym_icon2, and gym_icon3. The first tab links to the Web site of a local gym.
	2. The second tab displays the costs for the gym:

        Youth (ages 14–17) $25

        Adult (18 and over) $50

        Family/Household $75

        Active Senior: $50

	3. The third tab displays four photos. The images are named gym1, gym2, gym3, and gym4.
Conditions:	1. The pictures are provided with your student files.
	2. Use the same theme as the chapter project

Case Project 9–5: Go Web 2.0 Tablet App ★★★

Requirements Document

Application title:	Go Web 2.0 Tablet App
Purpose:	The Go Web 2.0 Tablet app displays eight screen shots (saved as .png files) of your favorite Web 2.0 technology sites.
Algorithms:	1. An opening screen displays three tabs at the bottom of the app. The tabs display the titles Screen Shots, URLs, and Link. Locate your own tab images. The first tab displays eight screen shots of Web 2.0 sites.
	2. The second tab lists the Web addresses of the eight sites.
	3. The third tab opens a link to your favorite Web 2.0 site.
Conditions:	1. Locate images from the Internet.
	2. Use the same theme as the chapter project.

Case Project 9–6: Pick Your Topic Tablet App ★★★

Requirements Document

Application title:	Pick Your Topic Tablet App
Purpose:	Get creative! Create an app with four tabs on a topic of your choice.
Algorithms:	1. Create four tabs, including a GridView and a Gallery object on different tabs.
	2. The tabs should have icons and text.
Conditions:	1. Select your own images.

CHAPTER 10

Move! Creating Animation

Unless otherwise noted in the chapter, all screen shots are provided courtesy of Eclipse.

In this chapter, you learn to:

- ◎ Create an Android application with Frame and Tween animation
- ◎ Understand Frame animation
- ◎ Understand Tween animation
- ◎ Add an animation-list XML file
- ◎ Code the AnimationDrawable object
- ◎ Set the background Drawable resource
- ◎ Launch the start( ) and stop( ) methods
- ◎ Add Tween animation to the application
- ◎ Create a Tween XML file that rotates an image
- ◎ Determine the rotation pivot, duration, and repeat count of a Tween animation
- ◎ Load the startActivity Tween animation in a second Activity
- ◎ Change the orientation of the emulator

Computer animation is widely used by television, the video game industry (as on Xbox, Vita, and Wii), and gaming applications on handheld devices. Animation displays many images in rapid succession or displays many changes to one image to create an illusion of movement. Animation is an integral part of many of the most popular Android apps at the Android Market, including *Words with Friends*, *Angry Birds*, *Cut the Rope*, and *Roller Ball*. Android developers see the value in using 3D graphics to create more graphical apps and in-demand games. Using Android animation, the chapter project named Wave Animation displays multiple photos of surfing the perfect wave controlled by a Start Frame Animation button that reveals the animated images frame by frame. The app contains four different surfing pictures in Hawaii. When the user taps the Stop Frame Animation button, the frame-by-frame animation stops and the last image of the surfer rotates around several times using Tween animation. A **motion tween** specifies a start state of an object, and then animates the object using a uniform transition type such as rotating a predetermined number of times or an infinite number of times. The Wave Animation Android smartphone application shown in Figure 10-1 allows the user to start and stop the animated images of a surfer riding a wave at different moments in a frame-by-frame sequence and then launches a second Activity that plays a rotation of the surfer image six times.

Four images are displayed during the Frame animation

EpicStockMedia/Shutterstock

Figure 10-1   Wave Animation Android app using frame-by-frame animation

The animation in the Android app in Figure 10-1 displays frame-by-frame animation where the time between each photo is measured in 100-millisecond intervals. The Start Frame Animation button begins displaying the surfing images, and the Stop Animation button stops the continuous Frame animation and begins the Tween animation of rotating the surfing image, as shown in Figure 10-2. The Tween animation rotates the fourth surfing image six times in a perfect circle. The orientation of the emulator is changed to landscape in Figure 10-2.

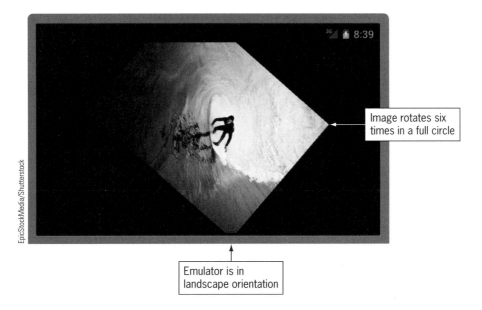

Image rotates six times in a full circle

Emulator is in landscape orientation

Figure 10-2   Wave Animation Android app using Tween animation

GTK
Professional Android animation can be created by using complex programs such as Maya or Cinema 4D. A freeware program named Blender develops 3D animated content in the gaming environment.

To create this application, the developer must understand how to perform the following processes:

1. Add the four images to the drawable folder.
2. Add a Frame animation XML file to the project.
3. Add the layout for the image and button objects in main.xml.
4. Set the duration between frames in the frame-by-frame animation.
5. Declare and instantiate the ImageView, Button, and AnimationDrawable controls.
6. Code the OnClickListeners for the Button controls.
7. Run the frame-by-frame Animation application.
8. Add a layout for an ImageView control for the Tween animation.
9. Add a Tween animation XML file to rotate the last surfing image.

10.   Create a second Activity named Tween.java to launch the rotation Tween animation.

11.   When the application executes, change the orientation of the emulator.

Android Animation

Android provides two types of animation: Frame and Tween animation. **Frame animation**, also called frame-by-frame animation, assigns a sequence of photos to play as in a slide show with a predefined interval between images. Frame-by-frame animation is typically created to show steps in a process such as fly-fishing or play a fast-paced sequence such as in a cartoon. To create the illusion of movement, a cartoon image can be displayed on the screen and repeatedly replaced by a new image that is similar, but slightly advanced in the time sequence.

Instead of using a sequence of images, **Tween animation** creates an animation by performing a series of transformations on a single image such as position, size, rotation, and transparency on the contents of a View object. Text can fly across the screen, an image of an engine can be rotated to display different angles, or the transparency of an image can change from transparent to solid. A sequence of animation instructions defines the Tween animation using either XML or Android code. In this chapter project, the application first displays a frame-by-frame animation. Code is added to the same application to display a second type of animation called a Tween rotation effect.

Adding the Layout for the Frame Image and Button Controls

The layout specifications for the chapter project reside within the main.xml file in a LinearLayout. The single ImageView control named imgSurf displays the surfing images in a frame-by-frame animation. The two Button controls named btnStart and btnStop start and stop the Frame animation, respectively. The layout is designed with a nested Relative layout within a Linear layout to place the two buttons side by side. In the Linear layout, an ImageView control displays the animation images. Insert this control and its properties in the main.xml file to specify precise settings for the control. Within the structured Linear layout, insert a Relative layout to arrange the buttons side by side, which the Linear layout does not allow. Later in the chapter, a Tween animation is added to the application and launched when the Frame animation ends. To begin the application and code the main.xml layout, follow these steps:

1.   Open the Eclipse program. Click the New button on the Standard toolbar. Expand the Android folder and select Android Project. Click the Next button. In the New Android Project dialog box, enter the Project Name **Wave Animation**. To save the project on your USB drive, click to remove the check mark from the Use default location check box. Type **E:\Workspace** (if necessary, enter a different drive letter that identifies the USB drive). Click the Next button. For the Build Target, select Android 4.0, if necessary. Click the Next button. For the Package Name, type **net.androidbootcamp.waveanimation**. Enter **Main** in the Create Activity text box.

The new Android Wave Animation project has an Application Name, a Package Name, and an Activity named Main (Figure 10-3).

Figure 10-3 Application information for the Wave Animation project

2. Click the Finish button. Expand the Wave Animation project in the Package Explorer. In the res/layout folder, double-click main.xml to display the XML code. If necessary, click the main.xml tab at the bottom of the window. By default, LinearLayout is set. Within the LinearLayout, delete the default four TextView XML codes (Lines 7–10). Add the ImageView control by typing the following custom XML code using auto-completion as much as possible:

```
<ImageView
    android:id="@+id/imgSurf"
    android:layout_width="wrap_content"
    android:layout_height="wrap_content"
    android:layout_gravity="center"
    android:minHeight="150px"
    android:minWidth="300px" />
```

The ImageView control is coded in main.xml (Figure 10-4).

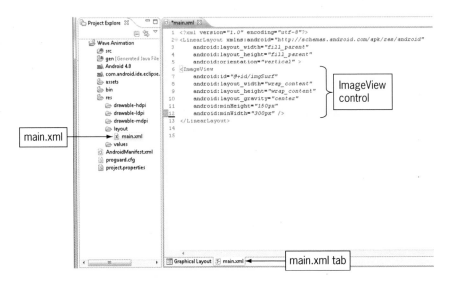

Figure 10-4   ImageView XML code

3. Press the Enter key, and then add the two Button controls within a Relative layout to place the buttons on the same line by typing the following custom XML code, using auto-completion as much as possible:

```
<RelativeLayout
        android:layout_width="fill_parent"
        android:layout_height="fill_parent" >
    <Button
        android:id="@+id/btnStart"
        android:layout_width="wrap_content"
        android:layout_height="wrap_content"
        android:layout_alignParentTop="true"
        android:layout_marginLeft="15dp"
        android:textSize="12dp"
        android:text="Start Frame Animation" />
    <Button
        android:id="@+id/btnStop"
        android:layout_width="wrap_content"
        android:layout_height="wrap_content"
        android:layout_alignParentRight="true"
        android:layout_marginRight="15dp"
        android:textSize="12dp"
        android:text="Start Tween Animation" />
</RelativeLayout>
```

The two Button controls are coded in main.xml (Figure 10-5).

```
X main.xml ⊠
 1  <?xml version="1.0" encoding="utf-8"?>
 2  <LinearLayout xmlns:android="http://schemas.android.com/apk/res/android"
 3      android:layout_width="fill_parent"
 4      android:layout_height="fill_parent"
 5      android:orientation="vertical" >
 6  <ImageView
 7      android:id="@+id/imgSurf"
 8      android:layout_width="wrap_content"
 9      android:layout_height="wrap_content"
10      android:layout_gravity="center"
11      android:minHeight="150px"
12      android:minWidth="300px" />
13  <RelativeLayout
14      android:layout_width="fill_parent"
15      android:layout_height="fill_parent" >
16  <Button
17      android:id="@+id/btnStart"
18      android:layout_width="wrap_content"
19      android:layout_height="wrap_content"
20      android:layout_alignParentTop="true"
21      android:layout_marginLeft="15dp"
22      android:textSize="12dp"
23      android:text="Start Frame Animation" />
24  <Button
25      android:id="@+id/btnStop"
26      android:layout_width="wrap_content"
27      android:layout_height="wrap_content"
28      android:layout_alignParentRight="true"
29      android:layout_marginRight="15dp"
30      android:textSize="12dp"
31      android:text="Start Tween Animation" />
32  </RelativeLayout>
33  </LinearLayout>
```

Two Button controls in a Relative layout

Figure 10-5 Two Button controls in XML code

Creating Frame-by-frame Animation

In the Wave Animation app, the frame-by-frame animation loads and displays a sequence of surfing images from the drawable folder. A single XML file named frame.xml lists the frames that constitute the surfing animation. You create frame.xml in a new res folder named drawable. In the XML code, an **animation-list** root element references four surfing images stored in the drawable folders. Each item in the animation-list specifies how many milliseconds to display each image. In the chapter project, each image is displayed for 1/10 of a second. The animation-list code includes a oneshot property, which is set to true by default. By setting the **android:oneshot** attribute of the animation-list to false, as shown in the following code, the animation plays repeatedly until the Stop Animation button is tapped. If the oneshot attribute is set to true, the animation plays once and then stops and displays the last frame. Note that you add the oneshot attribute to the code in the opening animation-list tag.

Code Syntax

```
<?xml version="1.0" encoding="utf-8"?>
<animation-list xmlns:android="http://schemas.android.com/apk/res/android"
android:oneshot="false" >
    <item android:drawable="@drawable/surf1" android:duration="100"/>
    <item android:drawable="@drawable/surf2" android:duration="100"/>
    <item android:drawable="@drawable/surf3" android:duration="100"/>
    <item android:drawable="@drawable/surf4" android:duration="100"/>
</animation-list>
```

When the XML file is added to the Android project, the Resource type Drawable is selected and animation-list is selected as the root element of the XML code. A folder named drawable is automatically added to the res folder. To copy the images into the drawable folder and code the animation-list XML code, follow these steps:

1. Save and close the main.xml file. To add the four image files to the drawable-hdpi folder, if necessary, copy the student files to your USB drive. Open the USB folder containing the student files. In the Package Explorer, expand the drawable-hdpi folder in the res folder. To add the four image files to the drawable-hdpi resource folder, drag the surf1.png, surf2.png, surf3.png, and surf4.png files to the drawable-hdpi folder until a plus sign pointer appears. Release the mouse button. If necessary, click the Copy files option button, and then click the OK button.

Copies of the four files appear in the drawable-hdpi folder (Figure 10-6).

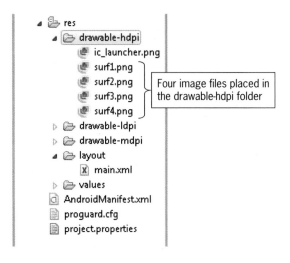

Figure 10-6   Copied images in the drawable-hdpi folder

2. Right-click the layout folder. Point to New on the shortcut menu, and then click Other. In the New dialog box, click Android XML File and click the Next button. The New Android XML File dialog box opens. In the Resource Type drop-down box, select Drawable. In the File text box, type the XML filename **animation**. In Root Element, select animation-list as the type of element that is added to the XML file.

An XML file named animation is created in a folder named drawable with the root element animation-list (Figure 10-7).

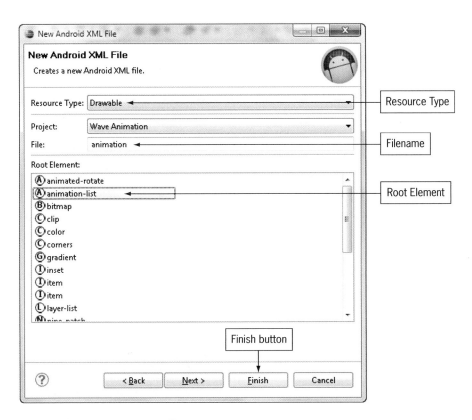

Figure 10-7   animation.xml file

3. Click the Finish button. The animation.xml file opens with the animation-list element already coded. Click the Source tag and then click before the closing tag > in Line 2. To add the oneshot attribute to create a continuous loop of animation, type **android:oneshot="false"**.

In animation.xml, the oneshot attribute is set to false in the animation-list code (Figure 10-8).

oneshot is
set to false

Figure 10-8   The oneshot attribute is set to false

4. Click Line 3 within the animation-list element to add the four list items that are displayed within the frame-by-frame animation. Type the following four lines to reference the images and millisecond durations:

```
<item android:drawable="@drawable/surf1" android:duration="100"/>
<item android:drawable="@drawable/surf2" android:duration="100"/>
<item android:drawable="@drawable/surf3" android:duration="100"/>
<item android:drawable="@drawable/surf4" android:duration="100"/>
```

In animation.xml, the four frames of the animation are entered as items in the animation-list element (Figure 10-9).

Four items in
animation-list

Figure 10-9   animation-list items

GTK

Android includes support for high-performance 2D and 3D graphics with the Open Graphics Library named OpenGL. OpenGL is a cross-platform graphics API that specifies a standard software interface for 3D graphics processing hardware and uses a coordinate system to map the image to the screen.

Coding the AnimationDrawable Object

The **AnimationDrawable class** provides the methods for Drawable animations to create a sequence of frame-by-frame images. In Android development, frame-based animations and image transitions are defined as drawables. The instance of the AnimationDrawable is instantiated as a class variable because it is used in multiple methods within the Main class. To instantiate the AnimationDrawable object in Main.java as a class variable, follow this step:

1. Save your work and then close the animation.xml tab. Expand the src and
    net.androidbootcamp.waveanimation folders, and then double-click Main.java
    to open its code window. Click at the end of the /** Called when the activity is
    first created. */ comment, press the Enter key, and type **AnimationDrawable
    surfAnimation;** to instantiate the object. Point to AnimationDrawable and click
    'Import AnimationDrawable' (android.graphics.drawable).

    *The AnimationDrawable instance named surfAnimation is coded within Main.java
    (Figure 10-10).*

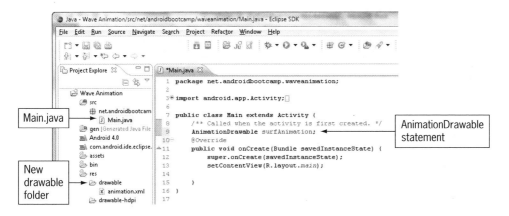

Figure 10-10   Instantiating AnimationDrawable

Setting the Background Resource

The ImageView control named imgSurf that was coded in main.xml must be coded in
Main.java to bind the Drawable resource files to the Background property. The Background
property of an image can be set to any full Drawable resource such as a .png file, a 9-patch
image file, or a solid color designated with hexadecimal code such as #FF0000 for red. A
special image, called a **9-patch image**, has predefined "stretching" areas that maintain the
same look on different screen sizes. These 9-patch graphics are named for their nine areas,
called patches, that scale separately. For example, a button may change sizes when it is
stretched across different form factors.

The images used in the Wave Animation application are .png files, referenced in
animation.xml as items in the animation-list. In the following code, a new instance of
ImageView named imgFrame is assigned to the ImageView control named imgSurf, which
was defined in the main.xml layout. The list of drawable images in the animation-list is
connected to the imgFrame instance by the imgFrame.setBackgroundResource method. The
setBackgroundResource method shown in the following code places the four surfing images
in the frame-by-frame display. Each frame points to one of the surfing images that were
assembled in the XML resource file.

Code Syntax

```
ImageView imgFrame=(ImageView)findViewById(R.id.imgSurf);
imgFrame.setBackgroundResource(R.drawable.animation);
surfAnimation=(AnimationDrawable) imgFrame.getBackground();
```

354

In the third line of the code syntax, the instance of AnimationDrawable called surfAnimation is assigned as the background of the four images to display in the animation. Android constructs an AnimationDrawable Java object before setting it as the background. At this point, the animation is ready to display the four images, but must wait for you to code the start( ) method, which actually begins the movement in the Frame animation. To instantiate the ImageView control and assign the four images to the Background property, follow these steps:

1. Click at the end of the setContentView (R.layout.main); line, press the Enter key, and then instantiate the ImageView that accesses imgSurf in the XML layout file by typing **ImageView imgFrame=(ImageView)findViewById(R.id.imgSurf);**. Point to ImageView and click Import 'ImageView' (android.widget).

    The ImageView control is instantiated (Figure 10-11).

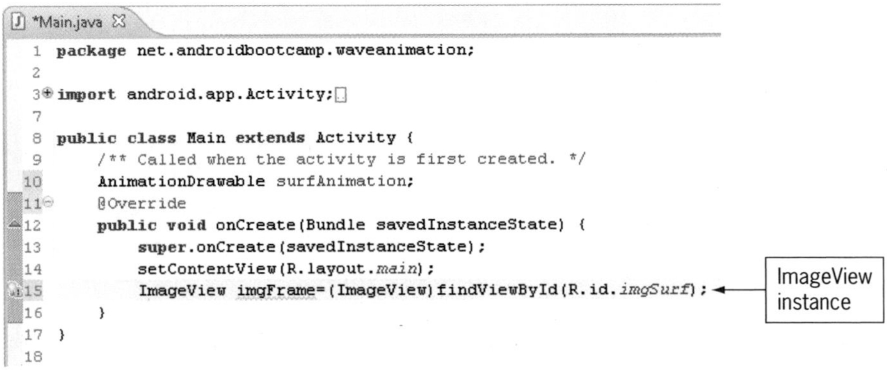

```
 J *Main.java ⊠
 1  package net.androidbootcamp.waveanimation;
 2
 3⊕ import android.app.Activity;☐
 7
 8  public class Main extends Activity {
 9       /** Called when the activity is first created. */
10       AnimationDrawable surfAnimation;
11⊖      @Override
12       public void onCreate(Bundle savedInstanceState) {
13           super.onCreate(savedInstanceState);
14           setContentView(R.layout.main);
15           ImageView imgFrame=(ImageView)findViewById(R.id.imgSurf);  ◄─  ImageView
16       }                                                                   instance
17  }
18
```

Figure 10-11   Instantiating the ImageView control

2. Press the Enter key to insert a blank line, and then set the background resource image for the animation-list in animation.xml by typing **imgFrame.setBackgroundResource(R.drawable.animation);**.

    The animation-list within animation.xml is set as the Background property of the imgFrame ImageView (Figure 10-12).

```
J *Main.java ☒
 1  package net.androidbootcamp.waveanimation;
 2
 3⊕ import android.app.Activity;▢
 7
 8  public class Main extends Activity {
 9      /** Called when the activity is first created. */
10      AnimationDrawable surfAnimation;
11⊖     @Override
12      public void onCreate(Bundle savedInstanceState) {
13          super.onCreate(savedInstanceState);
14          setContentView(R.layout.main);
15          ImageView imgFrame=(ImageView)findViewById(R.id.imgSurf);
16          imgFrame.setBackgroundResource(R.drawable.animation);  ◄──  setBackgroundResource
17      }
18  }
19
```

Figure 10-12   setBackgroundResource is set for the ImageView control

3. Next, access the AnimationDrawable object by "getting" the view object. Press the Enter key, and then type **surfAnimation=(AnimationDrawable) imgFrame.getBackground();**.

The AnimationDrawable is ready to display the four images (Figure 10-13).

```
J *Main.java ☒
 1  package net.androidbootcamp.waveanimation;
 2
 3⊕ import android.app.Activity;▢
 7
 8  public class Main extends Activity {
 9      /** Called when the activity is first created. */
10      AnimationDrawable surfAnimation;
11⊖     @Override
12      public void onCreate(Bundle savedInstanceState) {
13          super.onCreate(savedInstanceState);
14          setContentView(R.layout.main);
15          ImageView imgFrame=(ImageView)findViewById(R.id.imgSurf);
16          imgFrame.setBackgroundResource(R.drawable.animation);
17          surfAnimation=(AnimationDrawable) imgFrame.getBackground();  ◄──  getBackground
18      }
19  }
```

Figure 10-13   getBackground prepares the Animation drawable

IN THE TRENCHES
Common frame-by-frame animations include rotating timers, e-mail symbols, Activity icons, page-loading animations, cartoons, and other useful user interface elements.

Adding Two Button Controls

The Button controls in the Wave Animation project turn the frame-by-frame animation on and off. Both buttons use a setOnClickListener to await user interaction. To instantiate the two Button controls and add the setOnClickListener, follow these steps:

1. To code the first button, press the Enter key and then type **Button btFrame=(Button) findViewById(R.id.btnStart);**. Point to Button and select Import 'Button' (android. widget).

    The first Button control that begins the animation is instantiated (Figure 10-14).

```
 *Main.java

 1  package net.androidbootcamp.waveanimation;
 2
 3⊕ import android.app.Activity;
 8
 9  public class Main extends Activity {
10      /** Called when the activity is first created. */
11      AnimationDrawable surfAnimation;
12⊖     @Override
13      public void onCreate(Bundle savedInstanceState) {
14          super.onCreate(savedInstanceState);
15          setContentView(R.layout.main);
16          ImageView imgFrame=(ImageView)findViewById(R.id.imgSurf);
17          imgFrame.setBackgroundResource(R.drawable.animation);
18          surfAnimation=(AnimationDrawable) imgFrame.getBackground();
19          Button btFrame=(Button)findViewById(R.id.btnStart);   ◄——  First Button
20      }                                                               control instance
21  }
```

Figure 10-14   btFrame is the instance of the first button

2. To code the second button, press the Enter key and type **Button btTween=(Button) findViewById(R.id.btnStop);**.

    The second Button control that stops the animation is instantiated (Figure 10-15).

```
 *Main.java

 1  package net.androidbootcamp.waveanimation;
 2
 3⊕ import android.app.Activity;
 8
 9  public class Main extends Activity {
10      /** Called when the activity is first created. */
11      AnimationDrawable surfAnimation;
12⊖     @Override
13      public void onCreate(Bundle savedInstanceState) {
14          super.onCreate(savedInstanceState);
15          setContentView(R.layout.main);
16          ImageView imgFrame=(ImageView)findViewById(R.id.imgSurf);
17          imgFrame.setBackgroundResource(R.drawable.animation);
18          surfAnimation=(AnimationDrawable) imgFrame.getBackground();
19          Button btFrame=(Button)findViewById(R.id.btnStart);
20          Button btTween=(Button)findViewById(R.id.btnStop);   ◄——  Instance of second
21      }                                                              Button control
22  }
23
```

Figure 10-15   btTween is the instance of the second button

3. To code the first Button listener, press the Enter key and type **btFrame** followed by a period to open a code listing. Double-click the first setOnClickListener displayed in the auto-completion list. Inside the parenthesis, type **new on** and then press the Ctrl+spacebar keys to display the auto-completion list. Double-click the first choice, which is a View.OnClickListener with an Anonymous Inner Type event handler. If necessary, type **View.** before OnClickListener. Point to OnClickListener and select Import 'OnClickListener' (android.view.View). If necessary, insert a right parenthesis and semicolon after the closing brace for the auto-generated stub.

The onClickListener awaits user interaction for btFrame (Figure 10-16).

```
🗋 *Main.java ⊠
 1  package net.androidbootcamp.waveanimation;
 2
 3⊕ import android.app.Activity;▯
 9
10  public class Main extends Activity {
11      /** Called when the activity is first created. */
12      AnimationDrawable surfAnimation;
13      @Override
14      public void onCreate(Bundle savedInstanceState) {
15          super.onCreate(savedInstanceState);
16          setContentView(R.layout.main);
17          ImageView imgFrame=(ImageView)findViewById(R.id.imgSurf);
18          imgFrame.setBackgroundResource(R.drawable.animation);
19          surfAnimation=(AnimationDrawable) imgFrame.getBackground();
20          Button btFrame=(Button)findViewById(R.id.btnStart);
21          Button btTween=(Button)findViewById(R.id.btnStop);
22          btFrame.setOnClickListener(new View.OnClickListener() {
23              @Override
24              public void onClick(View v) {
25                  // TODO Auto-generated method stub
26              }
27          });
28      }
29  }
30
```

OnClickListener for first button

Parenthesis and semicolon inserted

Figure 10-16 First button OnClickListener

4. Press the Enter key after the semicolon to code the second Button listener. Type **btTween** followed by a period to open a code listing. Double-click the first setOnClickListener displayed in the auto-completion list. Inside the parenthesis, type **new on** and then press the Ctrl+spacebar keys to display the auto-completion list. Double-click the first choice, which is a View.OnClickListener with an Anonymous Inner Type event handler. If necessary, type **View.** before OnClickListener. If necessary, insert a right parenthesis and semicolon after the closing brace for the auto-generated stub.

The onClickListener awaits user interaction for btTween (Figure 10-17).

```
🗋 *Main.java ⊠
   1  package net.androidbootcamp.waveanimation;
   2
   3⊕ import android.app.Activity;☐
   9
  10  public class Main extends Activity {
  11      /** Called when the activity is first created. */
  12      AnimationDrawable surfAnimation;
  13⊖     @Override
  14      public void onCreate(Bundle savedInstanceState) {
  15          super.onCreate(savedInstanceState);
  16          setContentView(R.layout.main);
  17          ImageView imgFrame=(ImageView)findViewById(R.id.imgSurf);
  18          imgFrame.setBackgroundResource(R.drawable.animation);
  19          surfAnimation=(AnimationDrawable) imgFrame.getBackground();
  20          Button btFrame=(Button)findViewById(R.id.btnStart);
  21          Button btTween=(Button)findViewById(R.id.btnStop);
  22⊖         btFrame.setOnClickListener(new View.OnClickListener() {
  23⊖             @Override
  24              public void onClick(View v) {
  25                  // TODO Auto-generated method stub
  26                  surfAnimation.start();
  27              }
  28          });
  29⊖         btTween.setOnClickListener(new View.OnClickListener() {
  30
  31⊖             @Override
  32              public void onClick(View v) {
  33                  // TODO Auto-generated method stub
  34              }
  35          });
```

OnClickListener for second button

Parenthesis and semicolon inserted

Figure 10-17   Second button OnClickListener

GTK

As in earlier chapters, the figures in this chapter include @Override statements. Depending on your Eclipse installation, your code might not include these statements. If Eclipse doesn't insert these automatically, your code will run without any problems.

Using the Start and Stop Methods

After associating AnimationDrawable with the animation images and coding the buttons, you can use the start( ) and stop( ) methods of the drawable objects to control the Frame animation. When the user taps the Start Frame Animation button, the start( ) method begins the Frame animation continuously because oneshot is set to false. The Frame animation stops only when the user taps the Start Tween Animation button, which launches the stop( ) method and then initiates the startActivity, launching the second Activity named Tween.java. In the following code, the start( ) method is placed within the onClick( ) method for the Start Frame Animation button and the stop( ) method is placed within the onClick( ) method for the Start Tween Animation button:

Code Syntax

```
surfAnimation.start();
surfAnimation.stop();
```

The start( ) method launches the surfAnimation.xml file displaying the animation-list items and the stop( ) method ends the display of the animation-list. To add the start( ) and stop( ) methods, follow these steps:

1. Click at the end of the first // TODO comment (for btFrame), press the Enter key, and then type **surfAnimation.start( );**.

    The Start Frame Animation button is coded to start surfAnimation.xml (Figure 10-18).

```
22    btFrame.setOnClickListener (new View.OnClickListener () {
23        @Override
24        public void onClick(View v) {
25            // TODO Auto-generated method stub
26            surfAnimation.start();                    ← start( ) method
27        }                                                for btFrame
28    });
29    btTween.setOnClickListener (new View.OnClickListener () {
30
```

Figure 10-18   Entering the start( ) method

2. Click at the end of the // TODO comment for btTween, press the Enter key, and then type **surfAnimation.stop( );**.

    The Start Tween Animation button is coded to stop the Frame animation within surfAnimation.xml (Figure 10-19).

```
25        public void onClick(View v) {
26            // TODO Auto-generated method stub
27            surfAnimation.start();
28        }
29    });
30    btTween.setOnClickListener (new View.OnClickListener ()
31
32        @Override
33        public void onClick(View v) {
34            // TODO Auto-generated method stub        stop( ) method for
35            surfAnimation.stop();                 ←    btTween button
36        }
37    });
38    }
39 }
```

Figure 10-19   Entering the stop( ) method

3. To test the Frame animation, click Run on the menu bar, and then click Run to save the application and test it in the emulator. A dialog box requesting to run the application opens the first time the application is executed. Select Android Application and click the OK button. Save all the files in the next dialog box, if necessary, and unlock the emulator. The application opens in the emulator window where you can click the Start Frame Animation button to view the surfing animation.

The emulator displays the frame-by-frame animation (Figure 10-20).

Figure 10-20   Frame animation displayed in the emulator

Adding the Layout for the Tween Image

After the user taps the Start Tween Animation button, the Frame animation ends and a second Activity is launched. This second Activity is named Tween.java, and it defines a second layout with a single ImageView control identified with the id imgTween, referencing the fourth image named surf4. To code the tween.xml file layout to display an ImageView control, follow this step:

1. Close Main.java. In the res folder, right-click the layout folder, point to New on the shortcut menu, and then click Other. In the New dialog box, click Android XML Layout File, and then click the Next button. In the New Android Layout XML File dialog box, type **tween.xml** in the File text box to name the layout file. In the Root Element list, select LinearLayout. Click the Finish button. When the emulator window opens, click the tween.xml tab. Add the ImageView control by typing the following custom XML code beginning on Line 6, using auto-completion as much as possible:

```
<ImageView
    android:id="@+id/imgTween"
    android:layout_width="wrap_content"
    android:layout_height="wrap_content"
    android:layout_gravity="center"
    android:src="@drawable/surf4" />
```

A second XML layout named tween.xml displays an ImageView control (Figure 10-21).

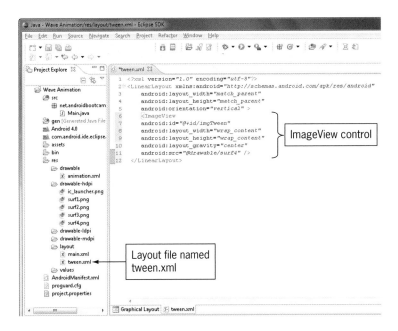

Figure 10-21 ImageView control coded in tween.xml

Creating Tween Animation

Instead of rendering several images in a sequence in Frame animation, Tween animation manipulates a Drawable image by adding tween effects. Defined in an XML file, **tween effects** are transitions that change objects from one state to another. An ImageView or TextView object can move, rotate, grow, or shrink. As shown in Table 10-1, Tween animations include a built-in library of tween effects. These effects are saved within an animation XML file that belongs in the res/anim/ folder of your Android project.

Tween effect	Purpose
alpha	Transitions an object from one level of transparency to another, where 0.0 is transparent and 1.0 is opaque.
rotate	Spins an object from one angular position to another. To rotate an object completely around, start at 0 degrees and rotate to 359 degrees (a full circle). A pivotX and pivotY percentage shows the amount of pivot based on the object's left edge.
scale	Transitions the size of an object (grow or shrink) on an X/Y scale.
translate	Moves the object vertically or horizontally a percentage relative to the element width (for example, deltaX="100%" would move the image one image width away).

Table 10-1   Tween animation effects

The four Tween animation effects in Table 10-1 can be coded in an XML file and individually configured or nested together to animate an object in any possible direction or size.

Coding a Tween Rotation XML File

In the Wave Animation application, the last image named surf4.png is rotated when the user clicks the Start Tween Animation button. Android uses an XML file-creator utility that supports 10 different Resource types. The default Resource type is Layout, but in the chapter project, you select Tween animation. After entering the XML filename as rotation.xml, click the root element of rotate to store the rotation.xml code for a Tween animation in the /res/anim folder. The XML file for a Frame animation is stored in the /res/drawable folder. The rotation.xml statements are shown in the following code:

Code Syntax

```
<?xml version="1.0" encoding="utf-8"?>
<rotate
xmlns:android="http://schemas.android.com/apk/res/android"
android:fromDegrees="0"
android:toDegrees="359"
android:pivotX="50%"
android:pivotY="50%"
android:duration="2000"
android:repeatCount="5"
rotate />
```

The rotation.xml code defines the attributes of the Tween animation. Notice the tween effect is set to rotate in the second line. The fromDegrees and toDegrees rotate attribute spins the object from 0 to 359 degrees, which equals 360 degrees for a full circle. The image in the chapter project completes several clockwise rotations. The pivotX and pivotY attributes pivot an object from its center by setting the pivot point, which can be a fixed coordinate or a percentage. By default, the object pivots around the (0,0) coordinate, or the upper-left corner of the object. Notice pivotX and pivotY are set to 50% in the code example, which determines that the pivot location is from the center of the object. The duration for each rotation is set for 2,000 milliseconds. The repeatCount represents how many times the object rotates after the initial rotation. You can set repeatCount to an integer or to "infinite" if you do not want the rotation to stop. Remember that the number of rotations is always one greater than the repeat value, so if you set the repeatCount to the integer 5, the object rotates six times. It rotates once initially and then repeats the rotation five more times. By creating an XML file, it is easier to make simple changes to fine-tune the animation. You might want to try different values in the rotation.xml file to see how the animation changes. To code the Tween animation to rotate an image, follow these steps:

1. Save and close the tween.xml layout file. To create a new rotation XML file, right-click the layout folder. Point to New on the shortcut menu, and click Other. In the New dialog box, click Android XML File and then click the Next button. The New Android XML File dialog box opens. In the Resource Type drop-down box, select Tween Animation. In the File text box, type the XML filename **rotation**. In Root Element, select rotate as the type of element that is added to the XML file.

The New Android XML File dialog box opens and the Resource Type, File, and Root Element are selected (Figure 10-22).

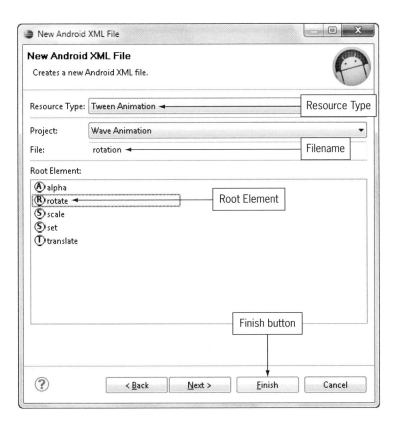

Figure 10-22 New Android XML File dialog box

2. Click the Finish button. The rotation.xml file opens with the rotate element already coded. Delete the closing rotate code and the right angle bracket (>) after rotate on Line 2. Click Line 3 and type the following code after the opening rotate root element:

```
xmlns:android="http://schemas.android.com/apk/res/android"
android:fromDegrees="0"
android:toDegrees="359"
android:pivotX="50%"
android:pivotY="50%"
android:duration="2000"
android:repeatCount="5" />
```

In rotation.xml, the Tween animation attributes are coded to rotate the image (Figure 10-23).

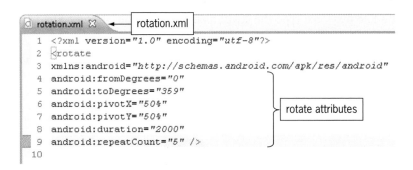

Figure 10-23   rotate attributes in rotation.xml file

IN THE TRENCHES
To change an image from transparent to opaque, code an alpha statement in an XML file such as <alpha xmlns:android=http://schemas.android.com/apk/res/android android:fromAlpha="0.0" android:toAlpha="1.0" android:duration="100">.

Coding a Second Activity to Launch the Tween Animation

When the user taps the Start Tween Animation button in the Wave Animation, two actions are triggered within the second onClick( ) method. The Frame animation is concluded with the stop( ) method and a startActivity intent launches a second Activity named Tween.java. To code a second Activity and launch the startActivity, follow these steps:

1. Save and close rotation.xml. To create a second class, right-click the src/net.androidbootcamp.waveanimation folder, point to New on the shortcut menu, and then click Class. Type **Tween** in the Name text box to create a second class that defines the Tween Activity. Click the Superclass Browse button, and then type **Activity** in the Choose a type text box. As you type, matching items are displayed. Click Activity – android.app and then click the OK button to extend the Activity class.

A new class named Tween.java is created (Figure 10-24).

Figure 10-24   Tween.java class

2.   Click the Finish button to finish creating the Tween class. To launch the Tween Activity class from the Main.java class, open Main.java. Scroll down to the statement surfAnimation.stop( ). Click at the end of the statement and press the Enter key. To launch an intent that starts the second Activity, type **startActivity (new Intent(Main.this, Tween.class));**. Point to Intent and then click Import 'Intent' (android.content).

A startActivity launches the Tween.java class (Figure 10-25).

Figure 10-25   Main.java launches the second Activity (complete code for Main.java)

IN THE TRENCHES

If you deploy an Android app and receive an error message similar to "Installation error: INSTALL_FAILED_INSUFFICIENT_STORAGE," the reason is the default internal storage is 64 MB. You can override this setting in the Eclipse launch configuration by clicking Run on the menu bar and then selecting Run Configurations. Click the Target tab and in the Additional Emulator Command Line Options box, type **-partition-size 1024**.

Coding a StartAnimation

Now that the layout, rotation XML file, and second Activity are ready, the Tween animation can be launched using the startAnimation method. Applying the Tween rotation animation, the **startAnimation** method begins animating a View object by calling the AnimationUtils class utilities to access the resources necessary to load the animation. To code the startAnimation method to launch the rotation, follow these steps:

1. Save and close Main.java. To code the onCreate method in Tween.java, click at the end of the public class Tween extends Activity { line, press the Enter key, type **public void onCreate(Bundle savedInstanceState) {** and press the Enter key. A closing brace for the onCreate method appears. Point to Bundle and then click Import 'Bundle' (android.os).

The onCreate method for Tween.java is coded (Figure 10-26).

```
🎵 *Tween.java ⊠
 1  package net.androidbootcamp.waveanimation;
 2
 3⊖ import android.app.Activity;
 4  import android.os.Bundle;
 5
 6  public class Tween extends Activity {
 7⊖     public void onCreate(Bundle savedInstanceState) {          ◄── onCreate method
 8
 9     }
10  }
11
```

Figure 10-26   onCreate method in Tween.java

2. To display the tween.xml layout, type **super.onCreate(savedInstanceState);**. Press the Enter key, and then type **setContentView(R.layout.tween);**.

A tween.xml layout is displayed for the Tween class (Figure 10-27).

```
🎵 *Tween.java ⊠
 1  package net.androidbootcamp.waveanimation;
 2
 3⊕ import android.app.Activity;☐
 5
 6  public class Tween extends Activity {
 7⊖     public void onCreate(Bundle savedInstanceState) {
 8         super.onCreate(savedInstanceState);
 9         setContentView(R.layout.tween);          ◄── setContentView layout
10     }
11  }
12
```

Figure 10-27   tween.xml layout is set

3. To instantiate the ImageView control named imgTween, press the Enter key and type **ImageView imgRotate = (ImageView) findViewById(R.id.imgTween);**. Point to ImageView and then click Import 'ImageView' (android.widget).

An instance of the ImageView control named imgRotate is instantiated (Figure 10-28).

```
🎵 *Tween.java ⊠
 1  package net.androidbootcamp.waveanimation;
 2
 3⊕ import android.app.Activity;☐
 6
 7  public class Tween extends Activity {
 8⊖     public void onCreate(Bundle savedInstanceState) {
 9         super.onCreate(savedInstanceState);
10         setContentView(R.layout.tween);
11         ImageView imgRotate = (ImageView) findViewById(R.id.imgTween);   ◄── Instance of
12     }                                                                        ImageView control
13  }
```

Figure 10-28   ImageView is instantiated

4. To begin the Tween rotation animation, press the Enter key and type **imgRotate. startAnimation(AnimationUtils.loadAnimation(this, R.anim.rotation));**. If necessary, point to AnimationUtils and then click Import 'AnimationUtils' (android.view.animation).

The Tween animation is started. The fourth image rotates six times and stops (Figure 10-29).

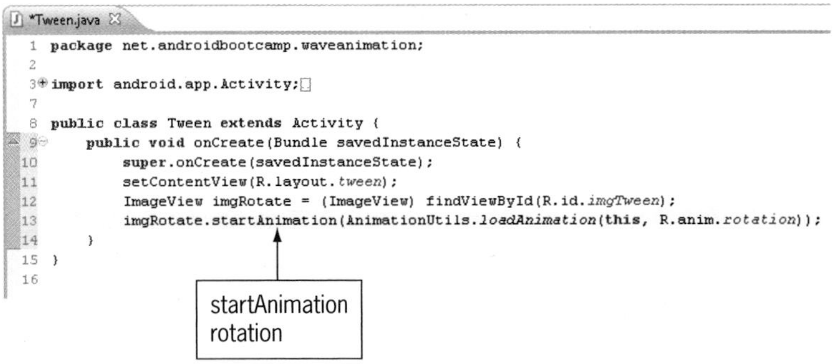

```
🗋 *Tween.java ⊠
 1  package net.androidbootcamp.waveanimation;
 2
 3⊕ import android.app.Activity;
 7
 8  public class Tween extends Activity {
 9⊝     public void onCreate(Bundle savedInstanceState) {
10         super.onCreate(savedInstanceState);
11         setContentView(R.layout.tween);
12         ImageView imgRotate = (ImageView) findViewById(R.id.imgTween);
13         imgRotate.startAnimation(AnimationUtils.loadAnimation(this, R.anim.rotation));
14     }
15  }
16
```

startAnimation
rotation

Figure 10-29   Image rotates using Tween animation (complete code for Tween.java)

5. Save your work.

Updating the Android Manifest File

The Android Manifest file must be updated to include the second Activity named Tween.java and to remove the title bar in the theme of both Activities to provide more display room for the animation. To add the second Activity to the Android Manifest file, follow these steps:

1. In the Package Explorer, double-click the AndroidManifest.xml file. To add the Tween class to the Android Manifest file, click the Application tab at the bottom of the Wave Animation Manifest page. Scroll down to display the Application Nodes section. In the Application Nodes section, click the Add button. Select Activity in the Create a new element at the top level, in Application dialog box. Click the OK button. The Attributes for Activity section opens in the Application tab. In the Name text box, type the class name preceded by a period (**.Tween**) to add the Tween Activity to the AndroidManifest.xml file.

The class .Tween is entered in the Name text box of the Attributes for Activity section (Figure 10-30).

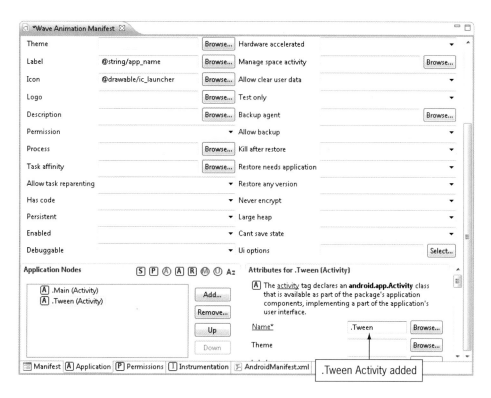

Figure 10-30 Adding the Tween Activity to the Android Manifest file

2. To change the Android theme, click the AndroidManifest.xml tab at the bottom of the window. Inside the Activity code, click at the end of the code that states android:name.Main. Press the Enter key to insert a new blank line. Type **android: theme="@android:style/Theme.Black.NoTitleBar"**. The theme also needs to be changed for the second Activity. Before the closing brace of <activity android: name=".Tween", press the Enter key. Type **android:theme="@android:style/ Theme.Black.NoTitleBar"**. If a right angle bracket does not appear at the end of the line, type > to insert the closing bracket.

The Android theme is coded within both Activities in the Android Manifest file (Figure 10-31).

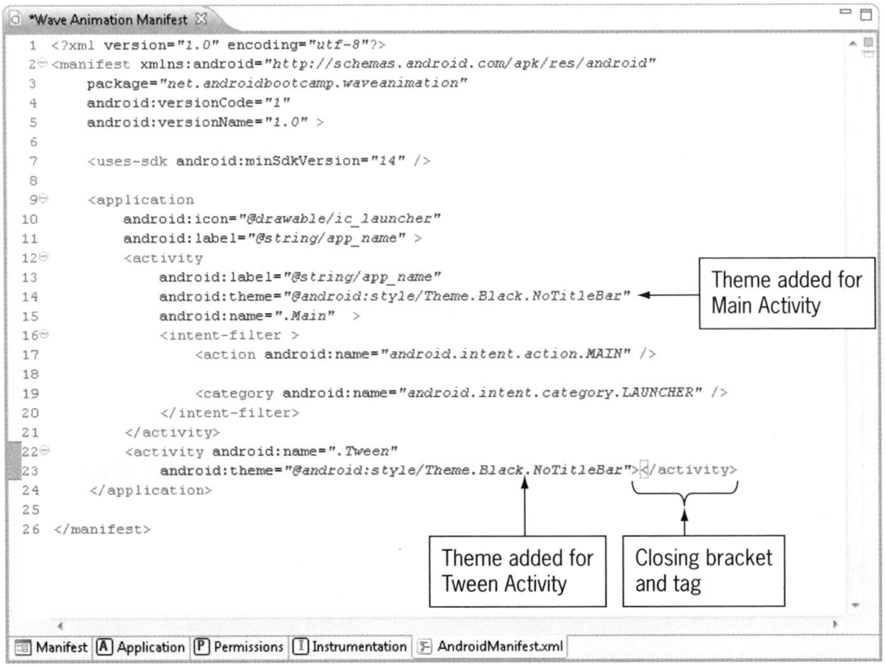

```
 1  <?xml version="1.0" encoding="utf-8"?>
 2  <manifest xmlns:android="http://schemas.android.com/apk/res/android"
 3      package="net.androidbootcamp.waveanimation"
 4      android:versionCode="1"
 5      android:versionName="1.0" >
 6
 7      <uses-sdk android:minSdkVersion="14" />
 8
 9      <application
10          android:icon="@drawable/ic_launcher"
11          android:label="@string/app_name" >
12          <activity
13              android:label="@string/app_name"
14              android:theme="@android:style/Theme.Black.NoTitleBar"
15              android:name=".Main"  >
16              <intent-filter >
17                  <action android:name="android.intent.action.MAIN" />
18
19                  <category android:name="android.intent.category.LAUNCHER" />
20              </intent-filter>
21          </activity>
22          <activity android:name=".Tween"
23              android:theme="@android:style/Theme.Black.NoTitleBar"></activity>
24      </application>
25
26  </manifest>
```

Theme added for Main Activity

Theme added for Tween Activity

Closing bracket and tag

Manifest A Application P Permissions I Instrumentation F AndroidManifest.xml

Figure 10-31 Adding the theme to the Android Manifest file

3. Close the Wave Animation Manifest tab and save your work.

Changing the Emulator to Landscape Orientation

Most Android phones and tablets automatically rotate the display from portrait to landscape orientation when the user turns the device 90 degrees. Throughout this text, the emulator has been shown in a portrait orientation because when you first install the Android emulator, the default screen orientation layout is vertical. To switch the emulator to a landscape orientation on a PC, press the Ctrl+F12 keys simultaneously (or press the 7 key on the keypad when Num Lock is turned off) when the emulator is displayed during execution, as shown in Figure 10-2. To rotate the phone emulator back to the initial portrait position, press the Ctrl+F12 keys again. Mac users can press the Fn+Ctrl+F12 keys to change the orientation.

Running and Testing the Application

With all this exciting animation, it is time to see both types of animation running in the Android emulator. Click Run on the menu bar, and then select Run to save and test the application in the emulator. Save all the files, if necessary, and unlock the emulator. The application opens in the emulator window where you can click the Start Frame Animation button to begin the Frame animation of the four surfing images, as shown in Figure 10-1. To end the Frame animation and begin the rotation shown in Figure 10-2, click the Start Tween Animation button. The Tween animation rotates the image six times in a complete circle and ends.

Wrap It Up—Chapter Summary

Android supports two types of animations: frame-by-frame and Tween animations, as shown in the Wave Animation application in this chapter. Frame-by-frame animation shows different drawable images in a View in the opening window. The second Activity displays a Tween animation that rotates an image. Using the animation methods provided in the Android environment, developers can explore the user interface layouts that provide more usability and interest.

- Android provides two types of animation. Frame animation assigns a sequence of images to play as in a slide show with a specified interval between images. Tween animation performs a series of transformations on a single image, such as to change its position, size, rotation, and transparency.

- To create a layout that displays two controls side by side, you can nest a Relative layout within a Linear layout.

- To create a Frame animation, you write code in an XML file to load a sequence of images from the drawable folder. In the XML code, an animation-list root element references these images. Each item in the animation-list specifies how many milliseconds to display the image.

- In the animation-list code, you can include the oneshot property to determine how many times to play the animation. The oneshot property is set to true by default, meaning the animation plays once and then stops. Set the oneshot property to false to have the animation repeatedly play through to the end and then play again from the beginning.

- When you add the XML file with the animation-list code to the Android project, select Drawable as the Resource type and select animation-list as the root element so that Android stores the XML file in the res/drawable folder.

- The AnimationDrawable class provides the methods for Drawable animations to create a sequence of frame-by-frame images. In Android development, frame-based animations and image transitions are defined as drawables.

372

- You can set the Background property of an image to any full Drawable resource such as a .png file. In Main.java, you must specify the ImageView control that contains the animation images so you can bind the Drawable resource files to the Background property. Assign a new instance of ImageView to the ImageView control that was originally defined in the main.xml layout. Use the setBackgroundResource method to connect the images in the animation-list to the instance of ImageView.

- In Main.java, also include an instance of AnimationDrawable and assign it as the background of the animation images. Android constructs an AnimationDrawable Java object before setting it as the background. The animation is now ready to display the four images, though it does not actually start playing them until the start( ) method is triggered.

- You can use the start( ) and stop( ) methods of the drawable objects to control a Frame animation. When the user taps one button, the start( ) method begins playing the animation continuously if the oneshot property is set to false. The animation stops only when the user taps another button to execute the stop( ) method. The code can then initiate a startActivity that launches another Activity.

- A Tween animation manipulates a Drawable image by adding tween effects, which are predefined transitions that change an object from one state to another. Save a tween effect within an animation XML file. Specify the Resource type of this XML file as Tween animation so that Android stores the file in the res/anim/ folder of your Android project.

- The XML file for a Tween animation defines rotate attributes such as the number of degrees to spin, the pivot location, the rotation duration, and the number of times to repeat the rotation.

- To launch a Tween animation, use the startAnimation method, which begins animating a View object by calling the AnimationUtils class utilities to access the resources it needs to play the animation.

- To switch the emulator to use a landscape orientation on a PC, press the Ctrl+F12 keys. To rotate the emulator to the original portrait position, press the Ctrl+F12 keys again. Mac users can press the Fn+Ctrl+F12 keys to change the orientation.

Key Terms

9-patch image—A special image with predefined stretching areas that maintain the same look on different screen sizes.

android:oneshot—An attribute of the animation-list that determines whether an animation plays once and then stops or continues to play until the Stop Animation button is tapped.

AnimationDrawable class—A class that provides the methods for Drawable animations to create a sequence of frame-by-frame images.

animation-list—An XML root element that references images stored in the drawable folders and used in an animation.

Frame animation—A type of animation, also called frame-by-frame animation, that plays a sequence of images, as in a slide show, with a specified interval between images.

motion tween—A type of animation that specifies the start state of an object, and then animates the object a predetermined number of times or an infinite number of times using a transition.

setBackgroundResource—A method that places images in the frame-by-frame display for an animation, with each frame pointing to an image referenced in the XML resource file.

startAnimation—A method that begins the animation process of a View object by calling the AnimationUtils class utilities to access the resources necessary to load the animation.

Tween animation—A type of animation that, instead of using a sequence of images, creates an animation by performing a series of transformations on a single image, such as position, size, rotation, and transparency, on the contents of a View object.

tween effect—A transition that changes objects from one state to another, such as by moving, rotating, growing, or shrinking.

Developer FAQs

1. What are the two types of built-in Android animation?
2. Which type of animation displays a slide show type of presentation?
3. Which type of animation is applied to a single image?
4. What is the root element of a Frame animation within the XML file?
5. Write the code that sets an attribute to play a Frame animation until the app ends.
6. Write the code that sets an attribute to play a Frame animation for three seconds.
7. Would the oneshot property be set to true or false in question 6?
8. Which type of Drawable image stretches across different screen sizes?
9. Name three types of Drawable objects that can be set as a Background drawable.
10. Which method launches a Frame animation?
11. Which method ends a Frame animation?
12. Name four tween effects.
13. Which tween effect shrinks an image?
14. Which tween effect changes the transparency of the image?
15. When you create a Tween XML file, which folder is the file automatically saved in?
16. If you wanted to turn an image one-quarter of a circle starting at 0 degrees, write two lines of the code necessary to make that rotation.

17. Write the attribute for a rotation that repeats 10 times.

18. When an emulator launches, which orientation type is displayed?

19. Which keys change the orientation of the emulator on a PC?

20. Which keys change the orientation of the emulator on a Mac?

Beyond the Book

Using the Internet, search the Web for the answers to the following questions to further your Android knowledge.

1. Research how smartphone animation games have changed the sales of console games in the gaming industry. Write at least 200 words on this topic.

2. Research OpenGL graphic development. Write at least 150 words on this topic.

3. A new player to the mobile platform is the Windows 8 smartphone. Research why this phone might or might not be successful in the long term. Write at least 150 words on this topic.

4. At the Android Market site, determine the top five grossing apps. Write a paragraph about each.

Case Programming Projects

Complete one or more of the following case programming projects. Use the same steps and techniques taught within the chapter. Submit the program you create to your instructor. The level of difficulty is indicated for each case programming project.

Easiest: ★

Intermediate: ★★

Challenging: ★★★

Case Project 10–1: Learn How to Make Biscuits App ⋆

Requirements Document

Application title:	Learn How to Make Biscuits App
Purpose:	A series of images use Frame animation to demonstrate the five steps in making biscuits.
Algorithms:	1. The opening screen displays the first image in the process of making biscuits (Figure 10-32).
	2. When the user taps the Make a Biscuit button, the five steps are each displayed for two seconds. After each image is shown once, the animation ends (Figure 10-33).
Conditions:	1. The pictures of the five steps in biscuit preparation are provided with your student files with the names biscuit1, biscuit2, biscuit3, biscuit4, and biscuit5.
	2. Display each image in the Frame animation with the size 250, 500.
	3. Code a theme with no title bar.

Make a Biscuit

Figure 10-32

iStockphoto/edenexposed

Figure 10-33

Case Project 10–2: Improve Your Golf Stroke App ⋆

Requirements Document

Application title:	Improve Your Golf Stroke App
Purpose:	A series of images use Frame animation to demonstrate the proper positions of the perfect golf swing.
Algorithms:	1. The screen displays six images, each showing the proper position during the process of making a golf swing. Display the images in a Frame animation with 0.5 seconds between each image. Each image should only be displayed once when the user taps the Perfect Golf Swing button (Figure 10-34).
	2. When the user taps the Rotate Your Swing button, rotate the fifth image around 270 degrees nine times with an interval of three seconds (Figure 10-35).
Conditions:	1. The pictures of the six golf positions are provided with your student files with the names golf1, golf2, golf3, golf4, golf5, and golf6.
	2. Display each image with the size 200, 400.
	3. Code a theme with no title bar.

Figure 10-34

Figure 10-35

Case Project 10–3: Droid Rotation App ★★

Requirements Document

Application title: Droid Rotation App

Purpose: As an advertisement at the end of a television commercial, a Droid phone rotates in a perfect circle four times.

Algorithms: 1. The opening screen displays a Droid phone in the center and automatically begins rotating the image four times in a perfect circle with an interval of 1.5 seconds.

Conditions: 1. The picture of the Droid phone is provided with your student files with the name droid.

2. Display the image with the size 100, 170.

3. Code a theme with no title bar.

Case Project 10–4: Cartoon Animation App ★★

Requirements Document

Application title: Cartoon Animation App

Purpose: A sequence of cartoon images is displayed to create the sense of motion.

Algorithms: 1. The opening screen displays one of four cartoon images of a man with an idea. When the user taps the Begin Cartoon button, each image is displayed for 0.15 seconds.

2. When the user taps the Stop Cartoon button, the current image rotates once and then stops.

Conditions: 1. The pictures of the cartoon are provided with your student files with the names cartoon1, cartoon2, cartoon3, and cartoon4.

2. Display each image with the size 200, 270.

3. Code a theme with no title bar.

Case Project 10–5: Flags of the World App ★★★

Requirements Document

Application title:	Flags of the World App
Purpose:	A sequence of flag images appears when the app starts.
Algorithms:	1. The opening screen displays images of seven world flags. When the user taps a World Flags button, a Frame animation displays each flag for 0.75 seconds until the app ends.
	2. When the user taps the Stop Flags button, the Frame animation stops. The last flag image fades away for 10 seconds until it is no longer visible.
Conditions:	1. The pictures of the seven world flags are provided with your student files with the names flag1, flag2, flag3, flag4, flag5, flag6, and flag7.
	2. Display each image with the size 400, 300.
	3. Code a theme with no title bar.

Case Project 10–6: Frame and Tween Animation Game App ★★★

Requirements Document

Application title:	Frame and Tween Animation Game App
Purpose:	Display images of your favorite game in action.
Algorithms:	1. Locate at least four images of your favorite game character (such as one in *Angry Birds*) and create a custom Frame animation of your choice.
	2. Create a Tween animation with one of the images that uses at least two of the tween effects.
Conditions:	1. Select your own images.
	2. Use a layout of your choice.
	3. Code a theme with no title bar.

Discover! Incorporating Google Maps

In this chapter, you learn to:

◎ Create an Android project displaying a Google map

◎ Install the Google API to the SDK

◎ Set up a Google API Android Virtual Device

◎ Locate your MD5 certificate

◎ Sign up for a Google Maps API key

◎ Understand security and permissions

◎ Access the MapView class

◎ Code the populate( ) method

◎ Add the onTap( ) method

◎ Set permissions for maps in the Android Manifest file

◎ Create a GeoPoint overlay

If you own a smartphone, using an online map to find directions to a friend's home, a new restaurant, or a business interview is most likely part of a typical week in your digital world. The most popular mapping application is owned by Google. In addition to simply using the built-in Android Google Maps application, you can embed it into your own applications to create a customized mapping app. Using Google Maps within your project, you can change the view of Google Maps, displaying a particular latitude and longitude of a location. The Maps application shown in Figure 11-1 displays a Google map with two pushpin images indicating the hometown locations of the author and the editor of this book.

Figure 11-1   Maps application

The Android app in Figure 11-1 allows the user to zoom in to see the map in more detail. Figure 11-2 displays the location of the hometown of the author of this text in Lynchburg, Virginia, and the editor's hometown in Madison, Wisconsin. The app uses the Google Maps API to bring the power of Google Maps to the Android platform.

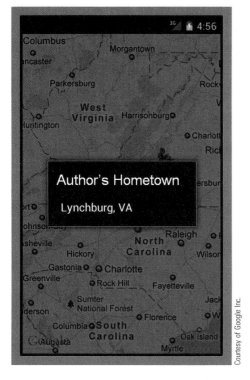

Author's Hometown

Lynchburg, VA

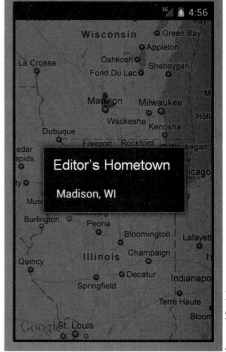

Editor's Hometown

Madison, WI

Figure 11-2   Hometown locations of the author and editor on the Android Google map

GTK

Google provides a text messaging service that includes Google Maps directions. Send a text message to Google with the from and to locations, and Google quickly responds with a text message containing complete, step-by-step directions. For example, you can send Google a text message similar to the following: Directions Atlanta, GA to Miami, FL.

To create this application, the developer must understand how to perform the following processes, among others:

1.   Install the Google API add-on to the SDK.

2.   Add the AVD that uses the Google API deployment target.

3.   Obtain a personal Maps API key from Google.

4.   Define a MapView inside a Linear layout in main.xml.

5.   Add permissions to the Android Manifest file to access the Internet and the Google library.

6.   Add a no title bar theme to the Android Manifest file.

7.   Add the pushpin image to the drawable folder.

8. Code the MapView in Main.java.

9. Add Overlay objects to the map.

10. Call the populate( ) method to read each Overlay object.

11. Display two GeoPoint overlays.

Using Google Maps

Google Maps is an online mapping service that contains a variety of features, such as turn-by-turn directions and GPS location services. Google introduced Google Maps in the United States in 2005 and has subsequently released versions throughout the world. Google Maps is an integral part of the Android experience, allowing apps to display information such as directions to a hotel, the distance of your morning run, street view images, bike path directions, possible traffic delays, and public transit routes. Google updates its maps frequently, especially in its version for Android.

Installing the Google API

To use Google Maps within an Android application, you must install the Google **API (application programming interface)**, a set of tools for building software applications, in the Android SDK. By installing the Google Maps API, you can embed the Google Maps site directly into an Android application, and then overlay app-specific data on the maps. The Android Google Maps API is free for commercial use providing that the site using it is publicly accessible and does not charge for access. If the app is for public sale, you must use Google Maps API Premier, which can be accessed for a per-usage subscription fee. The classes of the Google Maps Android library offer built-in downloading, rendering, and caching of mapping tiles, as well as a variety of display options and controls. Multiple versions of the Google Maps API add-on are available, corresponding to the Android API level supported in each version. This text uses Android 4.0 Google APIs by Google Inc. You must download the add-on to your computer and install it in your SDK environment to create an Android Google Maps app. To install the Android 4.0 Google API, follow these steps:

1. Open the Eclipse program. Click Window on the menu bar and then click Android SDK Manager to view the SDK files available.

    The Android SDK Manager dialog box opens with the current SDK packages listed (Figure 11-3).

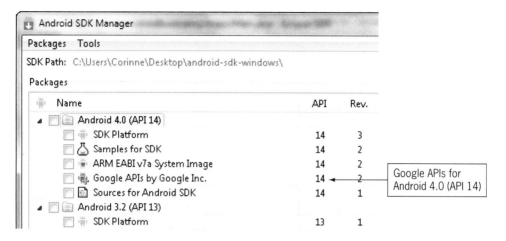

Figure 11-3   Android SDK Manager

2. In the Android 4.0 (API 14) category, check the Google APIs by Google Inc. check box, if it is not already installed (as indicated in the Status column). Click to remove the check mark from any other selected check boxes. Click the Install Packages button to install the Google API package. Close the Android SDK Manager after the installation.

    The Android SDK Manager is updated to include the Google APIs for use with the Google Maps features.

Adding the AVD to Target the Google API

After you install the Android Google API, you set the application's properties to select the Google APIs add-on as the build target. Doing so sets the Android Virtual Device (AVD) Manager to use the new Google API package. Make sure to select the version (by API level) appropriate for the Google API target. To target the Google API within the AVD Manager, follow these steps:

1. Click Window on the menu bar and then click AVD Manager.

    The Android Virtual Device Manager dialog box opens (Figure 11-4).

Figure 11-4   Android Virtual Device Manager dialog box

2. Click the New button. Type **Google_API** in the Name text box. Click the Target button, and then click Google APIs (Google Inc.) – API Level 14.

    A target device named Google_API is configured (Figure 11-5).

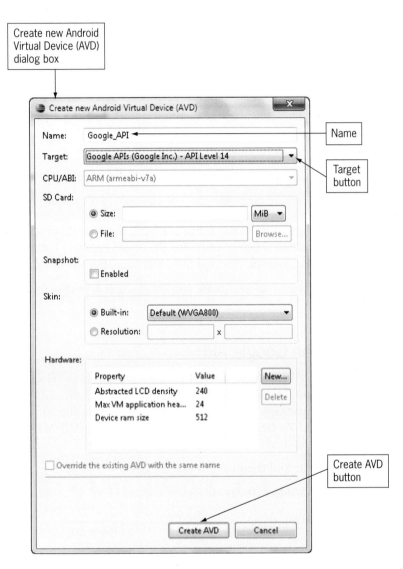

Create new Android Virtual Device (AVD) dialog box

Name

Target button

Create AVD button

Figure 11-5   Create new Android Virtual Device (AVD) dialog box

3. Click the Create AVD button.

    The Google_API is displayed in the Android Virtual Device Manager dialog box (Figure 11-6).

Figure 11-6   Google_API displayed in the AVD list

4.   Click the Close button to close the Android Virtual Device Manager dialog box.

The Android Virtual Device Manager dialog box closes after creating a new Android Virtual Device.

GTK

Android Google Map capabilities include instantly posting your present location on social networking sites.

Obtaining a Maps API Key from Google

Before you can run an Android Google Maps application, you need to apply for a free Google Maps API key so you can integrate Google Maps into your Android application. An Android map application gives you access to Google Maps data, but Google requires that you register with the Google Maps service and agree to the Terms of Service before your mapping application can obtain data from Google Maps. This applies whether you are developing your application on the emulator or preparing your application for deployment to mobile devices. Registering for a Google Maps API key is free. The process involves registering your computer's MD5 fingerprint. An **MD5 (Message-Digest Algorithm 5) digital fingerprint** is a value included as part of a file to verify the integrity of the file. Signing up with Google to register for a Google Maps API key is a task that needs to be performed only once and the purpose is mainly for security. A unique **Google Maps API key** is a long string of seemingly random alphanumeric characters that may look like this:

87:B9:58:BC:6F:28:71:74:A9:32:B8:29:C2:4E:7B:02:A7:D3:7A:DD

Certificate fingerprint (MD5): 94:1E:43:49:87:73:BB:E6:A6:88:D7:20:F1:8E:B5:98

The first step in registering for a Google Maps API key is to locate an MD5 fingerprint of the certificate used to sign your Android application. You cannot run a Google mapping application in your Eclipse Android emulator if it is not signed with your local API key. The Android installed environment contains a file named debug.keystore, which contains a unique identification. To locate the MD5 fingerprint of the debug certificate on your computer, follow these steps:

1. To generate an MD5 fingerprint of the debug certificate, first use Windows Explorer or the Finder to locate the debug.keystore file in the active AVD directory. The location of the AVD directories varies by platform:

    ◆ Windows 7 or Windows Vista: C:\Users\<user>\.android\debug.keystore

    ◆ Windows XP: C:\Documents and Settings\<user>\.android\debug.keystore

    ◆ Mac OS X: ~/.android/debug.keystore

   Note: The <user> portion of this path statement indicates your user account name on your computer. For example, using a Windows 7 computer, the location of the AVD directory on a computer with a username of Corinne is: C:\Users\Corinne\.android\debug.keystore.

   The location of the AVD directory is determined (Figure 11-7).

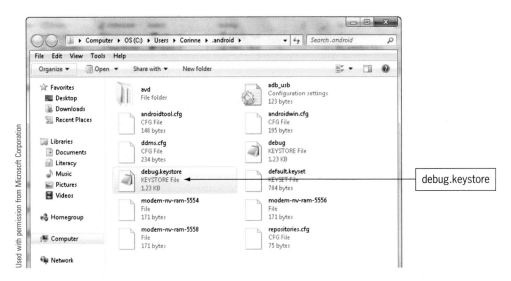

Figure 11-7   Location of the debug.keystore file on a Windows 7 computer

2. On a Windows 7 or Vista computer, click the Start button. Type **cmd** in the Search box and press the Enter key. On a Windows XP computer, click the Start button. Click Run. Type **cmd** and press the Enter key. On a Mac computer, on the Desktop toolbar, click the Spotlight button (upper-right corner). In the Spotlight box, type **terminal** and then press the Return key. To find the MD5 fingerprint of your computer, in the Command Prompt window, type the following command, replacing *<user>* with the name of the account:

In Windows 7 or Vista:

keytool.exe -list -alias androiddebugkey -keystore C:\Users*<user>*\\.android\\debug.keystore -storepass android –keypass android

In Windows XP:

keytool.exe -list -alias androiddebugkey -keystore C:\Documents and Settings*<user>*\\.android\\debug.keystore -storepass android –keypass android

In Mac OS X:

keytool -list -keystore ~/.android/debug.keystore

Press the Enter key.

On a Mac, when asked for your password, enter **android** and then press the Return key.

The MD5 fingerprint is displayed in the Command Prompt window (Figure 11-8).

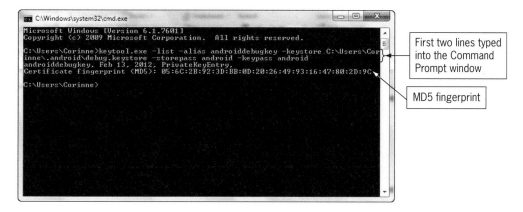

Figure 11-8   MD5 fingerprint in the Command Prompt window

3. To select the MD5 fingerprint in Windows, right-click the Command Prompt window and then click Mark on the shortcut menu. Select the MD5 fingerprint code, being careful not to include any extra spaces.

    On a Mac, drag to select the MD5 fingerprint code.

    The MD5 fingerprint is selected (Figure 11-9).

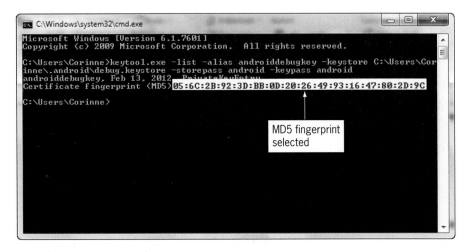

Figure 11-9 MD5 fingerprint selected

4.   To copy the MD5 highlighted code, press the Ctrl+C keys (Windows) or the Command+C keys (Mac) to copy the code to the system Clipboard.

The MD5 fingerprint is copied. You paste this code into a Web page in the next step.

Troubleshooting

If an MD5 fingerprint is not displayed when you perform the previous steps, refer to the following suggestions to solve the problem.

- *You receive a "keytool is not recognized" message*—If a message similar to "keytool is not recognized" appears after you enter the long keytool command, you need to locate the keytool executable file on your computer, which is stored in a subfolder of the Java folder. On Windows 7, this folder is:

```
C:\Program Files\Java\jdk1.7.0_01\bin
```

After locating the keytool executable file, open the Command Prompt window and enter the following command to change to the directory containing the keytool executable file:

```
cd C:\Program Files\Java\jdk1.7.0_01\bin
```

Enter the command to generate the MD5 fingerprint for your computer:

```
keytool -list -alias androiddebugkey -keystore
C:\Users\<user>\.android\debug.keystore -storepass android -keypass android
```

- *A fingerprint other than MD5 is generated*—After entering the long keytool command, a fingerprint such as SHA1 might appear instead of the MD5 fingerprint. To generate an MD5 fingerprint, add –v for version by entering the following command (for Windows 7) in the Command Prompt window:

```
keytool –v –list –alias androiddebugkey –keystore
C:\Users\<user>\.android\debug.keystore -storepass android –keypass android
```

Be sure to copy the MD5 fingerprint so you can register it with the Google Maps service.

Registering the MD5 Fingerprint with the Google Maps Service

Using the MD5 fingerprint, you can register with Google for a Maps API key. A single Maps API key is valid for all applications signed by a single certificate. After placing the MD5 fingerprint in the Google Registration page, a generated API key is displayed in the browser. You need a Gmail account to receive the API key, so sign up for a free Gmail account before completing the following steps, if necessary. Later in the chapter, you place the API key in the XML layout code. When the code is executed, it allows your application to connect with Google Maps. To register the MD5 certificate fingerprint with Google Maps service, follow these steps:

1. Start a browser and display the following Web site:
    http://developers.google.com/android/maps-api-signup

    The Android Maps API Key Sign Up Web page is displayed (Figure 11-10).

Figure 11-10 Android Maps API Key Signup Web site

2. Scroll down the page, if necessary, and check the I have read and agree with the terms and conditions check box. Click the My certificate's MD5 fingerprint text box and then press the Ctrl+V keys (Windows) or the Command+V keys (Mac) to paste the MD5 fingerprint code from the Command Prompt window.

The MD5 fingerprint code is pasted in the text box (Figure 11-11).

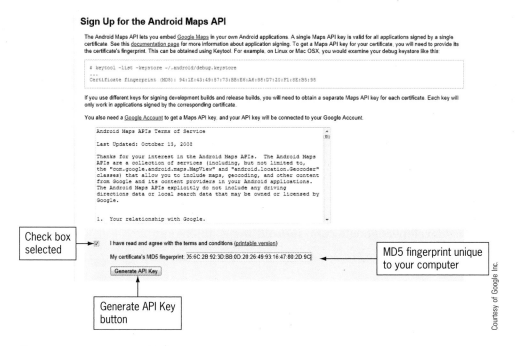

Figure 11-11 Unique MD5 fingerprint code

3. To display the Android Maps API key, click the Generate API Key button. If necessary, enter your Gmail e-mail address and password. (You need to create a Google account if you do not have one.)

The Android Maps API key is displayed. Because you need the API key later, do not close this window. You might want to take a screen shot of this key for future access (Figure 11-12).

Figure 11-12   Android Maps API key

GTK

If you receive a message similar to "The fingerprint you entered is not a valid Google Maps API key," you did not enter the MD5 fingerprint for your computer. See the Troubleshooting section earlier in this chapter to generate the MD5 fingerprint (not another type of fingerprint).

Adding the MapView Element in the XML Code

After obtaining the Google Maps API key, the next step is to create the Maps Android application in Eclipse. The API key attribute holds the Google Maps API key that proves your application and signed certificate are registered with the Google Maps service. To display a Google map in an Android app, the API key must be added to the main.xml layout file. To display Google Maps in your Android application, modify the main.xml file located in the res/layout folder.

To make it easier for you to add powerful mapping capabilities to your application, Google provides a Maps external library that includes the com.google.android.maps package. You must use the `<com.google.android.maps.MapView />` element to display the Google Maps in your Activity, as shown in the following code:

Code Syntax

```
<com.google.android.maps.MapView
  android:id="@+id/mapview"
  android:layout_width="fill_parent"
  android:layout_height="fill_parent"
  android:enabled="true"
  android:clickable="true"
  android:apiKey="0H1jqLj_jO8oBj4g8zSxyEuezie5-mE_56_UiXA" />
```

Note: Your generated apiKey will be different.

The apiKey in the last line of code can be copied and pasted from the browser window displayed in Figure 11-12. To begin the application and code the API key for the Google Maps in main.xml, follow these steps:

1. Click the New button on the Standard toolbar. Expand the Android folder and select Android Project. Click the Next button. In the New Android Project dialog box, enter the Project Name **Maps**. To save the project on your USB drive, click to remove the check mark from the Use default location check box. Type **E:\Workspace** (if necessary, enter a different drive letter that identifies the USB drive). Click the Next button. For the Build Target, select Google APIs (for platform 4.0) and then click the Next button. For the Package Name, type **net.androidbootcamp.maps**. Enter **Main** in the Create Activity text box.

The Build Target of Google APIs is selected. The new Android Maps project has a Project Name, a Package Name, and an Activity named Main (Figure 11-13).

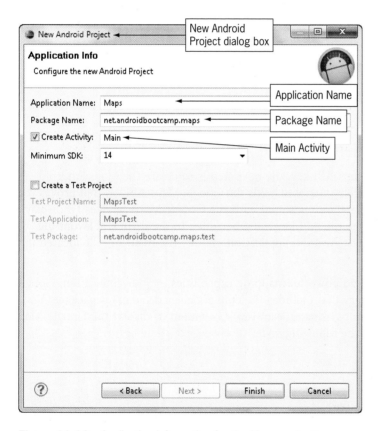

Figure 11-13   Application information for the Maps project

2. Click the Finish button. Expand the Maps project in the Package Explorer. In the res\layout folder, double-click main.xml. By default, LinearLayout is already set. Delete the TextView lines of code that display Hello World! Click the main.xml tab at the bottom of the window. To display a Google Android map using the unique API code for your computer, type the following code on Line 6, using auto-completion as much as possible:

```
<com.google.android.maps.MapView
    android:id="@+id/mapview"
    android:layout_width="fill_parent"
    android:layout_height="fill_parent"
    android:enabled="true"
    android:clickable="true"
    android:apiKey="Your API Code here" />
```

Note: Replace *"Your API Code here"* with your personal API code.

The Google map is coded in main.xml with the unique API code created earlier in this chapter (Figure 11-14).

```
 1  <?xml version="1.0" encoding="utf-8"?>
 2  <LinearLayout xmlns:android="http://schemas.android.com/apk/res/android"
 3      android:layout_width="fill_parent"
 4      android:layout_height="fill_parent"
 5      android:orientation="vertical" >
 6  <com.google.android.maps.MapView
 7      android:id="@+id/mapview"
 8      android:layout_width="fill_parent"
 9      android:layout_height="fill_parent"
10      android:enabled="true"
11      android:clickable="true"
12      android:apiKey="0H1jqLj_j08oBj4g8zSxyEuezie5-mE_56_UiXA" />
13  </LinearLayout>
```

Display the MapView by referencing the unique apiKey

Figure 11-14 Android Google Maps XML code

Adding Permissions to the Android Manifest File

Permissions are necessary in Android applications to prevent malicious outside applications from corrupting data and accessing sensitive information. The projects created in this text have not required any permissions thus far, but to access the Internet and connect with the Google mapping feature, the Maps application requires special permission. Typical permissions include full access to the Internet, your GPS location, your personal information, phone calls, SMS messages, and other system tools. The Android Manifest file can contain permission requests that are granted or denied when the application is run on the Android platform. With the permission tag in the Android Manifest file, you can mandate the level of access permitted. When you access Google Maps, the app requires permission to connect to the Internet. The following code gives permissions for this app to connect to the Internet and must be placed within the manifest element of the Android Manifest file:

Code Syntax

```
<uses-permission
    android:name="android.permission.INTERNET" />
```

In addition to the Internet permissions granted in the Android Manifest file, permissions are also necessary to inform the system that a Google library is being used. Because the actual maps reside at Google, your application requires permission to access this map data. As part of the application element within the Android Manifest file, include the following line to grant permissions to the Google library:

Code Syntax

```
<uses-library
    android:name="com.google.android.maps" />
```

In addition to the two permissions, the map display should have as much room as possible, so the Android Manifest theme is set to not display a title bar. To code the permissions and change the theme within the Android Manifest file, follow these steps:

1. Close main.xml and save your work. To add the permission request to access the Internet to the Android Manifest file, in the Package Explorer double-click the AndroidManifest.xml file. Click the AndroidManifest.xml tab at the bottom of the window. Inside the application code, click at the end of the line <uses-sdk android:minSdkVersion="14" />. Press the Enter key. Type **<uses-permission android:name="android.permission.INTERNET" />**.

   The Android permission for the Internet is coded in the Android Manifest file (Figure 11-15).

```
 1  <?xml version="1.0" encoding="utf-8"?>
 2  <manifest xmlns:android="http://schemas.android.com/apk/res/android"
 3      package="net.androidbootcamp.maps"
 4      android:versionCode="1"
 5      android:versionName="1.0" >
 6
 7      <uses-sdk android:minSdkVersion="14" />
 8      <uses-permission android:name="android.permission.INTERNET" />         Permission to access
 9                                                                            the Internet
10      <application
11          android:icon="@drawable/ic_launcher"
12          android:label="@string/app_name" >
13          <activity
14              android:label="@string/app_name"
15              android:name=".Main" >
16              <intent-filter >
17                  <action android:name="android.intent.action.MAIN" />
18
19                  <category android:name="android.intent.category.LAUNCHER" />
20              </intent-filter>
21          </activity>
22      </application>
23
24  </manifest>
```

Figure 11-15 Android Manifest code with the Internet permission

2. To add the permission request to access the Google library, click at the end of the line android:label="@string/app_name" > in the application. Press the Enter key. Type **<uses-library android:name="com.google.android.maps"/>**.

The Android permission for the Google library is coded in the Android Manifest file (Figure 11-16).

```
  *Maps Manifest ⊠
 1  <?xml version="1.0" encoding="utf-8"?>
 2  <manifest xmlns:android="http://schemas.android.com/apk/res/android"
 3      package="net.androidbootcamp.maps"
 4      android:versionCode="1"
 5      android:versionName="1.0" >
 6
 7      <uses-sdk android:minSdkVersion="14" />
 8      <uses-permission android:name="android.permission.INTERNET" />
 9
10      <application
11          android:icon="@drawable/ic_launcher"
12          android:label="@string/app_name" >
13          <uses-library android:name="com.google.android.maps"/>
14          <activity
15              android:label="@string/app_name"
16              android:name=".Main" >
17              <intent-filter >
18                  <action android:name="android.intent.action.MAIN" />
19
20                  <category android:name="android.intent.category.LAUNCHER" />
21              </intent-filter>
22          </activity>
23      </application>
24
25  </manifest>
```

Permission set for accessing the Google Maps library

Figure 11-16 Android Manifest code with the Google library permission

3. To remove the title bar from the theme, click at the end of the line android: label="@string/app_name" > in the application. Delete the closing brace of this line. Press the Enter key. Type **android:theme="@android:style/Theme.NoTitleBar">**.

The Android theme is changed to NoTitleBar in the Android Manifest file (Figure 11-17).

400

```
📄 *Maps Manifest ⊠

 1  <?xml version="1.0" encoding="utf-8"?>
 2⊝ <manifest xmlns:android="http://schemas.android.com/apk/res/android"
 3      package="net.androidbootcamp.maps"
 4      android:versionCode="1"
 5      android:versionName="1.0" >
 6
 7      <uses-sdk android:minSdkVersion="14" />
 8      <uses-permission android:name="android.permission.INTERNET" />
 9
10      <application
11          android:icon="@drawable/ic_launcher"
12          android:label="@string/app_name"
13          android:theme="@android:style/Theme.NoTitleBar">
14      <uses-library android:name="com.google.android.maps"/>
15⊝      <activity
16          android:label="@string/app_name"
17          android:name=".Main" >
18⊝      <intent-filter >
19          <action android:name="android.intent.action.MAIN" />
20
21          <category android:name="android.intent.category.LAUNCHER" />
22      </intent-filter>
23      </activity>
24      </application>
25
26  </manifest>
```

Theme is set to NoTitleBar

Figure 11-17   No Title Bar theme

GTK

Google Maps now extends beyond the Earth's surface boundaries. Google Maps now includes Google Sky, Google Moon, and Google Mars.

Understanding MapView

The Google mapping technology relies on the MapView class within Android. The **MapView class** displays and manipulates a Google map within the Android environment. The Main Activity must extend MapActivity instead of the default Activity to use the MapView class. The MapView class must be linked to the Google Maps API key in the XML code when it is instantiated. The following code instantiates the MapView control:

Code Syntax

```
MapView mapView = (MapView) findViewById(R.id.mapview);
mapView.setBuiltInZoomControls(true);
```

The instance of MapView named mapView has the setBuiltInZoomControls set to true. The **setBuiltInZoomControls** property allows the site visitor to use the built-in zoom feature. As the user pans the map, zoom controls are automatically shown at the bottom of the MapView display with a large plus and minus sign in the zoom controls.

Later in the code, a red pushpin will be overlaid on the map. The pushpin image needs to be placed in the res\drawable folder. To add the image to the drawable folder and instantiate the MapView control, follow these steps:

1. Close the Android Manifest file and save your work. To add the image file to the drawable-hdpi resource folder, drag pushpin.png from the student files to the drawable-hdpi folder until a plus sign pointer appears. Release the mouse button. If necessary, click the Copy files option button, and then click the OK button.

    A copy of the image file appears in the drawable-hdpi folder (Figure 11-18).

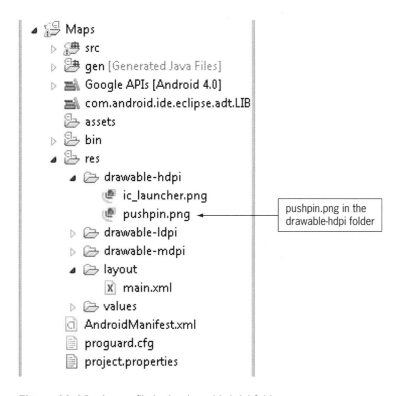

Figure 11-18   Image file in the drawable-hdpi folder

2. To instantiate the MapView control, double-click Main.java (in the src\net.androidbootcamp.maps folder) to open its code window. In the public class Main, change the extends Activity to extends **MapActivity**. Point to MapActivity and click Import 'MapActivity' (com.google.android.maps). Point to Main and click Add unimplemented methods.

    The Main Activity extends the MapActivity. The isRouteDisplayed auto-generated stub appears. This required method determines if the application is displaying any route information. This Maps app does not display a route, so false is returned (Figure 11-19).

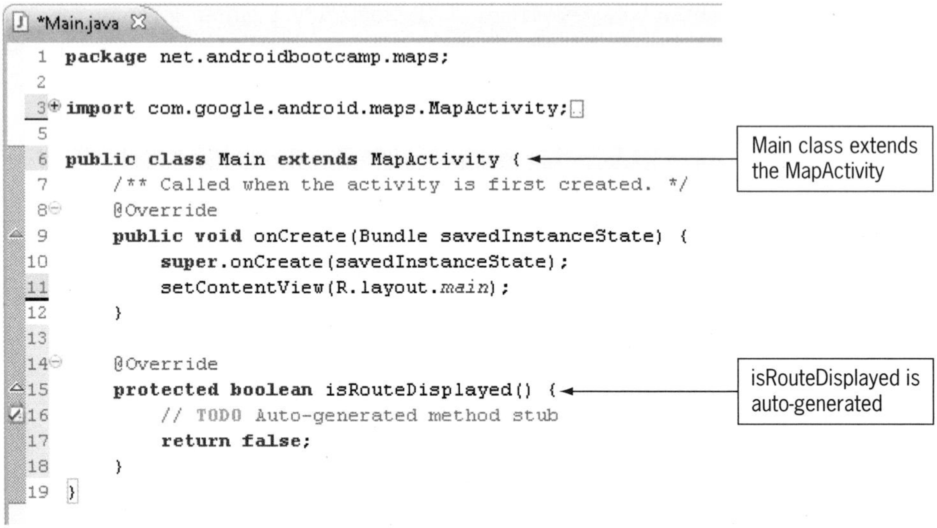

```
 1  package net.androidbootcamp.maps;
 2
 3  import com.google.android.maps.MapActivity;
 5
 6  public class Main extends MapActivity {
 7      /** Called when the activity is first created. */
 8      @Override
 9      public void onCreate(Bundle savedInstanceState) {
10          super.onCreate(savedInstanceState);
11          setContentView(R.layout.main);
12      }
13
14      @Override
15      protected boolean isRouteDisplayed() {
16          // TODO Auto-generated method stub
17          return false;
18      }
19  }
```

Main class extends the MapActivity

isRouteDisplayed is auto-generated

Figure 11-19   Main extends MapActivity

3. Click to the right of the setContentView statement and press the Enter key.
    Type **MapView mapView = (MapView) findViewById(R.id.mapview);**.
    Point to MapView and click Import 'MapView' (com.google.android.maps).
    Press the Enter key. To use the map's zoom in and zoom out controls, type
    mapView.setBuiltInZoomControls(true);.

    The instance of MapView is instantiated and the setBuiltInZoomControls are set to
    true to enable the zoom capabilities (Figure 11-20).

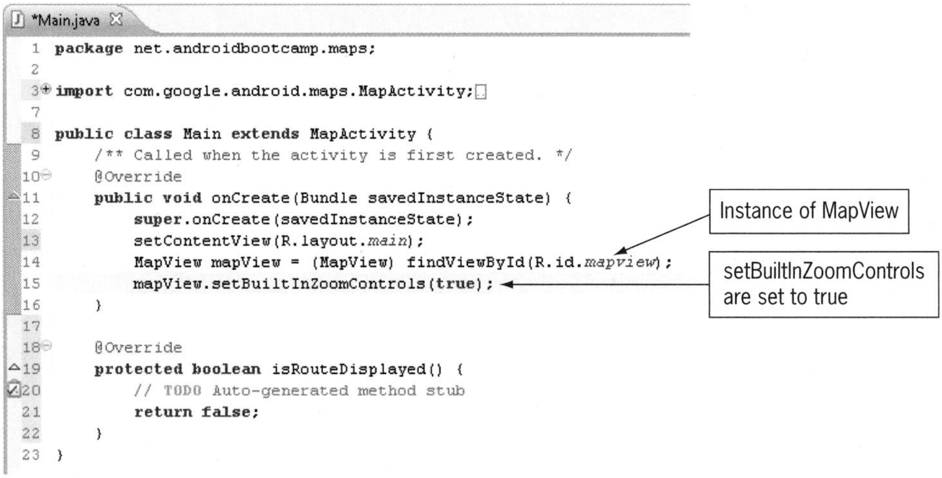

```
 1  package net.androidbootcamp.maps;
 2
 3  import com.google.android.maps.MapActivity;
 7
 8  public class Main extends MapActivity {
 9      /** Called when the activity is first created. */
10      @Override
11      public void onCreate(Bundle savedInstanceState) {
12          super.onCreate(savedInstanceState);
13          setContentView(R.layout.main);
14          MapView mapView = (MapView) findViewById(R.id.mapview);
15          mapView.setBuiltInZoomControls(true);
16      }
17
18      @Override
19      protected boolean isRouteDisplayed() {
20          // TODO Auto-generated method stub
21          return false;
22      }
23  }
```

Instance of MapView

setBuiltInZoomControls are set to true

Figure 11-20   Instance of MapView and the Zoom controls set to true

4. To view a zoomable map that loads the layout file and displays map tiles that allow the user to pan around the map, click Run on the menu bar. Select Run to save and test the application in the emulator. A dialog box requesting how you would like to run the application opens the first time the application is executed. Select Android Application and click the OK button. Save all the files in the next dialog box, if necessary, and unlock the emulator. The application opens in the emulator window where you can zoom in and out of the map.

A Google map appears in the emulator (Figure 11-21).

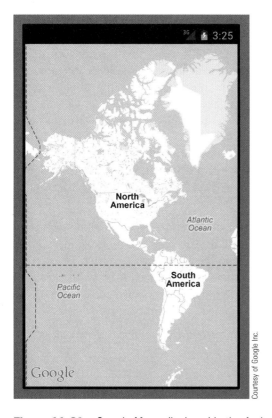

Figure 11-21 Google Maps displayed in the Android emulator

IN THE TRENCHES
As you zoom in and out of the map, be aware that Android defines 21 levels of zoom. At zoom Level 1, the equator of the Earth is 256 pixels long. Each successive zoom level is magnified by a factor of 2.

Adding Overlay Items

The map is displayed in Figure 11-21, but adding a specific location to a map customizes the application. In the Maps chapter project, two overlay objects are added to find particular locations on the Google map. The first location in Figure 11-2 displayed the author's hometown of Lynchburg, Virginia. The second map location was defined as the book editor's hometown of Madison, Wisconsin. A map marker, or **overlay**, uses a graphic image to indicate a specific location on a map. To add a map marker such as a red pushpin image to the map, an instance of the MapOverlay class is necessary. Several overlays can be placed on the same map. For example, you may have seen an app such as Yelp that displays dozens of popular restaurants by displaying red triangles within a city map as an overlay layer. To create an overlay, you must implement the **ItemizedOverlay class**, which manages the individual items placed as a layer on the map. A new Java class named Overlay is added to the Maps app and extends the ItemizedOverlay class. To add a second class that extends the ItemizedOverlay class, follow these steps:

1. Save your work. To create a second class, right-click the src/net.androidbootcamp.maps folder in the Package Explorer, point to New on the shortcut menu, and then click Class. Type **Overlay** in the Name text box to create a second class that defines the Overlay Activity. In the Superclass text box, type **com.google.android.maps.ItemizedOverlay**. Click the Constructors from superclass check box.

   A new class named Overlay.java is created to extend the ItemizedOverlay class (Figure 11-22).

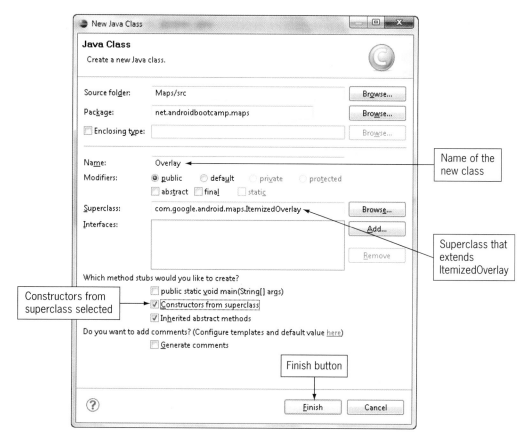

Figure 11-22   Overlay.java class

2. Click the Finish button. If necessary, click the Overlay.java tab.

    The Overlay class extends the ItemizedOverlay class with three auto-generated method stubs called constructors (Figure 11-23).

```
  J Main.java      J *Overlay.java ✕  ◄──────────────────────    Overlay.java tab

   1  package net.androidbootcamp.maps;

   2
   3⊕ import android.graphics.drawable.Drawable;□

   6
   7  public class Overlay extends ItemizedOverlay {

   8
   9⊖     public Overlay(Drawable defaultMarker) {
  10          super(defaultMarker);
  11          // TODO Auto-generated constructor stub
  12      }
  13
  14⊖     @Override
  15      protected OverlayItem createItem(int i) {      This argument might
  16          // TODO Auto-generated method stub        appear as int arg0;
  17          return null;                              the code will still run
  18      }                                             correctly
  19
  20⊖     @Override
  21      public int size() {
  22          // TODO Auto-generated method stub
  23          return 0;
  24      }
  25
  26  }
  27
```

Figure 11-23   Overlay.java class automated code

Adding Overlay Objects to an ArrayList

The Overlay class must first assign an array called an **ArrayList**, an expandable array that holds the overlay objects displayed in a layer on the map image. In the case of the chapter project, two pushpins are displayed as overlay objects. The context instantiation temporarily holds each of the items displayed in the array. Each of the constructors must be customized to define the default marker for each of the items in the Overlay array. For the app to actually draw the pushpin Drawable object, code must define where to place its boundaries. The center-point of the bottom of the image should be placed on the map using coordinates based on latitude and longitude. To do so, the four constructors are customized after the ArrayList and Context are instantiated, as shown in the following code:

Code Syntax

```
private ArrayList<OverlayItem> mOverlays = new ArrayList<OverlayItem>();
private Context mContext;
public Overlay(Drawable defaultMarker, Context context) {
        super(boundCenterBottom(defaultMarker));
        mContext = context;
        // TODO Auto-generated constructor stub
}
public void addOverlay(OverlayItem overlay) {
        mOverlays.add(overlay);
        populate();
}
@Override
protected OverlayItem createItem(int i) {
        // TODO Auto-generated method stub
        return mOverlays.get(i);
}

@Override
public int size() {
        // TODO Auto-generated method stub
        return mOverlays.size();
}
```

The first super constructor ties the overlay object to a default marker. The boundCenterBottom( ) method wraps the overlay object around the defaultMarker on the map. The addOverlay method is called each time a new OverlayItem is added to the ArrayList. A method called **populate( )** is necessary to add each new item in the ItemizedOverlay, which reads each of the OverlayItems such as the pushpin image and prepares for each image to be drawn on top of the map in a new visible layer. Each time the populate( ) method executes, the createItem(int) constructor retrieves each OverlayItem in the array. This method returns the OverlayItem from the position specified by an integer value. The size constructor returns the number of items being overlaid on the map. To code the ArrayList and Context and customize the constructors, follow these steps:

1. In Overlay.java, click the blank line after the statement beginning with public class Overlay to instantiate ArrayList and Context. Type **private ArrayList<OverlayItem> mOverlays = new ArrayList<OverlayItem>();**. Point to ArrayList and click Import 'ArrayList' (java.util). Press the Enter key and then type **private Context mContext;**. Point to Context and click Import 'Context' (android.content).

    The ArrayList and Context are instantiated (Figure 11-24).

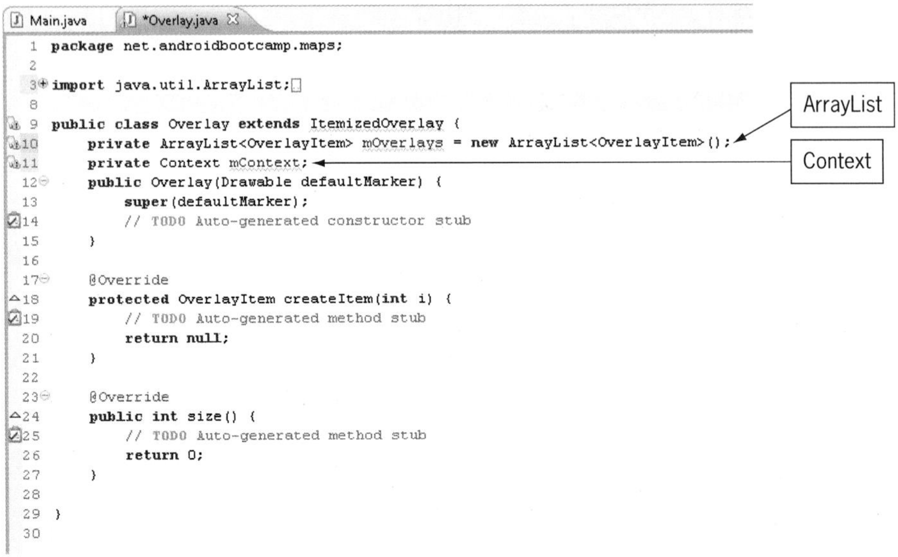

```
    Main.java        *Overlay.java
  1  package net.androidbootcamp.maps;
  2
  3  import java.util.ArrayList;
  8
  9  public class Overlay extends ItemizedOverlay {
 10      private ArrayList<OverlayItem> mOverlays = new ArrayList<OverlayItem>();
 11      private Context mContext;
 12      public Overlay(Drawable defaultMarker) {
 13          super(defaultMarker);
 14          // TODO Auto-generated constructor stub
 15      }
 16
 17      @Override
 18      protected OverlayItem createItem(int i) {
 19          // TODO Auto-generated method stub
 20          return null;
 21      }
 22
 23      @Override
 24      public int size() {
 25          // TODO Auto-generated method stub
 26          return 0;
 27      }
 28
 29  }
 30
```

ArrayList

Context

Figure 11-24   ArrayList and Context instantiated in the Overlay class

2. To customize the Overlay constructor to define a default marker for each item in the array, after defaultMarker in the statement beginning with public Overlay (Drawable defaultMarker), type **,** (comma and a space) and then type **Context context** within the parentheses. On the next line, change the statement to **super(boundCenterBottom(defaultMarker));** to bind the bottom center of the marker to a certain location. Press the Enter key. To assign the context to the instance of Context, type **mContext = context;**.

The Overlay constructor sets the boundary of the default Marker and the Context (Figure 11-25).

```
  1  package net.androidbootcamp.maps;
  2
  3⊕ import java.util.ArrayList;▯
  8
  9  public class Overlay extends ItemizedOverlay {
 10      private ArrayList<OverlayItem> mOverlays = new ArrayList<OverlayItem>();
 11      private Context mContext;
 12⊖     public Overlay(Drawable defaultMarker, Context context) {
 13          super(boundCenterBottom(defaultMarker));
 14          mContext = context;
 15          // TODO Auto-generated constructor stub
 16      }
 17
 18⊖     @Override
 19      protected OverlayItem createItem(int i) {
 20          // TODO Auto-generated method stub
 21          return null;
 22      }
 23
 24⊖     @Override
 25      public int size() {
 26          // TODO Auto-generated method stub
 27          return 0;
 28      }
 29
 30  }
 31
```

Overlay constructor is customized

Figure 11-25 Overlay constructor

3. To populate the overlay objects on the map, add a method named addOverlay by clicking after the closing curly brace below the first //TODO statement, pressing the Enter key, and then typing **public void addOverlay(OverlayItem overlay) {**. Press the Enter key. Type **mOverlays.add(overlay);**. Press the Enter key. To populate the overlay with the images in the array, type **populate();** and press the Enter key. If necessary, type a closing brace to complete the method.

The addOverlay method populates the overlay images in a layer over the map display (Figure 11-26).

```
   Main.java      *Overlay.java

 1  package net.androidbootcamp.maps;
 2
 3⊕ import java.util.ArrayList;
 8
 9  public class Overlay extends ItemizedOverlay {
10      private ArrayList<OverlayItem> mOverlays = new ArrayList<OverlayItem>();
11      private Context mContext;
12⊝     public Overlay(Drawable defaultMarker, Context context) {
13          super(boundCenterBottom(defaultMarker));
14          mContext = context;
15          // TODO Auto-generated constructor stub
16      }
17⊝     public void addOverlay(OverlayItem overlay) {                    addOverlay method
18          mOverlays.add(overlay);
19          populate();
20      }
21⊝     @Override
22      protected OverlayItem createItem(int i) {
23          // TODO Auto-generated method stub
24          return null;
25      }
26
27⊝     @Override
28      public int size() {
29          // TODO Auto-generated method stub
30          return 0;
31      }
32
33  }
```

Figure 11-26   The addOverlay method populates the pushpin images

4. Change the return type in the return null; line from null to **mOverlays.get(i)** to return the Overlay item from the position specified by the integer.

The return type is changed to return the correct Overlay item (Figure 11-27).

```
 J Main.java    J *Overlay.java ⊠
   1  package net.androidbootcamp.maps;
   2
   3⊕ import java.util.ArrayList;☐
   8
   9  public class Overlay extends ItemizedOverlay {
  10      private ArrayList<OverlayItem> mOverlays = new ArrayList<OverlayItem>();
  11      private Context mContext;
  12⊖     public Overlay(Drawable defaultMarker, Context context) {
  13          super(boundCenterBottom(defaultMarker));
  14          mContext = context;
  15          // TODO Auto-generated constructor stub
  16      }
  17⊖     public void addOverlay(OverlayItem overlay) {
  18          mOverlays.add(overlay);
  19          populate();
  20      }
  21⊖     @Override
  22      protected OverlayItem createItem(int i) {
  23          // TODO Auto-generated method stub
  24          return mOverlays.get(i);          ◄───────────────── Return type changed
  25      }
  26
  27⊖     @Override
  28      public int size() {
  29          // TODO Auto-generated method stub
  30          return 0;
  31      }
  32
  33  }
  34
```

Figure 11-27 OverlayItem method

5. Change the return type in the return 0; line from 0 to **mOverlays.size()** to return the Overlay item's current number of items in the ArrayList.

The return type is changed to return the correct number of items (Figure 11-28).

412

```
 1  package net.androidbootcamp.maps;
 2
 3⊕ import java.util.ArrayList;
 8
 9  public class Overlay extends ItemizedOverlay {
10      private ArrayList<OverlayItem> mOverlays = new ArrayList<OverlayItem>();
11      private Context mContext;
12      public Overlay(Drawable defaultMarker, Context context) {
13          super(boundCenterBottom(defaultMarker));
14          mContext = context;
15          // TODO Auto-generated constructor stub
16      }
17      public void addOverlay(OverlayItem overlay) {
18          mOverlays.add(overlay);
19          populate();
20      }
21      @Override
22      protected OverlayItem createItem(int i) {
23          // TODO Auto-generated method stub
24          return mOverlays.get(i);
25      }
26
27      @Override
28      public int size() {
29          // TODO Auto-generated method stub
30          return mOverlays.size();         ◄————  Change the return type
31      }
32
33  }
```

Figure 11-28   size( ) method

Coding the onTap Method

When the user taps the pushpin image on the Google map, a text message appears on the screen to identify whether this spot shows the author's or editor's hometown. The **onTap( )** method receives the index of the overlay item that was tapped by the user. The text message such as Author's Hometown Lynchburg, VA appears in an **AlertDialog box**, which is a simple dialog box that displays a message to the user about the overlay item. The AlertDialog box can contain a getTitle( ) method that displays a larger title at the top and a getSnippet( ) method that displays a message in a smaller font below the title. To actually display the alert dialog box, the show( ) method is used. The following code shows how the chapter project uses the onTap( ) method:

Code Syntax

```
@Override
  protected boolean onTap(int index) {
        OverlayItem item = mOverlays.get(index);
        AlertDialog.Builder dialog = new AlertDialog.Builder(mContext);
        dialog.setTitle(item.getTitle());
        dialog.setMessage(item.getSnippet());
        dialog.show();
        return true;
  }
```

In the onTap( ) method, notice that a return type is expected as a Boolean. Recall that a Boolean data type returns either true or false based on whether the user taps the overlay item. To code the onTap( ) method, follow these steps:

1. Click after the closing brace below the return statement and press the Enter key. To override the method, type **@Override** and press the Enter key. To code the onTap( ) method, type **protected boolean onTap(int index) {** and press the Enter key to create the closing brace. Point to the onTap method and select Add return statement. Change the return false; statement to **return true;**.

The onTap( ) method awaits user interaction with the overlay items (Figure 11-29).

```
 Main.java       *Overlay.java
   1  package net.androidbootcamp.maps;
   2
   3⊕ import java.util.ArrayList;
   8
   9  public class Overlay extends ItemizedOverlay {
  10      private ArrayList<OverlayItem> mOverlays = new ArrayList<OverlayItem>();
  11      private Context mContext;
  12      public Overlay(Drawable defaultMarker, Context context) {
  13          super(boundCenterBottom(defaultMarker));
  14          mContext = context;
  15          // TODO Auto-generated constructor stub
  16      }
  17      public void addOverlay(OverlayItem overlay) {
  18          mOverlays.add(overlay);
  19          populate();
  20      }
  21      @Override
  22      protected OverlayItem createItem(int i) {
  23          // TODO Auto-generated method stub
  24          return mOverlays.get(i);
  25      }
  26
  27      @Override
  28      public int size() {
  29          // TODO Auto-generated method stub
  30          return mOverlays.size();
  31      }
  32      @Override
  33      protected boolean onTap(int index)  {        ◄———————  onTap( ) method
  34          return true;
  35      }
  36  }
```

Figure 11-29   onTap( ) method

2. To instantiate the index value of the overlay item, click after the opening brace of the onTap( ) method and press the Enter key. Type **OverlayItem item = mOverlays.get(index);** and press the Enter key. To create an AlertDialog box, type **AlertDialog.Builder dialog = new AlertDialog.Builder(mContext);**. If necessary, point to AlertDialog and import 'AlertDialog' (android.app).

The instance of item holds the index of each overlay item and the AlertDialog box builds a message dialog box (Figure 11-30).

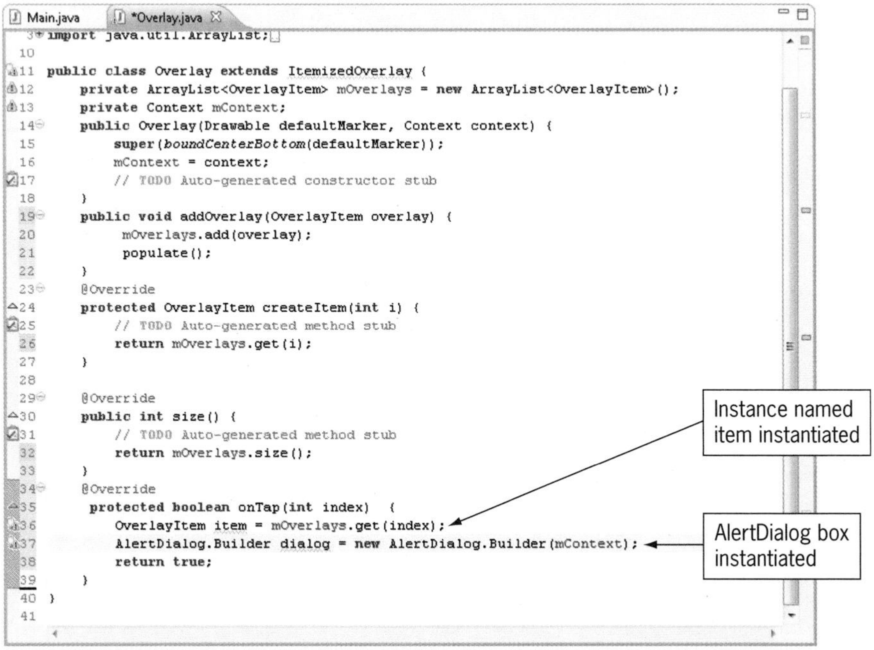

414

```
Main.java    *Overlay.java
    3  import java.util.ArrayList;
   10
   11  public class Overlay extends ItemizedOverlay {
   12      private ArrayList<OverlayItem> mOverlays = new ArrayList<OverlayItem>();
   13      private Context mContext;
   14      public Overlay(Drawable defaultMarker, Context context) {
   15          super(boundCenterBottom(defaultMarker));
   16          mContext = context;
   17          // TODO Auto-generated constructor stub
   18      }
   19      public void addOverlay(OverlayItem overlay) {
   20          mOverlays.add(overlay);
   21          populate();
   22      }
   23      @Override
   24      protected OverlayItem createItem(int i) {
   25          // TODO Auto-generated method stub
   26          return mOverlays.get(i);
   27      }
   28
   29      @Override
   30      public int size() {
   31          // TODO Auto-generated method stub
   32          return mOverlays.size();
   33      }
   34      @Override
   35      protected boolean onTap(int index) {
   36          OverlayItem item = mOverlays.get(index);
   37          AlertDialog.Builder dialog = new AlertDialog.Builder(mContext);
   38          return true;
   39      }
   40  }
   41
```

Instance named item instantiated

AlertDialog box instantiated

Figure 11-30   Instance named item and the AlertDialog box are coded

3. Press the Enter key. To set the title for the dialog box, type **dialog.setTitle(item.getTitle());** and press the Enter key. To set a message snippet below the title, type **dialog.setMessage(item.getSnippet());** and press the Enter key. To display the dialog box, type **dialog.show();**.

The dialog box's title and message are displayed (Figure 11-31).

```
Main.java      *Overlay.java

  1  package net.androidbootcamp.maps;
  2
  3⊕ import java.util.ArrayList;
 10
 11  public class Overlay extends ItemizedOverlay {
 12       private ArrayList<OverlayItem> mOverlays = new ArrayList<OverlayItem>();
 13       private Context mContext;
 14⊖      public Overlay(Drawable defaultMarker, Context context) {
 15           super(boundCenterBottom(defaultMarker));
 16           mContext = context;
 17           // TODO Auto-generated constructor stub
 18       }
 19⊖      public void addOverlay(OverlayItem overlay) {
 20            mOverlays.add(overlay);
 21            populate();
 22       }
 23⊖      @Override
 24      protected OverlayItem createItem(int i) {
 25           // TODO Auto-generated method stub
 26           return mOverlays.get(i);
 27       }
 28
 29⊖      @Override
 30      public int size() {
 31           // TODO Auto-generated method stub
 32           return mOverlays.size();
 33       }
 34⊖      @Override
 35       protected boolean onTap(int index)   {
 36           OverlayItem item = mOverlays.get(index);
 37           AlertDialog.Builder dialog = new AlertDialog.Builder(mContext);
 38           dialog.setTitle(item.getTitle());
 39           dialog.setMessage(item.getSnippet());
 40           dialog.show();
 41           return true;
 42       }
 43  }
 44
```

Figure 11-31   Complete code of Overlay.java

Coding the Drawable Overlay

To place the pushpin images on a separate transparent layer on top of the map grid, the MapView class allows you to supply a list of points of interest from the getOverlays( ) method to overlay on the Android map. By creating an instance named mapOverlays, as shown in the following code, the map locations can be listed by the pushpin image display:

Code Syntax

```
List<com.google.android.maps.Overlay> mapOverlays = mapView.getOverlays();
Drawable drawable = this.getResources().getDrawable(R.drawable.pushpin);
Overlay itemizedoverlay = new Overlay(drawable,this);
```

415

The pushpin.png file represents the map marker, which was saved in the res/drawable folder. The second class Overlay.java is instantiated in the code with an instance of itemizedoverlay. To create the List, Drawable, and the instance of the Overlay class, follow these steps:

1.   Close and save the Overlay.java file. In Main.java, click at the end of the mapView. setBuiltInZoomControls (true); line and press the Enter key. To create a list for the overlay items, type **List<com.google.android.maps.Overlay> mapOverlays = mapView.getOverlays();**. Point to List and click Import 'List' (java.util).

The getOverlays method is called to hold a list of items in the map (Figure 11-32).

Figure 11-32   List of overlay items

2.   To access the pushpin.png file from the drawable folder and set the image as the map marker, press the Enter key and type **Drawable drawable = this.getResources(). getDrawable(R.drawable.pushpin);**. Point to Drawable and import 'Drawable' (android.graphics.drawable).

The Drawable resource for the map overlay is set to pushpin.png (Figure 11-33).

Figure 11-33   The pushpin image becomes the map marker

3. To create an instance of the Overlay class and send the drawable image to the second Activity for display on the map, press the Enter key and type **Overlay itemizedoverlay = new Overlay(drawable,this);**.

The Overlay class is referenced (Figure 11-34).

```
*Main.java ⊠
1  package net.androidbootcamp.maps;
2
3+ import java.util.List;
9
10 public class Main extends MapActivity {
11      /** Called when the activity is first created. */
12      @Override
13      public void onCreate(Bundle savedInstanceState) {
14          super.onCreate(savedInstanceState);
15          setContentView(R.layout.main);
16          MapView mapView = (MapView) findViewById(R.id.mapview);
17          mapView.setBuiltInZoomControls(true);
18          List<com.google.android.maps.Overlay> mapOverlays = mapView.getOverlays();
19          Drawable drawable = this.getResources().getDrawable(R.drawable.pushpin);
20          Overlay itemizedoverlay = new Overlay(drawable,this);
21      }
22
23      @Override
24      protected boolean isRouteDisplayed() {
25          // TODO Auto-generated method stub
26          return false;
27      }
28 }
```

drawable image is referenced in the Overlay class

Figure 11-34 Instance of the Overlay class is created

GTK
Android devices typically include GPS (global positioning system) to show you where you are on the map using a similar method called MyLocationOverlay.

Locating a GeoPoint

By default, the Android Google Maps service displays the map of the United States when it is first loaded, but through the use of panning and zooming, any worldwide location can be found. After coding the Overlay class, the Main.java class is responsible for calling the Overlay class and displaying an exact location with the pushpin image in the Maps app. This map location is called a GeoPoint, and it contains the latitude and longitude coordinates. GeoPoint coordinates are specified in microdegrees (degrees * 1e6). For example, Lynchburg, Virginia, has the latitude and longitude coordinates of 37.4198°, -79.14°. To convert the latitude and longitude degrees to a GeoPoint location, each degrees value must be multiplied by one million. GeoPoint accepts integers only, so by multiplying by one million, the result is an integer value. When you multiply the coordinates of Lynchburg, Virginia, by one million, the GeoPoint location is (37419800, -79140000) using microdegrees. When an OverlayItem is created, it must have a GeoPoint location, a String title, and a String snippet before the item can be called by the populate( ) method.

IN THE TRENCHES
To locate the latitude and longitude coordinates of any location in the world, use the Web site
http://maps.google.com. On the Google Maps page, click the Maps Labs link in the lower-left part of the
page, and then click Enable LatLng Marker and Save changes. Next, right-click the map and then click Drop
LatLng Marker. A marker appears on the Google map with the coordinates of the location selected.

Coding the GeoPoint Location

Each GeoPoint location is defined with a microdegrees location representing latitude and
longitude. The GeoPoint is passed to an OverlayItem method identifying the String title and
String snippet that displays when tapped. In the Map app, the first GeoPoint is defined with
the coordinates to Lynchburg, Virginia. The second GeoPoint is set for Madison, Wisconsin.
The two GeoPoints are displayed as an overlay on the map with the add( ) method. To code
the two GeoPoint locations as an overlay for the map display, follow these steps:

1. To add the code to set a GeoPoint with the coordinates of Lynchburg, Virginia,
   press the Enter key, type **GeoPoint point1 = new GeoPoint(37419800,-79140000);**
   and point to GeoPoint to import 'GeoPoint' (com.google.android.maps). Press the
   Enter key. To set the GeoPoint as an overlay item with a title and text snippet,
   type **OverlayItem overlayitem1 = new OverlayItem(point1, "Author's
   Hometown","Lynchburg, VA");** and point to OverlayItem to import 'OverlayItem'
   (com.google.android.maps).

   The coordinates of the author's hometown are set in a GeoPoint location (Figure 11-35).

```
*Main.java
 1  package net.androidbootcamp.maps;
 2
 3⊕ import java.util.List;
12
13  public class Main extends MapActivity {
14      /** Called when the activity is first created. */
15⊖     @Override
16      public void onCreate(Bundle savedInstanceState) {
17          super.onCreate(savedInstanceState);
18          setContentView(R.layout.main);
19          MapView mapView = (MapView) findViewById(R.id.mapview);
20          mapView.setBuiltInZoomControls(true);
21          List<com.google.android.maps.Overlay> mapOverlays = mapView.getOverlays();
22          Drawable drawable = this.getResources().getDrawable(R.drawable.pushpin);
23          Overlay itemizedoverlay = new Overlay(drawable,this);
24          GeoPoint point1 = new GeoPoint(37419800,-79140000);
25          OverlayItem overlayitem1 = new OverlayItem(point1, "Author's Hometown","Lynchburg, VA");
26      }
27
28⊖     @Override
29      protected boolean isRouteDisplayed() {
30          // TODO Auto-generated method stub
31          return false;
32      }
33  }
```

point1 represents
the coordinates of
Lynchburg, Virginia

Figure 11-35 First GeoPoint

2. To add the code to set a second GeoPoint with the coordinates of Madison, Wisconsin, named point2, press the Enter key, type **GeoPoint point2 = new GeoPoint (43075900,-89400800);** and press the Enter key. To set the second GeoPoint as an overlay item with a title and text snippet, type **OverlayItem overlayitem2 = new OverlayItem(point2, "Editor's Hometown","Madison, WI");**.

The coordinates of the editor's hometown are set in a second GeoPoint location (Figure 11-36).

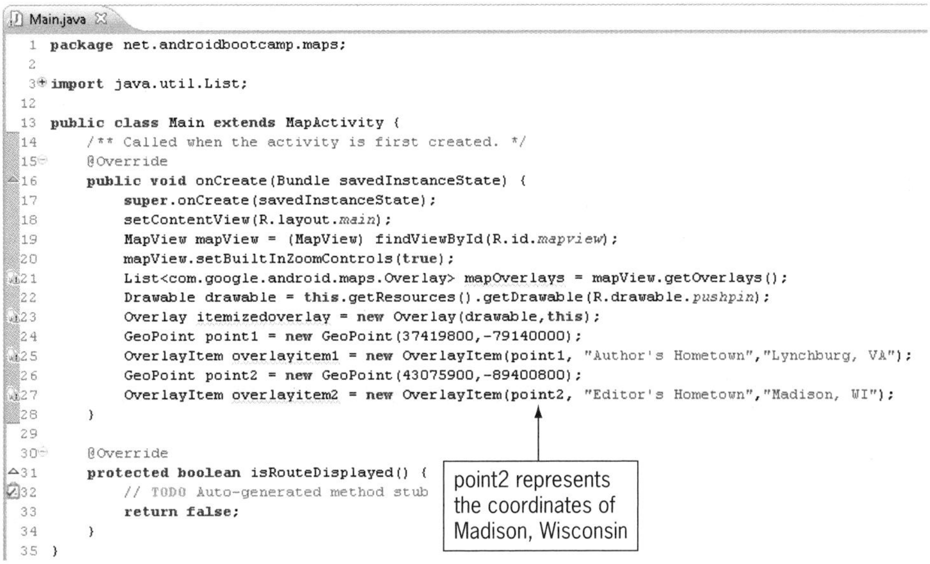

```java
Main.java
  1  package net.androidbootcamp.maps;
  2
  3+ import java.util.List;
 12
 13  public class Main extends MapActivity {
 14      /** Called when the activity is first created. */
 15      @Override
 16      public void onCreate(Bundle savedInstanceState) {
 17          super.onCreate(savedInstanceState);
 18          setContentView(R.layout.main);
 19          MapView mapView = (MapView) findViewById(R.id.mapview);
 20          mapView.setBuiltInZoomControls(true);
 21          List<com.google.android.maps.Overlay> mapOverlays = mapView.getOverlays();
 22          Drawable drawable = this.getResources().getDrawable(R.drawable.pushpin);
 23          Overlay itemizedoverlay = new Overlay(drawable,this);
 24          GeoPoint point1 = new GeoPoint(37419800,-79140000);
 25          OverlayItem overlayitem1 = new OverlayItem(point1, "Author's Hometown","Lynchburg, VA");
 26          GeoPoint point2 = new GeoPoint(43075900,-89400800);
 27          OverlayItem overlayitem2 = new OverlayItem(point2, "Editor's Hometown","Madison, WI");
 28      }
 29
 30      @Override
 31      protected boolean isRouteDisplayed() {
 32          // TODO Auto-generated method stub
 33          return false;
 34      }
 35  }
```

point2 represents the coordinates of Madison, Wisconsin

Figure 11-36 Second GeoPoint

3. To display the two GeoPoints as an overlay, press the Enter key and then type **itemizedoverlay.addOverlay(overlayitem1);** to add the first item to the overlay. Press the Enter key and type **itemizedoverlay.addOverlay(overlayitem2);** to add the second item to the overlay. Press the Enter key and type **mapOverlays.add (itemizedoverlay);** to display the overlay with both items on top of the map.

The overlay is populated with two items and displayed (Figure 11-37).

```
🗋 *Main.java ⊠
  1  package net.androidbootcamp.maps;
  2
  3⊕ import java.util.List;
 12
 13  public class Main extends MapActivity {
 14      /** Called when the activity is first created. */
 15⊝     @Override
⊝16      public void onCreate(Bundle savedInstanceState) {
 17          super.onCreate(savedInstanceState);
 18          setContentView(R.layout.main);
 19          MapView mapView = (MapView) findViewById(R.id.mapview);
 20          mapView.setBuiltInZoomControls(true);
⊕21          List<com.google.android.maps.Overlay> mapOverlays = mapView.getOverlays();
 22          Drawable drawable = this.getResources().getDrawable(R.drawable.pushpin);
⊕23          Overlay itemizedoverlay = new Overlay(drawable,this);
 24          GeoPoint point1 = new GeoPoint(37419800,-79140000);
⊕25          OverlayItem overlayitem1 = new OverlayItem(point1, "Author's Hometown","Lynchburg, VA");
 26          GeoPoint point2 = new GeoPoint(43075900,-89400800);
 27          OverlayItem overlayitem2 = new OverlayItem(point2, "Editor's Hometown","Madison, WI");
 28          itemizedoverlay.addOverlay(overlayitem1);
 29          itemizedoverlay.addOverlay(overlayitem2);
 30          mapOverlays.add(itemizedoverlay);
 31      }
 32
 33⊝     @Override
⊿34      protected boolean isRouteDisplayed() {
⊘35          // TODO Auto-generated method stub
 36          return false;
 37      }
 38  }
```

Two GeoPoints are
overlaid and added
to the map

Figure 11-37   Main.java complete code

Running and Testing the Application

To view the finished maps in the Android application, click Run on the menu bar, and then select Run to save and test the application in the emulator. If necessary, select Android Application and click the OK button. Save all the files in the next dialog box, if necessary, and unlock the emulator. The application opens in the emulator window where you can touch the map to zoom in and out. Touch each pushpin image to display each message, as shown in Figure 11-1 and Figure 11-2. If the application does not display a map, this indicates that you did not find your personal API key and place it within the main.xml file.

Wrap It Up—Chapter Summary

Using Google Maps within the Android environment provides a real-life application showing an exact location of a special interest. Two GeoPoint locations placed as an overlay on a map identified the locations of two cities in the United States in Main.java. The second class Overlay.java created an array list that held each overlay item.

- To use Google Maps in an Android application, you must install the Google API (application programming interface) in the Android SDK. You can then embed the Google Maps site directly into an Android application and overlay app-specific data on the map.

- After installing the Android Google API, you set the application's properties to select the Google APIs add-on as the build target, which sets the Android Virtual Device (AVD) Manager to use the new Google API package.

- Before you can execute an Android Google Maps application, you need to apply for a free Google Maps API key so you can integrate Google Maps into your Android application. To do so, you register your computer's MD5 fingerprint, which is a value in the debug.keystore file included in the Android installation. Using the MD5 fingerprint, you can register with Google for a Maps API key at the online Google Maps service. To display a Google map in an Android app, you must add the API key to the main.xml layout file in your project.

- Google provides a Maps external library that includes the com.google.android.maps package. You must use the <com.google.android.maps.MapView> element to display the Google Maps in your Activity.

- In general, Android apps use permissions to prevent malicious outside applications from corrupting data and accessing sensitive information. A mapping application needs permission to access the Internet and connect with the Google mapping feature. You add this permission request to the Android Manifest file, and the request is granted or denied when the application is run on the Android platform. The app also needs permission to use a Google library to access the current map data.

- Because Google mapping technology relies on the Android MapView class, your project's Main Activity must extend MapActivity instead of the default Activity to use the MapView class. When instantiating the MapView class in the XML code, you must link it to the Google Maps API key.

- An instance of MapView uses the setBuiltInZoomControls property. When set to true, this property allows site visitors to use the built-in zoom feature on the map in your Android app.

- A map marker, or overlay, uses a graphic image such as a pushpin to indicate a specific location on a map. To add an overlay to the map, first implement the ItemizedOverlay class, which manages the individual items placed as a layer on the map and then uses an instance of the MapOverlay class.

- The Overlay class assigns an ArrayList to hold the overlay objects, such as pushpin images, displayed in a layer on the map. The context instantiation temporarily holds each of the items displayed in the array. Customize each constructor to define the default marker for each item in the Overlay array. You must specify the center-point of the bottom of the overlay object using coordinates based on latitude and longitude.

- Use the populate( ) method to add each new item in the ItemizedOverlay to the map. This method reads an OverlayItem such as a pushpin image and prepares for it to be drawn on the map in a new visible layer. When the populate( ) method executes, a constructor such as createItem(int) retrieves an OverlayItem in the array, and then returns the OverlayItem from the position specified by an integer value. The size constructor returns the number of items being overlaid on the map.

- When the user taps an overlay object, such as a pushpin image, on the Google map, you can display a text message. To do so, use the onTap( ) method, which receives the index of the selected overlay item. The text message appears in an AlertDialog box. You can use a getTitle( ) method to specify a title for the dialog box and a getSnippet( ) method to display a message. To actually display the dialog box, use the show( ) method.

- To place overlay objects on a separate transparent layer on top of the map grid, use an instance of the MapView class to list points of interest from the getOverlays( ) method.

- By default, the Android Google Maps service displays the map of the United States when it is first loaded, but users can pan and zoom to find any location in the world. After coding the Overlay class, the Main.java class is responsible for calling the Overlay class and displaying an exact location. This map location is called a GeoPoint, and it contains the latitude and longitude coordinates. GeoPoint coordinates are specified in microdegrees (degrees * 1e6).

- When an OverlayItem is created, it must have a GeoPoint location, a String title, and a String snippet before the populate( ) method can call the item. Use the add( ) method to display the GeoPoints as an overlay on the map.

Key Terms

AlertDialog box—A simple dialog box that displays a message to the user about an overlay item.

API (application programming interface)—A set of tools for building software applications.

ArrayList—An expandable array, which, in this chapter, holds the overlay objects displayed in a layer on the map image.

Google Maps API key—A unique value consisting of a long string of seemingly random alphanumeric characters.

ItemizedOverlay class—A class that you must implement to create an overlay and manage the items placed as a layer on the map.

MapView class—A class that displays and manipulates a Google map within the Android environment.

MD5 (Message-Digest Algorithm 5) digital fingerprint—An algorithm that is widely used to verify data integrity. When the result of the algorithm is provided as part of a file, it verifies the integrity of the file.

onTap( )—A method that receives the index of the overlay item that was tapped by the user.

overlay—A map marker that uses a graphic image to indicate a specific location on a map.

permissions—A part of Android applications that prevents malicious outside applications from corrupting information and accessing sensitive information.

populate( )—A method necessary to add each new item in an ItemizedOverlay, which reads each of the OverlayItems such as the pushpin image and prepares for each image to be drawn on top of the map in a new visible layer.

setBuiltInZoomControls—A property that allows the site visitor to use the built-in zoom feature.

Developer FAQs

1. Which API is used with an Android mapping program?

2. Identify the following: 94:1E:43:49:87:73:BB:E6:A6:88:D7:20:F1:8E:B5:98

3. If the username of a Windows 7 computer is Daniel, what is the path statement for the debug.keystore file?

4. Name five permissions examples mentioned in the text.

5. Write a line of code to provide permission to access the Internet within the Android Manifest file.

6. Write a line of code to provide permission to access the Google library for maps within the Android Manifest file.

7. Which theme was used in the chapter project to provide more room for the map display?

8. When the setBuiltInZoomControls are set to true, what can the visitor use?

9. Where are the zoom controls displayed?

10. How many levels of zoom are available on the Android device?

11. Each time you tap the zoom control, the magnification increases by a factor of _____ .

12. What is another name for a map marker?

13. True or False? One map marker can be placed on an Android map at a time.

14. Which method is necessary to add each new item in an overlay?

15. GeoPoint coordinates are specified in _____ .

16. Convert the following latitude and longitude coordinates for use with GeoPoint: 49.128, -25.2229.

17. What are the latitude and longitude coordinates for the following microdegrees: 34000000, -17672000?

18. To display the AlertDialogBox message, what must the visitor do?

19. Which method reacts to the visitor's actions in question 18?

20. GeoPoints must be which data type?

Beyond the Book

Using the Internet, search the Web for the answers to the following questions to further your Android knowledge.

1. Research five different Android map applications at the Android Market (Google Play) site. Write a paragraph on the unique features of each.

2. Google Maps often acquires new mapping features. Write a summary of at least 100 words describing some of the latest features.

3. Another popular mobile mapping alternative is named OpenStreetMap. Write a summary of at least 150 words describing OpenStreetMap.

4. The fitness world is now using maps in several outdoor sports. Write a paragraph about four outdoor sports that use mobile mapping.

Case Programming Projects

Complete one or more of the following case programming projects. Use the same steps and techniques taught within the chapter. Submit the program you create to your instructor. The level of difficulty is indicated for each case programming project.

Easiest: ⋆

Intermediate: ⋆ ⋆

Challenging: ⋆ ⋆ ⋆

Case Project 11–1: Largest U.S. Cities App ⋆

Requirements Document

Application title:	Largest U.S. Cities App
Purpose:	An Android Google Maps program displays the three largest U.S. cities.
Algorithms:	1. A map displays the three largest U.S. cities—New York City (Figure 11-38), Los Angeles, and Chicago—using map markers.
	2. When the user taps each of the three largest cities on the map, the text *Largest City in US, Second Largest City in US, or Third Largest City in US* is displayed in a dialog box with the name of the city.
Conditions:	1. An image named greenlocator.png is available in the student files.
	2. Use Google Maps to determine the correct GeoPoint locations.

Figure 11-38

Case Project 11–2: New Year's Eve Celebrations App ⋆

Requirements Document

Application title:	New Year's Eve Celebrations App
Purpose:	An Android app displays the four top New Year's Eve celebration locations worldwide.
Algorithms:	1. The map displays a red pushpin for four of the top New Year's Eve celebrations (Figure 11-39) in Sydney, Australia, at the Sydney Harbor Bridge; in Berlin, Germany, at the Brandenburg Gate; in London, England, at Big Ben; and in New York City in Times Square.
	2. When the user taps each of the locator images on the map, the location of the celebration with the name of the city is displayed.
Conditions:	1. Use the same image for the pushpin used in the chapter project.
	2. Use Google Maps to determine the correct GeoPoint locations.

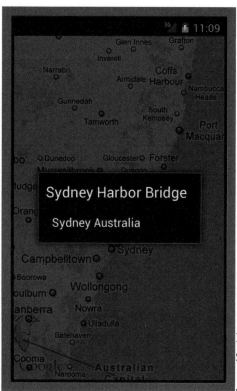

Courtesy of Google Inc.

Figure 11-39

Case Project 11–3: Olympic Cities App ⋆ ⋆

Requirements Document

Application title:	Olympic Cities App
Purpose:	The Olympic Cities app displays a green locator map marker on the last eight cities where the Olympics were held.
Algorithms:	1. Research the last eight Olympic cities and display a green locator for each city on the map.
	2. When the user taps each city's marker, a dialog box opens with the city's name and Olympic year.
Conditions:	1. An image named greenlocator.png is available in the student files.
	2. Use Google Maps to determine the correct GeoPoint locations.

Case Project 11–4: Personal Map App ⋆ ⋆ ⋆

Requirements Document

Application title:	Personal Map App
Purpose:	Create your own Android app showing a map with pushpins marking your hometown and your dream vacation location.
Algorithms:	1. Place a map marker on your hometown and dream vacation location.
	2. When the user taps your hometown and your dream vacation location, a dialog box opens describing the locations.
Conditions:	1. Find your own picture of the map marker image.
	2. Use Google Maps to determine the correct GeoPoint locations.

Finale! Publishing Your Android App

In this chapter, you learn to:

◎ Understand Google Play

◎ Target various device configurations and languages

◎ Prepare your app for publishing

◎ Create an APK package by exporting an app

◎ Prepare promotional materials

◎ Publish your app on Google Play

After all the work of designing your Android app, the time to publish it has arrived. Similar to the many Android devices available, an Android app can be published to a variety of application distribution networks. As an Android developer, you can publish your app to Google Play, Google's Android Market, as well as many others, such as Amazon Appstore, AppBrain, and SlideME. Because Google Play is the largest marketplace, this chapter targets the publication of apps on this Android network. The process to publish an app consists of preparing your app for publication, and then registering, configuring, uploading, and, finally, publishing it.

Before publishing an application, the developer must understand how to perform the following processes, among others:

1.   Test your app.

2.   Prepare the app for publication.

3.   Create an APK package and digitally sign your application.

4.   Prepare promotional materials.

5.   Publish your app to Google Play.

Understanding Google Play

Google Play (*https://play.google.com*) is a digital repository that serves as the storefront for Android devices and apps. It includes an online store for paid and free Android apps as well as music, movies, books, and games. Android phones, tablets, and Google television can all access the Google Play services. The Google Play Web site, as shown in Figure 12-1, includes the features and services of the Android Market, Google Music, and Google e-books. In addition, Google Play provides free cloud storage services, which saves space on an Android device. Google Play is entirely cloud based, so you can store all your music, movies, books, and apps online and have them always available to you. Over 130 countries around the world presently use Google Play. Competing companies such as the Apple App Store and Windows Store also market their applications within a similar structure. When you select an app on Google Play, the app installs directly to your Android device. Google Play is part of the default setup on new Android devices.

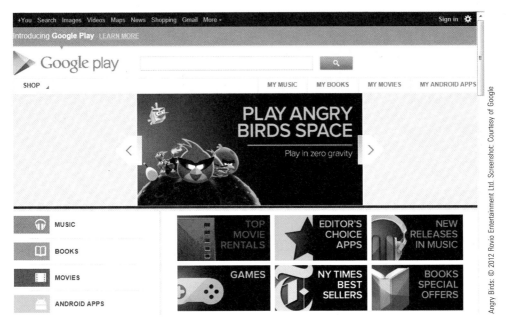

Figure 12-1   Google Play

GTK

With Google Play, you can store up to 20,000 songs for free using the cloud services.

Targeting Different Device Configurations and Languages

To reach a larger audience within the Google Play market, consider targeting multiple Android devices and translating your app into multiple languages. The Android platform runs on a variety of devices that offer different screen sizes and densities. With over a hundred Android handheld devices, using flexible design layouts that work on many screen sizes and resolutions ensures that your app works on a wider range of Android phones and tablets. Creating a custom experience for different screen sizes, pixel densities, orientations, and resolutions guarantees that each user feels that the app was designed specifically for his or her phone or tablet.

Android users live in every corner of the world and speak hundreds of different languages. As you design an Android app, you can provide alternate resources such as app text translated into multiple languages that change depending on the default locale detected on the device. For example, if your home country is Spain, most likely your phone's locale for the dialect selection is set to Spanish (Spain). If you want your application to support both English and Spanish text, you can create two resource directories in the strings directory (the strings.xml file). By customizing the strings resource files, you can write one application that recognizes many local languages. Instead of creating your app in English only, remember that the majority of the world does not speak English and consider extending your app's reach to a worldwide pool of Android users.

GTK

To translate the languages used in your app, you can use Google Translate (*http://translate.google.com*), a free translation service that provides instant translations among 58 different languages. If you use any translation service, it is still important to have a native speaker test your app.

Testing Your App on an Android Device

After completing your Android app, you must test your application on various devices before publication. Using different built-in emulators in Eclipse, you can test the design and functionality of your application on a wide range of devices. You can also see how your development application will perform in a real-world environment by using Eclipse to install and test it directly on an Android phone. With an Android-powered device, you can develop and debug your Android applications just as you would on the emulator. After you change the settings on your Android phone or tablet, you can use a versatile tool called the **Android Debug Bridge (adb)** to communicate with a connected Android device. To set up a device for testing your app, follow these steps:

1. On the home screen of an Android device, tap the Settings app to display the device settings. Select Applications and then select Development. Enable the USB debugging option and then click the OK button.

    The Android device changes the settings to enable USB debugging.

2. To set up your computer to detect your Android device, first install a USB driver for Android Debug Bridge on a Windows computer following the steps at **http://developer.android.com/sdk/oem-usb.html**. Each Android phone brand, such as Motorola and Samsung, has its own drivers that must be installed on your Windows computer.

    If you are using a Mac, you do not need to install a driver.

    The USB drivers are installed on a Windows computer.

3. Plug in an Android device to a USB cable. Run your application from Eclipse as usual. The Android Device Chooser dialog box opens listing the available emulator(s) and connected device(s). Select the device upon which you want to install and run the application, and then click the OK button.

    The Android application is tested on your Android device.

Creating an APK Package

After your Android application is successfully tested, you must create a release-ready package that users can install and run on their Android phones and tablets. The release-ready package is called an **.apk file (application package file)**, which is a compressed archive similar to a Zip file that contains the application, the manifest file, and all associated resources, such as image files, music, and other required content. An .apk file is a file format created by Google. Using the Eclipse Export Wizard, you can build a release-ready .apk file that is signed with your private key and optimized for publication. A private key digitally signs your application with your local system. All Android applications must be digitally signed with a certificate before the system can create an .apk package of your app for application distribution. The Android system uses the certificate as a means of identifying the author of an application and establishing trust relationships between applications. To create an .apk package that generates a private key for your local system, follow these steps:

1. Open a completed project in Eclipse that has been tested and runs properly. To export the project and create an .apk package, click File on the menu bar and then click Export.

The Export dialog box opens (Figure 12-2).

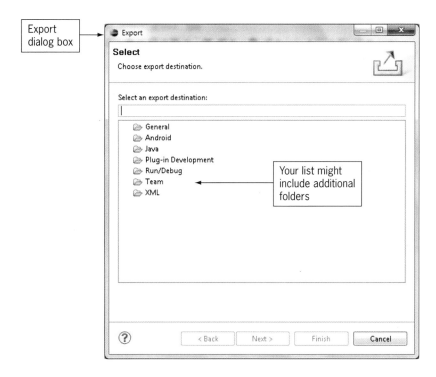

Figure 12-2 Export dialog box

2. Expand the Android folder in the Export dialog box. Click Export Android Application.

    The Export Android Application option is selected in the Android folder of the Export dialog box (Figure 12-3).

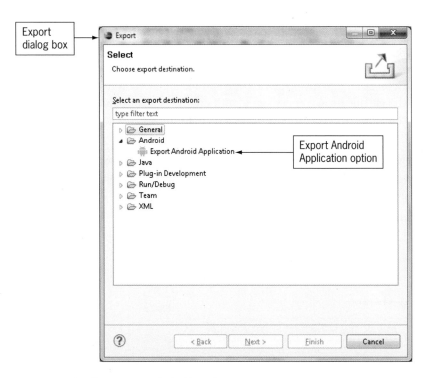

Export dialog box

Export Android Application option

Figure 12-3   Exporting an Android application

3. Click the Next button. In the Export Android Application dialog box, click the Browse button. The Project Selection dialog box opens. Click the name of the application that you are exporting.

    The present Android app project name is selected (Figure 12-4).

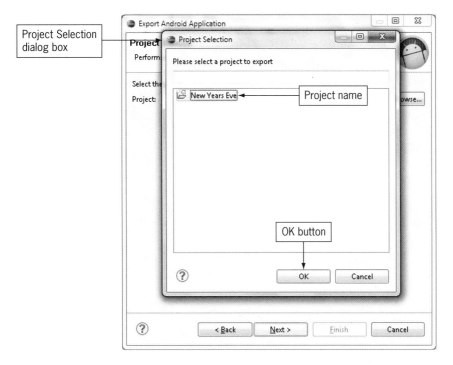

Project Selection dialog box

Project name

OK button

Figure 12-4 Selecting the project

4. Click the OK button, and then click the Next button.

    The Export Android Application dialog box asks whether you are using an existing keystore or a new keystore (Figure 12-5).

Export Android Application dialog box

Create new keystore option button

Figure 12-5   Selecting the keystore

5. Click the Create new keystore option button. In the Location text box, type the file path to your .android file and the name of the keystore file (such as C:\. . .\.android\debug.keystore.keystore).

    The debug.keystore file is selected in the Select Keystore Name dialog box (Figure 12-6).

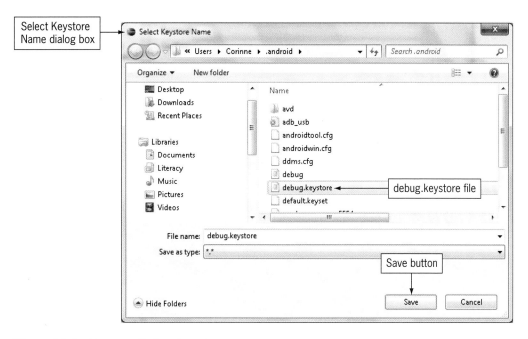

Select Keystore Name dialog box

debug.keystore file

Save button

Figure 12-6 Keystore file is selected

6. Enter a password of your own choosing in the Password text box. Type the same password again in the Confirm text box.

Your password is typed in twice in the Keystore selection (Figure 12-7).

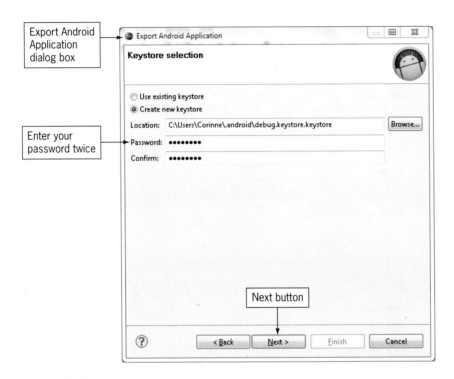

Figure 12-7   Entering a password

7. Click the Next button. To create a key, you must fill out the Key Creation form with your personal information. In the Alias text box, enter **androiddebugkey**. Use your keystore password again. In the Validity (years) text box, enter a valid number of years from 50 to 1,000 years. You can leave the Organization text box empty if you do not belong to an organization.

The Key Creation form is filled out with your personal information (Figure 12-8).

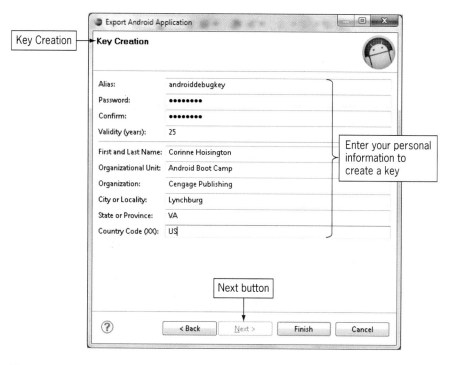

Figure 12-8 Key Creation form

8. Click the Next button. The Destination and key/certificate checks dialog box opens. Click the Browse button. Save the APK key file within the application folder.

The Destination APK file is saved within the application folder (Figure 12-9).

440

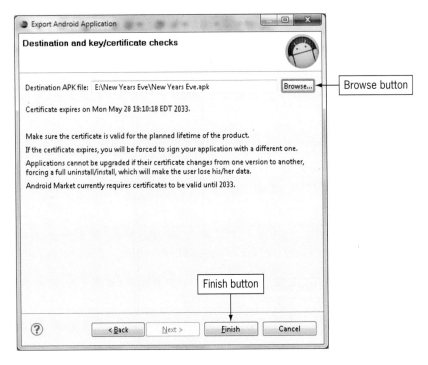

Figure 12-9   Destination APK file

9. Click the Finish button.

The Android app is now signed and ready to be saved to Google Play.

GTK
Android .apk files can be installed and run directly on an Android device.

IN THE TRENCHES
The keystore creates your private key for Android deployment. It is best to back up your keystore in a safe file location. If you lose your keystore file, you will not be able to upgrade your Android Google Play app.

Preparing Promotional Materials to Upload

When you publish your app in Google Play, you are required to post several images that accompany your app to assist with marketing. With hundreds of thousands of apps in the store, you must publicize your app so it stands out and is noticed by casual visitors. To leverage your app in the Google Play store, you can upload your app with screen shots, a video link, promotional graphics, and descriptive text, as in the Angry Birds Space page at Google Play, which is shown in Figure 12-10.

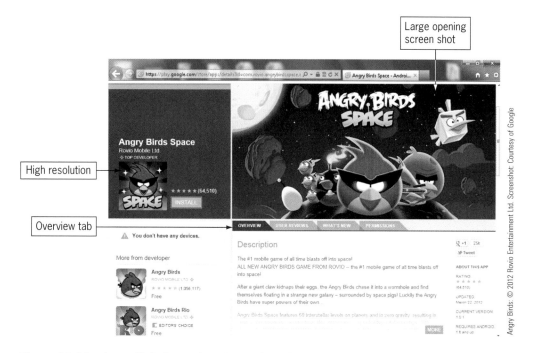

Figure 12-10   Angry Birds Space Android app from Google Play

Providing Images

In the Angry Birds Android app, a high-resolution application icon is displayed in the left pane by default. The application icon does not replace your launcher icon, but serves to identify and brand your app. The size of the application icon should be 512 × 512 pixels stored in a PNG file. In addition, Google Play requires a minimum of two screen shots of the app to display on the details page of your application. A large image (typically in the PNG format) is displayed at the top of the right pane (Figure 12-10) with any of the following dimensions: 480 × 320, 800 × 480, or 854 × 480 pixels. You can upload up to eight screen shots for the details page. The screen shots appear in the App Screenshots section of the details page, as shown in Figure 12-11. You can also display a video to demo your app, though Google Play does not require one. As an alternative, you can upload with your app a video link to your demo video from YouTube.com. The short video should highlight the top features of your app and last between 30 seconds and 2 minutes. Remember that these visual elements are the first impression potential users have of your app. Quality media helps improves an app's marketability.

442

Angry Birds: © 2012 Rovio Entertainment Ltd. Screenshot: Courtesy of Google

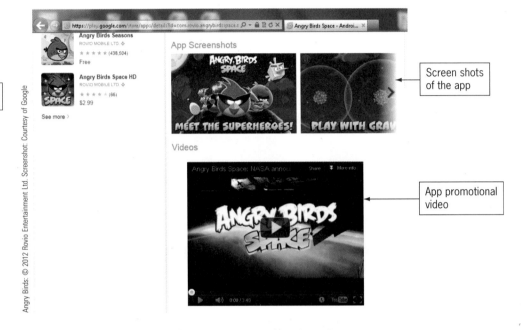

Figure 12-11   Angry Birds Space Android app Overview tab

Providing a Description

In addition to the promotional media items, an app description provides a quick overview of the purpose of the app and what it does. To intrigue your readers, you can include some of the features your application provides and describe why your app is unique in comparison with other competitors without mentioning their names. The description needs to sell your app to the widest audience possible. The description of the Angry Birds Space app in Figure 12-12 appeals to a gaming audience searching for a new Angry Birds experience in space. Notice the bullets used in the Angry Birds Space description showing the features and benefits of the app are clear and concise. A good description is written to motivate users to download the app. Revise the description with each update of your app, adding new information such as new features and user reviews.

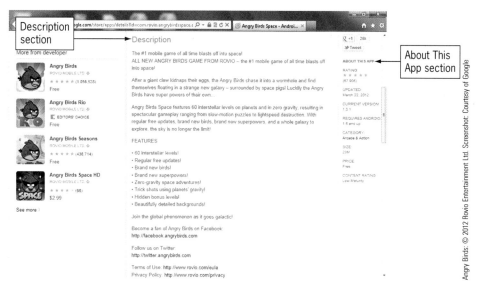

Figure 12-12 Angry Birds Space app description

Including App Information

In Figure 12-12, notice the ratings, date of last update, current version, Android platform requirement, category, size, price, and content rating in the right pane. Users search for the most popular apps as measured by their ratings. Prospective app buyers read user reviews to determine if your app is worth their time and money. When a visitor writes a good review about your application on the User Reviews tab (Figure 12-10), you can quote the review within your description. Customers value a large number of good reviews and are more likely to download your app if it has them. Notice in Figure 12-12 that the Angry Birds Space game is free. So how do the developers make money? The left column of the page lists other products created by this developer, including a second version of Angry Birds Space HD available for $2.99. Upon mastering the free game, users are often motivated to buy the full version of this product. As you price your app, consider that some users will never want to pay for an app, but many will pay for a great app. Consider also adding Facebook, Twitter, and other social networking links on your app's page at Google Play so users can also market your app within their friend networks.

When you upload your app into Google Play, you select one of the application categories shown in Table 12-1. If your app fits into more than one category, be sure to include each category to attract visitors in each category searched.

Category	Example of applications
Books & Reference	Book readers, reference books, textbooks, dictionaries, thesaurus, wikis
Business	Document editor/reader, package tracking, remote desktop, e-mail management, job search
Comics	Comic players, comic titles
Communications	Messaging, chat/IM, dialers, address books, browsers, call management
Education	Exam preparations, study aids, vocabulary, educational games, language learning
Finance	Banking, payment, ATM finders, financial news, insurance, taxes, portfolio/trading, tip calculators
Games	Arcade and action
	Brain and puzzles
	Cards and casino
	Casual
	Sports
Health & Fitness	Personal fitness, workout tracking, diet and nutritional tips, health and safety
Lifestyle	Recipes, style guides
Media & Video	Subscription movie services, remote controls, media/video players
Medical	Drug and clinical references, calculators, handbooks for health care providers, medical journals and news
Music & Audio	Music services, radios, music players
News & Magazines	Newspapers, news aggregators, magazines, blogging
Personalization	Wallpapers, live wallpapers, home screen, lock screen, ringtone
Photography	Cameras, photo-editing tools, photo management and sharing
Productivity	Notepad, to-do list, keyboard, printing, calendar, backup, calculator, conversion
Shopping	Online shopping, auctions, coupons, price comparison, grocery lists, product reviews
Social	Social networking, check-in, blogging
Sports	Sports news and commentary, score tracking, fantasy team management, game coverage
Travel & Local	City guides, local business information, trip management tools
Weather	Weather reports

Table 12-1   Application categories

(*Source:* Google Play support site: *http://support.google.com/googleplay/android-developer/bin/answer.py?hl=en&answer=113475&topic=2365760& ctx=topic*)

Registering for a Google Play Account

Google Play is a publishing platform that helps you distribute your Android apps to users around the world. Before you can publish apps through Google Play, you must register as a developer using your Gmail account username and password at *http://play.google.com/apps/publish*. Registering at Google Play requires a one-time-only payment of $25, which registers you as an Android application developer and enrolls you in a Google Checkout account.

The registration process requires you to have a Google account, agree to the legal terms, and pay the fee via your Google Checkout account. If you charge for your app, Google Checkout disperses revenue for application sales. If you register to sell applications, you must also be registered as a Google Checkout Merchant. As a developer, you have access to your app ratings, comments, and number of downloads. If you charge for your application, you will receive 70 percent of the application price with the remaining 30 percent distributed among the phone carriers. The profit after your first sale arrives in your Google Checkout account 24 hours later. After a purchaser buys and installs an app, his or her credit card is charged 24 hours later. If the user uninstalls the app before the 24-hour time period, Google issues a full refund of the purchase price. To register as a Google Play Android developer, follow these steps:

1. To register at Google Play, open a browser and go to the site **http://play.google.com/apps/publish**. Click the Continue button. If necessary, sign in with your Gmail account information. Enter your password for your Gmail account.

   Your Gmail account username and password are entered at the Google Checkout Web site (Figure 12-13).

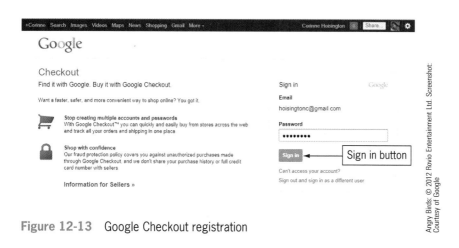

Figure 12-13   Google Checkout registration

2. Click the Sign in button to sign in with your Google account information. To register for a developer's Google Play account, in the Developer Name text box, type your name. In the Phone Number text box, type your phone number.

    On the Getting Started Google Play Android Developer Console page, the developer's name and phone number are entered (Figure 12-14).

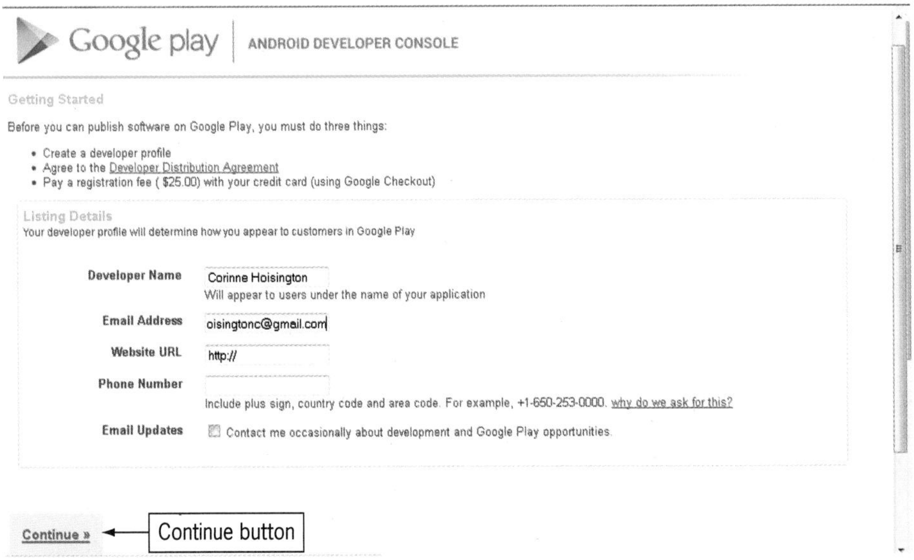

Figure 12-14   Google Play Android developer console

3. Click the Continue button to open the next page, which displays the Developer Distribution Agreement. Read through the Developer Distribution Agreement and click the 'I agree and I am willing to associate my account registration with the Developer Distribution Agreement' check box.

    The Developer Distribution Agreement displays with the details of the Google Play account (Figure 12-15).

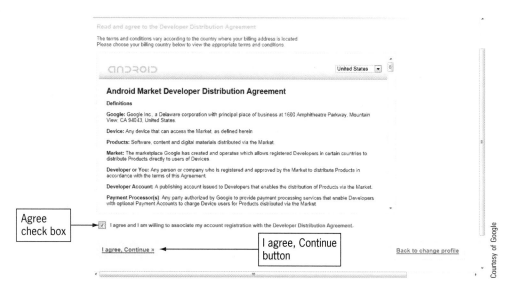

Figure 12-15   Developer Distribution Agreement

4.   Click the I agree, Continue button on the Developer's Distribution Agreement to open the Google Play Registration Fee page displaying the $25 registration fee.

The $25 registration fee for the Google Play developer's registration is displayed (Figure 12-16).

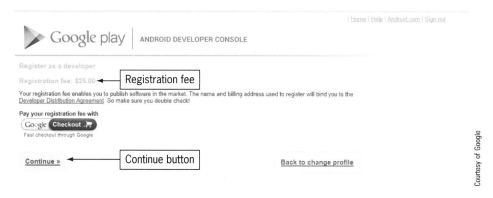

Figure 12-16   Google Play registration fee

5.   Click the Continue button to open the next page, where you can pay the registration fee. To pay a $25 registration fee for a developer's Google Play account, you can enter a credit card number and your address information.

The order details for your Google Play registration are entered. Your Web page might appear as a Google Checkout page (Figure 12-17).

Figure 12-17   Google Play account order

6. Click the Continue button to open the next page. If you would like to add additional users to your account, click the Invite a new user button and fill in the additional user's information.

    Additional users can be added to your Google Play account (Figure 12-18).

Figure 12-18   Add users to a Google Play account

IN THE TRENCHES

After creating your account in Google Play, it may take up to 24 hours for your account to be approved for Android app publication.

Uploading an App to Google Play

As you upload your app to Google Play, you will be prompted to enter information about your application. Once you create an account, the Developer Console pages take you through the steps to upload your unlocked application .apk file and the promotional assets. The maximum supported file size for the .apk file at Google Play is 50 MB. After your app is posted and rises in popularity, Google Play gives you higher placement in weekly "top" lists and in promotional slots in collections such as Top Free Apps. To upload an Android application to Google Play, follow these steps:

1. To upload your app at Google Play, click the Android Developer Console link, as shown in Figure 12-18, to open the All Google Play Android app listings page in a new browser window to upload an application.

    The Upload Application page opens and displays a list of any apps previously uploaded (Figure 12-19).

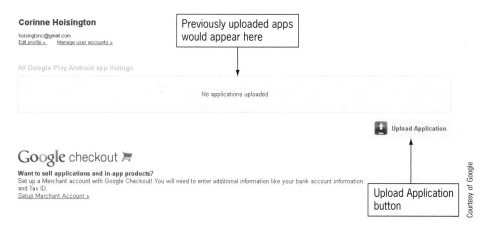

Figure 12-19   Upload application

2. Click the Upload Application button to upload the .apk file.

    The Upload new APK dialog box opens (Figure 12-20).

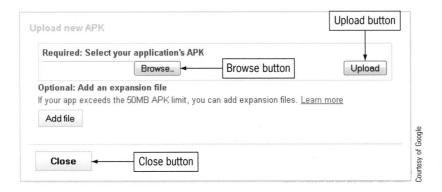

Figure 12-20   Upload new APK dialog box

3. To upload your .apk file, click the Browse button in the Upload new APK dialog box and locate the .apk file within your application folder. Click the .apk file and then click the Open button. Click the Upload button to upload the app to Google Play. Click the Save button after the .apk file uploads.

The Edit Application page opens within the browser (Figure 12-21).

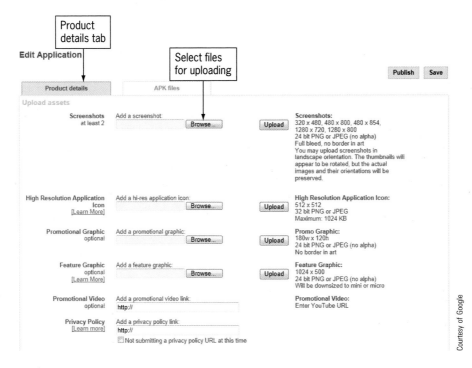

Figure 12-21   Edit Application page

4. On the Edit Application page, to upload the promotional assets such as the two required screen shots, the high-resolution application icon, and optional promotional graphics and a video link to YouTube, click the Browse button to the right of each asset listed on the Product details tab. The specifications are listed in the right column for each promotional asset. Scroll down the page after uploading the assets.

Scroll down the page to view the Listing details for the app (Figure 12-22).

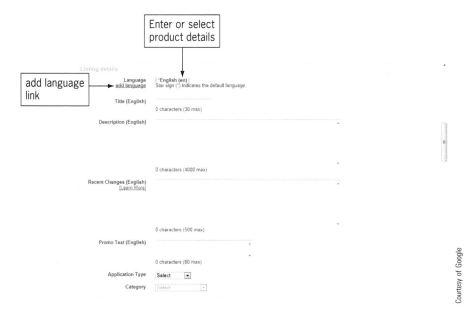

Figure 12-22 Listing details

5. In the Listing details section, you can add languages that you are using within your application by clicking the add language link. Enter your app's Title, Description text, Recent Changes, if necessary, and Promo Text in the text boxes provided. Click the Application Type box arrow, and then select Applications or Games. Next, select one or more categories for the app (see Table 12-1 earlier in the chapter). Scroll down the page after entering the requested listing details to view the Publishing options.

After scrolling down the page, the Publishing options for the app are displayed (Figure 12-23).

Select publishing
options

Figure 12-23   Publishing options

6. In the Publishing options portion of the page, you can apply copy protection, which may help prevent your application from being copied from a device. This feature is being updated in the near future. It is best to implement the Google Play licensing service for paid apps. Click the link for a free application to implement your own copy protection scheme if you are uploading a paid app. Select a Content Rating, which describes the age group or maturity best suited for your app, by clicking one of the four radio buttons. Usually, Everyone is selected for the Content Rating. If you plan to sell your app, click the Setup a Merchant Account at Google Checkout link and follow the steps. Typically all countries are selected to list your app for English speakers in those countries and for their Android devices. Scroll down the page to view the Contact information and Consent sections.

    After scrolling down the page, the Contact information and Consent sections are displayed (Figure 12-24).

Enter contact and consent information

This application is only available to devices with these features, as defined in your application manifest.

This application is available to over 0 devices.

Contact information

Website

Email   hoisingtonc@gmail.com

Phone

Consent

☑ This application meets Android Content Guidelines

☑ I acknowledge that my software application may be subject to United States export laws, regardless of my location or nationality. I agree that I have complied with all such laws, including any requirements for software with encryption functions. I hereby certify that my application is authorized for export from the United States under these laws. [Learn More]

Figure 12-24   Contact information and consent sections

7. In the Contact information section, enter at least one support channel for your app: Website, Email, or Phone. Click the two check boxes confirming that the application meets Android Content Guidelines and that the software application may be subject to United States export laws, regardless of your location or nationality. Before scrolling to the top of the Google Play form page to publish the app, click the Android Content Guidelines link.

    The Developer Program Policies page is displayed on a new browser tab (Figure 12-25).

anDROID   United States ▾

Android Market Developer Program Policies

The policies listed below play an important role in maintaining a positive experience for everyone using Android Market. Defined terms used here have the same meaning as in the Android Market Developer Distribution Agreement. Be sure to check back from time to time, as these policies may change.

Content Policies
Our content policies apply to any content your application displays or links to, including any ads it shows to users and any user-generated content it hosts or links to. In addition to complying with these policies, the content of your app must be rated in accordance with our Content Rating Guidelines.

*   **Sexually Explicit Material:** We don't allow content that contains nudity, graphic sex acts, or sexually explicit material. Google has a zero-tolerance policy against child pornography. If we become aware of content with child pornography, we will report it to the appropriate authorities and delete the Google Accounts of those involved with the distribution.

*   **Violence and Bullying:** Depictions of gratuitous violence are not allowed. Applications should not contain materials that threaten, harass or bully other users.

*   **Hate Speech:** We don't allow the promotion of hatred toward groups of people based on their race or ethnic origin, religion, disability, gender, age, veteran status, or sexual orientation/gender identity.

*   **Impersonation or Deceptive Behavior:** Don't pretend to be someone else, and don't represent that your app is authorized by or produced by another company or organization if that is not the case. Products or the ads they contain also must not mimic functionality or warnings from a user's operating system or other applications. Developers should not divert users or provide links to any other site that mimics Android Market or passes itself off as Android Market.

*   **Personal and Confidential Information:** We don't allow unauthorized publishing of people's private and confidential information, such as credit card numbers, Social Security numbers, driver's and other license numbers, or any other information that is not publicly accessible.

*   **Intellectual Property:** Don't infringe on the intellectual property rights of others, including patent, trademark, trade secret, copyright, and other proprietary rights. We will respond to clear notices of alleged copyright infringement. For more information or to file a DMCA request, please visit our copyright procedures.

*   **Illegal Activities:** Keep it legal. Don't engage in unlawful activities on this product.

*   **Gambling:** We don't allow content or services that facilitate online gambling, including but not limited to, online casinos, sports betting and lotteries.

*   **Malicious Products:** Don't transmit viruses, worms, defects, Trojan horses, malware, or any other items of that may harm user devices or personal data. We don't allow content that harms or interferes with the operation of the networks, servers, or other infrastructure of Google or any third-parties. Spyware, malicious scripts and password phishing scams are also prohibited on Android Market.

Network Usage and Terms
Applications must not create unpredictable network usage that has an adverse impact on a user's service charges or an Authorized Carrier's network. Applications also may not knowingly violate an Authorized Carrier's terms of service for allowed usage or any Google terms of service.

Figure 12-25   Developer Program Policies page

8. Click the Developer Console browser tab and scroll to the top of the page. Click the Publish button to publish your Android app with the promotional materials.

Your app is published in Google Play.

Wrap It Up—Chapter Summary

Before you can publish your application on Google Play, the app should be fully tested in the emulator and on multiple Android devices. To prepare your app for publishing, an APK package is exported using Eclipse. Successful app marketing requires paying attention to promotional materials that appear on Google Play, such as images, videos, and clear descriptions of the app. Publishing your app involves uploading the promotional materials that accompany the .apk file.

- Google Play is the storefront for Android devices and apps, and provides access to Android Market, Google Music, and Google e-books. It includes an online store for paid and free Android apps, music, movies, books, and games. Android phones, tablets, and Google television can access the Google Play services.

- To reach a larger audience within the Google Play market, you should target multiple Android devices and translate your app into multiple languages. Create a custom experience for devices with different screen sizes, pixel densities, orientations, and resolutions so that each user feels that the app was designed specifically for his or her phone or tablet.

- As you design an Android app, you can provide alternate resources such as strings of text translated into multiple languages that change depending on the default locale detected on the device.

- Before publishing an Android app, test it on various devices. Using different built-in emulators in Eclipse, you can test the design and functionality of your application on a wide range of devices and see how your development application performs in a real-world environment. Using the Android Debug Bridge (adb) tool in Eclipse, you can develop and debug an Android application on an Android device.

- After testing an Android app, you must create an .apk file (application package file), which is a release-ready package that users can install and run on their Android phones and tablets. An .apk file is a compressed archive that contains the application, the manifest file, and all associated resources, such as image files, music, and other required content. Using the Eclipse Export Wizard, you can build a release-ready .apk file that is signed with your private key and optimized for publication.

- When you publish your app in Google Play, you must post several images, including an application icon and screen shots. You can also post an optional video or link to a video that demonstrates your app. You must also provide a description that provides an overview of the purpose and features of the app. Finally, include app information such as ratings, Android platform requirement, category, and price.

- To publish apps through Google Play, you must register as a developer using your Gmail account username and password at *http://play.google.com/apps/publish*. The registration process requires you to have a Google account, agree to the legal terms, and pay a $25 fee via your Google Checkout account.

- After creating a Google Play account, the Developer Console pages at the Google Play Web site step you through uploading your unlocked application .apk file and its promotional assets.

Key Terms

.apk file (application package file)—A release-ready package of an Android app stored in a compressed archive similar to a Zip file that contains the application, the manifest file, and all associated resources, such as image files, music, and other required content.

Android Debug Bridge (adb)—An Android tool you use to communicate with a connected Android device.

Google Play—A digital repository that serves the Android Market and includes an online store for paid and free Android apps, as well as music, movies, books, and games.

Developer FAQs

1. What is the URL of Google Play?

2. Approximately how many countries use Google Play?

3. Name four services of Google Play.

4. What is the name of the two largest competitors to Google Play?

5. To increase your target audience in Google Play, what two considerations should you make?

6. How do you change your app to multiple languages?

7. What is the address of the Google Web site that assists with language translation?

8. What does adb stand for?

9. What does apk stand for?

10. Can you deploy your app to your Android phone?

11. Do you have to install adb drivers on a Mac computer?

12. Name four promotional assets that you can upload with your app at Google Play.

13. What is the maximum number of screen shots of your app in action that you can post in Google Play?

14. Where must you post your promotional video?

15. What are the minimum length and maximum length of the promotional video?

16. In which two social networking sites should you create a marketing presence?

17. Which category would you select at Google Play for a calendar app?

18. Which category would you select for a recipe app?

19. How much is the registration fee to publish Android apps at Google Play?

20. What is the maximum size of an .apk file at Google Play?

Beyond the Book

To answer the following questions, create an idea for an app that you think would sell well at Google Play.

1. Write about 200 words describing your Google Play app idea, beginning with a catchy title for the app.

2. Locate an image link that you would consider to be your application icon for your Android app. (If you plan to use the icon, you would of course need to properly obtain this image following copyright guidelines.)

3. Consider the price for selling your app. Write at least 150 words explaining why you selected this price after researching the Internet for price points for Android apps.

4. Create a short YouTube video to market your app idea, and provide the link to your instructor.

Glossary

.apk file (application package file) A release-ready package of an Android app stored in a compressed archive similar to a Zip file that contains the application, the manifest file, and all associated resources, such as image files, music, and other required content.

9-patch image A special image with predefined stretching areas that maintain the same look on different screen sizes.

ACTION_VIEW A generic action you can use to send any request to get the most reasonable action to occur.

Activity An Android component that represents a single screen with a user interface.

adapter Provides a data model for the layout of a list and for converting the data from the array into list items.

AlertDialog box A simple dialog box that displays a message to the user about an overlay item.

Android 4.0 Library A project folder that contains the android.jar file, which includes all the class libraries needed to build an Android application for the specified version.

Android Debug Bridge (adb) An Android tool you use to communicate with a connected Android device.

Android Manifest A file with the filename AndroidManifest.xml that is required in every Android application. This file provides essential information to the Android device, such as the name of your Java application and a listing of each Activity.

Android Market An online store that sells programs written for the Android platform.

android:oneshot An attribute of the animation-list that determines whether an animation plays once and then stops or continues to play until the Stop Animation button is tapped.

AndroidManifest.xml A file containing all the information Android needs to run an application.

AnimationDrawable class A class that provides the methods for Drawable animations to create a sequence of frame-by-frame images.

animation-list An XML root element that references images stored in the drawable folders and used in an animation.

API (application programming interface) A set of tools for building software applications.

array variable A variable that can store more than one value.

ArrayAdapter<String> i A ListAdapter that supplies string array data to a ListView object.

ArrayList An expandable array that holds the overlay objects displayed in a layer on the map image.

assets folder A project folder containing any asset files that are accessed through classic file manipulation.

break A statement that ends a case within a Switch statement and continues with the statement following the Switch decision structure.

Calendar class A class you can use to access the Android system date. The Calendar class also is responsible for converting between a Date object and a set of integer fields such as YEAR, MONTH, and DAY_OF_MONTH.

case A keyword used in a Switch statement to indicate a condition. In a Switch statement, the case keyword is followed by a value and a colon.

Change Gravity A tool that changes the linear alignment of a control, so that it is aligned to the left, center, right, top, or bottom of an object or the screen.

class A group of objects that establishes an introduction to each object's properties.

class variable A variable with global scope; it can be accessed by multiple methods throughout the program.

codec A computer technology used to compress and decompress audio and video files.

columnWidth A GridView property that specifies a fixed width for each column.

compound condition More than one condition included in an If statement.

constructor A part of Java code used to initialize the instance variables of an object.

DAY_OF_MONTH A date constant of the Calendar class that retrieves an integer value of the system's current day.

DAY_OF_YEAR A date constant of the Calendar class that retrieves the day of the current year as an integer. For example, February 1 is day 32 of the year.

DecimalFormat A class that provides patterns for formatting numbers in program output.

decision structure A fundamental control structure used in computer programming that deals with the different conditions that occur based on the values entered into an application.

element A single individual item that contains a value in an array.

emulated application An application that is converted in real time to run on a variety of platforms such as a Web page, which can be displayed on various screen sizes through a browser.

Entries A Spinner property that connects a string array to the Spinner control for display.

equals method A method of the String class that Java uses to compare strings.

event handler A part of a program coded to respond to the specific event.

final A type of variable that can only be initialized once; any attempt to reassign the value results in a compile error when the application is executed.

Frame animation A type of animation, also called frame-by-frame animation, that plays a sequence of images, as in a slide show, with a specified interval between images.

FrameLayout The part of a TabHost control that displays the tab content.

Gallery A View container that displays a horizontal list of objects with the center item displaying the current image.

gen folder A project folder that contains automatically generated Java files.

get The field manipulation method that accesses the system date or time.

getBaseContext( ) A Context class method used in Android programs to obtain a Context instance. Use getBaseContext( ) in a method that is triggered only when the user touches the Gallery control.

getInstance A method of the Calendar class that returns a calendar date or time based on the system settings.

GetSelectedItem( ) A method that returns the text of the selected Spinner item.

GetText( ) A method that reads text stored in an EditText control.

Google Maps API key A unique value consisting of a long string of seemingly random alphanumeric characters.

Google Play A digital repository that serves the Android Market and includes an online store for paid and free Android apps, as well as music, movies, books, and games.

GridView A control that displays objects in a scrollable grid, similar to the Gallery control. A GridView control is part of the View group and lets you specify the number of columns, column width, and column spacing.

hexadecimal color code A triplet of three colors using hexadecimal numbers, where colors are specified first by a pound sign followed by how much red (00 to FF), how much green (00 to FF), and how much blue (00 to FF) are in the final color.

459

hint A short description of a field that appears as light text in a Text Field control.

If Else statement A statement that executes one set of instructions if a specified condition is true and another set of instructions if the condition is false.

If statement A statement that executes one set of instructions if a specified condition is true and takes no action if the condition is not true.

ImageView control A control that displays an icon or a graphic from a picture file.

import To make the classes from a particular Android package available throughout the application.

import statement A statement that makes more Java functions available to a program.

instantiate To create an object of a specific class.

intent Code in the Android Manifest file that allows an Android application with more than one Activity to navigate among Activities.

isChecked( ) method A method that tests a checked property to determine if a RadioButton object has been selected.

item In a Spinner control, a string of text that appears in a list for user selection.

ItemizedOverlay class A class that you must implement to create an overlay and manage the items placed as a layer on the map.

Java An object-oriented programming language and a platform originated by Sun Microsystems.

launcher icon An icon that appears on the home screen to represent the application.

layout A container that can hold widgets and other graphical elements to help you design an interface for an application.

life cycle The series of actions from the beginning, or birth, of an Activity to its end, or destruction.

Linear layout A layout that arranges components in a vertical column or horizontal row.

ListActivity A class that displays a list of items within an app.

local variable A variable declared by a variable declaration statement within a method.

localization The use of the String table to change text based on the user's preferred language.

MapView class A class that displays and manipulates a Google map within the Android environment.

margin Blank space that offsets a control by a certain amount of density independent pixels (dp) on each of its four sides.

MD5 (Message-Digest Algorithm 5) digital fingerprint An algorithm that is widely used to verify data integrity. When the result of the algorithm is provided as part of a file, it verifies the integrity of the file.

MediaPlayer class The Java class that provides the methods to control audio playback on an Android device.

method A set of Java statements that perform a repeated task and can be included inside a Java class.

MONTH A date constant of the Calendar class that retrieves an integer value of the system's current month.

motion tween A type of animation that specifies the start state of an object, and then animates the object a predetermined number of times or an infinite number of times using a transition.

native application A program locally installed on a specific platform such as a phone or tablet.

nest To place one statement, such as an If statement, within another statement.

numColumns A GridView property that can be set to an integer value representing the number of columns to include, or to auto fit, which determines the number of columns to show based on the size of the Android screen and the image width.

object A specific, concrete instance of a class.

object-oriented programming language A type of programming language that allows good software engineering practices such as code reuse.

OnCreateDialog A method that creates a dialog box based on the argument passed by the showDialog method call.

onDateSet An event that is triggered when the DatePicker passes a value representing the year, the month, and the day. In other words, the onDateSet event is fired after the user selects a date.

onDestroy( ) method A method used to end an Activity. Whereas the onCreate( ) method sets up required resources, the onDestroy( ) method releases those same resources to free up memory.

onItemClick An event the OnItemClickListener processes when the user touches the Gallery display layout.

The onItemClick method is defined by OnItemClickListener and sends a number of arguments in the parentheses included within the line of code.

onListItemClick( ) A method called when an item in a list is selected.

onTap( ) A method that receives the index of the overlay item that was tapped by the user.

Open Handset Alliance An open-source business alliance of 80 firms that develop open standards for mobile devices.

overlay A map marker that uses a graphic image to indicate a specific location on a map.

Package Explorer A pane on the left side of the Eclipse program window that contains the folders for the current project.

padding property A property that you can use to offset the content of a control by a specific number of pixels.

Parse A class that converts a string into a number data type.

permissions A part of Android applications that prevents malicious outside applications from corrupting information and accessing sensitive information.

populate( ) A method necessary to add each new item in an ItemizedOverlay, which reads each of the OverlayItems such as the pushpin image and prepares for each image to be drawn on top of the map in a new visible layer.

position The placement of an item in a list. When an item in a list is selected, the position of the item is passed from the onListItemClick method and evaluated with a decision structure. The first item is assigned the position of 0, the second item is assigned the position of 1, and so forth.

prompt Text that displays instructions at the top of the Spinner control.

protected A keyword signifying that the method or variable can only be accessed by elements residing in its class.

RadioGroup A group of RadioButton controls; only one RadioButton control can be selected at a time.

Relative layout A layout that arranges components in relation to each other.

res folder A project folder that contains all the resources, such as images, music, and video files, that an application may need.

scope The scope of a variable refers to the variable's visibility within a class.

set The field manipulation method that changes the system date or time.

setAdapter A command that provides a data model for the Gallery layout, similar to an adapter, which displays a ListView control. Also a method that provides a data model for the layout of the GridView control. You use the setAdapter method to instantiate a custom BaseAdapter class called ImageAdapter and then apply it to the GridView.

setBackgroundResource A method that places images in the frame-by-frame display for an animation, with each frame pointing to an image referenced in the XML resource file.

setBuiltInZoomControls A property that allows the site visitor to use the built-in zoom feature.

setContent A method that indicates what to display in the tab content area of a TabHost control.

setContentView The Java code necessary to display the content of a specific screen.

462

setIndicator A method that sets the tab button caption and icon image in a TabHost control.

setListAdapter A command that projects your data to the onscreen list on your device by connecting the ListActivity's ListView object to array data.

smartphone A mobile phone with advanced computing ability and connectivity features.

soft keyboard An onscreen keyboard positioned over the lower part of an application's window.

sp A unit of measurement that stands for scaled-independent pixels.

Spinner control A widget similar to a drop-down list for selecting a single item from a fixed listing.

src folder A project folder that includes the Java code source files for the project.

startAnimation A method that begins the animation process of a View object by calling the AnimationUtils class utilities to access the resources necessary to load the animation.

state A stage in an Activity's life cycle that determines whether the Activity is active, paused, stopped, or dead.

static variable A program variable that does not vary and has the same value throughout execution of the application.

string A series of alphanumeric characters that can include spaces.

strings.xml A default file that is part of every Android application and holds commonly used strings in an application.

stub A piece of code that serves as a placeholder to declare itself, containing just enough code to link to the rest of the program.

Switch A type of decision statement that allows you to choose from many statements based on an integer or char input.

TabActivity A class that allows you to display tabs in a TabHost control, with each tab containing an Activity or view.

TabHost A control you use to wrap multiple views in a single window.

TableLayout A user interface design layout that includes TableRow controls to form a grid.

TabSpec A statement that specifies how the tabs in a TabHost control should appear.

TabWidget The part of a TabHost control that displays the tabs.

Text property A property that changes the text written within a control.

Text size property A property that sets the size of text in a control.

theme A style applied to an Activity or an entire application.

thread A single sequential flow of control within a program.

Timer A Java class that creates a timed event when the schedule method is called.

timer A tool that performs a one-time task such as displaying an opening splash screen, or performs a continuous process such as a morning wake-up call set to run at regular intervals.

TimerTask A Java class that invokes a scheduled timer.

toast notification A message that appears as an overlay on a user's screen, often displaying a validation warning.

Tween animation A type of animation that, instead of using a sequence of images, creates an animation by performing a series of transformations on a single image, such as position, size, rotation, and transparency, on the contents of a View object.

tween effect A transition that changes objects from one state to another, such as by moving, rotating, growing, or shrinking.

typeface A property that you can use to set the style of control text to font families, including monospace, sans_serif, and serif.

URI An acronym for Uniform Resource Identifier, a URI is a string that identifies the resources of the Web. Similar to a URL, a URI includes additional information necessary for gaining access to the resources required for posting the page.

URL An acronym for Uniform Resource Locator, a URL is a Web site address.

variable A name used in a Java program to contain data that changes during the execution of the program.

View A rectangular container that displays a drawing or text object.

Visibility property The Java property that controls whether a control is displayed on the emulator.

widget A single element such as a TextView, Button, or CheckBox control, and is also called an object.

XML An acronym for Extensible Markup Language, a widely used system for defining data formats. XML assists in the layout of the Android emulator.

YEAR A date constant of the Calendar class that retrieves an integer value of the system's current year.

Index